Woman President

Number Twenty-two
Presidential Rhetoric and Political Communication
Vanessa B. Beasley, General Editor

WOMAN PRESIDENT

Confronting Postfeminist Political Culture

KRISTINA HORN SHEELER AND KARRIN VASBY ANDERSON

Texas A&M University Press
College Station

♾ ♻
Library of Congress Cataloging-in-Publication Data
Sheeler, Kristina Horn, 1965–
    Woman president : confronting postfeminist political culture / Kristina Horn Sheeler
and Karrin Vasby Anderson. — 1st ed.
        p. cm. — (Presidential rhetoric and political communication ; no. 22)
    Includes bibliographical references and index.
    ISBN 978-1-60344-983-0 (book/cloth : alk. paper) — ISBN 978-1-62349-010-2 (e-book)
    1. Women presidents—United States. 2. Women presidential candidates—United States.
3. Gender mainstreaming—United States. 4. Sex discrimination against women—United
States. 5. Feminism and mass media—United States. 6. Mass media and women—United
States. 7. Presidents—United States—Election—Case studies. 8. Clinton, Hillary Rodham.
9. Palin, Sarah, 1964– I. Anderson, Karrin Vasby. II. Title.
JK516.S44 2013
306.2082'0973—dc23
                                                                                            2013010655

To
Ian Sheeler
and
Thad, Jaret, and Josh Anderson
with love and appreciation

Contents

Acknowledgments

This book, a collaborative project to which both authors contributed equally, is the second that has resulted from our complementary research agenda and strong friendship that began when we were graduate students at Indiana University. We thank our close network of "girlfriends"—Sarah Feldner, Krista Hoffmann-Longtin, Kelly McDorman, Claire Procopio, and Helen Tate—now in various positions and locations around the country, who created a community in support of research and professional success in its many forms. We also thank our colleagues at Indiana University Purdue University Indianapolis (IUPUI) and Colorado State University for their encouragement on this project. Thanks also go out to the many readers, reviewers, and advisors who have inspired us and helped us to push our work to be its best. We thank especially Vanessa Beasley, Mary Lenn Dixon, and the anonymous reviewers for Texas A&M University Press; your feedback allowed us to realize our vision for this project in improved form. We also want to acknowledge the financial support provided by the Carrie Chapman Catt Center for Women and Politics. Some of the material in chapter 5 originally appeared in the journal *Rhetoric & Public Affairs* as Karrin Vasby Anderson's article "'Rhymes with Blunt': Pornification and US Political Culture," 14, no. 2 (2011): 327–68, © 2011 by Michigan State University.

Kristina Horn Sheeler would like to extend a special thank you to Ian for his encouragement and support throughout the writing of this manuscript. Debates with him honed this project into a much stronger one and helped me fill in the assumptions I took for granted. Thank you for always believing in me, even when I did not believe in myself. To my parents, I appreciate your constant question, "How is the book coming along?" I am happy to answer, "Here it is." I don't know if this project would have made it to completion without the amazing support of my research and writing colleagues: Terri Carney from Butler University and Danna Kostroun, Tamara Leech, and Jennifer Thorington Springer from IUPUI. Our weekly meetings were always an inspiration and pushed me to "just write." This project is a testament to what supportive colleagues make possible. Finally, to my coauthor Kari, your writing still inspires me, and I count myself lucky to call you my coauthor and friend. Here's to many more collaborative projects in the future.

Karrin Vasby Anderson would like to thank those whose support makes projects like this one possible. Thad, thanks for encouraging me to dream bigger dreams and then helping to make those dreams come true; it's a pleasure and a privilege to partner with you. Jaret and Josh, thanks for bringing joy and laughter into my life; I appreciate your unique talents and your generous spirits. Mom and Dad, thanks for nurturing me emotionally and spiritually as I grew up and for always being there to lend a hand now. Kyle, thanks for your consistent support and commitment to our family. I am blessed to be surrounded by friends I can count on despite busy schedules, conflicting politics, and competing demands on our time and energy. To "The Village" (Lynn and E. J. Bodnar, Reagan and Randy Russell, Whitney and Kevin Williams, and all "our" kids) I extend my gratitude for serving as an extended family (GGs forever!). To the women who have been my soul mates since high school (Linda Baldini, Stacy Cook, and Tammy Kerr), thank you for continuing to inspire me, challenge me, and make me laugh. To my coauthor Kristy, thanks for your patience, good humor, and unflagging commitment to this project. I am inspired by the scholar and professional you have become, and I look forward to continued friendship and collaboration.

Finally, we both would like to acknowledge the efforts of the women who came before us to secure the right to vote, run for public office, and expand the meaning of democratic citizenship. We hope that this book contributes, in some small way, to women's journey to the Oval Office.

Woman President

Introduction

Gendered Presidentiality and Postfeminist Political Culture

In April 2012, the political public relations duo Stacy Lambe and Adam Smith used the blog platform Tumblr to launch a humorous feature called "Texts from Hillary," which paired photos of Secretary of State Hillary Clinton, wearing sunglasses and working on her smartphone, with photos of other famous figures texting. Lambe and Smith penned fictitious text exchanges between Clinton and political, journalistic, and pop culture personalities, with Clinton maintaining a witty, self-assured upper hand in each exchange. The inaugural image featured President Barack Obama reclining on a couch, asking, "Hey Hil, Watchu doing?" Her response? "Running the world."[1] With that, the "Obama Cool" of 2008 was cast in a negative light—one that showed the commander in chief loafing on the couch while Clinton took control.

Yahoo News quickly dubbed "Texts from Hillary" the "best political meme of 2012 thus far," and an MSNBC website asserted that the Tumblr creation "show[ed] Clinton at her coolest." The *Guardian* linked the enthusiasm for "the wildly popular Hillary-celebrating microsite" to the widespread appeal Clinton enjoyed in the spring of 2012, arguing that rather than fostering a Clinton craze, Lambe and Smith "rode the wave of Clinton's own growing popularity." By late April 2012, pundits were once again bandying about the "p-word." Howard Fineman noted that Clinton "wins solid marks as secretary of state, rides a wave of cult status on the web, and watches as the Beltway chattering classes wonder aloud whether she will be a candidate for president in 2016."[2]

Although "Texts from Hillary" was, itself, an enjoyable and insightful commentary on gender in political and popular culture, closer examination of the journalistic discussion that surrounded it, and the associated "Clinton craze" of spring 2012, reveals the machinations of postfeminist presidential culture. "Postfeminism" is a label that has been applied to a diverse set of reactions to the second wave of the feminist movement, but we use it here to describe the politically charged assertion that feminism's work is complete and, therefore, feminist politics are irrelevant, unnecessary, or passé.[3] Postfeminist discourses are strategically effective at undermining material feminist politics because they paradoxically embrace feminist ideals even as they reject cultural practices and political policies that promote those ideals. A postfeminist view of the US presidency embraces the conventional wisdom that "anyone" can be president and even promotes individual women candidates while denying, downplaying, or dismissing the structural and cultural inequities that contribute to women's political underrepresentation.

The discussion of Clinton's political persona in April 2012 frequently included an important contrast. As pundits hailed her newfound popularity, they also criticized her previous bid for the US presidency. After noting that "the past few weeks have been pretty good to Hillary Clinton," *Salon* reminded its readers that "four years ago this week, as she pressed on with her presidential campaign despite falling hopelessly behind in the delegate race, an ABCNews/*Washington Post* survey found that 54 percent of Americans viewed the former first lady unfavorably." On April 9, 2012, *Talking Points Memo*'s Benjy Sarlin cheerfully proclaimed, "What a difference four years makes: When she was running for the Democratic presidential nomination, Hillary Clinton was parodied as drab and calculated, especially compared with young and vigorous Barack Obama and winking and fresh-faced Sarah Palin. Now, she's fueling Internet jokes based on her own brand of badass cool."[4]

In his discussion of the multiple factors that could have contributed to the April 2012 "Hillary boomlet," Howard Kurtz suggested that it was due, in part, to a personal transformation: "The woman has always been so carefully controlled on the public stage, so guarded in keeping her emotions in check that a brief choking-up moment at a New Hampshire diner in 2008 was hailed as a breakthrough. These days . . . she seems considerably looser." Democratic partisan and Clinton supporter Paul Begala took Kurtz's critique one step further, asserting that her 2008 campaign was "a mess" and touting Clinton's "surprising and impressive" ability to blend "harmoniously . . . with Team Obama."[5] The narrative that emerged was a distinctly postfeminist one: women can and do capably run for president. They have the potential to be as popular with the US electorate as male candidates. Any failure of their candidacies should properly be ascribed to their personal shortcomings or strategic miscalculations rather than to the continued influence of sexism in US culture. Postfeminist views of both Hillary Clinton specifically and contemporary presidentiality more broadly ignore an important cultural reality: Americans have always preferred *potential* female presidential candidates to actual ones. That is one reason why the feisty, authoritative (and, importantly, fictional) Hillary Clinton showcased in "Texts from Hillary" could be widely embraced. Depictions of Hillary Clinton "running the world" are appealing only when she's not actually the one running it.

How, then, did we arrive at this point? In 1991, Susan Faludi argued that the gains of 1970s feminism had triggered a backlash against the movement, one that manifested itself in popular culture and journalistic media throughout the 1980s. She noted that the backlash was "at once sophisticated and banal, deceptively 'progressive' and proudly backward." Backlashes, Faludi contended, are "hardly random" and are "triggered by the perception—accurate or not—that women are making great strides."[6] In the 2008 and 2012 presidential campaign cycles, women made the greatest strides yet in their journey to the Oval Office. After Hillary Clinton became the frontrunner for the Democratic presidential nomination and Sarah Palin was added to the Republican ticket as John McCain's vice presidential running mate, the "new normal" of presidential politics required that at least one woman be present in even a Republican presidential primary field. No one blanched when, for a few weeks in 2011, the diminutive reactionary Michele Bachmann led the Republican pack after garnering the allegiance of the conservative Tea Party constituency. Notably, however, that support vanished the moment that Texas governor Rick Perry entered the race and put a more masculine face on conservative bona fides that matched Bachmann's. By December 2011, Bachmann had been dismissed by pundits as an "afterthought" and a "saucer-eyed looney tune."[7] The *Washington Post* declared her presidential hopes "all but counted out."[8] Like Clinton and Palin before her, Bachmann felt the sting of the backlash.

The purpose of this book is to examine the backlash against female presidentiality. We assess diverse public discourses that constitute US presidentiality in order to explicate the intransigent sexism that continues to constrain women in presidential politics. This backlash is informed by a rhetoric of postfeminism that emerged in popular culture in the 1990s and that has gained traction in twenty-first-century political culture. The 2008 campaign presents a unique opportunity to examine feminism(s) and political culture because both Hillary Clinton and Sarah Palin avowed "feminist" identities but operationalized what it means to be a "feminist" in very different ways. Additionally, analysis of the media's framing of each candidate reveals that insofar as postfeminism is supplanting antifeminism, postfeminism is the vehicle of the new backlash against female presidentiality—the "undeclared war" against the American woman president.

Women candidates have been running for US president since before they won the right to vote, but they have been stymied by a uniquely American milieu that combines narratives of hard work, equal opportunity, and limitless potential with a tacit but forceful proscription of women's political authority. Even as legal barriers to women's participation in electoral politics have been dismantled, their cultural, discursive, and rhetorical constituents remain. Scholars have begun to grapple with myriad explanations for women's inability to prevail in presidential contests, citing barriers such as the difficulties of raising the funds needed to run for president.[9] The paucity of women in the "launching roles" for the US presidency constitutes another barrier.[10] Other factors are a US electoral system that highlights candidates' personal identities over party loyalty or policy platforms and media bias.[11] Cultural prohibitions against women's political authority and the gendered nature of the US presidency further complicate women's efforts to reach the Oval Office.[12] What these salient explanations stop short of assessing, however, is the possibility that one of the most intransigent barriers to the election of a woman president is the persistence of a broad cultural backlash against female presidentiality.

In the pages that follow, we examine gendered presidentiality as it has been rhetorically constructed and contested in campaign oratory, political journalism, punditry, and popular culture. In assembling disparate discourses of presidentiality, we follow Michael Calvin McGee's admonition that a primary task of rhetorical critics is "text construction," insofar as "our first job as professional consumers of discourse is inventing a text suitable for criticism."[13] In order to understand the "'invisible text' which is never quite finished" but is "constantly in front of us," we must cast a wide net and draw together textual fragments that are diverse in type and tone, form and function.[14] In what remains of this introductory chapter, we lay the critical and theoretical foundation needed to understand gendered presidentiality as a text from a feminist rhetorical perspective.

In order to situate ourselves as feminist critics, we must define the words *feminism, antifeminism,* and *postfeminism.* Defining feminism is a tricky and potentially treacherous task because there are almost as many possible definitions of feminism as there are people who call themselves feminist. Two foundational principles for most feminists, however, are equality and gender justice. Feminists believe that people of all sexes and genders deserve equal value, treatment, and opportunity in social, cultural, relational, political, and economic spheres. When equal value, treatment, and opportunity are not accorded, feminists strive for gender justice. Achieving gender justice sometimes requires feminists to work within the system. At other times, the system itself must be critiqued, repurposed, or rejected. We join with second-wave feminists who seek to effect political change through collective agitation, but we also welcome third-wave feminists who engage politics in more individualized, personal ways. As scholars, we concur with Bonnie J. Dow and Celeste Condit that achieving gender justice "may include but can also go beyond the seeking of equality between men and women, to include understanding of the concept of gender itself as politically constructed."[15] Such an understanding requires reflexivity, thus acknowledging the intersections among gender and other systems that may not confer equal value, treatment, or opportunity.

Just as the construct "gender" is politically constructed, so too is the construct "president." If the scholarly aim of this book is to understand gendered presidentiality as a rhetorical phenomenon, the corresponding political goal is to determine why it has been thus far impossible to elect a woman president in the United States. As scholars, we want to more fully understand discourses of presidentiality. As feminists, we want to see a woman in the White House—but not just any woman. Ideally, we would prefer the first woman president of the United States to be someone who supports gender justice as opposed to someone who tacitly tolerates antifeminist positions or embraces a postfeminist world view. Both antifeminism and postfeminism compete with traditional feminism in the US political and cultural milieu, and both are instruments of backlash against female presidentiality.

Despite the real and significant gains made by women in the political sphere, antifeminism is rampant in political culture. Antifeminism often comes in the form of pundits or politicians suggesting that women are ill suited to presidential governance because they are women. In 2006, commenting on the victory speech Clinton gave after being reelected to the US Senate, MSNBC's Chris Matthews remarked, "We were watching Hillary Clinton earlier tonight; she was giving a campaign barn-burner speech, which is harder to give for a woman; it can grate on some men when they listen to it—fingernails on a blackboard, perhaps." When Clinton ran for president two years later, MSNBC's Pat Buchanan made what even he admitted was a "sexist comment" as he tried to explain the challenges Clinton might face during a debate with the sonically pleasant Obama because "when she raises her voice, and when a lot of women do, you know, it's as I say, it reaches a point where every husband in America has heard at one time or another." Writing for *New York* magazine near the end of Clinton's primary bid, Amanda Fortini noted that although "many women believed we had access to the same opportunities and experiences as men," after Clinton declared her candidacy, the "sexism in America, long lying dormant, like some feral, tranquilized animal, yawned and revealed itself." Fortini chronicled some of the more egregious examples, which included the Facebook group "Hillary Clinton: Stop Running for President and Make Me a Sandwich" (boasting forty-four thousand members), and the young men who followed the Clinton campaign and disrupted her political appearances by shouting, "Iron my shirt!" Marie Cocco asserted, "for all Clinton's political blemishes, the darker stain that [was] exposed [in 2008] is the hatred of women that is accepted as part of our culture."[16]

Scholarly assessments of the 2008 campaign confirmed Cocco's verdict. Diana B. Carlin and Kelly L. Winfrey's study of media framing during the 2008 campaign argues that media coverage of Clinton and Palin "incorporated gender stereotypes and gendered language that influenced the way both women were viewed." Erika Falk connects this journalistic trend to the broader history of the media's framing of women presidential candidates, saying that media bias against Clinton was "not surprising" given "historical trends [that] show that women candidates for president consistently receive less press coverage than equivalent men running in the same races." Falk also observes that "what was surprising was that such a disparity was present when the woman was the front-runner and that such a pattern, manifest in press coverage since 1884, still held in 2007."[17] Antifeminist objections to prospective female commanders in chief suggest that women are temperamentally ill suited to presidential leadership and/or would have difficulty being taken seriously by, for example, members of the military, terrorists, or foreign leaders. These comments, though common, are also readily labeled as "sexist" and often explicitly dismissed or derided by the majority.

If antifeminism rages against the feminist machine, postfeminism seductively suggests that feminism's work is complete and, therefore, that a politics of gender justice is irrelevant, unnecessary, and passé. Angela McRobbie defines postfeminism as a "process by which feminist gains of the 1970s and 80s come to be undermined," explaining that "through an array of machinations, elements of contemporary popular culture are perniciously effective in regard to this undoing of feminism, while simultaneously appearing to be engaging in a well-informed and even well-intended response to feminism."[18] Much of the scholarly attention to postfeminism has focused on its articulation and negotiation in popular culture.[19] However, the rise of Sarah Palin has prompted scholars to begin examining the ways in which Palin and her fellow "Mama Grizzlies" have infused electoral discourse with postfeminist politics.[20] This trend is noteworthy insofar as a defining characteristic of postfeminism has historically been depoliticization. The 2008 presidential campaign produced the explicit politicization of postfeminism insofar as strategies that previously were confined to entertainment and pop cultural spheres emerged forcefully to shape political dialogue. In her 2010 speech to the Susan B. Anthony List (an organization that funds anti-abortion women candidates), Palin likened the trend to a "stampede of pink elephants" converging on Washington, DC. She contrasted herself with "some left-wing feminists," some of whom (she alleged) "refused to admit I was even a woman, geez," as she hailed her postfeminist sisters "who are not put off by a gun-totin' pro-life mom of a fun, full family."[21] Of course, a feminist commitment to gender justice need not infringe on the Second Amendment and does not preclude either family or fun. The sustained appeal of Palin's breezy rhetoric, along with her persistent political relevance, suggests that postfeminism's flirtation with electoral politics is maturing into a complicated long-term relationship.

Gendered presidentiality is further complicated by the fact that presidentiality itself is a rhetorical process. Scholarship on the "rhetorical presidency" examines the ways in which US presidents employ rhetoric, reveals how discourse frames the presidency, and examines why presidential performances shape political culture and democratic society.[22] In order to fully engage the rhetorical presidency, however, scholars need to assess not only presidential rhetoric (oratory and other discourse produced by US presidents) but also the "ideological rhetoric that helps shape the cultural meaning of the institution of the presidency"—what Trevor Parry-Giles and Shawn J. Parry-Giles refer to as "presidentiality."[23] Presidentiality is shaped by historical narratives, oratorical discourse, journalism and punditry, and popular culture. Our analysis assesses many facets of gendered presidentiality: historical and contemporary, sober and satirical, inventive and banal. That analysis also is grounded in an understanding of presidentiality as performed, synecdochical, and normative.

Presidentiality has been performative since the inception of the role. Stephen E. Lucas notes that President George Washington "often referred to life as a drama and to himself as 'a figure upon the stage,'" and he details the ways in which Washington was mindful of "the rhetorical power of self-presentation." Leroy G. Dorsey asserts that "successful rhetorical leadership by presidents is distinguished by their performance, an unobtrusive performance given during moments transformed by their inventiveness to balance the expression of their decision-making skills and their sense of good will."[24] Performance characterizes all human interaction—whether labeling it "face-work," calling it a strategic response to "exigencies," "audiences," and "constraints," or viewing it dramatistically as an actor's own agency.[25] Scholars of human communication dating back to Aristotle have recognized rhetorical interaction as fundamentally performative. Presidential performances take on added cultural and political significance insofar as they "perform an ideology in the agon of politics."[26] Kurt Lancaster dubbed this process *dramapolitik,* in which "presidential character" is "created by means of a Barthesian myth—subsuming the values of an electorate in the public sphere," an arena that is "shaped by myth-making images," so that the "politician of *realpolitik* [is] replaced by the politician of *dramapolitik.*"[27] Lancaster argues that the rhetorical performances of presidents Abraham Lincoln and George W. Bush "utilized performative rhetoric that not only transformed themselves, but also transformed how their audience perceived them—and by doing so, the audience empowered their leaders to take the country in a new direction."[28] In this sense, presidential rhetoric has constitutive dimensions, as each "patriot in chief" performs presidential character in ways that not only promote a policy agenda but also shape US national identity.[29] Robert L. Ivie notes that "rhetoric is a constitutive force and a source of national identity essential to the operation of the public sphere and the constitution of the polity" and that "presidential oratory ... is equated with the construction of political culture."[30]

Presidential performance also is complicated by the diverse responsibilities assigned to US presidents. The presidency straddles regal and republican spheres insofar as the president is called upon to fulfill both civic/political and social/ceremonial roles. Lacking a monarchy, US citizens historically have turned to the first family in situations requiring government-sanctioned pomp and circumstance. Karlyn Kohrs Campbell explains that the US first lady historically has taken on many of the key ceremonial duties; therefore, "in terms of public performance, the first lady functions as a representative of the nation. She is expected to welcome heads of state, preside at state dinners, make public appearances, attend local and national celebrations, and become the patron saint of selected charities or projects."[31] In this regard, the US presidency is a "two-person career"—a performance that occupies the symbolic territory that some other countries split between heads of government and monarchs.[32] Consequently, presidentiality is a gendered synecdoche in which the president and first lady stand in for an idealized version of democratic citizenship and the American family.

The synecdochical nature of presidentiality shapes understanding not only of presidential leadership but also of the idealized American citizenship for which it stands. In their study of a televisual representation of a fictional presidency, Parry-Giles and Parry-Giles observe a truism that can be equally applied to fictive and actual US presidents: "simply put, individuals who occupy the presidency embody the national polity." Greg Goodale concurs, stating that "the person who occupies the presidency both represents and is representative of the American people." Indeed, the president has been a synecdoche for the ideal US citizen since the inception of the role. Lucas explains the way in which George Washington established the presidential archetype when he occupied that role as "military commander, republican hero, and modern Cincinnatus." Campbell and Kathleen Hall Jamieson discuss the ways in which presidential inaugural speeches enable the president to constitute a unified American public and position himself or herself as a surrogate for "fellow Americans." David Zarefsky explains that presidents since Washington have marshaled the strategic value of the synecdochical presidency, stating that Washington's "successors . . . have proved adept at construing their own interests as synonymous with the national interest and thereby at standing for the whole people." Indeed, as noted by James Darsey, the first president to disrupt the racial homogeneity of the US presidency based his campaign on a journey metaphor that functioned synecdochically, because if Obama could "succeed in making his campaign a journey that is coincident with our collective journey, then his campaign [would be] refigured: not the race of one man for the presidency of the United States but a vehicle for our common striving to get the country back on the right track toward our common destiny, the American Dream."[33]

Campbell explains that the (as of yet exclusively male) US president cannot stand in for the ideal citizen alone. He needs a spouse to complete the picture of the US president and first lady as "Mr. and Mrs. America, an ideal First Family expected to represent cherished US values."[34] For that reason, the few presidents who were unmarried identified substitutes to fulfill the social and ceremonial expectations of the first lady, and when presidential spouses were unable or unwilling to perform those duties, young female surrogates were selected.[35] Additionally, first ladies historically have conformed (at least explicitly) to traditional gender and familial norms. Molly Meijer Wertheimer notes that "all first ladies become symbols of American womanhood and as such they are expected to conform to the public's image of 'the ideal woman' of their times."[36] First ladies who resisted this model were considered controversial and often pilloried by the press and political opponents.[37] The perceived homogeneity of US first ladies has more to do with the media's collective memory and journalistic framing than it does with actual presidential spouses. Nonetheless, in journalism and political culture more broadly, "memories of a few presidential wives are recalled to establish the historical boundaries of first lady performance, which are then used to define proper behavior for contemporary first ladies."[38]

As a synecdoche for the ideal American family, the US presidency and first ladyship is a site on which cultural anxieties about gender and power are located, contested, and perpetually renegotiated. The prospect of a female president radically disrupts the established structure of the "first family"—a disruption made to seem more destabilizing because of the synecdochical nature of presidentiality. The perceived disruption is compounded by the fact that not only does the president and his or her spouse stand in for the national polity but presidential performances also establish and reinforce cultural and political norms, disciplining those who transgress familiar boundaries. Critical assessment of the US presidency's normative function produces greater understanding not only of presidentiality but of power as it is constructed in US political culture.

To understand the US presidency as normative, one must remember the dual senses of the term. According to the second edition of the *Oxford English Dictionary*, that which is normative can both "constitute" and/or be "derived from" a norm or standard. Thus, the US presidency both establishes and reflects political and cultural norms. Campbell and Jamieson argue that individual presidents fostered the expansion of executive power; they call the presidency an "amalgam of roles and practices shaped by what presidents have done."[39] Conversely, presidentiality is itself shaped by social and cultural norms. Even the popular press recognizes the normative nature of the US president. Writing for the *Washington Post*, Kathleen Parker observed that we have "certain cultural expectations, especially related to leadership. When we ask questions about a politician's beliefs, family, or hobbies, we're looking for familiarity, what we can cite as 'normal' and therefore reassuring."[40] Scholars have identified a number of norms salient to the US presidency; whiteness, Christianity, heterosexuality, and masculinity are among the most visible.[41] Although none of these norms can be easily separated from the others, the 2008 election provided compelling evidence of the ways in which masculinity is, perhaps, the most difficult norm to displace.

Mary E. Stuckey's review of academic research on the rhetorical presidency concludes that the "presidency is an important site where our national expectations of gender are performed and ritualized." As noted by Suzanne Daughton, "first and foremost, the president is the national patriarch: the paradigmatic American Man." Stuckey argues that the presidency is "a paternalistic office," one that has been so since "George Washington became the 'Father of Our Country.'" Michael Kimmel recounts the role played by gender norms during the 1840 presidential election, when William Henry Harrison defeated Martin Van Buren in a campaign Kimmel describes as "a political masterpiece of gendered speech"; he explains that "Harrison's manly virtues and log cabin birth were contrasted with Van Buren's ruffled shirts and his cabinet composed of 'eastern officeholder pimps.'" Kimmel concludes that "since 1840 the president's manhood has always been a question, his manly resolve, firmness, courage, and power equated with the capacity for violence, military virtues, and a plain-living style that avoided cultivated refinement and civility." Goodale traces the emergence of a distinctive "manly style" of speaking at the turn of the twentieth century and contends that "at the beginning of the twentieth century, the sound of the presidency changed in a manner that better represented an idealized American manliness."[42] John F. Kennedy was cast in a "heroic mold," Kimmel contends, as he "over[came] the perceived burdens of his aristocratic family lineage and youthful infirmity or injury—a World War II hero on PT-109, Kennedy presented a youthful vigor, a hardy manhood that, despite his chronic pain from a back injury, made him as comfortable sailing or playing touch football with his family on the lawns of their Hyannisport home as he was leading the nation into the New Frontier." Kimmel adds that when Lyndon B. Johnson had the presidential mantle forced upon him after Kennedy's assassination, he "appears to have been so deeply insecure that his political rhetoric dripped with metaphors of aggressive masculinity; affairs of state seem to have been conducted as much with the genitals as with political genius." As the twentieth century progressed, Jimmy Carter's "New Man" sensitivities were displaced by Ronald Reagan's rugged cowboy charm, and his successor, George H.W. Bush, struggled with the "wimp" charge after returning to "the 'kinder and gentler' policies of traditionally aristocratic noblesse oblige." Bush's reputation was saved, in part, after "he had some help in seizing the more-manly-than-thou mantle. Short, nerdy Democratic candidate Michael

Dukakis looked even more ridiculous riding around in a tank, complete with headgear, than Bush did in his hunting or fishing gear," yet even after his victory in the 1988 campaign, "Bush's years in office continued this preoccupation with demonstrating manhood," as he deposed Panamanian strongman Manuel Noriega and invaded Iraq in the first Gulf War.[43]

Postmodern presidentiality has been similarly masculinist. Much of the angst created by Hillary Clinton's activist approach to the role of first lady was spurred by the fact that her performance challenged and contested the traditional masculinity typically embodied by the presidency. As we have argued elsewhere, after Clinton's controversial attempts to reform the US health-care system, critics explicitly tied the policy defeat to a failure of presidential masculinity. Typical of journalistic accounts at the time was "Michael Barone's characterization of the health-care reform campaign as 'bossy social engineering.' As Barone saw it, Bill Clinton unwisely 'ceded' the health-care campaign to his wife, carrying 'the boomer liberal faith of feminism too far' and making himself look weak. That type of media commentary echoed Richard Nixon's admonition that 'If the wife comes through as being too strong and too intelligent it makes the husband look like a wimp.'"[44]

Brenton J. Malin asserts that the "late '90s scandals surrounding President [Bill] Clinton illustrate the '90s crisis of masculinity in an exemplary fashion" concluding that, "discussions of [Bill] Clinton's character indicate a sense of masculine, not merely presidential, crisis."[45] Of course, Clinton's tenure as president was followed by George W. Bush's return to a traditionally masculine presidential ethos, explicitly fashioned after Ronald Reagan. Like Reagan (and decidedly unlike his father, George H. W. Bush), Bush presented himself as a cowboy, riding his horse, chopping wood, and clearing brush on his Texas ranch. Kurt Lancaster argues that after "the crisis of 9/11" Bush molded "a persona from elements comprising a cowboy, a priest, and a soldier—qualities that embodied a leadership style strong enough to deal with a war on terror." When Democratic senator John Kerry challenged incumbent president George W. Bush in the 2004 campaign, his efforts were marred, as Anna Cornelia Fahey has argued, by his opponent's attempt to "Frenchify" him and construct him as a "feminine 'other.'"[46]

When considering the masculinity of the US presidency, it is important to note that, in particular, heterosexual manliness is the norm. Stuckey states that "presidents are allowed to be assertively if not aggressively heterosexual." Presidential heterosexism stems from the US culture's elision of homosexuality, from the synecdochical requirement that presidents (and their first ladies) stand in for the ideal US family, and from the expectation that US presidents should be classically masculine heroic leaders.[47]

If norms of masculinity have constrained even male presidents and presidential candidates, female contenders are forced to negotiate a more treacherous rhetorical terrain. One of the primary challenges faced by women political candidates since the 1960s is the "double bind" between femininity and competence, wherein society "expects a woman to be feminine, then offers her a concept of femininity that ensures that as a feminine creature she cannot be mature or decisive." As Jamieson explains, "The words commonly associated with the femininity/competence bind are 'too' and 'not . . . enough.' The evaluated woman has deviated from the female norm of femininity while exceeding or falling short of the masculine norm of competence. She is too strident and abrasive or not aggressive or tough enough. Or, alternatively, she has succumbed to the disabling effects of the feminine stereotype of emotionalism."[48]

Hillary Clinton's political career has received significant scholarly attention as an exemplar of someone whose public persona has been shaped by the double bind between femininity and competence.[49] We have previously assessed the ways in which "conflicts between role expectations trap women in double binds that curtail their options and circumscribe their power," and we focused on women as political spouses, candidates for representative offices, and those seeking positions in executive political leadership. Our earlier work considered the "variety of ways in which the double bind can influence a political persona," demonstrating the potential for double binds to function as both constraints and rhetorical resources. On one hand, the double bind serves as the context for the candidacy of any woman, a rhetorical constraint that must be negotiated. Conversely, however, the constraints established by the norms that surround femininity and leadership occasionally foster rhetorical ingenuity that allows political women to expand cultural understanding of what it means to be a good leader.[50]

Although women have made important inroads in the spheres of public leadership and political governance since the 1980s, the US presidency remains particularly elusive. The masculinity of the US presidency is a hegemonic cultural force, one that operates "on the terrain of 'common sense' and conventional morality."[51] Structural barriers, such as an uneven economic playing field and the paucity of women in the presidential "launching roles" of the US Senate, state governorships, and the vice presidency, plague women presidential candidates.[52] Insofar as the presidency is constructed as "the purview of men," female candidates will always be presented with "unique rhetorical challenges" unless the gendered nature of US presidentiality is re-visioned.[53]

Despite these and other barriers, however, some scholars, pundits, and citizens have embraced an air of inevitability when it comes to US voters electing a female president. In 2003, Robert P. Watson noted that "each accomplishment of the women's movement and each woman elected to public office have moved the country that much closer to the election of a woman to the presidency." Madeleine Kunin, author and former governor of Vermont, noted that "both women and African Americans have experienced centuries of struggle. Judging by large voter turnouts in the [2008] Democratic primaries, the country seems more poised than at any time in our history to write a new chapter for both." In 2007, when Hillary Clinton was still a viable presidential hopeful, Gallup News Service reported that "nearly 9 in 10 Americans, 88%, say they would vote for a woman for president." As one online discussant put it in response to a blog entry detailing the sexist responses to Clinton's presidential candidacy, "The very fact that [Hillary Clinton] was *there* . . . proves that sexism *is* dying and *is* in remnants of what it used to be. . . . No, sexism isn't dead, but yes, it is on its way out."[54] This book examines the merit of that claim. Unfortunately, our study suggests that rather than ushering sexism out, the 2008 presidential campaign illustrated the ways in which misogyny is being repurposed for public consumption—a task made easier by the postmodern media environment and the postfeminist cultural mood.

Reflecting on Obama's election as US president in 2008, Darsey optimistically asserted that "232 years after the publication of the document that set us off on our journey as a nation, [the United States] is finally at a point where an African American can be a serious contender for the nation's top leadership position," and he pointed to that fact as a sign that "the United States has, perhaps belatedly but at least finally, passed some check point on the way to the unachievable but ever-beckoning finish line of 'justice and equality for all.'"[55] For all? Women have acceded to increasingly powerful political roles, with both Democrats and Republicans promoting, for example, women as legislators, state governors, US secretaries of state, vice presidential nominees, and even one or two well-supported presidential hopefuls. Yet the distinctions earned by a handful of notable women function almost as a red herring, distracting the public from the broader reality that in 2010, nearly a century after earning universal suffrage in the United States, women still held just 16.5 percent of the seats in the US House of Representatives (72 out of 435, plus 3 delegates from Guam, the Virgin Islands, and Washington, DC), 17 percent of the US Senate seats (17 out of 100), and six state governorships.[56] Importantly, the office of US president remains just out of reach.

This book explains the ways in which hegemonic masculinity is a resilient and pernicious constraint of presidentiality. When viewed as a rhetorical performance, a synecdochical symbol, and a normative paradigm, the US presidency constitutes and is constituted by strong political and cultural expectations that any successful candidate must negotiate. In 2008, Barack Obama performed presidentiality in a way that allowed him to inhabit *both* a transformative multiracial space *and* a normative presidential space. Conversely, Hillary Clinton faced gendered constraints that precluded a similar transformation of gendered presidentiality. This book examines those constraints.

In chapter 1, we briefly review the historic bids women have made for the US presidency dating back to the pre-suffrage era. We assess the ways in which the "pioneer" metaphor has framed women candidates who have run for president throughout history, demonstrating how its elasticity has allowed it to be deployed for feminist, antifeminist, and postfeminist purposes. Chapter 2 examines fictional female presidentiality as it has been negotiated in popular films and television programs. We argue that these mediated texts operate on both propositional and suppositional levels. Propositionally, these films and television series contend that women are as qualified as men to serve as US president, and to the extent that sexism still exists in society, it is presented as outmoded, ridiculous, and/or corrupt. Suppositionally, however, each program reinforces the norms of presidentiality, such as masculinity, militarism, and whiteness. By characterizing fictional women presidents as primarily sexual, maternal, and humanitarian, each text paradoxically reifies the notion that women are ill suited to the US presidency. As such, texts that have been hailed as progressive actually feed the backlash experienced by real women candidates.

After laying the critical, historical, and pop cultural foundation for understanding discourses of female presidentiality, we transition to analysis of the 2008 presidential primary and general election campaigns. In chapter 3, we examine the ways in which Clinton and Palin introduced themselves to voters oratorically, noting that each candidate's performances deployed competing notions of "feminist" identity in order to negotiate the hegemonic masculinity of US presidentiality. Clinton's oratory was infused with a second-wave feminist sensibility, whereas Palin's exhibited characteristics of postfeminism. Chapter 4 takes a similarly narrative approach, assessing the stories told about Clinton, Palin, and feminism(s) in political media. We argue that in a postfeminist political context, campaign framing paradoxically suggests that barriers keeping women from the presidency have largely been removed even as it reinforces masculinist conceptions of presidentiality and antifeminist depictions of women candidates. Chapter 5 explicates the most explicit manifestation of the backlash during the 2008 campaign cycle: the "porning" of the presidential body. We argue that although both Clinton's and Palin's images were pornified, the pornification took different and distinct forms that were alternately informed by antifeminism and postfeminism. In chapter 6, we consider parodies of female presidentiality. Our examination of parodic episodes salient to the 2008 presidential campaign suggests that despite its oppositional design and rootedness in paradox, parodic presidentiality often normalizes rather than challenges traditional understandings of presidential power. In particular, although the parody of the 2008 campaign aptly skewered the mainstream media and questioned the partisan motives of candidates themselves, much of its humor was derived from reinforcement of, rather than challenge to, traditional gender norms. In that respect, parody contributed to the backlash against female presidentiality. We conclude our book by reflecting on the failed presidential/vice presidential bids of Hillary Clinton and Sarah Palin, arguing that although pundits point out specific missteps made by each campaign, too little attention has been paid to the broader cultural milieu that has constrained women presidential candidates for more than one hundred years.

To combat the force of hegemonic masculinity as a requirement of presidentiality, candidates and voters alike must have the political and cultural resources needed to credibly envision presidentiality as a gender-neutral role. For nearly a century, women politicians have been pushing the boundaries of what is possible and thus challenging established conventions of US presidentiality. In fact, women have been running for the office of US president since before they possessed the right to vote at the national level. In the chapter that follows, we examine the campaign strategies of women presidential candidates throughout history in order to more fully understand their impact on US presidentiality.

The First Shall Be Last

The "Pioneer" Frame as a Constraint for Women Presidential Candidates

The 2006 midterm election season seemed to portend a new era in US presidential politics. With buzz about the 2008 presidential campaign well under way, the August 28, 2006, issue of *Time* magazine put the junior US senator from New York, Hillary Clinton, on its cover, with seasoned political reporter Karen Tumulty claiming that "Hillary would step into the [US presidential] race as the instant front runner."[1] Clinton was popular with her New York constituents, had proven ability to raise money, and her candidacy was treated seriously—even enthusiastically—by many mainstream media outlets. The early buzz seemed to confirm polling data that suggested that US voters were willing to elect someone other than a white, heterosexual, Christian male to the highest office in the land. A 2005 poll conducted jointly by the White House Project and Roper Public Affairs reported that 79 percent of respondents stated that they were "very comfortable" or "somewhat comfortable" with a woman US president, with only 19.4 percent of respondents reporting to be "not very comfortable" or "not at all comfortable."[2] The results of a 2006 Gallup poll reported more modest support for women, with 61 percent of respondents indicating that "Americans are ready to elect a woman," followed closely by African American or black candidates (58 percent). The same poll rated public receptiveness for a woman president higher than that for presidential candidates "with other background characteristics, including Hispanic (41%), Asian (33%), Latter-Day Saint or Mormon (29%), Atheist (14%), or gay or lesbian (7%)."[3]

Since before woman suffrage, US women have envisioned the moment when they could lead the nation, yet, ninety years after the passage of the Nineteenth Amendment, US women held only a small percentage of seats in Congress and no woman presidential candidate from a major party had made it past the primaries.[4] According to a list compiled by the Interparliamentary Union and ranking the percentage of national parliamentary seats held by women worldwide, the United States ranked an abysmal seventy-second in the world in November 2010.[5] Similarly, in terms of presidential leadership, the United States lags behind countries as diverse as Ireland, New Zealand, the Philippines, Germany, Liberia, Great Britain, and Chile, among others, which each have elected women as heads of state.

Given the historical and cultural resistance to women leaders in the United States, it was no surprise that by October 2006, speculation favored the theory that Senator Clinton would leverage her considerable amount of Democratic funding to secure the role of Senate minority/majority leader, paving the way for the significantly less experienced US senator from Illinois, Barack Obama, to emerge as a popular Democratic presidential nominee in 2008.[6] In fact, an October 23, 2006, *Time* magazine cover announced journalist Joe Klein's theory under the headline "Why Barack Obama Could Be the Next President." Of course, cultural barriers exist that have typically precluded the election of any nonwhite male, and the national popularity of African Americans such as Obama and Colin Powell represents a broadening of the US presidential image. Nonetheless, despite Americans' professed willingness to admit women to the Oval Office, research demonstrates the resilience of the cultural, political, and economic barriers barring the door to women.

This chapter argues that the "pioneer" frame represents a significant discursive component impeding US women's presidential aspirations, one that is obscured by the rhetoric of postfeminism. When female candidates characterize themselves as pioneers or are framed as such by the media, two notions of the metaphor can be at play. A pioneer is someone who is first to do something, paving the way for those who follow. The assumption is that although "pioneering" individuals face hardship as they pursue a new goal, their efforts make the way easier for those who follow. Additionally, in the realm of electoral politics, the pioneer metaphor often invokes a distinctively western mythos that connotes frontier spirit, rugged individualism, and heroic masculinity.

More specifically, this chapter contends that the pioneer frame, which has been applied to each woman candidate for the US presidency since the nineteenth century, undermines the credibility of women candidates, underscoring the transgressive and oxymoronic quality of all woman presidential candidates. Although political women have benefited from the efforts of their predecessors, the pioneer metaphor obscures women's progress in the political sphere. The pioneer metaphor is potentially more debilitating for women than for men because: (1) the "first" metaphor situates women candidates as perpetual novices, (2) a male candidate will always exemplify the heroic masculinity implicit in the frontier narrative more authentically than a female candidate, and (3) postfeminist discourses inhibit recognition of the ideological, cultural, and political forces that contain women's agency and make the pioneer metaphor potentially debilitating. Women's presidential bids will gain traction only when one or more female presidential candidates displace the pioneer narrative and replace it with a story that locates women at the center of US political leadership, rather than at its periphery.

Women and Political Agency in US Presidential Politics

Decades of research on US women's political agency reveals that despite legal and social prohibitions against public, political action, women have worked since colonial times to assert their rights of citizenship and shape the public, political character of the United States. Although the purpose of this chapter is not to rehearse the history of women's political activities, it should be noted that women's path to the US presidency was paved by the founding mothers of colonial times, antebellum abolitionists, the temperance, suffrage, and labor activists of the Progressive Era, women candidates and officeholders of the mid- to late twentieth century, and women voters whose combined voice has the power to swing elections.[7]

In addition to enacting political agency as citizens, activists, voters, candidates, and officeholders, women have taken steps to run for the US presidency.[8] The burgeoning literature on women presidential candidates poses a number of explanations for the failure of women's presidential candidacies to gain traction. First, the office of US president is gendered masculine in ways that other elective offices are not.[9] Thus, the public, the major political parties, the media, and campaign funding sources have trouble framing women presidential candidates as legitimate contenders.[10] Second, women presidential candidates historically have had difficulty raising funds, even when they are proven, politically connected figures such as Elizabeth Dole.[11] Although funders will back women candidates for other political offices, the failure of any woman prior to the 2008 election to launch a successful presidential campaign has made enthusiasm for women candidates largely emotional rather than economic.[12] Additionally, women fail to fill presidential "pipelines," such as seats in the US Senate, state governorships, and the vice presidency, in large numbers, in part because of "role conflicts" that encourage them to opt into political service later in life than men and in part because of women's historic exclusion from the political sphere.[13]

Scholars of gender and US political culture have documented the ways in which archetypes of female identity are employed to frame female politicians and political candidates. Women are cast as "puppets" and "pioneers," as "beauty queens" and "bitches," as "Madonna" and "Eve."[14] Shanto Iyengar, Nicholas A. Valentino, Stephen Ansolabehere, and Adam F. Simon explain that cultural stereotypes reinforce gendered campaign frames, noting that "culturally ingrained expectations about the strengths and weaknesses of candidates serve as important filters for interpreting and understanding campaign communication. The typical voter lacks the motivation to acquire even the most elementary level of factual knowledge about the candidates and campaign issues. In low information environments, expectations based on visible cues—including a candidate's gender—take on special importance. Messages that confirm rather than cut against these expectations are more likely to be noticed, assimilated, and retained."[15] Such media messaging has significant consequences for women candidates. Diana B. Carlin and Kelly L. Winfrey document the ways in which "describing women in sexist terms reduces their credibility or may cause them to be seen as less human."[16]

Preliminary academic research on the 2008 campaign indicates that in 2007–8 the media continued its habit of framing women candidates in stereotypical ways.[17] This rich and still emerging research on women and the US presidency has given scant attention to the role that metaphor plays as a rhetorical constraint—one of the many barriers blocking women's entrance to the Oval Office.[18] What could be a frame that asserts a woman's strength, experience, and leadership qualifications instead exaggerates her difference.

Women Presidential Pioneers on a Wagon Train to Nowhere

When women presidential candidates are hailed as pioneers, the metaphor is often deployed as a positive moniker and one that signifies precedence. Presidentiality includes many potential "firsts" for women: the first woman to get her name on a ballot, the first woman to be nominated by any political party, the first woman to be included in a major-party primary process, the first woman to be a major-party frontrunner during the primaries, the first woman to be nominated by a major party, and so forth. This laundry list of "firsts" tacitly suggests that women are perpetually new to presidential politics while men are the familiar standard. This masculinized presidential history becomes problematic for women insofar as successful "candidates for president promise to be like the best of their predecessors, strong leaders in a nation whose political culture memorializes strong leadership."[19] The difficulty for women is not that they cannot demonstrate strong leadership but that it is more difficult for women to instantiate themselves into a thoroughly masculinized presidential history. Moreover, because there are so many "firsts" for women candidates, the media habitually apply a "novelty frame" to every woman candidate, making the proposition of backing a woman candidate seem risky.[20] Male presidential pioneers like Washington, Jefferson, and Lincoln are historical and cultural heroes; female presidential pioneers are either historical unknowns or cultural firsts.

When deployed in US political culture, the pioneer metaphor connotes much more than chronological precedence. It also invokes a frontier mythos. The notion of the frontier that has come to define US culture was advanced by Frederick Jackson Turner, whose essay, "The Significance of the American Frontier in American History" (1893), announced that the democratic, freedom-loving character of the United States arose from the frontier and the American West. Karen Dodwell explains that Turner's so-called "frontiersman" "defined what it meant to be an American as he moved west and left European influence behind. Most importantly, frontier life developed the individualism that promoted democracy, and it created a buoyant American character that thrived on freedom, strength, inquisitiveness, invention, and expansion." Ronald Carpenter argues that as a result of Turner's work, "a national hero emerged, one whose mythic character was capable of solving virtually any problem facing Americans, at any time." That "national hero," that "frontiersman," is the American president.[21]

The frontier hero has proven to be a relatively elastic metaphor for men, with ranchers (Theodore Roosevelt), celluloid cowboys (Ronald Reagan), and neo-westerners (George W. Bush) equally able to invoke the frontier mythos. Even men whose locational identities were far removed from the West benefited from identification with the frontier mythos. John F. Kennedy presided over the conquering of the "new frontier," deploying that metaphor to boost space exploration and launch the Peace Corps.[22] Barack Obama's 2008 campaign rhetoric aligned himself and his audience with "the pioneers who pushed westward against an unforgiving wilderness."[23]

Women presidential candidates have had a much more difficult time articulating an identity that resonates with the frontier pioneer in a way that harnesses its power. The frontier myth has proven challenging for women to negotiate in part because of the way it has been appropriated in the American psyche as something entirely masculine. Janice Hocker Rushing states that "the frontier has always been a patriarchal myth in which women were overwhelmingly dominated by men. Though necessary to life on the real frontier, women were rarely the center of action in the *myth*; those heroines who did appear were usually caricatures, masculine personalities in female bodies. Ever-present in the background as helpmates, mothers, captives of the Indians, schoolmarms, and saloon girls, women were nevertheless primarily *supplements*" [emphasis in original].[24]

Jenni Calder concurs, noting that "very, very few Western makers . . . have made convincing use of women's life in the West, either in terms of conveying something like the reality of their existence or of dramatising their mythic potential."[25] Despite these limitations, a handful of women politicians running for offices other than the US presidency—especially those from western states—have invoked the frontier mythos productively. In previous research, we have examined women governors who embraced the ethos of the pioneer and found that its populist dimensions "enabled them to appeal to the 'common people.'"[26] A few women have even negotiated successfully the hypermasculinity of the pioneer metaphor. When Ann Richards was governor of Texas, she crafted an unruly pioneer persona that complemented the "Lone Star mystique" of Texas, allowing her to "perpetuat[e] the mythos of the Texas frontier experience" in order to "create identification with her audience."[27] Even so, the Texas governorship is a relatively weak office since the governor shares executive power with five other independently elected officeholders. Consequently, what works symbolically for that office is not necessarily transferable to the US presidency. Even in Texas, Richards's appeal as the unruly pioneer lost its luster after just one term. She was unseated by George W. Bush, the neo-westerner destined to become cowboy in chief of the United States. Despite his pedigree as the wealthy, Yale-educated son of a US president, Bush's masculinity allowed him to convincingly inhabit the pioneer persona without the dimension of unruliness that ultimately disciplined Richards.

The pioneer metaphor, then, connotes both precedence and the frontier mythos. It is frequently deployed by candidates, the media, and historians who reflect on women presidential candidates, often in ways that align with feminist goals and values: women are as capable as men of presidential leadership and those who pave the way to the Oval Office should be lauded. What critics have been slow to examine, however, is how easily this framing also comports with postfeminist rhetoric, intimating that the election of a woman president is inevitable—only the passage of time and the industry of individual women candidates are needed in order for women to conquer the final frontier of the US presidency. Such framing actively displaces sexism as a barrier to female presidentiality while paradoxically bolstering the supposition that pioneering women candidates are perpetual presidential novices.

In what remains of this chapter, we provide a brief overview of women's historical bids for the US presidency, demonstrating the ways in which the pioneer metaphor has functioned as a debilitating frame for women candidates and tracing the development of the postfeminist narrative of the inevitability of female presidentiality. Our analysis is suggestive rather than exhaustive. Our intention is not to provide a complete examination of each candidate's rhetorical strategies. Instead, we focus on the ubiquity of the pioneer narrative as a frame for women presidential candidates in news accounts and historical narratives. Both primary and secondary sources are instructive in unmasking the durability of the pioneer metaphor because they demonstrate the fact that women are both framed as pioneers during their presidential campaigns and remembered as such well after their campaigns have ended. Moreover, our understanding of contemporary women candidates is shaped not just by the campaign rhetoric of their predecessors but also by the historiography that has framed women presidential candidates throughout history. After providing a brief overview of women's presidential bids throughout history, we examine the announcement speeches of Victoria Woodhull, Margaret Chase Smith, Elizabeth Dole, and Carol Moseley

Braun. These four speeches are significant because they typify the diverse strategies women candidates have used to assert their presidentiality and to instantiate themselves as feminists.

Women Who Would (Not) Be President

Victoria Woodhull's legacy always will include her status as a presidential pioneer. Representing the Equal Rights Party in 1872, she was the first woman to run officially for US president. Although she could not vote for herself, and indeed was confined to a jail cell on Election Day due to obscenity charges connected to political material published in her weekly newspaper, Woodhull is remembered by second-wave feminist icon Gloria Steinem as "the first woman to address Congress, the first to run for president, the first to originate and run her own weekly newspaper, and one of the few women to live out in public the principles of female emancipation and sexual freedom that were not only unusual in her day but illegal."[28] At the time, the radical free-love advocate's presidential candidacy was not taken seriously by the *New York Times,* which asserted that "the career of Victoria Woodhull cannot but be entertaining as she gains public attention by hook or by crook. . . . Mrs. Woodhull, with an ambition worthy of a female Napoleon, goes for the presidency and strikes immediately at the White House."[29] More recent narratives laud her candidacy's trailblazing impact. The online biography introducing the Victoria Woodhull-Martin Papers collected at Southern Illinois University at Carbondale's Morris Library notes that "Victoria Claflin Woodhull-Martin was the 'first woman' in many endeavors. She was the first woman to speak at the Capitol in Washington, DC, to open a bank on Wall Street, and to be nominated for President of the United States."[30] Similarly, in a column about Elizabeth Dole's 1999 presidential exploratory committee, Ellen Goodman describes Woodhull as "the most famous woman in America on April 2, 1870, when she claimed 'the right to speak for the unenfranchised women of the country' and announced her [US presidential] candidacy. At that moment, she had a personal story that the folks who put together the videos for today's national conventions would die for." Emphasizing the acknowledged symbolic nature of Woodhull's candidacy, Goodman writes, "Back in the days before women could vote, running for the presidency was an act of civil disobedience, not a career move. The difference between 1870 and 1999, says Lois Beachy Underhill, who wrote *The Woman Who Ran for President,* is 'Today, women run to win. She was running to make a statement.'"[31] Both historical and contemporary accounts of Woodhull, then, deploy the precedence argument and cast women presidential pioneers as important symbols despite their limited immediate political consequence.

Twelve years after Woodhull's run, Belva Ann Lockwood made a statement by claiming the nomination of the Equal Rights Party. One of the founders of the party, Lockwood ran for president in 1884 and again in 1888. Historical accounts note Lockwood's fight to claim her law degree when it was initially denied her and her status as the "first woman lawyer" to argue before the Supreme Court.[32] One scholar, writing in the *Journal of Supreme Court History*, claims "she pioneered—with Victoria Woodhull, Elizabeth Cady Stanton, and others—the radical idea of far-reaching political ambition on the part of women." Like Woodhull, she was radically outspoken, and some reports of her 1884 nomination suggest it was at best a surprise and at worst a joke.[33] In a letter sent to Marietta Stow, presumably in response to her nomination for the presidency, her radical persona shows through: "Why not nominate women for important places? . . . Is not history full of precedents of women rulers? . . . It is quite time that we had our own party[,] our own platform, and our own nominees. We shall never have equal rights until we take them, nor respect until we command it. Act up to your convictions of justice and right, and you cannot go far wrong."[34] This statement suggests that Lockwood recognized what many modern voters overlook: the pioneers of women's leadership were active centuries before Hillary Clinton and Sarah Palin. Consequently, applying a frame of precedence to contemporary women candidates elides the political work done by women throughout history.

Lockwood responded to her nomination with the utmost seriousness. She developed a "ten-point platform" and "initiated the first full campaign for the United States presidency carried out by a woman." Even so, political cartoonists lampooned Lockwood's candidacy, and she was even criticized by the National Woman Suffrage Association and Susan B. Anthony for being "imprudent" at a time when they believed woman suffrage would come by aligning with major political parties.[35] Lockwood experienced what many women candidates would come to endure—criticism from both feminists and antifeminists. Antifeminists often use humor to deploy derisive criticism of female presidential candidates. Although feminists would seem to be natural allies of women running for president, the movement's agenda on issues such as universal suffrage and abortion rights sometimes has conflicted with the priorities of individual women presidential candidates. Since feminists have traditionally aligned themselves with progressive political parties, Republican women presidential candidates have traditionally experienced the most friction between themselves and feminist activists.

Senator Margaret Chase Smith of Maine declared her candidacy for president on the Republican ticket in January 1964. Forty-six years later, on July 30, 2010, Kevin Miller of the *Bangor Daily News* penned a story on the unveiling of a portrait of Margaret Chase Smith at the Capitol in Washington, DC. The caption read, "Margaret Chase Smith paved the way, but will the governor's mansion remain elusive?" The story clearly painted Chase Smith as a pioneer of politics in her home state, noting that "history books" would "record the political barriers and gender walls that . . . Chase Smith broke down." She was "the first woman to serve in both chambers of Congress. The first female senator elected in her own right in a general election. The first woman to run for president in a major party."[36] History appears to remember Chase Smith's trailblazing status.

At the time of her declaration, however, the news media were less supportive and cast Chase Smith as a long shot with "no money, no time . . . and no organization." Assessing her announcement, *Time* magazine reported, "Actually, neither Victoria nor Belva Ann expected to win; they were merely highly vocal suffragettes [*sic*]. Not so Maine's trim, white-haired Republican Senator Margaret Chase Smith. Last week Maggie Smith, 66, confessed before the National Women's Press Club in Washington that she has no money, no time to campaign and no organization to speak of. Thereupon she announced saucily that she is going to run for the G.O.P. presidential nomination just the same."[37]

While the story suggests that Chase Smith perceived herself to be a viable candidate, the story does not paint her as such. *Time*'s particular selection of Chase Smith's words for its story does not present an identity that resonates with the rugged individualism of presidentiality: "'I am going to run my own campaign on my own record,' says she. 'I am running against no one. I'd like to be President. I think my experience and my record are greater than any other candidate or any other of the unannounced candidates. It's a real challenge, and that's one of the paramount things. When people keep telling you that you can't do a thing, you kind of like to try it.'"[38]

Recording linguistic hedges that typically are interpreted as a sign of feminine equivocation, the *Time* story fails to accord Chase Smith the requisite presidential gravitas.[39] Similarly, a song in support of her campaign titled "Leave It to the Girls" underscores her position as an outsider whose presidential potential was "mysterious," at best. The song begins:

> Leave it to the girls,
> Where there's a frill,
> And a powder puff there's greater skill
> Leave it to the chicks
> They've got a million magic tricks
> To change the course of history
> Their know-how is a mystery[40]

Chase Smith neglected to dip into this ostensible bag of tricks, refraining even from campaigning for the presidency when the US Senate was in session. Consequently, despite Chase Smith's assurances to the contrary, her candidacy cannot be viewed as a credible presidential bid.

Eight years after Chase Smith's nominal run, a member of Congress from New York, Shirley Chisholm, stepped into the presidential fray. Announcing her candidacy on January 25, 1972, her "double first for the Democrats" included being "the first woman and the first African-American to seek the nomination of the Democratic party for the nation's highest office." Feminist leader Jo Freeman's online diary of Chisholm's campaign characterizes her run as symbolic rather than strategic, noting, "Of course, she [Chisholm] didn't run with the expectation of being nominated, or to increase her clout in Congress. She ran 'to give a voice to the people the major candidates were ignoring.'"[41] In that respect, Chisholm's campaign echoed the efforts of Woodhull and Lockwood. Nevertheless, this candidacy of "double firsts" was credited with ushering in a new era in American politics. Sheila Tobias, then associate provost at Wesleyan University, evaluated the impact of the Chisholm candidacy: "We're moving, we're getting very close. And soon we'll be there."[42] Tobias's feminist optimism functions to feed what would eventually become a postfeminist narrative of inevitability—the historical "firsts" of each woman candidate argue enthymematically against the claim that sexism remains a barrier for women presidential candidates. Moreover, Chisholm was yet another presidential pioneer—launching the first "major" presidential bid by a woman in the twentieth century. Chisholm was heralded as an "'Unbossed' Pioneer" in her January 3, 2005, *New York Times* obituary, and a *Boston Globe* review of the PBS documentary *Chisholm '72—Unbought and Unbossed* called the program a "riveting portrait of a pioneer."[43] Yet, more than twenty-five years would pass before US voters would see another "major" female presidential candidacy—one hailed, again, as a "first" for women.

The twenty-five years between Shirley Chisholm and Elizabeth Dole witnessed five female presidential pioneers: Patsy Mink (1972), Ellen McCormack (1976, 1980), Sonia Johnson (1984), Patricia Schroeder (1988), and Lenora Fulani (1988, 1992). Each was a minor-party candidate or a Democratic candidate in just a few state primaries. Mink, "the first woman of color to serve in the US Congress," was an antiwar candidate in the Oregon Democratic presidential primary.[44] In a press release announcing the documentary *Pioneer Congresswoman Patsy Mink*, Franklin Odo wrote, "Patsy Mink offers a phenomenal political story, because she was so outside what you would expect of a woman, of a Japanese American and of a member of Congress." The press release identifies highlights of Mink's political career as follows: she was "the first woman of color to be elected to Congress," authored Title IX legislation, and was "the first Asian American to officially seek the presidency."[45] Ellen McCormack, an anti-abortion candidate in twenty Democratic primary contests, was "the first woman to qualify for federal campaign matching funds," and Jane H. Gilroy recounts McCormack's "pioneering effort" in her book *A Shared Vision*.[46] Sonia Johnson, running on the Citizens Party ticket, and Lenora Fulani, representing the New Alliance Party, both qualified for federal matching funds. Perhaps the best known of this group is Patricia Schroeder, who considered a "serious run for the presidency, but dropped out before the primaries because she could not raise the necessary funds."[47] She served twenty-four years in the House of Representatives and was a founding member of the Congressional Caucus for Women's Issues. True to the image of the pioneer as it is applied to female candidates, these women have many "'firsts' lining their biographies."[48]

When Elizabeth Hanford Dole announced that she had formed an exploratory committee for the presidential election of 2000, she was hailed as the "first serious female candidate for president," and "the first woman considered to have a real shot at becoming president."[49] Although early media reports touted her qualifications, fund-raising potential, and drive, most emphasized her appeal as a woman, to women.[50] The lead to a *Washington Post* story about Dole asserted that "the uniqueness of Elizabeth Dole's presidential candidacy is instantly obvious wherever she campaigns. The audiences are overwhelmingly female: younger women, older women, women with babies, women with husbands, women who are Republican Party veterans and women who have never participated in the political process before."[51] The *New York Times* reinforced Dole's "unique" appeal, stating, "She has said time and again that she is not running as a woman but instead is a woman running. Still, one of the most notable things about Elizabeth Dole's quest for the Republican Presidential nomination is the large number of women, especially young women not much involved in politics, who turn out whenever she makes a campaign stop."[52] By the summer of 1999 most media outlets were noting the lack of momentum in the Dole campaign, and after Dole withdrew her candidacy, postmortems of the campaign were laced with pioneer imagery. *ABCNews.com* reported that "frontrunner George W. Bush says Dole has been a friend, a trailblazer and an inspiration to many women."[53] The *Washington Post* headlined a story about Dole's withdrawal as follows: "One Small Step for Womankind: Elizabeth Dole's Candidacy Became Merely the Symbol She Avoided." Dole herself lauded the pioneering aspects of her campaign, even as she was angling for a possible vice presidential nomination. Answering questions after announcing her withdrawal from the campaign, Dole said, "I think what we've done is pave the way for the person who will be the first woman president. And I'm just delighted at what has happened because I feel like we've really made a great contribution."[54]

The next woman to make a contribution as a prospective presidential contender from a major political party was Carol Moseley Braun, a former US senator from Illinois. Her affiliation with a major national party and her inclusion in the Democratic primary debates, when coupled with her political credentials as a former US senator and ambassador, were enough to categorize her presidential bid as "serious." Her pioneer status was underscored by reports noting the "history-making potential" of her candidacy.[55] Yet, media reports indicated that she was "not considered a first-tier candidate" and called her "desperate" and "theatrical."[56] Even so, her candidacy was endorsed by the National Organization for Women (NOW) and the National Women's Political Caucus.

This brief summary of women's presidential bids prior to Hillary Clinton's in 2008, unique in their own right and spanning three centuries and multiple political parties, illustrates the resilience of the pioneer metaphor and related frontier imagery. Rather than helping women candidates identify with American exceptionalism and the rugged individualist persona that characterizes the public identity of so many successful male US presidential candidates, the pioneer image tags female presidential candidates as symbolic "trailblazers." Although the path to the White House has become well worn due to the efforts of women over several centuries, they ultimately are stopped short of their goal. Each woman is unique and interesting, but none emerge as credible presidential contenders. The appeal of their campaigns is dubbed largely symbolic. Their pioneering spirit paved the way into the history books but not the Oval Office. As a result, the notion of women's presidential leadership remains an exotic curiosity, or worse, an implausible oxymoron. Karlyn Kohrs Campbell notes that women's public participation itself used to be "oxymoronic."[57] One of the authors of this study has argued elsewhere that the strategic introduction of paradox and oxymoron may function as a strength of women's political participation rather than as a disadvantage.[58] Next, we explore the announcement speeches of four of the eleven women presidential candidates discussed in this chapter by considering the extent to which their speeches demonstrate a recognition of the challenges and opportunities associated with the pioneer narrative. Women presidential candidates have embraced, resisted, and/or attempted to recast the pioneer metaphor that has functioned as an intransigent campaign frame throughout history.

I Now Announce Myself as a Candidate for the Presidency

Victoria Woodhull, Shirley Chisholm, Elizabeth Dole, and Carol Moseley Braun each ran formidable, if unsuccessful, campaigns for the US presidency. Each woman cast her candidacy in terms that were appropriate to her situation and to her qualifications, acknowledging in different ways her position as a political pioneer. We examine each candidate's declaration to run for the presidency by assessing both fulfillment of the generic demands of such an address and by considering the ways in which each candidate negotiated the pioneer metaphor in asserting her fitness for the office. Judith Trent explains that the first stage through which a political campaign progresses is the "surfacing" stage, in which "predictable and specifically timed rhetorical transactions . . . serve consummatory and instrumental functions during the preprimary phase of the campaign."[59] During the surfacing phase, it is particularly important for candidates to demonstrate fitness for the office and establish an initially viable presidential identity. Fitness for office may be embodied in those myths, stories, and characteristics that have come to be associated with the presidency or political leadership in general. The announcement speech is the main public event of the surfacing period and arguably the most important for establishing the candidate's public persona, setting the tone of the campaign, and identifying the issues around which the initial campaign will revolve.

Victoria Woodhull, Pioneer as Radical Reformer

Woodhull, notably the most radical of the presidential candidates discussed here, was absolutely an outsider. Her pioneering efforts for women's equality and sexual freedom were not only socially proscribed but also illegal. A presidential candidate when women did not have the right to vote, Woodhull recognized that she would not be elected US president. Consequently, she relished her outsider, pioneer status even as it proved to be an unsuccessful vehicle toward presidential identity formation. In her defense of free love she set herself apart from the general public and admitted to the spiritualist activities for which she and her sister were known: "I have a better right to speak, as one having authority in this matter, than most of you have, since it has been my province to study it in all its various lights and shades. When I practiced clairvoyance, hundreds, aye thousands, of desolate, heart-broken men, as well as women, came to me for advice." Moreover, Woodhull asserted her status as pioneer of a new religious and ethical understanding, a pioneering prophet crying in the wilderness. She urged, "Do not criticize me, therefore, from a commonplace point of view. Question me, first, on the grounds of my faith. . . . My whole nature is prophetic. I do not and cannot live merely in the present."[60]

Woodhull formally announced her presidential candidacy on April 2, 1870, in a letter to the *New York Herald* that is excerpted in one of her political biographies. The letter forcefully asserted her fitness for office: "While others of my sex devoted themselves to a crusade against the laws that shackle the women of the country, I asserted my individual independence; while others prayed for the good time coming, I worked for it; while others argued the equality of women with man, I proved it by successfully engaging in business; while others sought to show that there was no valid reason why women should be treated, socially and politically, as being inferior to man, I boldly entered the arena of politics and business and exercised the rights I already possessed. I therefore claim the right to speak for the unenfranchised women of the country, and believing as I do that the prejudices which still exist in the popular mind against women in public life will soon disappear, I now announce myself as a candidate for the Presidency."[61]

Woodhull's statement is rhetorically intriguing insofar as it unites power feminist sensibilities with radical feminist goals.[62] Woodhull exemplified what Sonja K. Foss and Karen A. Foss have termed "repowered feminism," whereby "the power of symbolic interpretation is feminism's most powerful tool because it means that any feminist, no matter what her current condition, has the capacity to achieve the world she desires." Repowered feminism, informed by a "name it and claim it" philosophy, "recognizes and applauds the principles of power feminism and its focus on choice, the eschewal of victimhood, and the celebration of successes."[63] Woodhull embraced this ontological perspective, asserting that her "individual independence" allowed her to "boldly [enter] the arena of politics and business and [exercise] the rights" she believed she "already possessed."

Despite this power feminist mindset, Woodhull also was a radical reformer. Even to the point of urging rebellion, Woodhull campaigned for a government that recognized the citizenship rights of all. In her lecture on constitutional equality given in February 1871 she argued, "We mean treason; we mean secession, and on a thousand times grander scale than was that of the South. We are plotting revolution; we will overthrow this bogus republic and plant a government of righteousness in its stead, which shall not only profess to derive its power from the consent of the governed, but shall do so in reality."[64] In this respect, her speech illustrates the principle outlined by Stephen H. Browne, that "violence gives rise to certain interpretive possibilities, makes possible ways of reordering collective commitments and shared meanings." Browne's specific assessment of abolitionist Angelina Grimké easily could be applied to Woodhull—that her rhetoric "offered a compelling rationale for public life that could not—must not—be compromised by constraints imposed artificially by religion, race, or gender."[65] Woodhull's performed authenticity was integral to her candidate identity. Perhaps ahead of her time, Woodhull faced a general populace in 1872 that was not prepared for a radical female agitator as president. As an outsider, she clearly became the spectacle she sought but not the serious presidential contender demanded by the office. The radical pioneer reformer embodied the transgressive, oxymoronic nature of the pioneer metaphor. Unfortunately, Woodhull also serves as an illustration of power feminism's inherent challenges. Although Woodhull asserted her inalienable rights and pointed to her own individual successes in her announcement message, her rhetorical re-visioning was insufficient to the task of transforming presidentiality. Structural barriers proved more powerful than Woodhull's imposing repowered feminism.

Shirley Chisholm, a "Double" Pioneer

Nearly one hundred years later, on January 25, 1972, Shirley Chisholm delivered her presidential announcement address at the Concord Baptist Church in Brooklyn, New York. Those in the audience would have known her status as an elected official, her collaborative efforts in founding the National Organization for Women, and her pioneering work on the Equal Rights Amendment (ERA). However, Chisholm chose not to mention those efforts. Instead, her fitness for the office was communicated implicitly through the use of contrast: "Fellow Americans, we have looked in vain to the Nixon administration for the courage, the spirit, the character and the words to lift us. To bring out the best in us, to rekindle in each of us our faith in the American dream. Yet all we have received in return is just another smooth exercise in political manipulation, deceit and deception, callousness and indifference to our individual problems and a disgusting playing of divisive politics. Pinning [*sic*] the young against the old, labor against management, north against south, black against white. (Clapping.) The abiding concern of this administration has been one of political expediency, rather than the needs of man's nature."[66]

By contrast, Chisholm implied that she was fit for the office because she possessed "the courage, the spirit, the character" necessary. She represented honesty rather than "deceit and deception," concern rather than "indifference," unity rather than "divisive politics." She further demonstrated her fitness insofar as she had already engaged in the ritual expectation of the campaign trip: "I know from my travels to the cities and small towns of America that we have a vast potential, which can and must be put to constructive use in getting this great nation together." Yet, by indicating her fitness for the office implicitly through the use of contrast, Chisholm did not take advantage of her specific leadership experiences that would qualify her for the job. At this important event in the surfacing stage of the campaign, she needed to take advantage of the media attention and her own leadership experience to demonstrate rather than imply her fitness. Although the audience may already have known these details, explicit inclusion was necessitated not by the pragmatics of the situation but by the consummatory expectations of the announcement ritual.

Shirley Chisholm articulated her candidate identity through a Burkean strategy of identification. Kenneth Burke notes that "identification is affirmed with earnestness precisely because there is division. Identification is compensatory to division."[67] Illustrating the possibility of identification as a byproduct of division, Chisholm opened her remarks as follows: "I stand before you today as a candidate for the Democratic nomination for the Presidency of the United States of America. (Clapping.) I am not the candidate of black America, although I am black and proud. (Clapping.) I am not the candidate of the women's movement of this country, although I am a woman, and I am equally proud of that. (Clapping.) I am not the candidate of any political bosses or fat cats or special interests. (Clapping. Cheers.) I stand here now without endorsements from many big name politicians or celebrities or any other kind of prop. I do not intend to offer to you the tired and glib clichés, which for too long have been an accepted part of our political life. I am the candidate of the people of America. And my presence before you now symbolizes a new era in American political history."

Chisholm's political identity was thus premised on uniqueness. Her unique stature as a "double first" for the Democratic Party positioned her as a one-of-a-kind candidate. Paradoxically, she identified features of her political persona that made her unique and turned them around, using them to identify with audience members who may not have shared her identity characteristics.

The pioneering spirit of Shirley Chisholm resonated with a more traditional version of the frontier myth yet illustrates the double meaning of the mythos for female candidates. Chisholm concluded her announcement speech by urging her audience to "regain control of our destiny as we go down the Chisholm Trail for 1972." The "Chisholm Trail" imagery was repeated throughout the campaign and alluded to the frontier myth that functions to define American identity. In Chisholm's case, however, the imagery also encapsulated the candidate's recognition of the symbolic nature of her candidacy. She noted in her announcement that "my presence before you now symbolizes a new era in American political history." This statement underscored the aspect of the pioneer image that positions women at the periphery of US presidential leadership, marking their candidacy as transgressive.

As a supporter of the ERA and a founder of the New York chapter of the National Organization for Women, Chisholm was a key leader in the second wave of feminism in the United States, yet in her presidential announcement she told voters that "I am not the candidate of the women's movement of this country." Nonetheless, she was the first candidate to earn an endorsement from NOW, and feminist leaders campaigned on her behalf. Jo Freeman writes that "Chisholm was so outspoken in favor of women's rights that she was often criticized for not paying enough attention to black issues."[68] When asked about the discrimination she faced as both an African American and a woman, Chisholm stated, "When I ran for the Congress, when I ran for president, I met more discrimination as a woman than for being black. Men are men."[69] Chisholm's presidential candidacy, then, reflects the assumptions and perspectives of the liberal and radical feminism of the 1960s and 1970s. Unlike Woodhull and Chase Smith, Chisholm acknowledged the structural barriers, including patriarchy, that impeded her presidential prospects.

Elizabeth Dole, Pioneer as Public Servant
Elizabeth Dole detailed her leadership qualifications after a shaky beginning to her March 10, 1999, exploratory committee announcement speech. Her statement of intent in the speech's introduction was characterized by

a feminine qualifier: "As you know, I have been *thinking about* running for President" [emphasis added].[70] Quickly recovering, Dole began to list her political qualifications: "Yes, I've seen many Presidential campaigns up close. I know what they entail. And I know a run for the Presidency should be undertaken only if you believe in something so strongly that its accomplishment makes everything worthwhile." Dole demonstrated her fitness for the office by stating she had "spent a lifetime in public service." She then recounted résumé highlights such as the "opportunity to serve five presidents," "serv[ing] as a federal trade commissioner," and "of course I've just recently been serving as president of the American Red Cross, which is a $2.2 billion corporation." She went on to list the details: "Now at the Department of Transportation, my mission was really to oversee the management of material resources. At the Labor Department, it was human resources, and at the Red Cross, inner resources." Although Dole's political experience rivaled that of any male candidate, her choice to describe her work as "service" fit a more feminine model of women's political action as subordinated to the needs of others versus a masculine model of political leadership as individual agency and personal vision. She spoke of "public service" rather than politics, promoted teamwork over individual action, and spoke of the Department of Labor as a "mission field." She summarized this servant-leader image when she concluded the discussion of her qualifications, stating, "There is one overarching theme to my thirty plus years in public service, and I believe there [*sic*]; it's that I placed service over politics, consensus over confrontation. And I think it's important that you know that."

Although the image of a servant-leader is exemplified by the biblical, New Testament example of Christ, Dole's announcement discourse connoted a feminized version of servanthood that contradicted the heroic, individualistic masculinity of the US presidency. As Janis L. Edwards points out, Dole's "failure to alter her highly feminized campaign style for her first bid as a (presidential) candidate in 2000 has been criticized as a contributing factor to her failure to gain visibility in that race."[71] No doubt a conscious choice on Dole's part, the servanthood theme only reinforced her outsider status, which she, as a woman presidential candidate, needed to minimize rather than maximize.

This theme complemented the pioneer narrative insofar as it proposed a new model of presidential leadership: consensus rather than decisiveness, serving rather than leading, a "we" orientation rather than heroic individualism. Kim Reiser argues that Dole attempted to craft a "feminine presidency."[72] At one point late in her announcement address Dole acknowledged that American society does not hold public servants in high regard: "And as we raise regard for teachers, let's hope that we raise the regard for public servants. Because I think whether you're in the classroom or in government or whether you're working at the local Red Cross, public service brings out the best in ourselves." The point of her argument was clear. As a public servant she had acquired an abundance of leadership experience, and the office of president requires leadership experience. Even so, US culture has not traditionally regarded presidents as servants, and thus Dole's attempt to inhabit that role did not enhance her own presidentiality. Further, by her own admission, US citizens typically do not regard public servants highly. Thus, the choice to frame her leadership experience, metaphorically, as public service cast her as a pioneer embodying a new form of presidential leadership. Unfortunately, rather than expanding the myth of the US presidency, Dole's pioneering feminine leadership resided outside the mythic bounds of the Oval Office.

Dole was a presidential pioneer in another sense as well. In the aftermath of second-wave feminism, many cultural conservatives participated in the backlash against feminism. In 1996, Dole cautiously aligned herself with women's rights, even as she courted "family values" voters. When asked during an interview for *US News & World Report* whether or not she considered herself a feminist, Dole stated, "I think if it means that you had some sort of prepackaged answers that are handed down by the political correctness club, no. But if it means that you want equal opportunity for women, more freedom for women—absolutely."[73] Rather than repudiating feminism, Dole sought to refashion it for pro-life, pro-woman, conservative political purposes. Some feminist critics have categorized Dole with other postfeminists of the 1990s.[74] However, Dole's position on feminism was distinct from those who argued that the feminist movement had harmed women or that there was no longer any need for feminist agitation because the objectives of the movement had largely been achieved. Dole recognized the structural barriers to women's political and professional advancement—in part because she had negotiated many of them personally. Dole openly talked about the sexism she faced as one of 24 women (in a class of 550) to enter Harvard Law School in 1962, and her announcement speech emphasized the ways in which women's perspectives are needed at the presidential level. In fact, her feminism is reminiscent of that espoused by members of the Women's Christian Temperance Union in the nineteenth century: convinced of women's superior moral authority, they aligned themselves with the radical feminists of the suffrage movement in order to gain the political rights that would allow them to exert their moral authority more effectively. Dole, too, advocated a political agenda that was informed by religious conservatism. The fact that she was a woman seeking presidential authority, however, made her a de facto feminist reformer.

Carol Moseley Braun, a Pioneer with Experience

More than any woman featured in this chapter, Carol Moseley Braun demonstrated effectively her fitness for the office of president by presenting herself as a strong leader willing to "fight for the nomination." She delivered her announcement address three times in September 2003 and clearly engaged in the ritual expectations of the surfacing stage by embarking on a campaign tour: "Over the past several months I have traveled America, talking with people, listening to them, registering voters and engaging in a passionate debate about our country's direction. I am grateful to all those who opened their homes and their hearts, to those who shared their experiences with me, and who made it possible for me to explore the prospect of a Presidential campaign."[75]

Moseley Braun actively stated her political intentions, without qualifiers: "Today, I am officially declaring my candidacy for the Democratic nomination for President of the United States. I am running for the Democratic nomination because I believe this party ought to stand for inclusion, hope, and new ways to resolve old problems." With that beginning, she went on to argue that she had "the experience, the ability and the ideas to heal and renew America." She had "broken down barriers, built bridges and brought people together to achieve solutions that put the public interest first." Moseley Braun supported her claim with a list of examples that detailed her accomplishments:

> As a young federal prosecutor, I won a Justice Department award for my work to put an end to exploitation in housing policy. As a state representative, I fought for education, and passed laws to create the first local school councils and agriculture schools in Illinois. My colleagues voted me the "Conscience of the House" for my advocacy for the poor. As a county executive, I convened the first advisory council, and worked with organized labor to improve conditions for the employees and the public. When I left that office, it had become a profit center for Cook County, the workers were better off, and the public was better served. As a United States Senator, and as the first woman to serve on the Finance Committee, I passed laws for women's pension equity, and for environmental remediation and alternative energy, for school modernization and restoration of the interest deduction for college loans. As Ambassador, I was credited with improving relations on behalf of the United States, and was the first envoy to be made an honorary member of the Te Atiawa Maori tribe.

Carol Moseley Braun not only had a broad political résumé on which to base a presidential run but also was the only candidate to claim the title of president as her rightful political identity in her announcement speech. Near the end of her speech she stated, "As President, I will give you an America as good as its promise. I will reach out to bring us together to create an American renaissance, revival and renewal. I am uniquely qualified to do the job of President, and I offer the clearest alternative to this current administration, whose only new idea has been preemptive war and a huge new bureaucracy. I can fix the mess they have created, because I am practical, I am not afraid of partnerships and I am committed to making the world better for our children. By tapping the talent, the ideas, and the capacity that our whole society has to offer, we will expand the probability of succeeding together."

Moseley Braun's conceptualization of her political identity reveals the gradual but steady change in women candidates' articulations of self. If Woodhull had assumed the title of US president without acknowledging the obvious barriers between herself and the Oval Office, audience members would have dismissed her as delusional, rather than merely as radical. Although Moseley Braun's candidacy was only slightly more credible than Woodhull's, Moseley Braun could adopt the title of US president, at least within the confines of her announcement speech. That suggests that women have made progress since 1872. However, that progress will be limited as long as women presidential candidates continue to be viewed, first and foremost, as pioneers.

Carol Moseley Braun explicitly embraced the pioneer metaphor, not only noting her many political "firsts" but also contending that her leadership style would necessarily be different from that of the George W. Bush administration. Rather than waging a war on terror, she would build "partnerships for peace." Thus, she attempted to recast the pioneer metaphor paradoxically as well, but in a much more active, ego-oriented fashion than Dole or Chisholm had. She made use of her political experience even as she made it clear she intended to "shift gears, try another way, tap some of the talent that has been relegated to the sidelines of leadership." In other words, her identity was positioned as both inside and outside, as independent and collaborative, as experienced and fresh. The image of woman president as pioneer emerges explicitly in the anecdote Moseley Braun used to conclude her speech:

> Just last week, my little 9-year-old niece Claire called me in to her room to show me her social studies book. Turning to the pages on which all of our Presidents were pictured, she looked at me and complained: But Auntie Carol, all the Presidents are boys! I want Claire, and your daughters and sons[,] to know that in America, everyone has a chance to serve and contribute. . . . This campaign is our way of fighting to give Claire and every American girl or boy not only the opportunity to become President of this great country, but the freedom to decide to lead a quality private life if they choose to do so. There is no human power greater than a made up mind, and we have decided not to let them take away our liberty, our opportunity, our hope for a better future.

Moseley Braun's relationship to feminism was similar to that of Chisholm. Like Chisholm, Moseley Braun received the NOW endorsement when she ran for president. In that endorsement, Kim Gandy, NOW Political Action Committee chair, stated that "Moseley Braun's candidacy is a prime example of what feminists strive for—women moving up through all levels of political office."[76] Due, in part, to the gains made by women of Chisholm's generation, Moseley Braun was able to work for personal political advancement without needing to agitate simultaneously for women's collective rights in the outspoken manner that Chisholm did. In fact, although Moseley Braun alluded to the "hazing" she experienced as a junior senator, at the time she ran for president she asserted that "I've been treated, I think, the same [as other presidential candidates] in the sense that I've been given an opportunity to be heard."[77]

Each candidate examined in this chapter chose to articulate her fitness for the presidency by emphasizing character traits and personal experiences that not only were strengths for the candidate but also communicated to the electorate both unique expertise and an optimistic hope for a better future. For Woodhull it was an unabashed announcement of her female agency. Chisholm made an implicit appeal to ethics and unity. Dole articulated a commitment to public service, and Moseley Braun highlighted her broad political résumé. Each candidate further bolstered her claims to fitness by connecting her strengths to her distinctive candidate identity. Yet Moseley Braun and the other women presidential candidates have not entered into the annals of the American presidency. Perhaps this realization, more than any other, underscores the liability that the pioneer metaphor may present to female presidential candidates.

The Gendered History of Presidential Power

Our discussion in the introduction to this chapter gestured toward the possibility that Senator Hillary Clinton would be the next in a long line of female presidential pioneers. However, the speed with which her prospective candidacy was brushed aside by experienced journalists and political observers in favor of the less experienced but fresh Democratic face of Barack Obama points to the lingering challenges faced by women presidential candidates. Speaking on the October 22, 2006, edition of the *Chris Matthews Show, Time* columnist Joe Klein described the reception Obama was getting from voters in battleground states: "I was in Virginia, Maryland, Illinois, and another time in Iowa with him, and boy, the crowds are huge and he's terrific. He really is really good." All the panelists on that edition of the *Chris Matthews Show* gushed over Obama. MSNBC correspondent Norah O'Donnell referred to the message of unification Obama articulated in his keynote address to the 2004 Democratic National Convention, saying, "That's a very powerful message that he can use if he wants to run." Klein heralded Obama as "one of the most talented politicians I've seen in 37 years of doing this," and the BBC's Katty Kay topped off the praise by observing that Obama "is ridiculously good looking."[78]

That love fest, rarely seen among journalists discussing politicians, prompted host Chris Matthews to ask, "Does Obama have a better shot at being president than Hillary Clinton?" Matthews then cut to a clip of *New York Times* columnist Maureen Dowd, quoting political reporter Johnny Apple. She said, "I will give you a prediction from him, which is that it will be easier in 2008 for a black [*sic*] to become president than a woman, he thinks, because women have a track record of failure in this regard. And he thinks Colin Powell kind of got the American psyche ready for the idea." Acknowledging the racism embedded in American history, the panelists discussed Obama's appeal among white voters. Klein asserted, "When you see whites approaching Barack Obama, you know, they're ridiculous. They're, you know, they're practically salivating. It's unbelievable. They're all atwitter, you know? They love the guy." O'Donnell responded by noting that this enthusiasm could be attributed to Obama's version of his life story, which amounted to the "melting pot that is America." Klein agreed, stating more pointedly that "he's an African-American who doesn't grind their [whites'] noses in racial guilt."[79]

We recount this extended summary of one roundtable discussion of Obama versus Clinton as prospective Democratic presidential candidates to illustrate the problem women candidates still face. An African American man such as Obama can construct a personal history that places his political identity largely outside of the painful history of black America. His identity is constructed as African and as American—an outgrowth of his unique parentage and a perfect illustration of the popular melting pot metaphor at work. Women, conversely, cannot step outside the gendered history of US political power. Even someone like Hillary Clinton, who grew up with the advantages of education, cut her political teeth shaping policy somewhat behind the scenes at the gubernatorial level and with greater public exposure in the East Wing of the White House before being elected to the US Senate and then accepting an appointment as US secretary of state—even she is evaluated as potentially ineffectual as a presidential candidate. As the *Chicago Tribune*'s Clarence Page observed on the *Chris Matthews Show* broadcast, "Hillary Clinton carries political baggage with her right now, and as somebody said, Obama hasn't even got a carry-on."[80]

Our evaluation of women's bids for the US presidency is not meant to suggest perpetual failure. Rather, by highlighting the ways in which the pioneer metaphor has been wedded to women candidates and by explaining its potentially deleterious effects, we hope to expand the discursive space within which women presidential candidates are evaluated. Women need to move from the margins to the center of US politics. It is a move for which they have been strategizing in private and public discourses for centuries. Recognizing the importance of rejecting the pioneer metaphor is another small step forward. Replacing it is the next challenge.

As women candidates and voters develop new narratives of gendered presidentiality, they necessarily position themselves in relationship to feminism, antifeminism, and postfeminism. Our analysis of women presidential candidates' announcement addresses reveals the complexities associated with categorizing women candidates vis-à-vis feminism. Although Victoria Woodhull was active during feminism's first wave, she articulated a power feminist stance that has come to be associated with third-wave feminism. The presidential candidates most closely associated with second-wave liberal feminism (which is often critiqued as a movement that catered to middle-class white women) were African Americans Shirley Chisholm and Carol Moseley Braun. Although Elizabeth Dole is viewed by some as the conservative forerunner to Sarah Palin and Michele Bachmann, her rhetoric does not align neatly with a postfeminist world view. Examination of women's historical bids for the US presidency illustrates that presidential contests are not only magnets for antifeminist sentiments. They are also sites at which the meaning of feminism gets negotiated; how that negotiation develops will influence the prospects of future women presidential candidates.

Another place where presidentiality and feminism(s) get negotiated is the realm of popular culture. In the next chapter, we assess the depiction of fictional women presidential figures in television and film by examining the extent to which the pop culture presidency exhibits ideologies that are feminist, antifeminist, and postfeminist.

Fictional Presidentiality

Presidential Portrayals on the Large and Small Screens

n March 2000, a flash-forward episode of the popular cartoon series *The Simpsons* cast resident feminist and earnest overachiever Lisa Simpson as "America's first straight female president."[1] The episode's seemingly pre-scient storyline forces President Simpson to respond to a severe fiscal crisis. She strategizes the best way to break the news to the American public, dis-cussing her dilemma with her trusted advisor, Milhouse:

LISA. If I'm going to bail the country out, I'll have to raise taxes, but in my speech I'd like to avoid calling it a "painful emergency tax."
MILHOUSE. What about "colossal salary grab"?
LISA. See, that has the same problem. We need to soften the blow.
MILHOUSE. Well, if you just want to out-and-out lie—okay, we could call it a "temporary refund adjustment."
LISA. I love it.

Satirical television programs like *The Simpsons* give voice to viewers' frus-trations about American politics. Robert Hariman argues that insofar as it performs the task of "comic refunctioning," parodic television and "related forms of political humor" offer "essential resources for sustaining public culture." The aforementioned episode of *The Simpsons*, however, does more than poke fun at politicians' predilection for political euphemisms. It also portrays the US president as a woman. Although the cartoon characters on *The Simpsons* bear less mimetic resemblance to real life than do other fictionalized portrayals of presidentiality, Trevor Parry-Giles and Shawn J. Parry Giles assert that each pop cultural incarnation of a presidential figure helps to "define presidential leadership in powerful and meaningful ways, reflecting the cultural preoccupation with this institution and its place in our national culture." John M. Murphy concurs, explaining that "even as pundits decry the decline of politics and the degradation of the presidency, ordinary people applaud the heroism of fictional presidents and the durability of the institution."[2] When fictional presidential incarnations happen also to be female, they may contribute to the broader project of promoting women's political agency. As Marie C. Wilson, president of the White House Project, a national nonpartisan organization dedicated to advancing women's leadership, explains, "You can't be what you can't see. Once people see women in top leadership roles on the screen, they can imagine it happening."[3] Similarly, Donna Mullen Good, CEO of the Center for Women & Enterprise, asserts that "when kids grow up watching a show where a woman is president, when they are 18, seeing a woman's name on the presidential ballot is not going to be a strange thing."[4] Television critic Melanie McFarland concurs, lauding "television's ability to push culture forward" and asserting that "if viewers can buy a female president in primetime . . . perhaps electing a female president isn't such a distant reality after all."[5]

Of course, simply switching a fictional president's gender is not sufficient, either as a sign of attitudinal change or as a tool to promote said change. How women presidential figures are portrayed is consequential as well. An informed critique of filmic and televisual presidentiality promotes understanding of what Lynn Spigel and Denise Mann call media's "specific discursive functions" and the propensity of mass media to "produce, transmit, and at times transform the logic of cultural fantasies and practices." Following Spigel and Mann, Bonnie J. Dow advocates examination of "television programming as public discourse."[6] In the preceding chapter, we examined presidentiality as it has been enacted by women candidates throughout history. This chapter assesses gendered presidentiality as it has been articulated and negotiated in popular film and television. Evaluating the films *Kisses for My President* (1964), *Air Force One* (1997), and *The Contender* (2000), as well as the television series *Battlestar Galactica* (2004–9), *Commander in Chief* (2005–6), and *24* (2001–10), we argue that these texts operate on both propositional and suppositional levels.[7] Propositionally, these films and television series contend that women are as qualified as men to serve as US president, and sexism, to the extent that it still exists in society, is presented as outmoded, ridiculous, and/or corrupt. Suppositionally, however, each program reinforces the norms of presidentiality such as masculinity, militarism, and whiteness. By characterizing fictional women presidents as primarily sexual, maternal, and humanitarian, each text paradoxically reifies the notion that women are ill suited to the US presidency. As such, texts that have been hailed as progressive sometimes function to feed the backlash experienced by real women candidates. After briefly considering the scholarly import of fictionalized presidentiality, we examine the propositional and suppositional arguments that emerge in these six texts. We conclude by reflecting on the ways in which filmic and televisual presidentiality rehearses, reveals, and (occasionally) challenges cultural anxieties about women's presidential potential.

Presidentiality on the Large and Small Screens

One of the first challenges facing any critic of mediated discourse is the polysemous nature of texts.[8] Not only are complex mediated texts likely to be interpreted differently by members of active and diverse audiences, but their symbolic architecture can be described differently depending on one's critical focus. Leah Ceccarelli encourages critics to attend to "hermeneutic depth" in their critique of texts, recognizing the possibility that "*both* an interpretation *and* its opposite are sustained by the text" [emphasis in original].[9]

Attention to contradiction is a particularly important component of feminist media criticism. Marian Meyers explains that mediated representations of women in postmodern pop culture are "fractured" and as such are "inconsistent and contradictory, torn between traditional misogynistic notions about women and their roles on the one hand, and feminist ideals of equality for women on the other." Dow rightly notes that the "meanings offered by television are rarely direct, often contradictory, and never final." She explains that "the persuasive function of television is not so much to provide solutions to cultural conflicts but . . . rather to negotiate the parameters for the debate." Helene A. Shugart, Catherine Egley Waggoner, and D. Lynn O'Brien Hallstein suggest that in postmodern media contexts, resistive texts often are appropriated through "an aesthetic code of juxtaposition" in which "messages of resistance are coopted, commodified, and sold to audiences as a 'genuine imitation'—something whose code appears strikingly similar to the resistant discourse but, by virtue of strategic repositioning[,] is rendered devoid of challenge." Indeed, the presence of women presidential figures in popular media may be noteworthy, but, as Shugart points out, "visibility . . . is no guarantor of legitimacy."[10]

Stanley Kauffman explains that the US presidency "has long been an available ingredient of film-making. In earlier days the film president was either a historical figure (Walter Huston as Lincoln) or a dignified fictional chap (Walter Huston in *Gabriel over the White House*). Nowadays actual presidents get morphed into films (Johnson and Kennedy and Nixon in *Forrest Gump*, Clinton in *Contact*), or fictional ones are utilized in every which way."[11]

Presidents populate the small screen as well. The hit series *The West Wing* (1999–2006) is perhaps the best-known example of what Parry-Giles and Parry-Giles dubbed "prime-time presidentiality."[12] The US president also has been featured in other popular dramas, such as *24* and *Battlestar Galactica,* and in blockbuster films such as *Air Force One, Deep Impact* (1998), and *Independence Day* (1998).

Although audiences profess increasing levels of sophistication in their media use, Parry-Giles and Parry-Giles contend that "fictionalized representations of politics are powerful and accessible rhetorical forms, increasingly influential as they improve in technological sophistication and mimetic capacity. Such discourses play a central role in the definition and expression of political culture and political leaders."[13] Terry Christensen and Peter J. Haas concur, emphasizing the societal functions of political films but acknowledging that social scientists have been slow to treat them as a serious object of study because they do not lend themselves to quantitative analysis and because audiences respond to political films in multiple, and sometimes contradictory, ways. Although many depictions of the US presidency in popular culture underscore a simplified and stereotypical understanding of that role as hypermasculinized, militarized, and lacking ethnic diversity, Parry-Giles and Parry-Giles argue that the postmodern era has ushered in a more complex view of prime-time presidentiality that accommodates chaos and oppositionality, in which mediated texts often are "trapped between a more progressive, community-based notion of inclusivity and an individualistic image that perpetuates the traditional, conservative vision of a white/male hero embodying infinite power for righteous ends."[14]

Like the television series *The West Wing*, the texts considered in this chapter are characterized by the oppositionality Parry-Giles and Parry-Giles discuss. They explain that although *The West Wing* "disrupts the images of traditional political power, depicting a chaotic, inclusive, and communal presidentiality," this "ideological disruption of [*The West Wing*'s] postmodern take on the presidency is ultimately contained and controlled by its simultaneously conventional discourse of presidential politics."[15] Building on this observation, we argue that the texts considered in this chapter serve two distinct purposes, which, although they seem to oppose one another, are, in actuality, closely related. On one level, each text presents a propositional argument that women and men are equally qualified to serve as US president, and sexism, to the extent that it exists, is presented as outmoded, ridiculous, and/or corrupt. Because the propositional argument is explicitly performed by the characters, articulated through plot development, and confirmed by journalistic framing of the texts, the films and television series discussed in this chapter have sometimes been regarded as progressive and may appeal to audience members who value increased political agency for women. At the same time, however, the films and television series assessed here also were popular with a broad US audience. Their mass appeal required each text to reach beyond its "ideal" audience of progressives interested in women's political agency. We contend that the broad popularity of these six texts was fostered, in part, by suppositional arguments. Unlike the propositional argument, which is explicitly performed for the audience, suppositional arguments are unstated and their premises are assumed. Specifically, the texts considered in this chapter reinforce the norms of presidentiality by failing to critique its masculinity, militarism, and whiteness and by reinscribing women as sexual and maternal. The suppositional appeal of each text is enthymematic—it relies on the audience both to supply cultural assumptions about presidentiality *and* to do so without attending too closely to the implications of those assumptions. In other words, the presidentiality presented in these mediated representations is both progressive and reactionary, radical and conservative, feminist and antifeminist, fresh and familiar. Without the explicit claims about women's political competence performed propositionally in these discourses, each film or television series likely would have been dismissed as an outmoded caricature of political leadership. At the same time, however, if the texts disrupted the norms of presidential power too dramatically, they would lack fidelity to broader narratives about US political leadership and likely would have failed to garner widespread audience appeal. By examining both propositional and suppositional arguments, critics and citizens not only become better equipped to think critically about fictional depictions of gendered politics but also may begin to understand why the prospect of a woman president has, thus far, been relegated to the realm of popular fiction.

Because our analysis of gendered presidentiality in film and television constitutes just one chapter of this book, our assessment of each series and film is necessarily brief. Rather than accounting fully for the ideologies, themes, and strategies present in each text, we trace the contours of presidentiality as they emerge in the performances of primary characters, the storylines of selected episodes, and the journalistic and academic framing of each text. Our assessment is meant to be suggestive of broad trends in popular incarnations of fictional presidentiality rather than representative of the complexities present in each text. While more detailed analysis would produce additional insights and might suggest oppositional interpretations, our assessment of the propositional and suppositional arguments present in all six texts reveals the ways in which presidentiality continues to be gendered even in a postmodern media environment.

Screening Madam President

We begin our analysis with the prototypical depiction of female presidentiality seen in the short-lived television series *Commander in Chief*. Of all the texts analyzed in this chapter, *Commander in Chief* was the only program for which the exploration of gendered presidentiality was its raison d'être; thus, it serves as a suitable place to begin our analysis.

Commander in Chief, a Network Television First

When writer/producer Rod Lurie's series about the first female US president premiered on September 27, 2005, both the series and subsequent journalistic coverage emphasized a narrative of historic firsts. *Commander in Chief* was the first major network television series to feature a female lead character in the role of the first woman president of the United States. Lurie's screenplays for the inaugural episodes focused on firsts, as evidenced by episode titles such as "First Choice," "First Strike," "First Dance," "First ... Do No Harm," and "First Scandal."[16] Lurie explained that the emphasis on firsts was intentional, saying that "we absolutely went into this with the agenda of making America comfortable with the idea of a female president."[17] The import of these fictional firsts was acknowledged by organizations like the White House Project and the Center for Women & Enterprise. The head of the White House Project gushed, "For us, *Commander in Chief* is historic. . . . When push comes to shove in Hollywood, women are still portrayed as leading ladies but not as leaders. One of our goals with the project is to help people understand how these images they see on television and the movies are really shaping their opinion." The CEO of the Center for Women & Enterprise claimed that "the fact that a woman is portrayed as president in a television show that's not science fiction or fantasy driven is about the path of social change. . . . This show is important for women in politics."[18]

Enthusiasm for the show was not limited to those for whom seeing a woman chief executive was a personal and professional project. Early in its run, viewers embraced the show. The *New York Times* estimated the audience for the premiere to be 16.15 million, making it "the night's most-watched program." The *Tampa Tribune* reported, "After an impressive debut in September, *Commander* shot up in the ratings for three consecutive weeks, indicating it was a hit on a tough, competitive night."[19] The show's star power, which likely contributed to its initial popularity, included Hollywood heavyweights Geena Davis and Donald Sutherland, cast, respectively, as President Mackenzie Allen and her political rival, Speaker of the House Nathan Templeton. Davis won a Golden Globe for her performance, but even her A-list talent could not carry the show to a second season. The series was plagued by behind-the-scenes chaos and subjected to unfavorable scheduling changes that resulted in series cancellation after just one season.[20]

Commander in Chief's pilot episode features Vice President Mackenzie Allen assuming the presidency after the sudden death of President Theodore Roosevelt Bridges. Allen's constitutionally mandated ascent is presented as a controversial move. On his deathbed, President Bridges asks Allen to resign the vice presidency to make way for Templeton to step in since Templeton, unlike the politically independent Allen, shares Bridges's conservative political philosophy. Templeton reveals that Allen was added to the ticket as a publicity stunt and an attempt to curry favor with women voters. When Allen convenes the Cabinet, she faces hostility and resistance. The *New York Times* reported that Lurie's decision to have Allen inherit the presidency via the death of President Bridges was "not a comment on the likelihood of a female presidential candidate being elected in real life." Instead, the series setup served a narrative purpose. Lurie explained, "I thought that it would be more dramatic to have her inheriting the job, because that way more people would be opposed to her."[21]

Positioning Mackenzie Allen to stand firm despite fierce opposition serves the series' propositional argument that women are as qualified as men to serve as US president. Even before she assumes the presidency, Allen is strong and resolute, a factor highlighted by her independent political affiliation, her determination to assume the presidency despite the wishes of President Bridges and his Cabinet, and her willingness in the first episode to embark on a just but potentially unpopular military strike. In fact, Allen's strength and independence are established even before the opening credits of the series premiere, in the following exchange with President Bridges's chief of staff, Jim Gardner:

GARDNER. Look, we've got hell on earth afoot. We've got Korea, Syria, Iran . . . things are too unstable, we don't need the world . . .

ALLEN. [*interrupts*] the world to see a soft, indecisive woman commanding the troops, as opposed to Nathan "Bloody Hell" Templeton.

GARDNER. Madam Vice President, I really must insist that you strongly consider—

ALLEN. Jim, you're not in a position to insist how I take my coffee.[22]

The series premiere shows Vice President Allen being comfortable leading not only the government but also the military. While aboard Air Force Two, she confirms with a top general that, if word of the president's condition leaked out, "we would move to a higher DEFCON [defense condition]." The general replies, "Yes, ma'am, that's SOP [standard operating procedure]." Vice President Allen replies definitively: "Okay. I'd like to elevate our readiness posture now. Let's not wait." The general agrees, but Gardner, the chief of staff, questions the decision. Allen waves him off then asks to move the fleet into hot spots. An irked Gardner blurts out, "What do you suggest I tell the president when he asks why you put our navy on high alert?" As if channeling the aura of the presidency, Vice President Allen replies, "He won't ask. He'll know." That prediction comes true when she briefly speaks with Bridges at his bedside, before his death.

President Allen's competence as commander in chief also is invoked explicitly at the conclusion of the series premiere, when she orders a military strike to rescue a Nigerian mother and baby. The mother is being held for adultery, facing death by stoning. Although Templeton, among others, advises against official US involvement in this matter, President Allen insists, telling the Nigerian ambassador, "If you think that I am going to stand by and watch a young woman be executed, tortured, for having sex, you are sorely mistaken." The extraction is a success, and episode two indicates that the move produced a spike in President Allen's approval ratings.

In addition to underscoring a woman's performance of presidential competence, *Commander in Chief* articulates the propositional claim that sexism, to the extent that it still exists in society, is outmoded, ridiculous, and/or corrupt. Vice President Allen acknowledges common stereotypes about women and leadership with frankness and sarcasm. In a closed-door meeting with Templeton, when she is debating whether or not to accede to the presidency, the aging, white-haired Speaker of the House dates himself by invoking old-style assumptions about women as leaders:

TEMPLETON. The world's in turmoil, Mac, it could go any which way. This is not the time for social advances made for the sake of social advances.
ALLEN. Meaning a woman in the Oval Office?
TEMPLETON. No, meaning a woman as the leader of the free world. How many violent states do you think would follow the edicts of a woman?
ALLEN. [*sarcastically*] Well, not only that, Nathan, but we'd have that once a month "will she or won't she press the button" thing.

Templeton's overt sexism is underscored when he responds to that comment with a sincere, "Well, couple of years and you're not going to have to worry about that anymore," invoking the impending onset of menopause.

Commander in Chief's propositional arguments in favor of women's competence and in opposition to sexism are developed in tandem with series elements that tell a more familiar story of US presidentiality. Parry-Giles and Parry-Giles explain that fictional depictions of US presidentiality are often "contained and controlled" by ideologies of "militarism, masculinity, and whiteness."[23] Militarism is central to *Commander in Chief*, but its virtues are extolled suppositionally. The series unfolds with militarism as an unquestioned component of presidentiality. Consider the series title: *Commander in Chief*. Reservations about the viability of women presidential candidates often raise the issue of whether a woman could credibly act as commander in chief during a time of war. In the post-9/11 context, the United States is perpetually engaged in the "war on terror"; thus, credible presidential figures (real or fictional) must demonstrate their ability to lead the military capably.

Commander in Chief addresses this expectation in its premiere episode. As noted previously, one of Vice President Allen's first official actions after President Bridges's hospitalization is to put the US Navy on high alert. The premiere episode itself revolves around the military effort to rescue a captive Nigerian woman from death by stoning. The episode ends as President Allen addresses the nation, with images of the military strike appearing as she makes the speech. As President Allen promises to "vigorously defend our Constitution," the shot cuts to an image of three soldiers leaping from US helicopters and running, guns drawn, to rescue the Nigerian woman and her baby. Episode three of *Commander in Chief* also revolves around a military crisis. After several US Drug Enforcement Agency agents are murdered in the fictional South American country of San Pasquale, President Allen devises a military, rather than political, solution to the problem. In retaliation for the killings, President Allen proposes bombing the coca crop to decrease the local dictator's wealth and power. She appears to come up with this plan on the spot in the Situation Room, after her legal and military advisors have failed to present her with workable options. Her chief of staff reacts, complimenting her plan as "bold. Decisive. You're going after the drugs, not the citizens. I like it." Simultaneously, the background score swells with the type of music that often accompanies successful military missions in action movies. Later, reluctant vice presidential nominee and maverick Warren Keaton approaches her chief of staff, who is also the president's husband and who had been preparing him for his confirmation hearings, and says, "I saw something in that Situation Room. It's not often that I find somebody I'm willing to follow."[24]

Some might argue that the valorization of militarism is itself an outgrowth of the norm of masculinity that is entwined with US presidentiality. That *Commander in Chief* would reify presidential masculinity is somewhat surprising, considering the series' propositional arguments in favor of a woman president. Suppositionally, however, masculinity is normalized in select scenes. In episode two, for example, President Allen is seeking someone to serve as her vice president. She wants to appoint Warren Keaton, her Democratic opponent in the previous campaign and a man known for frank opinions and strong character. He resists her invitation initially and only begins to consider it when she invokes a stereotypically masculine presidential persona:

KEATON. Vice president is really being secretary of the useless.
ALLEN. Then why did you join Crawford's ticket?
KEATON. He offered me State.
ALLEN. He offered you State?
KEATON. What can I tell you? If you want a man that's worth a damn in this job, you gotta make the job worth a damn. No offense.
ALLEN. You want to know something, Warren? For all your shoot from the hip, hoo ha bravado, you are absolutely full of crap.
KEATON. Beg your pardon?
ALLEN. You're here. That tells me you do want the job. I want you to have it. I'm not going to give you State. You should consider this an honor, Warren. Salute, and join the team. It's time to step up and be a man.[25]

President Allen may be able talk a masculine game, but *Commander in Chief* suppositionally reminds viewers that President Allen is unlike other occupants of the Oval Office. First, and perhaps most surprisingly given the show's setup, Allen is cast as not particularly political. An independent, Allen discusses the fact that her reelection to a second term as president is unlikely, a fact that frees her up to make politically unpopular decisions. Later, when Allen comes to possess an old but politically damaging video of Templeton, her husband, Rod Calloway, encourages her to use it:

CALLOWAY. Stop turning the other cheek, Mac.
ALLEN. I'm not going to destroy a man's life over something he said nearly half a century ago, no matter how hateful it is.
CALLOWAY. Look, if he had this on you he wouldn't hesitate to use it.
ALLEN. I'm not going to make Nathan Templeton my role model.
CALLOWAY. He's a politician.
ALLEN. I'm not going to turn into that.[26]

Of course, this exchange is meant to valorize Allen's choices as a mark of good character. It also suggests that one thing the American public holds in lower regard than female leaders is "politicians." Midway through the season, Allen indicates her intention to run for a second term; however, she resists the glad-handing and fundraising that any modern presidential campaign requires, telling her husband that "I'm going to do more than just run for president for the next two years. I want to be president."[27] After the series' untimely cancellation, Mackenzie Allen lost out on the opportunity either to govern or to campaign for another term.

President Allen's differences extend to her feminine attractiveness and sex appeal, which garnered significant coverage in press write-ups about the series. The *Washington Post*'s Robin Givhan rightly notes that, in politics (real or fictional), "sex appeal and charisma seem intertwined" and that Mackenzie Allen "made a convincing argument that a skirt belongs in the Oval Office." Television critic Tom Shales's assessment of Allen's charisma, however, was little more than journalistic leering: "Geena Davis can veto my legislation anytime. Starring as the first woman to hold the highest office in the land, Davis reminds us what we have missed in most of our past, real-life presidents: cuteness. She's got a twinkle in her eye, a twinkle in her smile, a twinkle everywhere. She's President Twinkle—just what we need to tame the extreme, charm the militant, inspire the troops." Later in his review Shales continues, "Davis is bountiful, beautiful, believable. You can accept that maybe, under the right set of quixotic circumstances, she might ascend to the position of leader of the free world. She certainly does wear more lipstick than any of her predecessors." Comments like these were so common in coverage of the series premiere they prompted Connie Schultz of the *Cleveland Plain Dealer* to lament, "It sure would be a welcome leap out of middle school if reviewers stopped opining on the president's pouty mouth and whether her lips are too red. That's so last year—when the coverage of [the spouse of the Democratic vice presidential candidate] Elizabeth Edwards focused on the stretch of her waist instead of the far reach of her mind."[28]

Another defining characteristic of Mackenzie Allen's presidentiality, besides her sex appeal, is her status as a wife and mother. The premiere episode makes clear that Allen and her husband have a happy, mutually respectful marriage. By giving the president and her husband different surnames, however, series creators also signal Allen's personal independence. Nevertheless, the first gentleman chafes under the confines of his socially focused "office." In addition to his wife frequently being too tired at the end of the day to have sex, Calloway is frustrated when he is removed as his wife's chief of staff and asked to behave like a more traditional political spouse. After repeatedly complaining about his symbolic role and ceremonial duties, Calloway considers accepting a job offer to be the commissioner of Major League Baseball. When a scandal erupts at the White House, Allen asks him to stay, and in the next episode Calloway outlines his expectations:

CALLOWAY. You said you were going to offer me a legitimate role in your administration and instead you're asking me to be secretary of pillow talk.
ALLEN. I am way too tired for this, okay, I just asked what you think.
CALLOWAY. Okay. You want to know what I think. Because I'm going to be honest with you, which no one else in the West Wing is going to be. You have no focus. No forward motion. No game plan. And, guess what, the guy who could help you make one, the guy who wants to help you make one, he's too busy picking out drapes for the Vermeil Room.[29]

In this short exchange, the series suggests not only that Allen's success depends on the counsel and involvement of her husband but also that the position of presidential spouse (which accomplished women have been filling since the election of the first US president) is trivial and meaningless—namely because it has been women who have filled the position and the duties are construed as feminine. Calloway indicates that if Allen does not create a more formal political role for him, not only will he be professionally dissatisfied but she will be jeopardizing their marriage. Sadly, Allen is not the only fictional female president whose political success threatens her marriage. Several texts examined in this chapter suggest that female presidentiality can be hazardous to matrimonial health and harmony.

Calloway and Allen have three children: twin teenagers and a younger daughter. Lurie has stated that one of his goals in creating *Commander in Chief* was to explore the tensions experienced by a woman trying to balance multiple personal roles with her presidential duties.[30] For President Allen, this often manifests itself in the odd juxtaposition of the personal and the presidential. Early in episode one, Vice President Allen talks to her husband about pressing matters of state and domestic concerns in the same breath, illustrating the norm that women (even as vice president of the United States) assume the mental duties critical to family functioning. She says, "They will bury this woman up to her neck in sand and stone her to death. That can't be the first result of my presidency. Oh, the twins, the Secret Service is getting them home?"[31] President Allen repeatedly replaces the sugary breakfast provided to her youngest daughter by the White House staff with fresh fruit, and on the way to her first big national address, her daughter spills juice on her white shirt. With the aplomb of a working mom used to multitasking, the president obscures the stain with an aide's silk scarf, makes up with her husband, who is miffed over losing his position as chief of staff, and then—with her mind cleared of domestic stresses—proceeds to address the nation.

Of course, presidentiality and motherhood do not always mix well, and sometimes the series narrative reveals the ways in which the demands of the presidency curtail President Allen's efforts to remain an attentive and effective parent. Although Allen will interrupt her schedule at any time if her children want to see her, when she actually engages them she is often distracted—too distracted to see that more parental attention is needed. On the eve of her first important state dinner, Allen's teenage daughter, Rebecca, is entertaining a boy from school at the White House. Earlier in the episode, the boy was revealed to be someone of low character out to score with willing girls. Sensing the danger faced by his twin sister, Allen's son, Horace, steps in to try to persuade his sister not to get involved with the boy. When that attempt fails, he bribes his younger sister, Amy, to stay in the same room with the couple while he and his parents are busy at the state dinner.[32] Interestingly, although Horace and Rebecca are twins, in this particular episode Horace is presented as mature and thoughtful, while Rebecca is portrayed as selfish and impulsive—a subtle but familiar suppositional statement about masculinity and femininity.

Although women's roles as nurturers may be conflicting for them in terms of managing their daily responsibilities, *Commander in Chief* also argues suppositionally that a female perspective provides women with a more ethical, humanitarian approach to governance than men have. The notion that women are, by nature, more moral than men dates back to the nineteenth-century cult of "true womanhood," which hypothesized that women's sanctuary within the private sphere kept them pure and moral and that such morality was needed in order to rear ethical children.[33] While contemporary US women are not legally barred from public, political activity, some critics have theorized a "feminine ethic of care" that translates into more humane policymaking.[34]

President Allen embarks on military action not to exercise her power or bolster her poll numbers but strictly for moral and humanitarian reasons. In a conversation with Templeton that convinces Allen to defy President Bridges's wishes and accede to the presidency, they discuss the Nigerian case and motivations for becoming president:

TEMPLETON. You know that your vice presidency was never ever intended to be a presidency. It was done as a stunt. You can see that. You're female. You're an independent. You're a teacher.

ALLEN. University chancellor.

TEMPLETON. Philosopher queen. But the point is, it was all done as pure theater, and you got great reviews, but now you should get off the stage while your audience still loves you and before they figure out that your vice presidency was a whole lotta nothing, because when they get a look at that go away mission he sent you on to Nigeria for, what's her name? The adulteress?

ALLEN. Orea Medulla.

TEMPLETON. Yeah. It was supposed to be another piece of theater. But then you up and went to France and asked them for their assistance. France? You asked guys who can't get elected without the Muslim vote to intercede in the verdict of Nigeria's sharia court? Come on, Mac! And we're going to end up looking silly and ineffectual because you're never going to be able to save her, and we're gonna lose face, and for whom? A lady who couldn't keep her legs together.[35]

At that point, Allen folds her resignation speech, puts it on the table, and states her intention to take the oath of office. Templeton asks her why she wants to be president.

ALLEN. For the same reason that Teddy Bridges did. Because I believe that the people of America deserve a president—

TEMPLETON. No, in this room, with just you and me, just the two of us, the answer that you should be giving me is that you want to be president because you want the power, you want the power to control the universe!

ALLEN. That's not me.

TEMPLETON. Well that's the problem.

President Allen's principled commitment to human rights is underscored at the end of episode one, when, in her address to the nation, she promises to "recognize, as Harry Truman said, that the responsibility of a great state is to serve the world, not to dominate it. For while human rights is not just an American issue, we must consider it an American responsibility."

Mackenzie Allen's commitment to human rights is similar to that of other fictional female presidents discussed in this chapter. Although presented, propositionally, as an inherent good, Allen's humanitarianism supports the suppositional claim that women leaders are primarily motivated by humanitarian impulses and that those impulses may override their political and/or tactical sensibilities. Just as the "cult of true womanhood" was invoked to keep women away from the polls prior to universal suffrage, the stereotype that women are more humanitarian than men may suppositionally count against women's efforts to become the commander in chief.

By subscribing to the assumption that women and men inherently govern differently, *Commander in Chief*'s narrative suppositionally reifies stereotypes about masculinity and femininity more broadly. In the episode "First Dance," Allen prepares for her first state dinner, held for Russian president Dmitri Kharkov. After Kharkov dominates several joint press conferences and Allen's impulsive action places her at a tactical disadvantage, she prepares for the state dinner unsure if President Kharkov will even show up. The only productive conversation Allen has that day is an unofficial exchange with Kharkov's spouse. In conversation with another woman, President Allen is both thoughtful and effective, and Mrs. Kharkov, indeed, persuades her husband to turn up for the state dinner. President Allen, dressed in an off-the-shoulder ball gown, gives a moving toast about Kharkov's father. A touched Russian president invites the American president to dance—much to the horror of her staff. Shrugging off their concerns, Allen lights up the dance floor and engages in the day's only successful moment of diplomatic negotiation with Kharkov. The emotive musical score invokes other filmic depictions of women in ball gowns. Of course, the fact that President Allen looks good in a ball gown and dances freely with the Russian president is not, in and of itself, particularly gendered. Presumably a woman president would wear an attractive gown at a black-tie affair. More problematic is the suppositional story arc that presents Allen as most effective when participating in more feminine settings—an intimate conversation with the Russian first lady and the social moments of a diplomatic visit.

Crucial to understanding *Commander in Chief*'s initial appeal—as well as its eventual demise—is the fact that the series was written as a modern melodrama. As John Mercer and Martin Shingler explain, modern melodrama often "deals with highly-charged emotional issues, characterized by an extravagantly dramatic register" and "an overtly emotional mode of address."[36] Unlike political dramas such as *The West Wing, 24,* and even *Battlestar Galactica, Commander in Chief* is not a complex, oppositional, postmodern text. Its characters bear less mimetic resemblance to real-world individuals than those on other popular, politically minded television series. Morality is starkly defined, narrative twists and turns are more dramatic than action as it unfolds in real life, and music is earnest and sometimes intrusive. Mercer and Shingler note that in the early days of film production, melodrama "proved eminently suitable for adaptation to the new cinematic medium, providing an obvious appeal for filmmakers seeking the widest and largest possible audience for their new product."[37] Seeking to establish a large audience share, contemporary television producers often employ melodramatic techniques as well. Scholars of modern melodrama often have focused on a subgenre, the Hollywood family melodrama, which consists of the following characteristics:

1. Central protagonist who "tends to be privileged by a high degree of audience identification"
2. Unsympathetic father figure who often is "absent or deceased"
3. Direct portrayal of characters' "psychological situation," with music used to "mark the emotional events, constituting a system of punctuation, [and] heightening the expressive and emotional contrasts of the storyline"
4. "Wish fulfillment and the tendency to culminate the drama in a happy ending. However, there are many cases when such an ending appears, realistically, to be impossible or at least highly improbable."[38]

Although *Commander in Chief* may not come immediately to mind as a classic example of the Hollywood family melodrama, in many ways the criteria fit. Producers certainly want audience members to identify with Mackenzie Allen, and Donald Sutherland's Nathan Templeton serves as a sufficiently unsavory father figure. In the series, Templeton is a Republican, but he does not necessarily represent the mainstream Republican viewpoint. That role is fulfilled by Allen's Republican teenage daughter, Templeton's chief of staff, and other Republican characters on the show. Templeton, conversely, is shown to have articulated racist sentiments early in his political career, and his own chief of staff sometimes goes behind his back to disrupt plans that even she believes to be too extreme.[39] Templeton, then, is the ultimate out-of-touch authority figure—or, as one television critic put it, "thoroughly unctuous."[40] The "emotional events" in the series may not be visceral outbursts, like those in a film such as *Rebel without a Cause;* however, the rousing speeches and historic signings indulge the audience's (perhaps sublimated) desire for politics to be meaningful. Additionally, unlike *The West Wing, Commander in Chief*'s narrative is a domestic story, not of the president and his staff, but of the president, her family, and their lives inside (both wings of) the White House. With music exacerbating every narrative twist and turn, the weekly plotlines seek the fulfillment of political fantasies and the happy ending of a government that functions ethically and effectively. To put it another way, as did *Slate*'s Dana Stevens, "*Commander in Chief* is *The West Wing* with extra cheese. Rather than a hardheaded, ripped from the headlines political drama, it's a political fantasy that takes place in a Beltway Neverland, where bipartisanship becomes tripartisanship and the fate of the free world is decided by an ill-placed sexist jibe."[41] That sentence subtly underscores the fact that *Commander in Chief* was often assessed by critics who subscribed (perhaps unconsciously) to a postfeminist world view. Reacting to "an ill-placed sexist jibe" is presumed to be not only unpresidential but also unnecessary—a dated, liberal feminist overreaction to a problem (sexism) that has largely been solved in postmodern, postfeminist society.

The weaknesses of the melodramatic genre are illustrated in *Commander in Chief*'s last episode, "Unfinished Business."[42] Upon hearing about the death of the house speaker for the Illinois legislature, a man who also happened to be a staunch opponent of women's rights, President Allen decides that his death presents her with an opportunity to finally pass the ERA. The show's narrative assumes that for the thirty-five states that did ratify the ERA in 1972, their ratification would remain intact—meaning that President Allen needed only to secure ratification from three more states for the US Constitution to be successfully amended.[43] She articulates her rationale for the proposed change at a press conference: "In the Declaration of Independence, the first truth to be held as self-evident is that 'all men are created equal.' Since women didn't win the right to vote until about a century and a half later, I'm afraid that we have to assume that they did mean 'men.' Now, we can't amend the Declaration, but we can and must amend the Constitution to ensure women have equal rights."

After being told by one of her aides that "no Democrat, no Republican, no one wants to go near this in an election year," Allen, with a determined smirk on her face, responds, "Except me." With that, the narrative establishes Allen as the melodramatic heroine seeking wish fulfillment through completion of an almost unattainable goal. Throughout the show, Allen faces resistance from conservatives like her daughter and the Joint Chiefs of Staff, gets encouragement from ERA supporters like her mother and members of her staff, and proves adept at potentially persuading even a skeptical female Republican from Florida's state senate to support the legislation. The episode ends with the future of the ERA still to be determined but with Allen and Templeton facing off over the issue at a town hall meeting in front of an audience of college students. An out-of-touch Templeton attempts to relate to his student audience by using references to the popular culture of the mid-twentieth century. Allen, conversely, addresses their questions and concerns directly. The melodramatic climax concludes (as it does in many episodes of *Commander in Chief*) with Allen waxing eloquent. A student queries whether the ERA is "obsolete," and Templeton replies that the fact that the United States has a woman president suggests, in fact, that it is. Allen answers with a characteristically stirring speech. She explains that "the Equal Rights Amendment is not for the first female president. It's for the girl who wants equal opportunity in school. It's for the single mother who can't get a mortgage or a small business loan, for the woman who faces harassment in her office and violence in her home. The ERA isn't going to solve all of these problems, but it will help." Propositionally, Allen articulates a liberal feminist argument about the structural discrimination women continue to face in modern society. Suppositionally, however, the speech (and the series) ends with an underscoring of the inevitability of women's progress—suggesting that all that is needed for sexism to subside is the passage of time. Allen states, "Moments ago, the Illinois general assembly ratified the ERA [applause]. The amendment has now been ratified by 36 states [applause]. . . . And so, like Alice Paul and so many others before her who have fought for equality, [music begins] tonight, we take one step forward. And know this. We will fight on!" When even the anachronistically sexist Templeton joins in the standing ovation the audience gives Allen, the series' narrative confirms that gender justice is a postfeminist inevitability. The series subtly suggests that we live in a society where the necessary majority of states *could*, even *would*, ratify the ERA because US citizens are broadly committed to gender equity. That narrative obscures the intransigent sexism and antifeminism that not only continues to disadvantage women and girls but also hampers the efforts of women presidential candidates.

Unfortunately, the melodramatic heroine Mackenzie Allen never witnessed the culmination of her efforts, since the series was canceled before the ERA could be fictitiously ratified by the requisite number of states. She also was unable to launch her quixotic quest for a second term, in which the likelihood of a win was hampered by her independent party status, her promise not to take funds from large campaign donors, and her determination to "do her job" rather than spend her time out on the stump campaigning. Although Allen's actions defy the logic of political strategy, they fulfill the generic requirements of a melodramatic heroine. So, if the audience identified with Allen, why did they stop watching *Commander in Chief?*

As noted previously, the series suffered from behind-the-scenes personnel problems and an unfavorable time slot change. Reviews of the series, however, illustrate that *Commander in Chief*'s melodramatic tone was also at least partially responsible for the series' lagging performance after the first few episodes. In *Salon* Heather Havrilesky chastised the show for "veering into schmaltzy or sentimental territory." In *Newsweek* Joshua Alston critiqued the show's oversimplification of characters, describing Allen as "stereotypically feminine, pretty, empathic and family-oriented" and noting that "we don't live in these small-screen utopias."[44] Lurie, who was fired as showrunner after the first few episodes and replaced by veteran television writer Stephen Bochco, expressed his frank opinion that the show suffered not just from melodramatic oversimplification, but from explicit sexism. As reported in *Newsweek*, "In Bochco's retooling, the male characters came to the fore. 'She was always turning to her husband or to a man for advice or approval, so the show was beginning to become not about why we should have a female president, but why we should not have one,' Lurie says. 'I don't know if I can call myself a feminist, but I know that Bochco is not.'"[45]

Lurie's frustration at the direction his series took in his absence articulates the potential gains, and losses, that come from fictional presidentiality. The remaining case studies in this chapter assess a variety of approaches to portraying fictional women presidents and vice presidents. Some are idealized but farcical. Some are nuanced and complicated. Others are tragically flawed. But each portrayal is significant, not just because of what it may teach viewers about presidentiality. They are significant because of what we all can learn about presidential norms and expectations once we dissect how those norms are rehearsed and challenged on screen.

Woman President as Farcical Foil in *Kisses for My President:*

Although *Commander in Chief*'s Geena Davis was hailed as the first actor to portray a female US president, Polly Bergen earned that distinction forty-one years earlier when she played President Leslie McCloud in the 1964 comedy *Kisses for My President.* Ostensibly carried into office by a bipartisan tide of women voters participating in US politics in the aftermath of woman suffrage, Leslie McCloud was the only fictional woman president to be *elected* until 2008, when the television series *24* introduced President Allison Taylor. *Kisses for My President* was designed as a vehicle for star Fred MacMurray, who played a befuddled "male first lady" finding himself at a loss in his new role. Bergen's President McCloud is confident and competent, steering the ship of state with wisdom, humor, and a steady hand, though the film revolving around her is designed to emphasize how farcical the notion of a woman US president really is. The film resolves this conundrum when, in the closing scene, President McCloud announces that she is pregnant and, upon the advice of her doctor, resigns her post for the safety of her baby.

Even in 1964, before *Roe v. Wade,* Title IX, or pay equity legislation, the notion that a woman could serve in the Oval Office as competently as a man was plausible enough to shape the character of President Leslie McCloud. Early in the film, her husband articulates the movie's propositional claim of women's presidential competence by reinforcing her credentials for the position: "You have a better background than some of the previous tenants. Daughter of an ambassador, niece of a senator, former judge, wife, mother, and a graduate of Radcliffe. What other president can make that statement?" During the course of the film, President McCloud interacts confidently with congressional leaders, roots out corruption in a US aid agreement, interacts productively with the press, and exhibits keen sensitivity to public perceptions.

The film also clearly addresses the propositional argument that, even in 1964, blatant sexism was outmoded. President McCloud demonstrates agility in fending off the advances of male politicians she encounters in the Oval Office. In one scene, President McCloud welcomes a senator and former political rival:

McCloud. I'm sorry to keep you waiting, Senator Walsh.

Walsh. May I say that it is always an honor to call on the president, but indeed a pleasure to find so lovely a creature behind such a noble desk.

McCloud. Thank you, senator, but I remember a different approach when you were running against me.

Later, she encounters visiting dictator Raphael Valdez (played for laughs by Eli Wallach), who is seeking continued financial aid from the United States. He says, "Never before in the line of duty have I been welcomed into the chambers of a woman so beautiful as you." McCloud curtly responds, "Sit over there, please. This is an office and it belongs to the people of the United States."

Images of sexuality were significantly more demure in the films of the mid-twentieth century than they are in the twenty-first, and, consequently, references to President McCloud's sexuality are understated compared to those in some of the texts considered in this chapter. Nevertheless, one of the primary comic devices in *Kisses for My President* revolves around the first gentleman's inability to secure the private affection of his wife. Perpetually stymied by the telephone, her fatigue, or classified presidential business, Mr. McCloud's frustration grows as the film unfolds. This element of the plot was not appreciated by 1960s-era film critic Bosley Crowther. Reviewing the movie at the time of its release for the *New York Times,* Crowther criticized the filmmakers' decision not to have the president of the United States fulfill her marital obligation: "Indeed the most galling annoyance that Claude Binyon and Robert G. Kane have contrived for this unprecedented 'First Lady' is the deprival of the solace of his mate. They propose that it is highly amusing that he should be constantly stymied in love."[46] Despite the fact that the film's humor revolves around the first gentleman's inability to rendezvous with his wife, the forty-something Leslie McCloud manages to get pregnant while in office. That portion of the propositional narrative subtly reinforces the sexist notion that women presidential candidates' perpetual potential for pregnancy makes them less suited to the job than men.

The suppositional argument that female presidentiality is, ultimately, unnatural is underscored by the genre of the film. Unlike the other texts considered in this chapter, which are categorized as dramas and/or thrillers, *Kisses for My President* is a farce. Jessica Milner Davis defines farce as a genre that "delights in taboo violation, but which avoids implied moral comment or social criticism and which tends to debar empathy for its victims." Davis goes on to explain that "the more respectable the comic victims are, and the more successfully moral implications are avoided, the funnier the farce will be."[47] As previously noted, *Kisses for My President* focuses not on the narrative of the first woman president but instead on the many ways in which her husband is bewildered by his new duties. The farcical tone of the film is highlighted on the videotape cover art, which features Bergen's character solemnly taking a telephone call in the Oval Office and MacMurray's character standing beside his wife and wearing a conservative suit, a flowery woman's hat, and a befuddled expression on his face. Rather than satirizing gender roles, this film reifies them to comic effect. The fact that Mr. McCloud is a supportive spouse who gamely attempts to make the best of his new situation allows viewers to align themselves and their sympathies with him. They can admire President Mc-Cloud's pluck and even condemn the sexism of the male politicians in the film without challenging the traditional gender roles that inspire the film's humor. If the film were a satirical send-up of gender roles, President McCloud's forced retirement at the end of the film would highlight the inequities woven into the fabric of twentieth-century political culture. Instead, her decision to replace governance with nurturance feels like the happy ending that restores sanity and order to the world of the erstwhile patriarch, Mr. McCloud.

Presidential Surrogate as Supplicant in *Air Force One*

If the generic constraints of farce inhibited a progressive critique of gender roles in 1964, 1997's *Air Force One* illustrates the ways in which the expectations of the summer blockbuster proved even more constraining. *Air Force One* is diametrically opposed, in theme and tone, to *Kisses for My President*. The late nineties blockbuster features Harrison Ford as James Marshall, president and action hero. When the presidential airplane is hijacked with the president and his family on board, Vice President Kathryn Bennett (played by Glenn Close) steps in to manage the situation on the ground. Although Bennett never assumes the role of the president, she does act as presidential surrogate during the portions of the film when the president is absent and/or unable to make tactical decisions. Moreover, the prospect of the president's death at the hands of the hijackers thrusts Bennett into the position of potential presidential successor.

Of the six female executives considered in this chapter, Vice President Bennett displays the least amount of personal agency and individual strength. That is, perhaps, no surprise. As Denise Bostdorff argues, the US vice presidency is "in effect, a traditional female role" that requires vice presidents of either gender to "submerge their independence and individualism to perform their day-to-day duties which consist mainly of abject 'feminine' servility."[48] Even so, the simple fact that director Wolfgang Petersen chose to make his vice president a woman was an unexpected and progressive move in the summer of 1997, when *Air Force One* was released. The genre of the film is particularly relevant here. Unlike *The Contender,* a thoughtful reflection on issues of privacy, gender, and public power, *Air Force One* was a successful summer blockbuster—a popcorn movie. This star vehicle for Harrison Ford, packed with outrageous stunts and special effects, was not intended to make audiences think critically about US political culture and gender relations. When

Bennett disembarks from a military helicopter to assess the situation on the ground after Air Force One has been hijacked, her female gender stands out as something new—an infrequently seen statement about the proper role of women. The fact that this woman was played by Glenn Close, a respected Hollywood heavyweight, lent credibility to her role as well. Propositionally, then, *Air Force One* suggests that women are present at the highest levels of political leadership and should be taken seriously.

Vice President Bennett enters the film inquiring about the president's status and lamenting, "How the hell did this happen? How the hell did this happen?" Quickly regaining her composure, she calmly assesses the situation, asking about remaining fuel in the plane, likely destinations if the hijackers remain in control, and ally notification. Throughout the movie, Vice President Bennett maintains command of the Situation Room, making decisions that are unpopular but that support and assist President Marshall's heroic efforts on the plane. Ultimately, although she violates constitutional protocols and defies the wishes of the Cabinet, her instincts are proven correct and she is partially responsible for the president's safe return. The film propositionally valorizes Bennett's ability to carry out the duties of the vice presidency. Importantly, however, Bennett's agency (like that of Joan Allen's Senator Hanson in *The Contender*, discussed later in this chapter) is contained by the fact that the president is portrayed as the final authority to whom she answers.

Like the two texts assessed earlier in this chapter, *Air Force One* articulates the propositional claim that sexism is outmoded and/or corrupt. The most explicitly sexist statements in the film are uttered either by the terrorist hijackers or the gutless secretary of defense, who is prepared to sacrifice the president and the lives of the other hostages. During negotiations with Vice President Bennett, when the hijacker, Korshunov, thinks the president used an escape pod to flee Air Force One, Korshunov ridicules the vice president's gender and criticizes the president for a perceived lack of heroic masculinity:

BENNETT. I would like to speak to the first lady.
KORSHUNOV. No, why?
BENNETT. I need to know that they're safe.
KORSHUNOV. The president is safe. But then you must know that. He ran from here like a whipped dog. I'm sure you can't wait for him to get back to making the decisions so that you can stop sweating through that silk blouse of yours.

Similarly, Secretary of Defense Walter Dean (played by Dean Stockwell) circles the room making impatient demands, uttering unproductive asides, and ineffectually asserting his dominance over the vice president: "If you'd just try and relax, Kathryn, I'm in charge." She replies, "Oh, I don't know, Walter, it seems to me that they're in charge."

This small exchange illustrates well how the film functions, simultaneously, at propositional and suppositional levels. Propositionally, Dean's power play looks foolishly sexist. Suppositionally, however, Bennett's response underscores her own lack of control, while the film's narrative ultimately establishes that the presidential patriarch was really the one "in charge"—asserting his authority and single-handedly overpowering the terrorists. The most memorable line of the film comes near the end, when President Marshall and Korshunov are wrestling next to the aircraft's open emergency exit. Gaining the upper hand, Marshall hurls Korshunov off of Air Force One, exclaiming, "Get off my plane!" A relieved first lady waits in the wings to greet the president with grateful kisses.

The preeminence of presidential masculinity is suppositionally illustrated throughout *Air Force One* in the embodiment of Ford's president and Close's vice president. The commander in chief is a physically strong, courageous, and heroic male whereas the vice president exhibits powerless speech forms and looks to men for input and guidance. For example, when arguing with the secretary of defense about who should be in charge on the ground, the secretary tells a presidential aide, "It's not her decision." "Oh?" she replies. The secretary of defense says, "This is a military decision. I'm the secretary of defense. Check your regs. In the absence of the president, the buck stops here." The vice president retorts, "Get the attorney general and a copy of the Constitution. We have, oh my God, nineteen minutes! I'm going to consult with President Petroff."

Later, in a private telephone conversation with President Marshall, he appears as the steady leader, while Vice President Bennett poses questions rather than options and seems unwilling to make the "tough calls." It is not until the president begins to quote children's literature that she agrees with his position:

MARSHALL. We cannot release Radek.
BENNETT. They're going to shoot a hostage every half hour until we do. I don't want a plane full of dead people. Jim, they shot Jack Dougherty.
MARSHALL. Oh, Christ. Kathryn, we can't give in to their demands. It won't end there.
BENNETT. And if you die in that plane? Does it end there?
MARSHALL. Kathryn, we've got a job to do, whatever the cost.
BENNETT. Mr. President, I—
MARSHALL. Kathryn, if you give a mouse a cookie . . .
BENNETT. He's gonna want a glass of milk.

Air Force One is not a nuanced text. Its over-the-top action and exaggerated masculinity serve as filmic shorthand, cueing the audience to provide the requisite stereotypes about presidentiality in order to appreciate the film's action and feel rewarded by its ending. Filmic depictions of US presidentiality are not always so explicitly stereotypical. Three years after President Marshall physically expelled a terrorist from his plane, Hollywood produced a slightly more thoughtful rumination on the challenges of presidential leadership.

Embodied Presidentiality in *The Contender*

The notion of a woman as second in command forms the backdrop for the 2000 political thriller *The Contender*, written and directed by *Commander in Chief* creator Rod Lurie. In this film, the sudden and unexpected death of the US vice president prompts Democratic president Jackson Evans (played by Jeff Bridges) to attempt to "secure his legacy" by appointing a woman as the next vice president. The fact that the nominee, Senator Laine Hanson (played by Joan Allen), is a woman ensures that this film interrogates the question of gender and the US presidency; however, it is important to note that unlike Lurie's subsequent television series *Commander in Chief,* the issue of gender is not the central theme of the film. Released on the heels of Bill Clinton's presidency, *The Contender* critiques the national obsession with the private lives of public officials. When accusations surface that Senator Hanson participated in group sex as a college student, she refuses, on principle, to answer the charges, asserting, "I simply can't respond to the accusations because it's not okay for them to be made." Elizabeth Ann Haas quotes film critic Roger Ebert's discussion of *The Contender*'s central theme: "When I asked its star, Jeff Bridges, if the plot was a veiled reference to Monicagate, he smiled. 'Veiled?' he said. 'I don't think it's so veiled.'"[49] In the end, the film both betrays and reinforces its thematic convictions. Senator Hanson maintains her public silence on the issue, and the president himself secures her confirmation with a rousing speech made to a joint session of Congress. Viewers, however, are treated to a private conversation between Hanson and President Jackson in which she confirms that the allegations are false. *The Contender*'s propositional argument is that women are equal to men and that both should be granted the right to privacy, even when they hold public office. Suppositionally, however, the film focuses on the presidential body, suggesting that female sexuality is dangerous and deviant, whereas male bodies are suited to heroic leadership.

One of *The Contender*'s early scenes indicates that this film will address stereotypes about women, sexuality, and leadership. The scene opens to a couple making love in an office. The telephone rings, and the conversation develops as follows:

MR. HANSON. Yeah, that's good. You like that.
MRS. HANSON. Yeah, I like that. [*telephone rings*] [*breathless*] Don't answer it. Don't answer it.

MR. HANSON. I've got to get it. No, it's the red line.

MRS. HANSON. [*pleading*] No, no, no, no. no . . . [*laughs*]

MR. HANSON. Hanson here. Yeah. Of course I'll hold. Laine, quiet! Hello, sir. I'm great, sir. Thank you. Yes, as a matter of fact we're watching him on C-SPAN now. Yes she is. One second, sir. [*to his wife*] It's the president. He wants to talk to you. You want to speak to him?

MRS. HANSON. [*sits up*] Uh, hello, sir, this is Senator Hanson speaking.

A viewer who came to the film without prior knowledge of the plot would be led to assume, according to the construction of the scene, that the couple is in the husband's office and that he, therefore, is the senator. By turning the tables the film announces its intention to expose and challenge stereotypes about women and leadership.

The Contender's Laine Hanson is a moderate Washington pol. The daughter of a popular Republican governor and a respected senator herself, Hanson displays cool confidence in the face of a brutal confirmation process in which she is subjected to both tough policy questions and embarrassing personal attacks. Even her archrival, Republican senator Sheldon Runyon (played by Gary Oldman), acknowledges her appeal. Runyon is in a conference with his choice for the vice presidency, Democratic governor Jack Hathaway, and a young Democratic member of Congress who is serving on the confirmation committee, Reginald Webster. Runyon explains to Webster why he thinks the president wants Hanson, saying, "Jackson Evans has chosen to make putting a woman in office his swan song. Laine Hanson is the only reasonable choice in your party. . . . [She] is attractive. She's a looker. The mere fact that she was a Republican means that she can't be too far to the left. It's a perfect pedigree. We can't get you in by convincing him that you're the right man for the job. We have to convince him that she's wrong." Senator Hanson lives up to her "perfect pedigree" by performing well under pressure, displaying more strength and personal conviction than any of the male characters in the film, and ultimately securing the vice presidency. Thus, at a propositional level, the film argues that women and men are equally suited to the office of US president.

The film reinforces this propositional argument by portraying objections to Hanson's candidacy as outmoded, sexist, and corrupt. *The Contender*'s Senator Runyon, whose character is meant to epitomize the socially conservative wing of the Republican Party during the late 1990s, parrots to the president's press secretary sexist explanations of why even successful women political leaders lack credibility:

RUNYON. Look, I don't mind she's a woman. But I'm not confirming a woman just because she's a woman. Laine Hanson has an extra burden. She has to come onto the world stage with perfect credentials.

PRESS SECRETARY. Margaret Thatcher didn't have perfect credentials. The world respected her.

RUNYON. The world accepted Margaret Thatcher because they knew she had to answer to Ronald Reagan. A woman better be pretty damn qualified to have nobody to answer to, and Laine Hanson is not that.

In the ensuing conversation Runyon, Webster, and Hathaway are plotting Hanson's demise. A private investigator Runyon brought in to dig up dirt on Hanson tells the group, "We have to gut the bitch in the belly. We all have to understand, we're going to obliterate a life." Thus, the film's narrative exaggerates the fact that those who seek to impede women's political agency are both out of touch and willing to engage in the politics of personal destruction for their own political gain.

Despite the film's strong propositional contention about women's political equality, *The Contender* also constructs female sexuality as potentially dangerous and deviant. As previously noted, audiences are introduced to Laine Hanson lying prone on a desk, making love with her husband. This healthy, and slightly racy, image of adult sexuality is paired with much more graphic and prurient flashbacks of a supposed nineteen-year-old Hanson performing oral sex at a fraternity party. During the confirmation hearings, it is divulged that Senator Hanson met her current husband when he was her campaign advisor. Despite the fact that his wife was one of her best friends, she engaged in an affair with him that led to the breakup of his first marriage and their subsequent union. That chain of events prompts an explosive conversation with the president in which Senator Hanson echoed her position that her private life was not of public relevance, and because she was not married at the time of the affair, she is not, technically, an adulterer (a charge she had denied under oath). The president, visibly enraged because the adultery charges caught him by surprise, states, "Your husband may be an adulterer, you're not. Fine. What you are is a sex-crazed homewrecking machine. The female Warren Beatty. Runyon knows that you're clean of the perjury, but he's got the world thinking that you're something out of a bad soap opera!"

When the feminine body is not being portrayed as inappropriately sexual, it is regarded as potentially problematic in terms of its connection to motherhood. Laine Hanson's status as the mother of a six-year-old boy does not intrude on her public duties in the same way that Mackenzie Allen's motherhood does. If anything, Hanson is portrayed as underinvolved with family matters. In one scene, she and her son are shown on a visit to her father's home. At first, it appears to be a family-oriented visit. Later, however, the film reveals her father to be a prominent Republican and former governor. The purpose of the family visit is for Senator Hanson to secure her father's endorsement of her as the vice presidential nominee. Thus, Hanson might be seen as a woman who puts her political ambition above her family responsibilities. Later in the film, her status as a mother reappears during the following exchange in the confirmation hearings:

SENATOR RUNYON. Madam Senator, tell us a little bit about your family. You have a son.

SENATOR HANSON. Yes, I have one six-year-old boy, Timothy.

SENATOR RUNYON. It's a very nice age. Uh, I see here that when you had your son, Timothy, you were absent from your duty for a few months' maternity leave.

SENATOR HANSON. Yes, I believe it's the right and responsibility of every mother to be able to take maternity leave.

SENATOR RUNYON. Paid maternity leave.

SENATOR HANSON. Yes, I don't believe we should penalize our citizens for having children.

SENATOR RUNYON. Fine. I think I'm on safe grounds saying that valuing motherhood is quite nonpartisan. Were you to get pregnant again, do you plan to take maternity leave?

SENATOR HANSON. Uh, well, I've not given that any consideration.

SENATOR RUNYON. No? Are you still able to bear children?

SENATOR HANSON. Yes, I believe I am, yes.

SENATOR RUNYON. Yet you have not given this matter any consideration? Perhaps that means that you . . . no, strike that! Madam Senator, let us assume you ascended to the presidency and you were to have a child during your term, would you cede your duties to your vice president and for how long?

REPRESENTATIVE WEBSTER. [exasperated] Mr. Chairman, would the chair expect the designate to assure the committee she would have her tubes tied before she assumes office? Mr. Chairman, I humbly request a point of order.

SENATOR RUNYON. You will be afforded one when I am finished . . .

SENATOR HANSON. The truth, excuse me, the truth is that while we have not put a seal on the concept of having another child, my husband and I practice birth control.

What is particularly interesting about that scene is it is the first question to which Senator Hanson does not have a perfectly polished, pre-rehearsed answer. She seems taken aback by the prospect of getting pregnant while in office and only regains her composure after Representative Webster objects to the question on principle. Because the film presents the question of pregnancy in the context of Runyon's questioning, it is held up as an inappropriate and sexist question. Nevertheless, pregnancy and childbearing are cast as both fundamental to the female experience and incommensurate with the duties of the presidency. In that respect, this twenty-first-century film is not much different from 1964's *Kisses for My President*.

As *The Contender* constructs the female body as fundamentally sexual, potentially dangerous, and perpetually maternal, the male presidential body retains its heroic masculinity. Unlike in a film such as *Air Force One*, the president's heroic masculinity is not manifested in hand-to-hand combat. Rather, at the film's conclusion, Senator Hanson's bid for the vice presidential confirmation is successful not because of her experience, her principled action, or her deft negotiation of the committee's questioning. Her success is clinched, instead, by an unprecedented presidential address to a joint session of Congress demanding an immediate roll call vote to confirm his vice presidential appointee. The president's speech concludes with the following call to action: "I will not be deterred by partisanship. I will not be deterred by misogyny. I will not be deterred by hate. You have now come face to face with my will. Confirm my nominee. Heal this nation, and let the American people explode into this new millennium with the glory of being true to this democracy. Thank you [*standing ovation from the full chamber*]."

The melodramatic happy ending undercuts the film's propositional argument about the complexities of postmodern political leadership. If members of Congress confirm Hanson as vice president, they do it in response to an idealized version of white, male presidentiality. He orders members of Congress as if they were royal subjects rather than republican interlocutors. Most importantly, Hanson's efforts alone are not enough to secure confirmation. She must be assisted by the male presidential authority. Her victory enhances his legacy.[50] Consequently, *The Contender* leaves intact the white, heroic masculinity of postmodern presidentiality.

If Lurie's two attempts to constitute female presidentiality presented little challenge to the traditional presidential persona, it might be that the task of rewriting presidentiality is difficult when situated within the familiar contours of the Oval Office, the White House, and contemporary US political culture. The next text we examine removed presidentiality from its terrestrial constraints, taking presidentiality where no woman had gone before.

Woman President as Sci-Fi Fantasy in *Battlestar Galactica*

When *Battlestar Galactica* premiered on December 8, 2003, it was a "reimagining" of the 1970s series of the same name. Both series were set "in a distant galaxy" where the "Twelve Colonies of Man" respond to an attack by an "empire of machines, the Cylons, who were created generations before as worker drones for [humanity]."[51] Whereas the original series was designed to appeal to viewers "still thrilled by *Star Wars* and hungry for more action-packed sci-fi," the updated version had a broader intellectual purpose.[52] Woody Goulart and Wesley Y. Joe contend that showrunner Ronald D. Moore (who cut his television writing and production teeth on several *Star Trek* spinoff series) employed a storytelling technique that "deliberately distorts what viewers may deem as 'normal' or 'expected' perspectives on people, politics, organized religion, and moral issues."[53] Goulart and Joe argue that the purpose of this "different prism" is to "convince *Battlestar Galactica's* audience to look at individual political, religious, and human moral issues from a variety of perspectives. By bringing the ambiguity of these issues into the foreground, *Battlestar Galactica* challenges average citizens to think about the potential merits of perspectives they oppose and the drawbacks of perspectives they embrace."[54]

The cerebral dimensions of *Battlestar Galactica* did not inhibit commercial success. According to the *New York Times,* as of July 2005 the series was "the most successful original program in the Sci-Fi Channel's history." Premiering just two years after 9/11, *Battlestar Galactica's* narrative explores issues that were hotly contested in real-world arenas during its television run. Moore stated that as he was reconceptualizing *Battlestar Galactica* he knew that the audience would "feel a resonance with what happened on 9/11." *New York Times* contributing writer John Hodgman reported that "the echoes of the war on terror were unapologetic and frequently harrowing; what happens when an advanced, comfortable, secular democracy endures a devastating attack by an old enemy that it literally created . . . ?"[55]

Battlestar Galactica is an important text of gendered presidentiality because in the aftermath of the Cylons' initial nuclear strike on the Twelve Colonies, the remnant of the colonial government is led by President Laura Roslin (played by Mary McDonnell).[56] Previously the secretary of education and forty-third in line for the presidency, Roslin accedes to high office after the nuclear holocaust kills the president, his cabinet, and all other governmental officials who precede her in the constitutionally mandated presidential line of succession. Scholars of gender and the US presidency are likely to appreciate the wry irony that it takes a nuclear holocaust and the elimination of forty-two governmental officials for a woman to rise to the presidency, even in a place and time far removed from our own.

Academics who have assessed *Battlestar Galactica* praise it for its egalitarian portrayal of gender. Sarah Conly calls the universe of the Twelve Colonies an "androgynous society—one where social roles aren't limited by sex. . . ." Similarly, Goulart and Joe note that "unlike in the real world, where both politics and the military are male-dominated, the *Battlestar Galactica* audience encounters a completely gender-blind political and military infrastructure."[57] It is true that women are represented in key leadership roles. In addition to President Roslin, the *Galactica's* best fighter pilot is a woman (Kara Thrace, call sign "Starbuck"), military women serve in the same combat and support capacities as men, and the character introduced in season two as the fleet's senior military officer is a woman, Admiral Helena Cain. Yet the presence of women does not equate to numerical parity. In the miniseries premiere, seven of the major characters are male while four are female. Throughout the series there are more male military officers than female, more male fighter pilots than female, and even the twelve Cylon models feature seven males and five females. The fact that scholars regard this environment to be "completely gender blind" is telling.

Considerations of gender, of course, go beyond a numerical tally of the gender assigned to each character. Throughout the series, female power often is associated either with mysticism and emotionalism or with betrayal and corruption.[58] In that respect, the women of the *Galactica* sometimes function as tokens. Dana L. Cloud explains that when members of "subordinate" groups achieve positions of power and authority in the dominant society, they sometimes trade "group identity, politics, and resistance" for "cultural capital within popular cultural spaces."[59] The "cultural capital" amassed by portraying a woman president or female fighter pilot comes at the expense of a narrative that elides the gendered barriers to women's political and military advancement that exist even in the *Battlestar Galactica* universe. One minor but telling marker that identifies Roslin as a token is the way in which crew members address President Roslin as "sir." Because the linguistic habits of characters on the series tend to parallel contemporary US grammar, this deviation is notable and reinforces the notion that presidential leadership is a masculine activity.[60] Roslin may be a credible president in the *Battlestar Galactica* universe, but she is still performing a man's job.

Although our analysis is not primarily concerned with the intent of the directors, producers, and screenwriters who develop each artifact, it is useful to acknowledge evidence that showrunner Moore intended to play with gender stereotypes from the conception of the series reimagining. In the original series, one of the most beloved characters was Starbuck, a dashing male fighter pilot played by the actor Dirk Benedict (who went on to play a lead character in the 1980s action series *The A-Team*). Fans of the original series, many of whom had supported a *Battlestar Galactica* reboot, were aghast when Moore revealed that in the character's new incarnation, Starbuck would be a woman. Hodgman documented the fan outrage in the aftermath of the announcement: "'Starbuck is a guy. A GUY! A GUY!!!' posted a fan named Rhonda on the forums of battlestargalacticaclub.com in December 2002. Moore was accused of bowing to political correctness, of dishonoring the memory of the original actors, of requiring a beating."[61]

Hodgman also recounts the actions of John Dipalmero, who started a Yahoo group called "Ron Moore Sucks" and bragged, "In every 'Battlestar Galactica' Yahoo group, I would call him the MooreRon, and it became very popular."[62] Hodgman notes that despite the initial fan resistance, the series garnered excellent ratings, and "many of the fan sites that had originally opposed Moore and [series co-creator David Eick's] vision now actively or passively support it. Discussion of the show has migrated somewhat, from the fan boards to political blogs, where the issues it raises about security, religion and the ethics of android torture inspire heated debate, as well as praise from conservatives and liberals alike."[63]

The preceding discussion of fan response to Moore's gender bending points to an important conclusion: Moore's reimagining of the series included some components designed to challenge gender norms, and despite initial resistance, audiences ultimately responded well to these challenges. We contend that the suppositional arguments deployed by the *Battlestar Galactica* narrative disciplined the propositional progressiveness of Moore's character development. In order to fully understand the gendered framing of the women and men on *Battlestar Galactica*, it would be necessary to examine character traits, character development within the series narrative, and the polyvalent nature of each character. For the purposes of this chapter, however, we focus exclusively on the character of President Roslin.

Specifically, we argue that *Battlestar Galactica* portrays President Roslin as credible because she actively resists "politics" and did not actively seek political power. Further, the series casts Roslin as humanitarian, spiritual, and emotional in contrast to Commander Adama's pragmatic, rational, military leadership. Finally, the "happy ending" of the series is premised, in part, on Roslin and Adama's consummation of a romantic relationship. The suppositional argument becomes even more consequential in light of the fact that the series was heralded for its thoughtful negotiation of complex political questions. As viewers were encouraged to reflect critically on their own assumptions about religion, war, and what it means to be human, they simultaneously were observing a portrait of gendered presidentiality that maintained fidelity to dominant gender norms.

Like Mackenzie Allen, Laura Roslin accepts the presidential mantle in spite of the fact that the president under whom she served had asked for her resignation prior to his death. She had resisted President Adar's request for her to step down as secretary of education after she peacefully negotiated the end of a strike by the teachers' union.[64] Roslin nonetheless asserts her constitutional authority to be president of the Twelve Colonies in the aftermath of the Cylon attack. Importantly, however, viewers do not learn of the conflict between Adar and Roslin until well into season two. In the premiere miniseries, Roslin is cast as a reluctant public servant, though one with an instinctive grasp of political leadership. The series begins with Roslin headed for the *Galactica*—a time-worn battleship being decommissioned after years of service—in order to participate in the decommissioning ceremony. After the *Galactica*'s commander, William Adama (played by Edward James Olmos), announces the nuclear attack to the fleet, Roslin confronts her shuttle's pilot, who confirms the report. As she steadies his trembling hand, the visibly shaken pilot says, "I—I guess I should go make an announcement or something." Roslin replies, "I'll do it. I'm a member of the political cabinet. It's my responsibility." Roslin then begins her transformation from secretary of education to political authority, issuing orders to the pilot: "While I'm doing that I would ask that you [*notable pause*] contact the ministry of civil defense and see what we can do to help." The pause indicates that Roslin's political duties thus far have not prepared her to automatically know the protocol and procedures for a situation like this one. However, her quick decision making marks her as someone with leadership capability.[65]

In the next scene, Roslin informs the political dignitaries and staff members aboard the shuttle about the attack. She is the only one who does not panic. Her authority is called into question immediately, however, when a public relations official aboard the ship queries, "Wait a minute. Who put you in charge?" Roslin responds, "Well, that's a good question. The answer is no one, but this is a government ship and I am the senior government official, so that puts me in charge, so, why don't you help me out and go down into the cargo area and see about setting it up as a living space. Everyone else, please, please try and stay calm. Thank you."

As she will do throughout the series, Roslin invokes the authority of the democratically sanctioned chain of command and, in turn, quiets the objections of her detractors. Her quiet assertion of her position is presented as a duty foisted upon her rather than a political office for which she campaigned. The stakes are raised when an automated message reveals that the president, his cabinet, and many other senior government officials are deceased or missing. Faced with the possibility that she might actually become president, she converses with Captain Lee "Apollo" Adama (son of Commander William Adama), who asks, "How far down?" Roslin tells him, "I'm forty-third in line of succession. I know all forty-two ahead of me. From the president down. Most of us served in his first administration . . . some came with him from the mayor's office . . . I was there on his first campaign. Never really liked politics. Kept telling myself I was getting out after his first term. But he had a way about him . . . you just couldn't say no to him. You just couldn't say no."

That exchange establishes Roslin as someone who not only never sought elective office herself but also professes not to "like politics." Additionally, her interest in public service is intertwined with her feelings for President Adar, a man with whom, the series later reveals, she shared a romantic relationship. Thus, the potency of a woman leading the Twelve Colonies is tempered by the narrative assurance that she harbors little political ambition and that she gained access to power primarily through a male leader. Mary McDonnell confirmed that the narrative intent of the show was to establish Roslin's lack of personal political ambition. She stated, "Laura Roslin's presidency was unique in that she became president during war and cataclysm without the energy of ambition fueling her decisions. This was a woman who hadn't a clear political ambition. This made her very different from the women in power that we see on TV."[66]

Despite her lack of ambition, the duty of the presidency falls to Roslin. In the series, however, she shares power with Commander Adama, the ranking military officer and the *Galactica*'s commander. Through the characters of Roslin and Adama, the series narrative propositionally explores the tensions between military and civilian power, especially during times of war. Suppositionally, however, a more basic struggle between stereotypically masculine and feminine leadership styles is played out during the series' four seasons. This dichotomy is introduced shortly after Roslin becomes president. Unaware that Roslin has inherited the presidency, Adama instructs his communications officer, "Send the following message to all colonial military units. Use the priority channel. Message begins: 'Am taking command of fleet.'"[67] Shortly thereafter, Apollo relays Adama's military announcement to the new president:

PRESIDENT ROSLIN. Captain Apollo, send a message to Commander Adama informing him that we're engaged in rescue operations and require his assistance. Ask how many hospital beds they have available and how long will it take them to get here.
APOLLO. I, uh . . .
PRESIDENT ROSLIN. Yes?
APOLLO. I'm not sure he's going to respond very well to that request.
PRESIDENT ROSLIN. Tell him this comes directly from the president of the Colonies and it's not a request.

In these two short scenes, the series narrative establishes that both Adama and Roslin are decisive leaders who act with confidence and conviction. Both leaders also have legitimate claim to the position of leader of the fleet. The conflict is addressed at the end of the miniseries premiere, when President Roslin and Commander Adama meet face to face:

PRESIDENT ROSLIN. If this civilization is going to function it's going to need a government. A civilian government run by the president of the Colonies.
ADAMA. You're in charge of the fleet, but military decisions stay with me.
PRESIDENT ROSLIN. Agreed.
ADAMA. Then I think we have a deal, Madam President.

As the scene concludes, Roslin and Adama stand opposite one another, shaking hands in a gesture of shared leadership. Although the propositional argument advanced in the verbal and visual components of the scene suggests that Adama and Roslin are equals, by assigning military authority to Adama, the series narrative sidesteps what is arguably the most significant barrier to women's presidential leadership in the real world: the problem of being perceived as a credible commander in chief. This division between woman/man, civilian/military is exacerbated by the ways in which Roslin's leadership is depicted as primarily humanitarian, emotional, and mystical.

Like other fictional women presidents, Laura Roslin is portrayed as being motivated by humanitarian, rather than military, priorities. In the miniseries premiere, the public relations official who earlier had questioned her authority welcomes Apollo on board Roslin's shuttle:

PR OFFICIAL. Personally I'd feel a lot better if someone qualified were in charge around here.
APOLLO. Is there something wrong with your pilot?
PR OFFICIAL. No, it's just that he's not the one giving orders.

When Apollo confronts Roslin, he discovers that her primary concern is with the safety of civilians present in the fleet:

ROSLIN. Start the cargo transfer and prep bay three for survivors.
APOLLO. I'm sorry—survivors?
ROSLIN. As soon as the attack began the government ordered a full stop on all civilian vessels, so now we've got hundreds of stranded ships in the solar system. Some are lost, some are damaged, some are losing power. We have enough space on this ship to accommodate five hundred people; we're going to need every bit of it.
PR OFFICIAL. But we don't even know what the tactical situation is out there.
ROSLIN. The tactical situation is that we are losing, right, Captain?
APOLLO. Right.
ROSLIN. So we pick up as many people as we can and we try to find a safe haven to put down. Captain, I'd like you to look over the navigational charts for a likely place to hide from the Cylons. That's all.
APOLLO. [ruefully, to the PR official] The lady's in charge.

Roslin's determination to retreat is contrasted with Commander Adama's announcement to *Galactica*'s troops after the attack that "the best thing we can do is get this ship into the fight." After Roslin is sworn in as president of the Colonies, she continues to clash with Adama over humanitarian versus military objectives. Wanting to leave *Colonial One* and the other civilian ships, Adama confronts Roslin with his intention to return to battle. Addressing her as "Miss," Adama indicates that he does not yet fully accept her presidential authority:

ADAMA. Miss Roslin, my priority at this moment is the repair of *Galactica* and the resumption of combat operations against the enemy.

PRESIDENT ROSLIN. Correct me if I'm wrong, Commander, but as far as we know, isn't *Galactica* the last surviving battlestar?

ADAMA. We don't know how many battlestars or how many other elements of the fleet may have survived.

The two argue about the status of the other ships in the fleet, and Adama asserts,

ADAMA. We're going after the enemy. We're at war. That's our mission.

PRESIDENT ROSLIN. I don't know why I have to keep telling you people this, but the war is over.

ADAMA. I don't accept that.

After continued arguing, an exasperated Adama asks,

ADAMA. And what do you want me to do? Run?

PRESIDENT ROSLIN. Yes! That's absolutely right! The only sane thing to do here is exactly that, run. We leave this solar system and never look back.

ADAMA. And go where?

PRESIDENT ROSLIN. I don't know. Another star system, another planet— somewhere the Cylons won't find us.

ADAMA. You can run if you want. This ship is going to stand and fight.

PRESIDENT ROSLIN. You don't get it, do you? The human race is about to be wiped out. We have fifty thousand people left and that's it. If we want to even survive as a species, then we need to get the hell out of here and start having babies.

For dramatic purposes, *Battlestar Galactica* benefits from having two leaders struggling against one another. The fact that Roslin represents civilian power and Adama represents military power is not, in and of itself, explicitly gendered. However, when Adama states his intent to "stand and fight" and Roslin summarizes her wish to "get the hell out of here and start having babies," it's not a stretch to suggest that Adama is cast as a masculinized military leader and Roslin inhabits a more traditionally feminine persona governed by what Carol Gilligan calls "an ethic of nurturance, responsibility, and care."[68] In the next episode, it becomes clear that *Galactica* is unable to outrun the Cylons, and thus Adama becomes the clear-eyed realist while Roslin's plan is shown to be ineffectively idealistic.

Throughout *Battlestar Galactica*'s four seasons, Adama and Roslin clash repeatedly over humanitarian versus military objectives. At times, Roslin's stubbornness suggests an inability to capably lead. As Jason P. Blahuta notes, Roslin "is willing to sacrifice *Colonial One*, including what's left of the civilian government, in order to save the disabled *Gemenon Liner 1701* and two

CHAPTER 2

other defenseless civilian ships when the Cylons attack. But does she save the other ships? No. She refuses to leave the crippled ships behind, but she has no plan for how to save *Colonial One*—a noble, yet stupid decision. If the Cylons destroy *Colonial One*, the entire civilian government would be obliterated along with the other ships shortly thereafter. Fortunately, Apollo saves the day by taking matters into his own hands."[69]

As the series develops, President Roslin, in addition to being governed by an (overly) idealistic humanitarianism, makes decisions that are increasingly informed by a mystical belief in Colonial legend/religion. George A. Dunn explains: "Laura Roslin discovers her destiny after coming to believe she's the 'dying leader' whom Pythia foretold would 'lead humanity to the promised land.'" From that point on, "Roslin's identity is based on locating herself within this story, a religious narrative that assigns her a particular destiny."[70] Similarly, Elizabeth F. Cooke contends that President Roslin is motivated by "religious hope," which stands in contrast to Adama's "hopeful pragmatism" and Apollo's "political hope."[71] Women and femininity have long been linked to spirituality, in contrast to men's/masculinity's rationality. In democratic societies like the Twelve Colonies or the contemporary United States, excessive spirituality is deemed unsuitable to political governance because of the need to keep democracies from devolving into theocracies. If men are perceived to be more democratic and pragmatic than women, men will, necessarily, be viewed as more appropriately presidential.

The presentation of President Roslin as excessively mystical is enhanced by the fact that Roslin's religiosity leads her to make decisions that appear to compromise the safety of the fleet and thus belie even her own humanitarianism. Goulart and Joe recount an illustrative example. At the end of season one, President Roslin persuades "the military's most skilled combat pilot, Starbuck," to embark on a solo mission that would "allegedly enable the president to fulfill an ancient religious prophecy of leading the humans to Earth." An alarmed Adama stages a military coup based on the rationale that "Roslin's political skills, including her power to appeal to broadly held religious beliefs, [could] compromise Adama's command authority to an extent that could ultimately jeopardize the military's capacity to protect the human community." Adama becomes convinced that "Roslin is a 'religious fanatic' of questionable mental competence."[72]

What is telling about this storyline is not just that Roslin is aligned with religiosity and her competence is questioned. As the narrative plays out, Starbuck's mission proves to be helpful and Roslin is at least partially vindicated. However, her rationale for her decisions remains suspect; just because Starbuck's mission was a success does not mean that Roslin's dubious mysticism will always lead to the best course of action. Indeed, Starbuck's success can be read as either a lucky break or a prophetic turn of events. Goulart and Joe point out that "Adama's skepticism of the president's claims of prophetic destiny is arguably the only sane analysis of the political community's security situation.... Decisions to seize key military assets and undermine the senior military officer's command authority in the service of fulfilling religious prophecy can lead a reasonable person to believe that the president is incapable of serving as a wartime head of state."[73] Herein lies the crux of the problem. As the *Battlestar Galactica* narrative unfolds, it argues, suppositionally, that women are more prone to religiosity, humanitarianistic sentimentality, and nurturance. In a time of war, these values must sometimes be subordinated to the more masculine traits of pragmatism, rationality, and military strength.

Because Roslin's presidential tenure stretches over four seasons, her character (and the narrative in which it is situated) is more complex than that of many of the other fictional presidents considered in this chapter. As a result, she typifies the imperfect postmodern leader described by Parry-Giles and Parry-Giles. Like Adama, Roslin is neither all good nor all bad, neither completely capable nor totally incompetent. Both leaders exhibit wisdom, courage, and conviction. Both fall prey to hubris and poor judgment. What is interesting about the trajectories of Roslin's and Adama's character development is that, on the whole, Roslin is portrayed as a more nurturing and spiritual leader, whereas Adama is cast as a stronger military presence. At key moments, Adama is also shown to possess a stronger moral compass.

For example, Blahuta notes that Roslin sometimes adheres to "Machiavelli's counsel: the only way to maintain a strong and stable state when surrounded by corruption is to discard conventional morality. Adama, however, holds fast to the values that define Colonial society."[74] Blahuta points to the following exchange, when Adama and Roslin are faced with the prospect that a corrupt Gaius Baltar may become the next Colonial president:

ADAMA. Do we steal the results of a democratic election or not? That's the decision. Because if we do this, we're criminals. Unindicted, maybe, but criminals just the same.
PRESIDENT ROSLIN. Yes, we are.
ADAMA. You won't do it. We've gone this far, but that's it.
PRESIDENT ROSLIN. Excuse me?
ADAMA. You try to steal this election, you'll die inside. Likely move the cancer right to your heart. People made their choice. We're gonna have to live with it.[75]

Roslin relents and democratic ideals are safeguarded, but it is Adama, not Roslin, who upholds civilian democracy. Thus, whereas Adama can capably act as a principled military *and* political leader, Roslin seems willing to betray her principles in order to retain political power.

As illustrated in the preceding example, Roslin is frequently assisted by male figures, characters who protect, counsel, and challenge her. An important introduction to Roslin's reliance on men occurs in the miniseries premiere, when her shuttle is targeted by a Cylon missile following the initial nuclear strike. Apollo intercepts the missile and saves the shuttle. After his fighter is disabled, Roslin's shuttle picks up Apollo, establishing a symbiotic relationship between Apollo and Roslin that will develop throughout the series. Apollo's heroics protect the *Gemenon Liner* and the rest of the fleet after Roslin's decisions leave the fleet vulnerable.[76] During a military coup Roslin relies on Apollo and another white male character, Tom Zarek, to oppose Adama's efforts and restore her to the presidency.[77] More broadly, over the course of the series, Apollo and another young, white, male character, Karl "Helo" Agathon, exhibit the most consistent character and sense of principle.[78] Thus, white masculinity retains its position even within a series that embraces leaders as complex and flawed individuals.

Although Roslin is not sexualized in the same way as, for example, Caprica Six, the concluding episodes of the series do follow Roslin and Adama as they consummate a sexual relationship that had been brewing for years.[79] Blogger Kate O'Hare describes it as a "torrid, possibly doomed, romance," but the sexual tension between Adama and Roslin seems to stem less from sheer physical attraction and more from the shared struggle of mutually respectful partners.[80] Because Roslin and Adama form two halves of the governing authority throughout the series, it may seem "natural" for their partnership to evolve into a sexual relationship as the Cylon threat is subdued and the fleet finds a safe home. Equally as important, however, is the narrative impulse woven throughout western literature and popular culture that a "happy" ending requires the romantic union of male and female lead characters. In the case of *Battlestar Galactica,* the end belies a tragic romance as opposed to a "happily ever after" fairy tale. No longer needing the titles of "president" and "commander," Adama comforts a dying Roslin, whose cancer (revealed in the miniseries premiere) is finally taking its toll. Adama tenderly carries Roslin to his rebuilt jet and takes her up to survey the planet that will become the new home of the Twelve Colonies. As Roslin's life slips away, Adama tells her that he is "just looking for a quiet little place for that cabin" they discussed sharing after their romantic relationship commenced. When he notices that she is gone, he takes her hand, kisses it, and begins to weep. Then he places his wedding ring on her finger, a gesture that brings this unconventional series to an exceedingly conventional end.[81] This conclusion is satisfying for the viewer, in part, because it confirms and instantiates not only the preeminence of heterosexual romance but also the centrality of romance to human fulfillment.

Battlestar Galactica treats female presidentiality with depth and complexity, exploring issues of gender, power, and political agency with more nuance than is typically found in a television series. In some ways, its fantastical genre allowed the series more leeway than, for example, that given to a series such as *Commander in Chief.* As showrunner Moore stated, "The networks are terrified of controversy, but in sci-fi, they don't notice or care so much—you get a free pass."[82] When the strictures of real-world drama are enforced, the result is less transformative and more reactionary. Nothing illustrates that claim more clearly than an examination of female presidentiality as portrayed in the Fox television drama *24.*

Female Presidentiality as Personal and Political Tragedy in *24*

When *Newsweek* columnist Joshua Alston reflected on the series finale of the popular Fox series *24,* he lamented the fact that he had "hoped for a more optimistic ending for President Allison Taylor . . . who by the final seconds of *24* is disgraced for participating in a cover-up and on the verge of submitting her resignation." Alston concluded that although "buildings and cars and entire city blocks were destroyed by all manner of weapon," nothing "sustained more damage in *24* than the image of the presidency."[83] Taylor's embattled presidential journey began optimistically, with *24*'s executive producer Howard Gordon discussing the introduction of Taylor's character at the beginning of season seven by announcing, "It's time to go back to an idealized president—a well-articulated and idealized president."[84] The fact that *24*'s return to idealized presidentiality would be led by a woman prompted speculation about the similarities between Taylor and one-time Democratic presidential frontrunner Hillary Clinton. As noted in 2007 by Reuters's Nellie Andreeva, "'24' producers had been contemplating having a female president next season for some time. Their decision to go for it might reflect the closely watched Democratic Party's presidential race, in which Hillary Clinton is the frontrunner."[85] Similarly, *If* magazine declared, "Hillary Clinton fans, rejoice—*24* made your dream into TV reality."[86] What began as a dream at the outset of season seven quickly deteriorated into a personal and political nightmare for President Allison Taylor. Taylor's tragic end is not surprising considering the larger tragic frame that dominates the narrative of *24.*[87] None of the presidents in the *24* universe fare particularly well, but the contours of Taylor's downfall illustrate the ways in which *24*'s suppositional claims eclipsed the propositional progressiveness of casting a woman in the role of Jack Bauer's commander in chief.[88]

24 earned both high ratings and critical acclaim throughout its eight-season run on the Fox television network. Steven Peacock dubs *24* a "cultural phenomenon" that "garnered near-unanimous acclaim from critics and viewers alike." Daniel Chamberlain and Scott Ruston herald the series as "stylistically bold, narratively engaging, culturally relevant, and blessed with commercial and critical success."[89] *24* featured star Kiefer Sutherland in the role of Jack Bauer, a government agent working for the US Counter Terrorism Unit (CTU). Bauer's willingness to resort to extraordinary measures (often involving violence, intimidation of civilians, and torture) in order to preserve national security, along with the series' innovative real-time format, has prompted popular, critical, and scholarly interest in this polyvalent text.[90] For our purposes in this chapter, *24* presents the most recent network television incarnation of a woman president—one that both reifies heroic white masculinity and serves as a cautionary tale about the risks of female presidentiality.

Allison Taylor (played by Cherry Jones) enters the *24* universe after being elected to office. This detail differentiates her from screen predecessors such as Mackenzie Allen and Laura Roslin. For Taylor, democracy rather than catastrophe sweeps her into the Oval Office. Viewers are introduced to her during the season seven prequel, "Redemption," as she prepares to be inaugurated. Walking through the White House on her husband's arm, their good-natured marital banter lays the foundation for Taylor's "Day 7" (season seven) persona:

HENRY TAYLOR. How are you feeling?

PRESIDENT-ELECT TAYLOR. Excited. Nervous.

HENRY TAYLOR. You should be. In a few hours you're going to be the most powerful person in the world, as if you're not already hard enough to live with.

An outwardly confident, inwardly conflicted Taylor leans (literally and figuratively) on her husband, who has perfected the dutiful, supportive first gentleman persona. He recedes into the background as Taylor is briefed on the situation that will frame the Day 7 narrative: political unrest in the fictional African nation of Sengala. Television critic Cynthia Fuchs summarizes the plot as follows: "Taylor is stuck between hard places: she's promised the former/exiled prime minister of Sengala, Motobou (Isaach de Bankolé) to send US troops to stop the genocide being perpetrated by General Juma (Tony Todd) and his vengeful ally Dubaku (Hakeem Kae-Kazim). The latter, mad because Jack killed his brother in Africa, is working inside the US with terrorists who, during the first hour, seize control of the nation's infrastructure (including ATC, power grids, water supplies), displaying their power quite spectacularly by nearly crashing two passenger jets at JFK."[91]

President-elect Taylor is immediately positioned as the idealistic humanitarian in a closed-door briefing with outgoing President Noah Daniels, who points out that the United States risks getting "caught up in another civil quagmire halfway around the world. Now that is a hard sell. Especially when there's nothing in Sengala worth protecting—no natural resources, no substantial economic ties, nothing that threatens our national security." The briefing continues:

PRESIDENT-ELECT TAYLOR. The last time Juma made a power grab he ignited a tribal war that killed tens of thousands of civilians. Our involvement could avert a genocide.

PRESIDENT DANIELS. And this war will be tragic too. But it isn't our war. Which is why I've ordered the ambassador to begin evacuating all non-military nationals.

PRESIDENT-ELECT TAYLOR. I think that's a mistake.

PRESIDENT DANIELS. I don't want any Americans caught in the crossfire when Juma starts shooting.

PRESIDENT-ELECT TAYLOR. Closing our embassy sends a signal to the world that we are willing to sell out a democratic ally to a war criminal.

PRESIDENT DANIELS. I appreciate your idealism.

PRESIDENT-ELECT TAYLOR. I can't say the same for your cynicism.[92]

Like Mackenzie Allen and Laura Roslin, Allison Taylor begins her presidential tenure as a principled humanitarian, illustrating that the "cult of true womanhood" notion of women's elevated morality rings true even in the morally relativistic *24* universe. Even so, in the complex *24* landscape, matters of public policy are not as clear cut as they were, for example, in Mackenzie Allen's White House in *Commander in Chief.*

On the heels of the "Redemption" prequel, Day 7 commences just a few months into President Taylor's tenure. After economic sanctions have failed to curtail Juma's actions, Taylor discusses military action against Juma with the Joint Chiefs of Staff. Although her generals report that they are likely to face "minimal" resistance from Juma, Taylor faces opposition from her own secretary of state, Joe Stevens, who voices his concerns in front of the Joint Chiefs: "Madam President, my objection to this operation isn't a secret to anyone in this room. For us to be wading into the middle of another civil conflict halfway around the world. . . ." President Taylor replies, "We're done debating this, Joe. The UN's been issuing reprimands and economic sanctions while Benjamin Juma has slaughtered over two hundred thousand of his own people. That number will continue to grow if we don't stop him now. And if you can't get behind what we're doing I'll find a secretary of state who can. But I am done with your hand wringing."[93]

That exchange establishes Taylor's confidence and credibility; however, as the narrative unfolds, Taylor receives increasing resistance from her male cabinet members and advisors. Her resolve is challenged when forces that infiltrated the nation's infrastructure grid make demands tied to the military response to General Juma. Speaking to the president directly, Juma's right-hand man, Dubaku, instructs the president to make "a complete and immediate withdrawal of the US naval strike force" in order to avoid an attack on American civilians.[94] With American lives in the balance, Taylor's advisors strongly urge her to pull back on the military response to Juma.

At this point, the Day 7 plot enters narrative territory familiar to many presidential dramas: a terrorist is making demands on a US president. As viewers of blockbusters such as *Air Force One* know, the cardinal rule of US domestic and foreign policy is never to give in to terrorist demands. Presidents who stand their ground in the face of personal and political jeopardy (such as Harrison Ford's President Marshall in *Air Force One*) are typically cast as heroes and their efforts are usually rewarded. Not so for President Taylor. Although she convincingly articulates the rationale for not giving in to terrorist demands, her advisors counsel a different course of action, with some viewing the threat against American lives as a convenient rationale for ditching the messy humanitarian mission in Sengala. Taylor articulates the moral dilemma in a conversation with her chief of staff, Ethan Kanin, saying, "Unless I order our forces to stand down, I'll be condemning innocent Americans to death. And if we capitulate, thousands of Sengalins will be slaughtered. . . . And now to have to decide between two impossible choices." Kanin pushes Taylor away from the humanitarian mission (and toward capitulation to terrorist demands), saying, "Well, at least one of those choices does stand a good chance of preserving American lives."[95] Ultimately, Taylor unilaterally decides to follow the long-standing US practice of not negotiating with terrorists. The consequences are swift and dramatic. As Taylor and Kanin watch through a window in the Oval Office, Dubaku uses a device to divert air traffic control signals, causing two airplanes to crash into one another.[96] Just months into the tenure of this fictional woman president, hundreds of innocent lives are lost after she fails to heed the counsel of her male advisors.

Meeting with her cabinet after the crash, Secretary of State Stevens urges, "Madam President, this is a catastrophic loss of American life and it's only going to get worse. We have to withdraw our forces before the next deadline."[97] Eventually, the risk to the US public is mitigated by the heroic action of Jack Bauer and his former CTU colleague Tony Almeida, who also manage to uncover a conspiracy within the US government. Bauer convinces President Taylor that he and his CTU colleagues are the only people she can trust until the conspirators have been uncovered. Bauer's cavalier assertion of authenticity and authority are illustrated when, in a secret meeting in the Oval Office, Taylor questions his reliability, saying, "You resigned from government service and the Senate regards you as having been a renegade agent. How am I supposed to know where your loyalties really lie?" Bauer replies definitively, asserting, "With all due respect, Madam President, ask around."[98] Even though Bauer is a flawed hero, he is a hero nonetheless, and his determination to act in the nation's best interest is one of the few constants throughout *24*'s eight seasons. Thus, when he begins to order around the president of the United States, his actions achieve narrative fidelity not only with gender norms but also with the storyline of *24*.

Despite Bauer's involvement, the early days of Taylor's presidency are marked, as noted in a news broadcast during the 3:00 A.M.–4:00 A.M. hour of Day 7, by "an unprecedented series of terror attacks" that "left people all over the country shaken and demanding answers."[99] The early episodes of season seven make the suppositional argument that even when a strong, principled woman is elected by democratic majority into the office of the presidency, it does not take long for her allies to turn against her, the safety of US citizens to be jeopardized, and her own confidence and conviction to be shattered.

Taylor's status as a mother also is integral to the plot development of *24*'s season seven. Rather than being portrayed as a working mother balancing the competing demands of presidentiality and motherhood (as was, for example, *Commander in Chief*'s Mackenzie Allen), Taylor's children are grown and bring a different set of challenges to her presidential narrative. First, *24* establishes Taylor's ability to resolutely do her job despite the recent death of her son. Early on Day 7, Kanin warns Taylor that involving her husband, Henry Taylor, in political matters may not be a good idea given his instability following the death of their son. Convinced that his son's death was murder rather than suicide, Henry obsessively pursues evidence of a plot—evidence that initially only he believes exists. Kanin confronts Taylor:

KANIN. I don't mean to sound like a broken record, but I'm not sure your husband is up to handling Aldridge.
PRESIDENT TAYLOR. Henry's fine.
KANIN. He's better, I realize that, but . . .
PRESIDENT TAYLOR. It's going to take more than a few months. He lost a son.
KANIN. So did you. And you haven't let your loss interfere with your job. Your husband's a strong man, but he doesn't have your resilience.
PRESIDENT TAYLOR. [*visibly irritated*] It's not a matter of resilience, Ethan. [*tearing up*] There's not a day that goes by, not a moment when I don't think about my son. But I'm about to take this nation to war and grief is a luxury I can't afford right now.[100]

As the plot of Day 7 unfolds, Henry's suspicions surrounding his son's death are confirmed, but his search for evidence leads to his eventual kidnapping and later to a shooting that leaves him hospitalized. In the aftermath of the terrorist attack on the civilian airplanes, Taylor's self-confidence is further shaken by her failure to believe and support her husband. This plot twist disciplines Taylor for the presidential resolve she articulated in her earlier conversation with Kanin and confirms that even when Henry Taylor appeared to be off balance and obsessive, he still was a better judge of circumstances than was his wife. An emotional Taylor confides to Kanin, "What happened to Henry was my fault, Ethan. He never believed our son committed suicide. And he was right and I didn't listen to him. And if I had we wouldn't be here right now. Henry wouldn't be fighting for his life."[101] Here, the narrative of *24* chastises Taylor both as an ineffective president and as a bad wife.

Reeling from disclosure of evidence that points to corruption in her own administration, Taylor closes ranks and makes another decision that implicates her status as a mother as something that conflicts with presidentiality. Taylor invites her daughter, Olivia Taylor, to step in and act as a presidential advisor. Her first task is to assist her mother in naming a new chief of staff after Kanin's resignation. Taylor's decision to admit her daughter into the presidential inner circle was surprising, since the Day 7 narrative reveals that Olivia had been dismissed from Taylor's presidential campaign staff due to unethical behavior. Olivia's return is characterized, first, as a family moment. After inviting her daughter to serve as acting chief of staff until a replacement for Kanin can be found, Taylor implores, "Livy, I need someone I can trust, especially after everything that's happened today. You're not going to say no to your mother, are you?"[102] Taylor's trust in her daughter is quickly betrayed, however, when Olivia uses her position to hire a hit on the man who killed her brother. When her plan is uncovered, Olivia confesses to both parents and a conversation about parental versus presidential priorities ensues:

PRESIDENT TAYLOR. How could you do this, Olivia? How could you do something so stupid?
OLIVIA TAYLOR. I'm sorry, I tried to call it off, I swear.
PRESIDENT TAYLOR. It doesn't matter, darling, it happened.
HENRY TAYLOR. For God's sake, Allison, stop yelling at her. Hodges killed our son.
PRESIDENT TAYLOR. I know what he did.
HENRY TAYLOR. Then you know, if anyone deserves to die it's him. All you should be thinking about now is how to protect our daughter.[103]

Despite her husband's wishes, Taylor refuses to help her daughter cover up the murder. Henry details the cost, not of his daughter's actions but of his wife's position:

HENRY TAYLOR. You're Olivia's mother.
PRESIDENT TAYLOR. And I'm also the president of the United States.
HENRY TAYLOR. And our family's already paid a steep enough price for that. . . . Your job cost our son his life.[104]

President Taylor refuses to participate in a cover-up of her daughter's crimes. As a result, her daughter is incarcerated and her husband leaves her.

The Day 7 storyline concludes as an antifeminist cautionary tale about the potential costs to women who pursue presidential leadership.

In the short span of *24*'s Day 7, a woman president is challenged by her cabinet, her decision making results in the deaths of several hundred American civilians, she hastily installs her daughter as chief of staff, her daughter uses the office of the presidency to have someone killed, and the day ends with her daughter in jeopardy, her marriage in shambles, and the country reeling from devastating acts of terror. If this were the close of Allison Taylor's story, some solace could be gained from the fact that she ends the season with her integrity intact. Day 8, unfortunately, proves that President Taylor's tenure in office is not only a personal tragedy for herself and her family; it also ushers in a political tragedy for the American public.

As noted at the beginning of our discussion of *24*, things do not end well for President Allison Taylor. Since all of the presidential figures in *24* eventually encounter tragedy, Taylor's demise is not particularly unusual. Of note for the purposes of this chapter, however, is the way in which the *24* narrative discredits her. Day 8 opens with President Taylor on the verge of negotiating an historic peace treaty with Omar Hassan, president of the Islamic Republic of Kamistan (IRK). Taylor is once again held up as a humanitarian, but her plans for Mideast peace are interrupted when members of Hassan's own government turn against him, obtain materials for a dirty bomb, and threaten to set it off in New York City unless Hassan is handed over to them. Numerous advisors urge her to surrender Hassan in order to avert detonation of the dirty bomb. Valuing the peace process above all else and once again unwilling to give in to terrorist demands, Taylor articulates her rationale for protecting Hassan, saying, "President Hassan is a guest of this country. He is my partner in peace. And I will not sell him out to the very terrorists we are determined to defeat."[105] Taylor also reminds her cabinet members that the terrorists cannot be trusted to abide by their promise not to detonate the bomb and that capitulation to terrorist demands weakens US national security.

As in all seasons of *24*, Day 8 is packed with plot twists and turns. After a series of events leads to President Hassan's death, Taylor attempts to resuscitate the peace process by working with Hassan's widow, Dalia Hassan. The two women initially personify principled leadership, courage, and grace as they cooperate to salvage the peace process. Unfortunately, the narrative reveals that Russian leaders, critical third signatories of the peace accord, orchestrated Hassan's kidnapping and death in order to stall the peace process. When they threaten to leave the negotiations, President Taylor is desperate to bring them back to the table. In her desperation, Taylor turns to former US president Charles Logan—a character known to *24* fans for his hand in the assassination of David Palmer, the beloved president from *24*'s early seasons. Repeating the mistake she made in Day 7 and once again receiving counsel from questionable sources, President Taylor allows Logan to engage the Russians on her behalf. As details of Logan's arrangement with the Russians emerge, Taylor discounts the input of her trusted advisor, Ethan Kanin, who says, "Madam President, you covered up the Russians' involvement. That's grounds for impeachment—possibly a criminal indictment. You crossed the line, Madam President. But it may not be too late to step back and limit the damage." President Taylor, looking both chastened and emotional, asks him how. Kanin encourages Taylor to come clean. Momentarily convinced, Taylor informs Kanin of her intention to do the right thing; however, when conferring with Logan, he persuades her to expand the cover-up by detaining and torturing a key informant in order to secure and bury evidence of the conspiracy. When Kanin learns of Taylor's intention to authorize the witness's detainment and torture, a debate ensues:

KANIN. Keeping the truth from Jack Bauer is one thing, but authorizing the illegal detention and torture of a prisoner? How far are you willing to go to protect this lie?
PRESIDENT TAYLOR. As far as necessary to preserve this treaty. It's vital to the security of this nation. And what I am doing is for the greater good.
KANIN. This was Logan's idea, wasn't it?
PRESIDENT TAYLOR. The decision was mine and I stand behind it.
KANIN. Allison, please listen to what I am saying. I think this is about more than the greater good. I think your presidency has cost you your marriage and your children and you think that this treaty will somehow redeem that loss.
PRESIDENT TAYLOR. Ethan, that's enough.
KANIN. Allison, you've made this personal and you've lost your way.[106]

Kanin states his intention to resign if Taylor proceeds. Desperate and emotional, Taylor pleads, "Ethan, please. We are almost there. You can't just abandon me like this."[107]

The preceding exchange between Kanin and Taylor is critical—not only because it propels the Day 8 narrative to its tragic conclusion but also because it exemplifies the tragedy of female presidentiality. First, the conversation underscores the flaw inherent to Taylor's humanitarian impulses. Rather than exemplifying principled character, Taylor's obsession with the peace process causes her to betray her ally, Dalia Hassan, and to commit impeachable offenses. Second, Kanin emphasizes that the reason Taylor was willing to go so far was not a calculation of the greater good (a motivation that frequently inspires Bauer) but rather was an outgrowth of her failures as a wife and mother. Transitioning from presidential advisor to authoritative patriarch, Kanin refers to Taylor by her first name and chides, "You've made this personal and you've lost your way." By invoking Taylor's predilection for the "personal" over the "political," Kanin taps into an ancient association of femininity with the intimate realm of emotions, contrasted with Kanin's rational masculinity. Put another way, in his review of *24*'s final season, *Newsweek*'s Alston laments the fact that Taylor becomes "a flighty nitwit" who exhibits a "troubling tendency to blindly follow the most recent suggestion from one of her male advisers."[108]

As Day 8 winds down, Taylor continues to rebuff Kanin's appeals to principle. The *24* narrative conflates humanitarianism with naked political ambition as Logan works to keep Taylor involved with the cover-up. "Believe me," Logan says, "I know how hard you worked for this—how you sweated, and prayed, the sleepless nights—I know! The power to make a difference, that's why we came into politics. How few of us get to achieve it! But you have. You so nearly have."[109]

Persuaded, Taylor asks Bauer to stop investigating the murder of his friend, Renee Walker, because she knows that his investigation will expose the Russian conspiracy and her administration's cover-up. Taylor entreats Bauer, saying, "The peace process is back on track. Dalia Hassan will represent her country at the signing. The Russians have accepted her and have undertaken to support the treaty." Bauer attempts to persuade the president of the merits of continuing the investigation until he begins to realize that she does not want the truth to come to light. "You don't want to know the truth," Bauer says. "What I want is to keep the Russians at the table," she replies. After continued argument, an emotional President Taylor informs a cool and collected Bauer that "this peace treaty is in the interests of the United States and of the world. That makes it a good in itself and certainly more important than your desire for revenge." Bauer responds that he wants justice rather than revenge. Taylor concludes, "And I want peace."[110]

Ultimately, Jack Bauer's personal quest for justice *and* revenge leads him to discover the cover-up of the Russians' involvement in Hassan's murder. President Taylor herself actively participates in the cover-up, giving multiple orations on the importance of preserving the peace process at any cost until the last hour of Day 8. One pivotal scene juxtaposes a press conference in which President Taylor extols the peace process with images of someone being tortured per presidential authorization. Humanitarianism, which is construed as a feminine virtue in a variety of presidential narratives, is cast as an empty ideal that predisposes the president to corruption.

As the series draws to a close, President Taylor, in a belated act of courage, tearfully withdraws from the peace accord and confesses her part in the conspiracy to the nation, saying, "Grave crimes have been committed in the run up to this treaty. I have participated in a conspiracy to hide those crimes. And before there can be a meaningful peace, justice must be served."[111] In the *24* universe, the only person consistently positioned to pursue justice is hero Jack Bauer.

The importance of gender to the *24* narrative is not immediately apparent to all critics. Paul Delaney argues that conflict in *24* is not gendered because "the women of *24* are on both sides. Some fight side by side with Bauer, others fight him with equal ruthlessness."[112] Yet gender norming cannot be gauged simply by examining who the protagonists and antagonists are. Instead, the construction of the female characters, such as (for our purposes) President Taylor, must be read alongside the narrative of heroic white masculinity that forms the foundation and framework of *24*. Jack Bauer, to be sure, is a flawed hero. His failings led him to cheat on his wife, disappoint his daughter, become addicted to drugs, and routinely participate in rogue acts of torture. Despite all that, however, the sustained storyline of *24* vindicates Bauer again and again, as he uncovers key information no one else can obtain, outwits and overpowers his adversaries, selflessly completes his missions, and saves countless civilian lives. One television critic explains that, when Bauer is facing indictment at the beginning of season seven for allegedly engaging in illegal acts of torture, "it's everyone else who doesn't get what it takes, echoing the show's constant theme of Bauer as a misunderstood hero."[113] *Newsweek*'s Alston concurs, describing Bauer as "the ultimate rogue agent, constantly squaring off against his superiors when they lack the stomach for his brand of instinct-driven, red-tape-cutting heroics."[114] In fact, *24* exhibits many of the narrative characteristics of what Parry-Giles and Parry-Giles call "postmodern romance." They explain that "contemporary romance discourse, like the political culture that produces it, can reflect a deep-seated ideological dissonance, making the distinctions between good and evil more ambiguous in the postmodern age." Consequently, despite the moral ambivalence that comprises Bauer's character, he nonetheless fulfills the function of a tragic hero. Because white masculinity is so deeply instantiated in Bauer's character, *24* has had the narrative latitude to experiment with diversified incarnations of presidentiality while reinforcing the preeminence of white masculinity.[115]

As the series finale builds to its conclusion, Bauer finds himself on a mission to exact justice on those responsible for killing Renee Walker and participating in the ensuing cover-up. Bauer's journey is portrayed as both a murderous quest for revenge and a methodical pursuit of justice. One scene underscores the fact that although Bauer's obsession is consistent with the conflicted morality his character displays throughout the series, the blame lies not with Bauer but with President Taylor. With a gun to the head of one of the conspirators, Logan's assistant Jason Pillar, Jack explains on what grounds he derives his moral authority:

PILLAR. I don't understand something. You've spent your entire career working outside the system but you've always had a good reason, but this? It's just blood lust. You're destroying an agreement that took years to put together.

BAUER. An agreement made by murderers and liars.

PILLAR. Murderers? You're the one killing people in cold blood.

BAUER. Everybody I took out had a hand in today's attack.

PILLAR. Well, who makes you judge and jury?

BAUER. President Taylor. When she agreed to the cover-up. I would have accepted justice by law. But that was taken away from me by people like you. So you're right. I am judge and jury. Now step back. Turn around.[116]

At the last minute, however, Bauer's blood lust is tempered after Pillar begs for his life and tells Bauer he has a young daughter. A father himself, Bauer relents. That last-minute act of restraint reminds the audience of Bauer's moral compass.

In Day 8's final conversation between Bauer and Taylor, the president (and the episode's narrative) places the blame for the day's events squarely on her own shoulders, saying, "I wanted this peace so badly, Jack, and for that I have betrayed every principle that I have ever stood for. And I betrayed you. If I had listened to you none of this would have happened." Taylor concludes, "I would give anything to take back the time."[117] Of course, in the *24* universe, time marches on. Just as the passing of time is a narrative imperative, so too is the masculinization of authority. Although at the outset of Day 7, *24* raised the propositional possibility that women can lead as courageously and effectively as men, by the end of Day 8 that possibility is eclipsed by the personal and political tragedies of female presidentiality.

Why Fictional Presidentiality Matters

Despite the fact that Allen, McCloud, Bennett, Hanson, Roslin, and Taylor develop divergent presidential personae, each character's program functions (at least initially) as a propositional argument that women can serve as chief executives equal to men and that, to the extent that sexism endures in US society, it is recognized as anachronistic, ridiculous, or corrupt. In media, propositional arguments are the most explicit messages at the surface—those that nearly every audience member is equipped to recognize. Propositional arguments are likely to "ring true" to most audience members, either because they fit conventional narrative structures, they reinforce accepted cultural ideals, and/or because they fulfill audience desires. Were the propositional argument about women's competence put forth without any recognition of the sexism that the first woman president surely will face, it would undercut the argument's force. Each fictional work addresses this challenge by recognizing the continued existence of sexism but marking it as out of step with the mainstream, as ridiculous, and/or as corrupt. Because each fictional work discounts the rhetorical force and material consequences of sexism in contemporary society, the corresponding narratives reinforce postfeminist ideology. The shortcomings of postfeminism have been articulated at length and are typified by Bonnie J. Dow's contention that postfeminism promotes "a kind of rugged individualism on the part of exceptional women whose lives are cushioned by privileges of education, race, and class." Dow continues, explaining that postfeminism encourages citizens to "overlook the profound inequalities that burden women" who lack access to such privileges.[118] The important point to note is that postfeminism is recognized by most feminist scholars as a false feminism, an argument that denies, rather than responds to, the constraints of patriarchy.[119]

Insofar as presidentiality is informed by norms of militarism, whiteness, masculinity, and heroic individualism, we argue that these cultural assumptions, reinforced in historical narratives, news media, and popular culture, form the foundation for the suppositional arguments that emerge in our six texts.[120] A suppositional argument functions below the surface of the propositional argument and can either bolster or deny the explicit claims made at the text's most obvious level. Suppositional arguments, though not hidden or unarticulated, may be more difficult for audience members to recognize, either because the assumptions are so widely held as to be taken for truth or because audience members want to resist their existence or rhetorical force. The fictional works assessed in this study argue suppositionally that US presidents are militaristic, white, male, and heroic. Additionally, the texts reinforce long-held cultural assumptions that women's identity is defined by their sexuality, their potential for childbearing, and the superior moral character that comes from their role as mothers.

At the suppositional level, then, these texts reinforce traditional stereotypes, both about the office of US president and about women. As a result, the suppositional argument contradicts and disciplines the proposition that women and men can serve as US president equally well. The contradiction between propositional and suppositional claims is present in both television and film, comedy and drama. It informs blockbuster successes and ratings flops. Despite the differences (in medium, tone, genre, and purpose) illustrated by the texts assessed in this chapter, they share a suppositional view of women presidents as (overly) humanitarian, sexual, and maternal. They fail to effectively disrupt the hegemonic white masculinity of the postmodern presidency. Perhaps most importantly, their appeal relies on a clever pairing of propositional and suppositional arguments, proving that explicitly and unproblematically sexist texts are (thankfully) no longer as convincing as they used to be. But moments of disruption and challenge in these texts of presidentiality are contained by the suppositional narrative fidelity to a cultural understanding of the US presidency as a masculinized role. Therefore, our critique of fictional presidentiality may not be surprising, but it is consequential because it reveals why so many real-world women candidates fail to reach that elusive bar of credibility as a "qualified" presidential contender.

In order for popular films and television series to live up to the liberatory potential heralded by the White House Project's Marie Wilson, cultural assumptions that reside at the level of supposition will have to be recognized and then challenged. This can be done through a variety of channels: interpersonal, journalistic, academic, and even pop cultural. This chapter illustrates the ways in which films and television series are particularly well suited to negotiation of multiple perspectives. Not only do they develop complex characters and address weighty political issues, they also articulate a multilayered argument. When women's equality is valued at *both* the propositional and suppositional levels, we may be nearing the day when a female commander in chief is more than just a prime-time president.

In 2006–7, many, if not most, political pundits and strategists thought that day was upon us. Hillary Clinton's commanding lead early in the 2008 Democratic primary campaign led journalists and voters to speculate that one of the remaining glass ceilings in US public culture was about to be shattered. It was not, but the 2008 presidential campaign was a history-making election nonetheless. Sarah Palin became the first woman to be nominated as a vice presidential candidate on a Republican ticket, and Barack Obama's election proved that the hegemonic whiteness of the US presidency was more malleable than was its hegemonic masculinity. Because the 2008 campaign was a pivotal moment in the history of presidentiality, the rest of this book examines its rhetoric. Rather than providing a chronological examination of the campaign or a detailed accounting of the candidates' stump speeches, we use a series of case studies to examine presidentiality as it was negotiated in 2007–8. The rhetoric of presidentiality takes many forms and includes traditional speeches, journalistic narratives, viral videos, campaign kitsch, and comedic displays. The case studies that follow focus explicitly on issues of feminism, antifeminism, and postfeminism as articulated and contested in candidate oratory, media framing, the pornification of the presidential body, and political parody.

Presidential Campaign Oratory

Two Faces of Feminism

"▐ 'm in. And I'm in to win."[1] On January 20, 2007—two years to the day
before the next president would be inaugurated—Senator Hillary Clinton
took to the Internet to announce her bid for the US presidency. With
money in the bank, a respected record in the US Senate, and the advantage of the Clinton political machine, she was the first woman frontrunner
for a major party nomination. Being in that position required Clinton to
buck more than two hundred years of American tradition, but to succeed she
would also have to recast the face of US presidentiality. Conversely, when
Alaska governor Sarah Palin became the first woman to accept the Republican Party's vice presidential nomination, her equally historic oratorical performance complemented the masculine visage of presidentiality. The 2008
campaign oratory of Clinton and Palin was important, not only because of
the symbolic significance of each of their campaigns but also because, as they
introduced themselves to US voters, they embodied two competing feminist identities. Hillary Clinton's candidacy represented the liberal feminist
promise of women's political equality. Sarah Palin's candidacy embodied the
persistence of patriarchy in postfeminist political culture.

In this chapter we examine the ways in which Clinton and Palin introduced themselves to voters oratorically, and we note how each candidate's
performances deployed competing notions of "feminist" identity in order
to negotiate the hegemonic masculinity of US presidentiality. We begin by
reviewing key oratorical moments that have instantiated the heroic masculinity of presidentiality. Although this rhetoric poses challenges for all candidates with diverse identities, women presidential hopefuls are particularly
constrained.

Masculinity as Oratorical Strategy in Demonstrating Presidentiality

Presidential candidates routinely employ political oratory that capitalizes
on strategies of hegemonic masculinity to demonstrate presidential fitness.

As we argue in the introduction, cultural understandings of the US presidency as rhetorical performance, synecdochical symbol, and normative paradigm reinscribe expectations of hegemonic masculinity, making it difficult to imagine a woman as commander in chief. Candidates also routinely feminize their opponents of either gender in an effort to demonstrate their rivals' lack of fitness for the office, further widening the gap between notions of presidentiality and the ability of a female body to perform presidentiality. Even in instances when women are involved in presidential performances, such as convention introductions by political spouses, the strength and patriarchal character of the candidate come through in stark contrast to the female speaker. In fact, political spouses routinely are used to help male presidential candidates perform their heterosexual masculinity. In this section, we briefly review the literature on presidential oratory, noting the central role masculinity plays as a strategy in the performance of presidentiality.

In Suzanne Daughton's examination of the convention discourse of the Democratic and Republican nominating conventions between 1972 and 1992, she notes that there exists a "predisposition to link the role of president to some primitive concept of *machismo*." This trend intensified in 1980, when Ronald Reagan not only relied on masculinity to prove his fitness but also condemned his rivals for their "impotence." Daughton's analysis demonstrates the ways in which masculinity is a strategic asset when demonstrating presidential fitness while femininity typically is cast as unpresidential.[2]

After Reagan's presidential tenure, George H. W. Bush became the "apprentice" who claimed "his master's visual and verbal language during his own tenure in the White House, . . . [and tried] to fashion himself first and foremost as the decisive and forceful commander-in-chief who fathers and protects his country through the exertion of his masculine powers."[3] Karin Wahl Jorgensen explains that during the 1992 campaign, "competing visions of the American male" emerged.[4] An accomplished athlete and military hero, Bush had a biography that bolstered his masculine fitness for the office. Unfortunately for him, during his first term he was characterized as a "wimp," and his appeal to make America a "kinder, gentler nation" reinforced that characterization.[5] Additionally, George H. W. Bush's blueblood image excluded him from the cowboy persona that aligns with the frontier narrative and served Reagan, and later George W. Bush, so well.

Bush's opponent, Bill Clinton, also faced challenges to his masculinity. He was not a war hero or sports champion, and he did not have a traditional family background. Additionally, some viewed his politically active, career-oriented spouse as a liability who undercut his presidential manliness.[6] However, even Clinton was able to construct a sufficiently masculine persona through oratory that functioned as an important complement to his "feel your pain" sensitivity. Jorgensen argues that Clinton regularly discussed politics using the language of football, positioning himself as the coach who never lets up. The result was "an image of brutal and ruthless exertion of force. It reduces politics to a simple, dichotomous game of win and lose. . . . The coach, a pet metaphor of US political leaders, . . . conveniently encapsulates the paternalistic guidance embedded in the president's job description. As a strategic pathfinder and overseer for his team—the country—he brings the best out in his citizens, taking advantage of their unity to control them."[7]

Similarly, Daughton finds that Clinton's 1992 campaign oratory included "plenty of statements to demonstrate that he had the strength required for the office. . . . Clinton not only demonstrate[d] his willingness to use force, but criticize[d] George Bush for not being 'man enough' to stand up to oppressive governments around the world."[8]

Elizabeth Dole's introduction of candidate Bob Dole during the 1996 Republican National Convention "served to underscore his heroic masculinity."[9] Delivering perhaps one of the most memorable, intimate addresses by a political spouse in support of her husband, Elizabeth Dole stepped down from the convention's "very imposing podium" to walk among the convention attendees and discuss "the man I love."[10] Although Dole stated that she moved away from the lectern because "it's just a lot more comfortable for me" to speak about her husband "down here with you," her physical performance positioned her deferentially below an image of Bob Dole that popped up during the speech and loomed large over the convention hall. Elizabeth Dole's image provided a stark contrast to candidate Bob Dole, a war hero whose "sheer masculine strength and determination enabled him to recover from his injuries." As a result, Elizabeth Dole "encouraged the audience to view her husband as an archetype of the US presidency—strong, independent, and able to care for those he governs."[11] By contrast, she performed the role of supportive heterosexual spouse. Just as Shawn J. Parry-Giles and Trevor Parry-Giles find that the presence of "feminine style" in the campaign films of presidential candidates masks the patriarchal nature of the institution of the presidency and "the stereotyped roles of women as wives and mothers," Elizabeth Dole's performance demonstrates the ways in which women must sublimate themselves to the presidential patriarch in order to promote the male candidate's fitness for office.[12]

During the 2000 presidential debates, candidates George W. Bush and Al Gore employed "conceptual metaphors" that align with conservative and progressive political ideologies: the strict father and the nurturant family.[13] Alan J. Cienki concludes that Bush relied on the strict father model to define his fitness for the office.[14] According to the linguist George Lakoff, the strict father model is an elaboration of a masculine ideal premised on metaphors of control: moral strength, moral authority, and moral order. The strict father model also assumes a natural hierarchy in the world, asserts that evil exists and must be punished, and characterizes the "good person" as one who exhibits discipline, obedience, and self-reliance. In relying on strict father morality, Bush demonstrated his masculine fitness for the office of president and continued the trend of deploying masculinity as a strategy of presidential campaign oratory. This persona was intensified after 9/11. Jon Roper argues that "during the 18 months after September 11, 2001, in defining the war on terror in a way that allowed his image to be projected as the nation's heroic leader, George W. Bush was able to cast his shadow over the contemporary presidency." Kevin Coe, David Domke, Meredith M. Bagley, Sheryl Cunningham, and Nancy Van Leuven concur, noting that "anyone who can be associated with constructions of femininity—or even simply non-hegemonic conceptions of masculinity—is suggested to be unfit for public office."[15]

The most looming challenge Democratic presidential nominee John Kerry faced in 2004 was the war on terror and the image of presidentiality as it had been constructed during George W. Bush's first term. Kerry attempted to demonstrate his fitness to be commander in chief during wartime in his campaign rhetoric. The opening line of his convention acceptance address declared, "I'm John Kerry, and I'm reporting for duty."[16] The convention itself was designed to be one long testament to Kerry's bravery in war, a theme that was delivered through the words of his fellow soldiers. Yet, the image of Kerry that resonated was not Kerry the war hero but Kerry the "flip flopper" who was both "French and feminine." As Anna Cornelia Fahey argues, the campaign discourse of George W. Bush capitalized on an anti-French sentiment during the Iraq war to characterize John Kerry as "French" and, by extension, feminine and unfit for the presidency. Fahey explains that the "Frenchification of Kerry helped both to preserve established hierarchies of power based on gender and to maintain politics in this country and in the world as a patriarchal system. It also feminized and thereby devalued dissent in times of war."[17]

Clearly, the moment at which political women face the most daunting rhetorical challenge is during times of national crisis, when citizens look to their commander in chief for reassurance and protection against enemy-others. In their work noting the electoral successes of female candidates in the 1990s and early 2000s, Dianne G. Bystrom, Mary Christine Banwart, Lynda Lee Kaid, and Terry A. Robertson acknowledge that the 1990s "was an era dominated by domestic concerns. Female candidates were often fighting an issue battle that focused on their own natural turf; issues such as education and health care allowed them to play to their strengths and often forced male candidates to turn their own campaigns to feminine issues." They acknowledge, however, that the post-9/11 landscape "would seem to put female candidates at a disadvantage, particularly in races with national import." Ann Gordon and Jerry Miller concur, noting that "at a time when the military becomes more important, such as during wartime, women may be at a disadvantage." People may have a difficult time envisioning a woman as commander in chief. Similarly, Jennifer Lawless argues that, in our post-9/11 political culture, "citizens prefer 'masculine' traits and characteristics in their leaders and believe that men are more likely than women to possess these qualities. Moreover, voters continue to deem men more qualified to handle military crises, whereas women receive an edge when the issues at stake revolve around poverty, women, and children." According to Erika Falk and Kate Kenski, "Citing terrorism, homeland security, and/or US involvement in Iraq as the most important problem facing the nation is significantly associated with being more likely to say that a male president would do a better job handling the national issue most important to the respondent."[18]

In January 2007 Clinton entered this rhetorical fray, determined to demonstrate her fitness for office. With the US economy and its standing in the world on the decline, voters were primed for an alternative to the "strict father" persona exhibited by George W. Bush and many of his predecessors. The contrasting voice Clinton developed was rooted not only in her Democratic political philosophy but also in her liberal feminist politics.

Candidate Oratory in 2008

The 2008 presidential campaign unfolded as a tale of two feminisms: liberal second-wave feminism and conservative postfeminism. Although the second wave of feminism in the United States produced the educational, social, and political conditions necessary for women to occupy key positions at the top of almost every profession, by 2007 the US presidency remained stubbornly off limits to women.

Clinton's Liberal Feminist Presidentiality

Bonnie J. Dow notes that "job equity" is a "key representative anecdote for liberal feminism in the public mind."[19] Hillary Clinton's bid to break the "highest, hardest glass ceiling" was viewed by many as the potential moment when women would finally become fully vested in the American democratic system.[20] Clinton's candidacy raised the possibility that feminism's second wave would finally pay off, but that return on investment also posed a price. What Karlyn Kohrs Campbell observed in 1973 about feminist rhetoric generally is also true of Clinton's presidential oratory specifically—that, "no matter how traditional its argumentation, how justificatory its form, how discursive its method, or how scholarly its style, it attacks the entire psychosocial reality, the most fundamental values, of the cultural context in which it occurs."[21] It should have come as no surprise that the woman who came of age during the height of second-wave feminism would draw on its philosophical underpinnings and rhetorical characteristics as she forged a new genus of presidentiality. For Clinton, that meant incorporating the stylistic features of consciousness-raising rhetoric into her presidential announcement speech. When Clinton announced that she was "forming a presidential exploratory committee," she espoused a rhetoric of conversation and collaboration ensconced in a digital veneer.

Clinton's historic announcement came not from the storied steps of an American landmark, with the candidate flanked by citizen supporters. Instead, she reached out to voters from the indeterminate recess of cyberspace, announcing her candidacy via Internet video and e-mail message. Clinton's Internet announcement was designed to revitalize a political brand that, for some US voters, had grown stale. The timing of her announcement was significant. January 20, 2007, was the day before President George W. Bush's State of the Union address. January 20 was also the date on which the next president would be inaugurated in two short years. However, Clinton's chronemic attempt to capitalize on presidential symbolism was her only nod to presidential tradition. Instead, Clinton attempted to demonstrate her freshness by feminizing aspects of her performance, directly countering the heroic, individualistic masculinity that is endemic to US presidentiality.

Clinton delivered the address in what appeared to be a living room, with soft lighting, flowered pillows, and family pictures displayed in the background. It was a small group setting rather than a large oratorical event. Her red jacket was the singular nonverbal sign of power, but even that was softened by its feminine tailoring and Clinton's choice to position herself seated on the couch, with hands primly folded on her lap. Clinton stated her intention to keep her campaign located in that sphere when she said, "While I can't visit everyone's living room, I can try. And with a little help from modern technology, I'll be holding live online video chats this week." Clinton's choice to meld modern technology with an intimate rhetorical style was understandable. It was a strategy productively employed by Ronald Reagan.[22] However, Clinton's rhetoric, unlike Reagan's, was infused with a second-wave feminist philosophy that complemented her political style.

Campbell explains that the consciousness-raising rhetoric of feminism's second wave was characterized by small group "rap sessions" in which "all are considered expert."[23] Clinton began her video message by saying, "I'm not just starting a campaign, though, I'm beginning a conversation—with you, with America. Because we all need to be part of the discussion if we're all going to be part of the solution." Rather than taking up the mantle of heroic leadership, Clinton suggested that, if elected, her political power would be diffuse—shared equally with her fellow citizens. The e-mail announcement that accompanied her video message deployed the conversation metaphor similarly, asking readers to join her "not just for the campaign but for a conversation." The conversation Clinton envisioned was both intimate and informal. In her video message she implored, "Let's talk. Let's chat. Let's start a dialogue about your ideas and mine."

During the 1970s, the goal of consciousness raising was "to make the personal political," underscoring the fact that "what were thought to be . . .

individual problems [were] common and shared."[24] In 2007, Clinton sought strategic advantage when she employed rhetorical strategies designed to suggest to voters that the daily struggles they faced were the responsibility of the president and Republicans in Congress rather than being isolated, personal failings. Clinton noted that "the conversation in Washington has been just a little one-sided lately, don't you think?" Her question was peppered with equivocations and tag questions—markers of feminine speech that can be evaluated as powerless speech forms.[25] This risky strategy aligned with the consciousness-raising tradition, in which a speaker's equivocations activate her audience and they find themselves nodding in agreement. Clinton was attempting to point out to her audience the exclusionary politics of the current administration and enlist their participatory response.

A key characteristic of second-wave feminism is that it was a leaderless movement. Appropriating that aspect of liberal feminism may seem an odd choice for someone who was campaigning to be the leader of the free world; however, Clinton was well acquainted with the double bind between femininity and competence.[26] At earlier points in her political career, she was roundly disciplined when she transgressed the boundaries of appropriate femininity.[27] In her announcement e-mail, although Clinton touted the need for "a new president," she refrained from explicitly casting herself in that role, exemplifying instead the leaderless ethos of second-wave feminism. This approach was strategically sound insofar as it made Clinton less threatening to voters who might object (even subconsciously) to a woman "taking over." Clinton stated, "Only a new president will be able to undo Bush's mistakes and restore our hope and optimism. Only a new president can renew the promise of America. . . . And only a new president can regain America's position as a respected leader in the world. I believe that change is coming November 4, 2008. And I am forming my exploratory committee because I believe that together we can bring the leadership that this country needs."

By stopping short of naming herself the heir to the presidency, Clinton exhibited a new style of presidential leadership premised on the feminist value of collaboration. In her announcement video message she inflected the requisite laundry list of policy initiatives with a more collaborative, participatory tone: "Let's talk about how to bring the right end to the war in Iraq and to restore respect for America around the world. How to make us energy independent and free of foreign oil. How to end the deficits that threaten Social Security and Medicare. And let's definitely talk about how every American can have quality affordable health care."

The construction of the preceding sentences suggests that Clinton sought assistance from her audience. Her announcement e-mail message intensified the appeal to collaboration, intimating that Clinton would seek the presidency in concert with voters: "I need you to be a part of this campaign, and I hope you'll start by joining me in this national conversation. As *we* campaign to win the White House, *we* will make history and remake our future." Clinton concluded with a liberal feminist rallying cry: "we can only break barriers if we dare to confront them, and if we have the determined and committed support of others."

Employing a conversation metaphor was not a new strategy for Clinton. In 1993, as first lady of the United States and chair of President Bill Clinton's Task Force on Health Care Reform, Clinton dubbed her health care reform campaign speeches "conversations on health" and contended that the Clinton plan for health care reform was the "result of literally thousands, and tens of thousands, of conversations."[28] Similarly, in 1999, when she "was assembling support to run for a US Senate seat" in New York, Clinton embarked on a "listening tour"—a strategy that, according to Julie Vorman of the Center for Public Integrity, "worked" insofar as it "helped to sell voters on her credentials as a New Yorker."[29] Thus, it is perhaps not surprising that Clinton sustained her second-wave feminist rhetoric of conversation and collaboration throughout the 2008 Democratic primary campaign.

Casting her political opponents in the role of authoritarian patriarch, Clinton chastised the Bush administration's "top-down" approach, charging that it bred "cynicism" and "let us down."[30] Using imagery reminiscent of Betty Friedan's "problem that has no name," Clinton frequently argued that the "middle class and hard working families don't even exist to this Administration. It's like they're invisible."[31] Clinton's conversational oratorical style sought to raise the consciousness of an audience that had been ignored for too long. Her collaborative approach distinguished her from her opponent in the Democratic primary, Senator Barack Obama, as well. Clinton said, "Well, some people believe you make change by demanding it. Some people believe you make change by hoping for it. I believe you make change by working hard for it. That's what I've done all my life and that is what I will do for you."[32]

Consensus was a key component of Clinton's collaborative vision, and conversation was the vehicle for cultivating consensus. Clinton urged, "Equally important to having a plan, we have to have a political consensus and that is what I am trying to develop as I talk about healthcare and engage in a conversation with the American people."[33] In a speech built around the theme of innovation, she stated, "I want to hear your ideas and to work with you. Call this version 1.0 of my innovation agenda, so after collaborating with some of you we'll perhaps tweak it and fine tune it, but the ultimate consequence of this has to be leadership that once again sets our sights on the stars and gives us the tools to get there."[34]

Clinton situated her collaborative progressivism in the practical, private space of a kitchen table. Clinton has frequently advocated the "kitchen table" view of politics at various points in her political career—perhaps most notably in her speech to the 1996 Democratic National Convention in which she mused, "I wish we could be sitting around a kitchen table, just us, talking about our hopes and fears, about our children's futures."[35] The metaphor was particularly well suited to the "kitchen table politics" of the primary season—when candidates literally connect with voters in the private spaces of their homes. In her remarks to the Urban League, she stripped out the overt domesticity of the kitchen but retained the collaborative sentiment, saying, "I will call everyone to the table. One of the things I really believe in, is getting everybody out there together, and rolling up our sleeves, and starting to act like Americans again."[36] Similarly, she told a New Hampshire audience, "Together we are going to take back our birthright. We are going to have the confidence and optimism to start rolling up our sleeves and solving our problems again. That will begin with once again restoring and rebuilding the American middle class."[37] Her collaborative approach to leadership extended to everyone a seat at the table.

Clinton's liberal feminism informed her foreign policy rhetoric as well. On the campaign trail, Clinton articulated a world view premised on "global interdependence." She declared that the "biggest challenge" Americans face is "restoring leadership by once again valuing alliances, respecting our values, and understanding that American strength is more than just a show of force."[38] Similarly, she promised, "When I am President, my White House will welcome you. Our government will be a partner with you." For Clinton, restoring "America's position" in the world required finding "common ground." Clinton also emphasized the ways in which her liberal feminist presidentiality was an alternative to George W. Bush's "strict father" approach to foreign relations, saying, "When I am president, there will be a very simple message that goes out across the world—the era of cowboy diplomacy is over. We're going to start working with people again."[39]

As the campaign evolved throughout 2007, the demands of a hotly contested primary and the looming Republican opposition encroached on Clinton's alternative voice, prompting her to strike a balance between normative presidentiality and her alternative vision of presidentiality. She became more assertive in laying claim to the presidential title but retained her collaborative vision, saying, "I'm running for president because I believe if we set big goals and we work together to achieve them, we can restore the American dream today and for the next generation."[40] She paired metaphors of conversation with more traditional images of sports and war, citing her "experience standing up and fighting for what I believe. . . . As president, I will continue those fights."[41] She told one campaign audience, "If I'm your nominee, you'll never have to be worried that I will be knocked out of the ring because I do have the strength and experience to lead this country and I am ready to go toe to toe with Senator McCain whenever and wherever he desires."[42] In December 2007 she told an audience in Clear Lake, Iowa, that "standing up for America's values and protecting our country and our people is the first job of the President. Bringing us together to end the war, fixing our economy, and taking on big challenges like immigration, health care, energy independence, climate change and so much else is what I will do."[43] Later, she underscored the importance of marrying presidential toughness with an ethic of collaboration, saying, "You have to know how to balance it; how to stand your ground and how to find common ground."[44] Similarly, she urged, "We need a president who understands there is a time for force, a time for diplomacy, and a time for both, who understands that we enhance our international reputation and strengthen our security if the world sees the human face of American democracy in the good works, the good deeds we do for people seeking freedom from poverty, hunger, disease, illiteracy, and oppression." Clinton concluded, "We need a president who knows how to deploy both the olive branch and the arrows."[45]

The preceding analysis of Clinton's presidential persona as articulated through the oratory she used to introduce herself to voters is, of course, not exhaustive. It does not account for the complexities of individual rhetorical situations, nor does it examine Clinton's campaign rhetoric in toto. Instead, by excavating key dimensions of Clinton's political style, we have illustrated the ways in which second-wave feminism informed an alternative notion of presidentiality. Unfortunately, not even someone as experienced, well funded, and well connected as Hillary Clinton could effectively displace the hegemonic masculinity of normative presidentiality. In fact, during the 2008 general election campaign, normative presidentiality made a resurgence, shaping the vice presidential persona of Sarah Palin.

Palin's Postfeminist Vice Presidentiality

Women have been nominated as vice presidential candidates for major US political parties only twice: the Democratic Party nominated Representative Geraldine Ferraro of New York to run on the ticket with Walter Mondale in 1984. Twenty-four years later, the Republican Party nominated Alaska governor Sarah Palin as John McCain's running mate. That women should appear on the presidential ticket so infrequently is notable, since, as Denise M. Bostdorff points out, "the contemporary vice presidency is, in effect, a traditional female role." Bostdorff explains that "although vice presidents must seem to have enough strong 'masculine' traits to ensure their competence during national emergencies, they must submerge their independence and individualism to perform their day-to-day duties which consist mainly of abject 'feminine' servility."[46] Additionally, Bostdorff asserts that vice presidential figures are comically enmeshed in the scene of presidentiality, which robs them of much of their individual agency. She states that vice presidential candidates "must succumb to a gradual sublimation process whereby they become more and more submerged in the persona of the presidential nominee and therefore, more and more controlled by the scene around them."[47]

Assessment of the oratory that introduced and defined Palin as prospective vice president confirms and expands Bostdorff's insights. By examining the campaign oratory that introduced Palin to the electorate as a prospective vice president, we illustrate the ways in which her vice presidential persona not only reified norms of presidentiality but also situated those norms within postfeminist political culture.

When McCain unveiled Palin as his choice for a vice presidential running mate, his speech was constructed to suggest that his decision was a dramatic departure from the norms of presidential politics. Before revealing the identity of his running mate, McCain praised the individual's personal characteristics while assiduously avoiding the use of gendered pronouns. He stated, "I found someone with an outstanding reputation for standing up to special interests and entrenched bureaucracies; someone who has fought against corruption and the failed policies of the past; someone who's stopped government from wasting taxpayers' money on things they don't want or need and put it back to work for the people; someone with executive experience, who has shown great tenacity and skill in tackling tough problems."[48]

The passage continued with a familiar laundry list of qualities and qualifications that characterize successful US political leaders. McCain attempted to demonstrate the unpredictability of his choice, however, when he announced that his decision made him "especially proud" during "the week we celebrate the anniversary of women's suffrage." At that point, well into his speech, he proceeded with the big reveal, describing his running mate as "a devoted wife and a mother of five."[49] The rhetorical climax was created by McCain's attempt to generate a Burkean "perspective by incongruity," violating the "proprieties" of presidentiality by nominating a "devoted wife and mother of five" to be the next US vice president.[50]

The problematic aspects of McCain's choice would emerge later, after Palin participated in disastrous interviews with ABC News anchor Charles Gibson and CBS News anchor Katie Couric.[51] At the time of the announcement, however, the rhetorical genius of McCain's pick, and her subsequent introductions to the American public, was the fact that as a prospective vice president, Palin seemed to both challenge *and* reinforce the norms of presidentiality. On its face, Palin's presence on the Republican ticket bolstered the postfeminist narrative suggesting that a woman, like a man, could easily inhabit a presidential persona, even in the context of a socially conservative national political party. Palin performed her potential presidentiality by embracing the pioneer persona. For Palin, the pioneer frame functioned not to diminish her candidacy as merely symbolic, as it had for so many female presidential hopefuls. Instead, the trope was inflected with a regional tone of authenticity. First Palin described her husband, Todd Palin, as a "lifelong commercial fisherman, lifetime Alaskan ... a production operator in the oil fields upon Alaska's North Slope, and he's a proud member of the United

Steelworkers Union, and he's a world champion snow machine racer." Then, after introducing her children, Palin described herself as "just your average 'hockey mom' in Alaska" who became "chairman of the Alaska Oil and Gas Conservation Commission," fought corruption where she found it, and "stood up to the old politics as usual, to the special interests, to the lobbyists, the Big Oil companies and the 'good old boy' network."[52] In her Republican National Convention (RNC) vice presidential acceptance address, Palin addressed the complex problem of Iranian control of a large segment of the world's oil supply by encouraging domestic oil and gas exploration. Her expertise on this issue was articulated via a colloquialism that came to define her political ethos: "take it from a gal who knows the North Slope of Alaska: we've got lots of both [oil and gas]."[53] As it did for former Texas governor Ann Richards, the pioneer image "worked to her advantage" and enabled Palin to advance "populist and progressive appeals."[54]

In addition to plying the pioneer metaphor to strategic effect, Palin cheerfully inhabited the persona of an "unruly woman." In this respect, as well, Palin mirrored strategies perfected by Richards, another bombastic female governor. As noted in our earlier work, "the image of an unruly woman can be an empowering one," and Palin, like Richards before her, recognized the value of posing as "rule breaker, joke maker, and public, bodily spectacle."[55] In her vice presidential acceptance speech, Palin again identified herself as an "average hockey mom" and then delivered the joke that became the most frequently quoted line from her 2008 RNC address: "You know they say the difference between a hockey mom and a pit bull: lipstick [*sic*]."[56] That joke both embraced the unruly toughness of a pit bull and disciplined its unruliness with a nod to domestic maternalism and feminine attractiveness. In fact, one of the reasons that Palin could perform her unruliness so explicitly was because it was tempered by markers of traditional femininity. That is where Palin differed from Richards, whose performance was more likely to subvert markers of traditional femininity through her unruly humor. According to Mary L. Kahl and Janis L. Edwards, Palin's "greatest unruliness may be that she [had] the audacity to simultaneously conform to and challenge both traditional and feminist standards for femininity. Palin's persona combines the extremes of femininity (pretty, fertile, and youthful) with the extremes of masculinity (macho, fearless, self-sufficient)."[57]

Even as her introduction to the voting public figured Palin as a postfeminist vice presidential figure, the oratory that announced Palin's candidacy simultaneously articulated what Katie L. Gibson and Amy L. Heyse have called a "femiphobic" political rhetoric—one that underscores the hegemonic masculinity of presidential leadership.[58] In their assessment of Palin's address at the 2008 RNC, Gibson and Heyse argue that speakers there "followed traditional hegemonic scripts to celebrate John McCain's masculinity and to emasculate Barack Obama. What resulted was the continuation of a conservative masculinist script that is anchored to gender dualities and relies on a fierce denigration of the feminine." Gibson and Heyse further contend that Palin participated in this performance of hegemonic masculinity by constructing a "faux maternal performance" that functioned "to bolster the RNC's celebration of conservatism and hegemonic masculinity."[59] The man her discourse was designed to celebrate, of course, was McCain. In this way she fulfilled the expectation outlined by Bostdorff—that of sublimating herself to the man at the top of the ticket—while reinforcing postfeminist themes of maternalism, individualism, and traditional heterosexual marital relationships.

Palin's 2008 RNC address was replete with markers of her own traditional femininity. While touting McCain's qualifications to be the next commander in chief, Palin described herself as "just one of many moms who'll say an extra prayer each night for our sons and daughters going into harm's way." Discussing her entrée into politics, Palin claimed that she was "just your average hockey mom, and signed up for the PTA ... because I wanted to make my kids' public education even better." Her description of an ideal vice president was a person possessing "a servant's heart." Finally, Palin underscored presidential masculinity by defining the qualifications for office in starkly masculinist terms, promoting McCain alone to the position of warrior in chief, stating, "There is only one man in this election who has ever really fought for you, in places where winning means survival and defeat means death, and that man is John McCain."[60]

That Palin's oratory reinforced presidentiality's hegemonic masculinity is not unusual. In fact, it aligns with the rhetorical situation facing all vice presidential candidates. Bostdorff explains that whereas citizens "want the president to control events in our country," vice presidents as "seconds-in-command" are "subject to the demands of political tradition and the president they serve, just as women historically have been constrained by the cultural norms and the men that surround them."[61] Vice presidentiality, then, is fundamentally servile, and when Palin spoke at the RNC she explicitly inhabited a servile posture. After listing a litany of characteristics that qualified McCain for presidential leadership—including "resolve and toughness, and strength of heart"—Palin emphasized that McCain, alone, embodied true presidentiality, stating, "As the mother of one of those troops [in Iraq], and as the commander of Alaska's National Guard, that's the kind of man I want as our commander in chief." She continued, saying that "to serve as vice president beside such a man would be the privilege of a lifetime."[62]

If McCain had won the 2008 presidential contest, he would have been the oldest person elected to a first term as US president. Despite his age and his bout with cancer, the McCain-Palin campaign downplayed the prospect of a Palin presidency during Palin's surfacing stage.[63] In fact, during the 2008 campaign vice presidential announcement phase, Palin acceded to the feminized norms of vice presidentiality in her oratory in ways that confirmed and even exacerbated the hegemonic masculinity of presidentiality. Although billed as a political maverick, McCain and his running (help)mate performed a version of presidentiality that was both familiar and traditionally normative.

With two months remaining in the campaign, there was ample time to proceed through the rest of the discursive phases of vice presidentiality identified by Bostdorff: confrontation, vindication or resignation, and submission. During confrontation, "citizens, journalists, and others, like stereotypical in-laws-to-be, scrutinize and confront the second on issues, past or present, where compatibility does not appear to exist."[64] Confrontation can take one of two forms: differences of opinion between the second and the presidential candidate, or charges of unworthiness. In the next chapter we assess Palin's confrontation phase closely, examining the ways in which news media framed her as potentially unworthy of either the vice presidency or the presidency in light of her poor performance in journalistic interviews, the unplanned pregnancy of her teenage daughter, a scandal involving the cost of her campaign wardrobe, and charges that she abused her power as Alaska's governor in order to precipitate the firing of her former brother-in-law, an Alaska state trooper.[65] For the purposes of this chapter, it is important to note that after each potential scandal unfolded in quick succession during the confrontation phase, Palin's oratorical strategies changed. Palin attempted to vindicate herself—not by demonstrating appropriate vice presidential submission but by asserting her status as a co-president.

During the final six weeks of the campaign, Palin's oratory followed the same stock format. At the beginning and end of each stump speech, Palin spoke as a conventionally submissive running mate, praising McCain's character and experience and exhorting her audience to vote for McCain. For example, she told an audience gathered in Johnstown, Pennsylvania, that "John McCain is his own man . . . always put his country first . . . he has overcome adversity . . . and will get this economy put back on the right track."[66] In multiple addresses Palin praised McCain for his toughness, courage, experience, boldness, fairness, good judgment, wisdom, and truthfulness.[67] However, aside from the conventional bookends, the majority of Palin's stump speech positioned herself beside McCain as an equal presidential partner, suggesting that policy initiatives, plans, and actions were theirs together or, in some cases, hers alone. The language changed from "McCain will" to "John and I" and "we will." Importantly, the "we" in Palin's stump speeches usually referred to herself and McCain, rather than the more common construction in stump speeches, where "we" refers to the candidate and the audience. For example, in different stump speeches Palin made the following promises: "Together John and I will complete education reform,"; "John and I are going to set this country on a path firmly toward energy independence"; "we'll bring tax relief to every American ... we're gonna let more of you keep what you earn"; "we will balance the budget by the end of *our* first term."[68] That last sentence is particularly telling, insofar as presidential terms are typically assigned exclusively to the president. Palin's linguistic choice claims the "first term" as "ours"—hers and McCain's together, intimating that the two are a team—co-presidents with a shared policy agenda.

As a point of contrast, compare Palin's language on the stump to that of Joe Biden. When he spoke as Obama's running mate, he was careful to attribute policy proposals exclusively to Obama. Biden stated, "Barack Obama will reform our tax code. He'll cut taxes for 95 percent of the American people who draw a paycheck. That's the change we need." In subsequent paragraphs of the same speech, Biden repeated that sentence construction, promising that "Barack Obama will" "make energy a genuine national priority," "invest in the next generation of teachers," "bring down health care costs," and "put more cops on the streets," concluding each sentence with the exhortation that Obama's plans represented "the change we need." Similarly, while addressing a group of Obama supporters, Biden touted Obama's leadership skills, saying, "I have great respect and have had great respect for a long time for Barack Obama, but I've never, I never thought I'd have the kind of respect I have after watching him assemble probably the finest economic team that's been put together in the history of this country, Democrats and Republicans. You should see him orchestrate these meetings we have with 18 of the best minds in the world, from both parties. There's no doubt about who's [in] charge."[69]

Conversely, in her stump speeches, Palin devoted long stretches of time to telling audiences "a little bit about my own track record."[70] Highlighting her maverick identity, Palin discussed her activities as mayor of Wasilla and governor of Alaska, emphasizing the ways in which *she* reduced taxes, instilled pro-business reforms, eliminated wasteful spending, and challenged the status quo. She highlighted her plans for US energy independence, which were predicated on increased domestic drilling and mining. She encouraged audience chants of "drill, baby, drill" and "mine, baby, mine," which became mainstays of her performances on the stump.[71] Although a relatively small component of her stump speech, this call-and-response pattern is particularly revealing in terms of the ways in which it highlights the postfeminist nature of Palin's political persona. The chant shifts attention away from McCain and toward Palin—certainly McCain was not the "baby" to which the crowd was energetically referring. Thus, the chant underscored Palin's budding status as co-president, but it also intimated another source of Palin's popularity: her sex appeal. Recall that one tenet of postfeminism is that an important source of women's agency is their sexuality. As such, the argument goes, it can and should be deployed in any context that would benefit the individual woman. Shortly after the chant "drill, baby, drill" became a mainstay of Palin's performances on the stump, Internet T-shirt vendors began selling shirts featuring taglines such as the following: "Oil. Palin. Two Things in Alaska I'd Like to Drill."[72] In chapter 5, we explore the implications of "pornified" campaign paraphernalia in more detail. For the purposes of this chapter, however, the example illustrates Palin's predilection for playfully deploying her sexual power in her oratory in ways that the more liberal feminist Hillary Clinton did not.

On a few occasions during her stump speeches, Palin also placed herself at the center of the Oval Office. This strategy was most notable when Palin addressed the issue of special needs children. She promised that families with special needs children would "have an advocate in the White House," and she positioned herself as that advocate to the exclusion of McCain.[73] In her Johnstown, Pennsylvania, remarks, for example, Palin devoted one-third of the thirty-minute speech to the topic of special needs families, during which time McCain virtually disappeared from the address.[74] Significantly, McCain's name was mentioned only seven times in the last third of the Johnstown speech.

The preceding analysis of Palin's campaign oratory during the fall of 2008 is, of course, not exhaustive. Instead, our aim, as it was with analysis of Clinton's oratory, is to assess key speeches in order to gauge the influence of feminist logics on Palin's discourse. As Palin rhetorically constructed a complex vice presidentiality, she infused it with postfeminist appeal. In her RNC acceptance speech, Palin played up the traditional maternalism and conventional femininity that are key aspects of postfeminist ethos. She proved that a woman need not be a "radical" (or even liberal) feminist in order to inhabit a prominent place in national politics. This performative claim functioned to repudiate Clinton's second-wave feminism even as Palin attempted to court Clinton's supporters. Our analysis demonstrates the ways in which Palin's performance maintained fidelity to the familiar narrative of US presidentiality, even when the McCain campaign ostensibly challenged presidential tradition by placing a woman on the ticket. In addition, the fact that Palin's disciplined (post)femininity was particularly well suited to vice presidentiality illustrates the ways in which postfeminism's alleged individual agency is often emptied of its political authority. Women's political agency is most readily accepted when it is appropriately subordinated to men's.

Political Journalism and Punditry

Framing the "Dangerous" Campaigns of Sarah Palin and Hillary Clinton

On August 27, 2008, the second night of the Democratic National Convention (DNC), Senator Hillary Clinton gave a rousing speech of support for Senator Barack Obama's nomination to represent the Democratic Party in the 2008 presidential election. Those viewing the event on MSNBC, however, might have been led to believe that the outcome of Clinton's speech was far from a foregone conclusion. Although anchor Keith Olbermann noted that "the defeated's role" is always to "stand before the convention now dominated by the winner and sell that winner," MSNBC anchor Chris Matthews asserted instead that it was "soap opera night." Hillary Clinton and Bill Clinton nabbed the starring roles in Matthews's version of a *DNCs of Our Lives* soap, leaving the pundits breathless with anticipation in wondering whether the Clintons would graciously cede the spotlight to Obama. In a bizarre flurry of words characteristic of Matthews's campaign coverage, he speculated on the question by assigning Bill and Hillary soap opera stage names: "It's one of those, I expect her name should be Brad. You know, what do you think Brad will say? What will Alice say tonight? What will Hillary say tonight about Barack Obama that appeals to the friends of Hillary Clinton? It's very interesting."[1]

Less interesting are the predictable metaphors and narrative frames deployed each election season by journalists and pundits who seek to pique the interest of an apathetic voting (or nonvoting) public by characterizing campaigns as competitions, wars, and romances. As a bombastic Olbermann tagged Hillary Clinton's DNC address the "Clintonian speech of epic proportions," he and his cohort relied on familiar metaphors to describe the evening's events. They deployed sports metaphors, noting that in Clinton's speech "it was like she was passing the ball to the guy who was going to carry on, like the baton in a relay. It was a relay." They employed war metaphors, likening the rift between Clinton and Obama supporters to "Northern Ireland, yes, there's a power-sharing agreement that's been signed but right below the surface is a seething historic tension between the two camps. . . .

This peace treaty has not been fully accepted." Despite that lingering tension, however, war metaphors also were used to explain the way in which Clinton herself was soldiering on. Matthews stated, "Hillary Clinton did such a good job of arming Barack Obama tonight and putting him on the horse and sending him forward." They even found a way to incorporate romance metaphors. Roundtable discussant Pat Buchanan doubted Clinton's ability to deliver her voters to the Obama camp because "Hillary Rodham Clinton doesn't have supporters. She has a following. . . . These women out there are in love with Hillary Clinton." Finally, an exchange between Olbermann and Tom Brokaw captured the metaphorical mixing that characterized the evening's reporting. Olbermann addressed Brokaw, saying, "Tom, the—the response to that from her supporters, I don't know that this can be emphasized enough, it is impossible to think that, you know, an ocean liner . . . it's impossible to turn one of those around on a dime. Was there anything missing from this speech in terms of trying to get that done, in trying to say, as Chris has suggested, to continue to mix these metaphors, that you have to accept this baton being passed from the Clinton campaign to the Obama campaign?" Brokaw responded, "Yes, the passing of the baton from the Clinton campaign to the Obama campaign and then mounting him on a horse, I am keeping track of these metaphors, keep in mind, and turning the ocean liner around all at the same time."[2] One is tempted to conclude that this discussion, which devolved into a metaphorical morass, is a product of unscripted live television or the demands of the twenty-four-hour news cycle, yet research demonstrates that this excerpt typifies the tone of presidential campaign coverage.

In this chapter, we examine the journalistic framing of Clinton's and Palin's presidential and vice presidential bids. Although scholars have documented the impact of campaign frames on political engagement, less attention has been paid to the ways in which seemingly gender-neutral frames position women outside the realm of presidentiality. In a postfeminist political context, campaign framing paradoxically suggests that barriers excluding women from the presidency have largely been removed, even as it reinforces masculinist conceptions of presidentiality and antifeminist depictions of women candidates. After briefly reviewing the scholarly literature on the rhetoric of campaign framing, we assess the postfeminist and antifeminist framing of Palin and Clinton.

Campaign Frames from Racehorses to Romance

Robert Entman explains the framing process of political news as one of selection and salience.[3] According to Entman, framing is defined as "selecting and highlighting some facets of events or issues, and making connections among them so as to promote a particular interpretation, evaluation, and/or solution." He goes on to identify two classes of frames: substantive and procedural. Substantive frames define causes or effects, endorse remedies, or convey moral judgments, while procedural frames suggest "evaluations of political actors' legitimacy, based on their technique, success, and representativeness." The news media frequently rely on procedural frames employing horserace or game metaphors, which, as Entman argues, downplay deliberation of policy issues on the campaign trail.[4]

Entman explains that "framing works to shape and alter audience members' interpretations and preferences through *priming*. That is, frames introduce or raise the salience or apparent importance of certain ideas, activating schemas that encourage target audiences to think, feel, and decide in a particular way."[5] According to Thomas Patterson, framing campaigns as contests or games "dominates the journalist's outlook in part because it conforms to the conventions of the news process," including a dynamic plotline, inherent conflict, and the illusion of novelty.[6] The strategic frame is not benign, however. Entman sees political news as playing "a major role in the exertion of political power, and the frame in a news text is really the imprint of power—it registers the identity of actors or interests that competed to dominate the text."[7] The ability of a candidate to develop a presidential image worthy of the power associated with the office is directly connected to the frame through which that candidate is conveyed to the public. Metaphors such as "battleground" states, a campaign's "arsenal," and "lobbing" negative attacks become literalized as true, making it difficult for voters or journalists to envision campaigns in alternate ways.

Female candidates face particular challenges, given the prevalence of frames that place them outside the realm of presidentiality. The strategic frames of sports and war reinforce notions of heroic masculinity and rugged individualism that undermine a female candidate's ability to inhabit a presidential persona. Writing on the subject of athletic masculinity, Michael Messner argues that "the competitive hierarchy of athletic careers encouraged the development of masculine identities based on very narrow definitions of public success ... serving to construct a masculine personality that disparaged anything considered 'feminine' in women, in other men, or in oneself."[8] Implicit in metaphors of sport that frame political reporting are masculine values that the sporting arena has constructed as oppositional to femininity. Nicholas Howe argues that the use of sports and war terminology in political journalism may work to position women outside of political power, and Sue Curry Jansen and Don Sabo identify the sport/war frame as the key rhetorical resource reinforcing patriarchal values and upholding the hegemony of white masculinity in US foreign policy. When coupled with the frontier myth, the ideological consequences of which are documented by Ronald Carpenter, this framing doubly underscores the heroic masculinity of presidentiality.[9]

Within the strategy frame that positions politics as a competition, the romance frame suggests a more seductive narrative in which candidates compete for the affection of the feminized electorate. According to Dan Hahn, "Gender-based discourse is basic in American political communication, and ... manipulation of that discourse by political elites without corresponding understanding by the citizenry is dangerous." Here, the political actor or suitor "woos" the public, who then vote either to accept or reject *his* advances. The use of the masculine pronoun is intentional, for the political candidate is always placed in the masculine role and the electorate in the feminine role. Citizens develop a relationship based on "false intimacy," according to Hahn, which allows the candidate to share secrets with the electorate, claim to be listening, and foster "dependency via the 'savior' role." In Hahn's discussion of the presidential inaugural as a marriage ceremony, he argues that "both the president and the groom sometimes are depicted and perceived as men 'on white horses' who will rescue the nation or the damsel from some unsavory fate."[10] Hahn continues: "Hence, candidates 'woo' the voters, who say 'yes' or 'no.' If the answer is yes and the person is elected, there is a public ceremony that 'cements' the bonds, called the 'Inaugural,' in which the person elected vows fealty to the Constitution (a kind of 'til death do us part' pledge). This is followed by a honeymoon, after which the 'marriage' proceeds until the president dies in office or is replaced at the polls by a new suitor or is impeached."[11]

Like the game frame, the romance frame for political campaigns is more than just a metaphoric way to position citizens and their presumptive representatives. Media frames are consequential because they shape the ways in which people understand and participate in a democracy. When voters are sidelined by sports metaphors or seduced by romance metaphors, they become passive observers of the political system rather than engaged participants. Journalists focus on the excitement of daily fluctuations in the polls rather than spending time assessing complicated policy proposals. Kathleen Hall Jamieson highlights the ways in which this system exacerbates the cynicism about politics that already plagues many citizens.[12] Studying frames is important, however, not just in the interests of invigorating voter participation or combating cynicism; by explicating the logology of campaign frames, critics can unmask the values and motives that shape political dialogue, contextualize candidate identity, and create US political culture. In this chapter, we take up that task by assessing the debilitating frames through which the media assessed the candidacies of Sarah Palin and Hillary Clinton in 2008.

Maverick Mom to Dangerous Diva

In the years since Palin's vice presidential campaign, her persona—like that of many public figures—has become little more than a caricature. It is worth remembering, however, the relative complexity encapsulated in media narratives immediately after Palin was named McCain's running mate and the first female vice presidential nominee of the Republican Party. The *Washington Post* described Palin as "a 44-year-old mother of five who hunts caribou and was once a beauty queen" and noted that she "rose to the statehouse by challenging the corruption that has become endemic in Alaska, even if it meant taking on the Republican establishment there, including the former governor and the state's congressional delegation."[13] Present in that description are three facets of Palin's identity crucial to her initial framing in the media: maverick appeal, rugged individualism, and appropriate femininity.

Palin was instantly branded a maverick—a label that the McCain campaign assiduously cultivated. *Time* noted that the "obscure . . . governor and mother of five from tiny Wasilla . . . reinforces John McCain's narrative of a maverick conservative crusader." The *Washington Post* concurred, announcing in a headline, "With Pick, McCain Reclaims His Maverick Image." Similarly, the *Dallas Morning News* reported, "McCain picks Alaska's governor, a fellow 'maverick,'" and the *Washington Times* touted "Palin's rise" as "a model for maverick politicians." Once Palin's maverick persona took hold, she seemed an obvious match for McCain. *Time* concluded, "The real surprise . . . is that it's such a surprise."[14]

As a self-styled maverick, Palin easily inhabited the rugged individualism endemic both to presidentiality and postfeminism. The *Weekly Standard* profile published a few weeks after McCain's announcement gave Palin a Lincolnesque origin story, explaining that she "grew up in what was virtually a one-room house in Wasilla with a wood stove for heating and whatever the family shot and caught for food."[15] Emerging literally from the Alaskan frontier, Palin was described as McCain's "mooseburger-eatin,' salmon-fishin,' guntotin' pick for running mate."[16] In fact, her predilection for "totin'" guns was noted by multiple media outlets.[17] Support for gun rights is a calling card for many conservative politicians. For Palin it also underscored her frontier ethos and a power feminist inclination to take personal safety into her own hands. Her pro-gun street cred was substantiated not only by her affiliation with the National Rifle Association but also by the "dead grizzly bear in her office."[18] She was living the strenuous life—Teddy Roosevelt style. Camille Paglia likened her to "Annie Oakley, a brash ambassador from America's pioneer past."[19]

Like many of her powerful female predecessors, Palin brandished an assertiveness that earned her begrudging admiration. While both opponents and supporters embraced her high school moniker—"Sarah Barracuda"—most early reports echoed CBS News, which praised her "aggressive style and her willingness to take on corruption in a state notorious for its Wild West ethics."[20] Sentiments expressed on the Fox News program *Hannity & Colmes* on the day of McCain's announcement reflected the rugged individualist frame, with panelists calling Palin a "crusader," lauding her as a "prosecutor," hailing her for "challeng[ing] the corrupt Republican establishment of Alaska," effusing that "she walks on water in Alaska," and concluding, "This woman is a heroine."[21]

Perhaps because of her assertive independence, her popularity, and her relatively young age, Palin did not hesitate to self-identify as a "feminist." One month after McCain named Palin his running mate, CBS News anchor Katie Couric asked her if she considered herself a feminist. Palin's reply illustrates a conflation of feminism with postfeminism, and it demonstrates the ways in which Palin's postfeminism was wrapped up in her rugged individualism: "I do. I'm a feminist who believes in equal rights, and I believe that women certainly today have every opportunity that a man has to succeed and to try to do it all anyway. And I'm very, very thankful that I've been brought up in a family where gender hasn't been an issue. You know, I've been expected to do everything growing up that the boys were doing. We were out chopping wood and you're out hunting and fishing and filling our freezer with good wild Alaskan game to feed our family. So it kinda started with that. With just that expectation that the boys and the girls in my community were expected to do the same and accomplish the same. That's just been instilled in me."[22]

Palin's response exhibits defining characteristics of postfeminism: the notion that structural inequalities have been effectively dismantled ("women certainly today have every opportunity that a man has to succeed") and that industrious individuals are capable of simply asserting their own equality ("I've been expected to do everything growing up that the boys were doing"). Postfeminist Palin downplays the need to push for gender justice, assuming instead that "gender" is not "an issue." When Couric pressed Palin to define the word *feminist* specifically, Palin provided a classically liberal feminist definition of the term, calling a feminist "someone who believes in equal rights. Someone who would not stand for oppression against women." Yet, when Couric quizzed Palin about her opposition to the Ledbetter Fair Pay Act, Palin reinforced the postfeminist notion that institutional discrimination is largely a relic of the 1960s and thus new pay equity legislation is unnecessary. She stated, "The Ledbetter pay act—it was gonna turn into a boon for trial lawyers who, I believe, could have taken advantage of women who were many, many years ago who [*sic*] would allege some kind of discrimination. Thankfully, there are laws on the books, there have been since 1963, that no woman could be discriminated against in the workplace in terms of anything, but especially in terms of pay." For Palin, workplace discrimination, like other manifestations of patriarchal power structures, is simply something that occurred "many, many years ago."

Palin's maverick persona as a rugged individualist was moderated by her prominent and appropriate femininity. In fact, her traditionally feminine bona fides likely made it more possible for her to explicitly claim a "feminist" identity, even as she enacted a postfeminist world view. A young, attractive mother of five, Palin presented herself as a "self-styled hockey mom."[23] This theme was quickly picked up in the national press. In a story headlined "'Hockey Mom' Gets the Nod," the *Chicago Sun-Times* quoted one prospective voter's assessment of Palin: "She's a working mother with a child in Iraq and a Down syndrome son. That pulls a lot of heartstrings." Similarly, the *Atlanta Journal-Constitution* included GOP delegate Linda Evans's description of Palin in its story, saying, "Palin is a reformer who's telegenic, has a large family—her eldest son is in the military—and is raising a young child with Down syndrome." The *New York Times* described Palin as a "church-going mother of five," whereas *MSNBC.com* put a slightly more progressive spin on the theme, asserting that "with five children and a state government to run, she's the epitome of the high-energy working mom."[24]

By foregrounding Palin's maternity, the early framing of her candidacy embodied what Ashli Quesinberry Stokes argues is the "subtle" language of postfeminism, which "employs a language of liberation while selling society traditional values, such as motherhood and domesticity."[25] These traditional credentials became a necessity when, just days after Palin's nomination, she revealed that her unmarried teenage daughter, Bristol, was pregnant. Palin garnered "GOP support" from the crisis because of her "consistent pro-life message."[26] As the Associated Press reported, "Prominent religious conservatives . . . predicted that the announcement [of Bristol Palin's pregnancy] would not diminish conservative Christian enthusiasm for the vice presidential hopeful, a staunch abortion opponent. In fact, there was talk it might help." After Palin was buffeted by critics who saw Bristol's pregnancy as the unfortunate outcome of abstinence-only sex education, Palin received a gallant defense from Republican allies. A *New York Post* headline proclaimed, "This Is No Way to Treat a Lady—GOPers Stand Up for Sarah."[27]

International coverage of Palin's nomination focused less on Palin's social conservatism, softening her identity by playing up her feminine attractiveness. The *Express*, a British newspaper, announced, "McCain's secret weapon, a beauty queen"; in that article, journalist Macer Hall described Palin as a "44-year-old Governor of Alaska, a mother-of-five and former beauty queen." The *Daily Telegraph* in London claimed that a "feminine touch lifts McCain's campaign" and characterized Palin as a "former beauty queen." The *Birmingham Post* declared "Miss Alaska runner-up could make history."[28]

Less than a week after McCain announced Palin as his running mate, she introduced herself to the nation at the Republican National Convention. Her speech was well received. Forty-two percent of respondents to a Gallup poll rated Palin's convention speech as excellent, a percentage that was higher than the figure for those who rated Obama's speech similarly. In addition, Gallup reported an uptick in the percentage of respondents who indicated that having Palin on the ticket would make them more likely to vote for

McCain, from 18 to 29 percent.[29] Frank Newport of *Gallup.com* explained that "the convention and/or McCain's selection of Sarah Palin as his vice presidential running mate not only had the effect of moving the horserace needle in McCain's direction, but also increased several measures of enthusiasm for the GOP." ABC News explained on its morning show that "people seem to relate to a mom who is unafraid to mix things up. She's the hockey mom as candidate."[30]

Following the convention, Palin was featured on covers of serious news magazines, including *Time, Newsweek,* and the *New Yorker,* as well as tabloid weeklies such as *OK, People, Us,* and the *National Enquirer.* Enthusiasm for Palin was at an all-time high. In its convention coverage, CBS News effused about "Palin mania," the Republican "superhero ticket," and "GI John and Superwoman."[31] Palin was the "it girl" of Republican politics, a one-woman postfeminist force with which to be reckoned. Importantly, such narratives rarely presented Palin as successor to women who preceded her, paving the way to a more gender-inclusive presidentiality. Instead, she was the rugged individualist, a postfeminist candidate who pulled herself up by her Alaskan bootstraps. This narrative proved palatable to the public. According to a September 10, 2008, poll conducted by the Pew Research Center for the People and the Press, after the convention the public perceived news coverage of Palin to be "fair" and the stories covered "important."[32]

An even stronger postfeminist narrative emerged in the blogosphere: Sarah Palin as "everywoman." That frame exhibited another of the key markers of postfeminism: the generalization of middle-class women's concerns and values to every woman.[33] For example, Media Lizzy & Friends wrote, "McCain's choice ... demonstrates a keen political insight. She is every woman. . . . Let's just think about our society and pop culture—then ponder how this former mayor and mother of five will win the hearts of America." The entry concluded with gushing enthusiasm for the McCain-Palin ticket because of this "spectacular decision" that "brings ... home" the reality that "America is OUR nation. All of us. We are all equal." Similarly, in anticipation of Palin's convention speech, Ed Kilgore strategized, "A little bit of Everywoman, and a first effort to look like Superwoman, is all she needs for now." On the *QandO Blog: Free Markets, Free People,* MichaelW discussed the reaction of evangelicals to news of Bristol Palin's pregnancy, writing that the story "struck close to home" for some. The result: "Palin as Everywoman." Michelle Bernard argued that "what makes [Sarah Palin's] achievements so unique is the fact that she is everywoman, an average homemaker who cared enough to get involved in local politics and deal with everyday problems affecting everyday people."[34]

Of course, not everyone embraced the "everywoman" frame. A *Huffington Post* headline scoffed, "RNC Speech Proves Sarah Palin Is Not 'Every Woman.'" The *Guardian* headlined its article, "Will the Real Sarah Palin

Please Stand Up?" with its correspondent, Sarah Wildman, observing that Palin "pretends to be a representative of the American everywoman (whoever that really is, I'd love to know—though I guess it has something to do with watching a child play team sports). Yet outside of talk of theoretical football match side conversations, she had nary an argument about what these women actually need or want—or what women's rights might be in the US circa 2008."[35]

Wildman's charge highlights the ways in which a postfeminist "everywoman" narrative empties women's political achievements of gender politics. If "any" woman is "everywoman," gender justice is sacrificed in the service of an individual woman's success. That success is then cited as proof that feminist organizing is no longer needed. Taken to the extreme, this narrative asserts that postfeminism is the new feminism. Postfeminist gadfly Camille Paglia summed up that particular sentiment, asserting that "in terms of re-defining the persona for female authority and leadership, Palin has made the biggest step forward in feminism since Madonna channeled the dominatrix persona of high-glam Marlene Dietrich and rammed pro-sex, pro-beauty feminism down the throats of the prissy, victim-mongering, philistine feminist establishment."[36]

After a whirlwind courtship, Palin's honeymoon with the media was predictably short lived. Palin agreed to two key interviews after the Republican National Convention, the first with ABC's Charles Gibson and the second with CBS's Katie Couric.[37] Neither went well. Palin bobbled answers to foreign policy questions, could not explain the so-called "Bush Doctrine" (a label applied to many aspects of President George W. Bush's military and foreign policy), and came up empty when asked to list the newspapers and magazines she read.[38] Although the news media was right to call out Palin's muddled vernacular and her lack of knowledge on key issues, journalistic discussion of each interview also reflected the gendered framing that subsequent scholarly analyses have documented.[39] Of particular interest is the way in which Palin's independent maverick persona was molded into something more staged, deferential, and amateurish.

A *New York Times* headline announced that Palin was "Showing a Confidence, in Prepared Answers," and a subsequent editorial dubbed her performance "visibly scripted." A third *New York Times* account chastised Palin for "appearing to hew so closely to prepared answers that she used the exact same phrases repeatedly."[40] *ABCNews.com* similarly observed Palin's tendency to stick "closely to the McCain talking points," and the *Birmingham Post* called Palin an "'eager student' who repeated talking points." The *Washington Post*'s Howard Kurtz minimized Palin's gubernatorial record, writing that Palin "handled herself well for someone who three years ago was worried about the books in the Wasilla Library." *Slate* announced, "Palin vs. Gibson, Round 1: The ABC Anchor Flummoxes the GOP amateur." That article cast Palin as an inexperienced schoolgirl in its description of her bobbling of the "Bush Doctrine" question, noting, "Palin attempts to fake it for 25 seconds with a swirl of generalities before Gibson, showing all the gentleness of a remedial social studies teacher, interjects."[41]

The notion of a female vice presidential candidate as inexperienced student hearkens back to what was arguably the most famous retort uttered by the only other major party woman vice presidential candidate: Democrat Geraldine Ferraro. In her 1984 debate with Vice President George H. W. Bush, Bush offered to "help [her] with the difference" between Iran and Lebanon. Ferraro went on the offensive, saying, "I almost resent, Vice President Bush, your patronizing attitude that you have to teach me about foreign policy."[42] Unfortunately for Palin, her performance in early interviews reinforced, rather than challenged, the assumption that she was too inexperienced to be commander in chief. In his opinion piece for *Time*, Romesh Ratnesar characterized the Couric interview as "Sarah Palin's Foreign Policy Follies" and took a patronizing tone of his own, saying, "It takes a hard heart not to like Sarah Palin. She has a winning personal story. She can be poised, charming and funny. . . . But we should stop pretending that she is ready now or will be ready anytime in the foreseeable future to be Commander in Chief." In the Couric interview (which, according to an *LA Times* blog, made even conservatives wince), Palin "offered rambling and often disjointed explanations . . . [about] McCain's credentials as a Wall Street reformer and why Russia's proximity to Alaska gave her foreign policy experience."[43] Couric followed up on a statement Palin made during the Gibson interview, one in which she attempted to bolster her foreign policy credentials by noting that Russians were "our next-door neighbors, and you can actually see Russia from land here in Alaska, from an island in Alaska." After comedian Tina Fey famously parodied Palin on *Saturday Night Live* by asserting, "I can see Russia from my house," the real Palin reacted to the ways in which she had been "mocked," saying, "It's very important when you consider even national security issues with Russia as Putin rears his head and comes into the airspace of the United States of America, where do they go? It's Alaska, it's just right over the border. It is from Alaska that we send those out to make sure that an eye is being kept on this very powerful nation, Russia, because they are right there; they are right next to our state."[44]

Whether or not one accepts that proximity to a country such as Russia affords a governor legitimate foreign policy experience, the linguistic patterns present in both interviews illustrate why Palin's performance was roundly criticized. Replete with vagaries and grammatical errors, Palin seemed to be searching for both words and answers to questions that, as Alaska's governor, she had never faced. In her 2009 memoir, *Going Rogue*, Palin discussed her frustration at the McCain campaign's penchant for scripting her answers during those early weeks of the campaign. That reflection suggests that media reports that criticized Palin for appearing to be "on script" were accurate.

The Gibson and Couric interviews slowed Palin's initial momentum in the campaign; paradoxically, however, they also played to her advantage by lowering expectations for her performance in the vice presidential debate. A *New York Times* editorial stated it succinctly: "We cannot recall when there were lower expectations for a candidate than the ones that preceded Sarah Palin's appearance in Thursday night's vice-presidential debate with Joseph Biden." Mitchell S. McKinney, Leslie A. Rill, and Rebekah G. Watson demonstrate the ways in which Palin's capable debate performance was more highly rated by viewers because she exceeded expectations. The media echoed this reaction while casting Palin in strikingly feminine terms, attributing her positive rating to factors like charm and emotionalism. *NBC Nightly News* correspondent Andrea Mitchell reported that "Republicans were ecstatic that Sarah Palin got past the debate" but added that "she tried to charm her way through the hour and a half." Tom Brokaw told NBC's Matt Lauer that "what she probably did was give the campaign an emotional boost just when they needed it." Writing for the *New York Times*, Alessandra Stanley noted that "every now and then, [Palin] cocked her head, winked, and nudged [Biden] hard—like a little sister who knows her older brother cannot hit back." Joe Klein loaded multiple gendered terms into the lead paragraph for his story in *Time*, crediting Palin with "an ability ... to repeat, with a fair amount of credibility, the formulations that her handlers had given her," as evidenced by the fact that "practically the first words out of her mouth were 'Go to a kids' soccer game.'" Klein continued, saying, "She had that folksy thing down—although I did notice ... that when she tried to get cutesy with her folksiness, it didn't work."[45]

In order to keep the presidential contest interesting, the media first built Palin up as a rugged maverick and then tore her down as a scripted cutie pie. Her "gun-totin'" authenticity was recast as "that folksy thing." Of course, all politicians are susceptible to this cycle, but considering the relatively short duration of Palin's vice presidential campaign, the number of times her persona was run through the media mill is notable.

Shortly after the vice presidential debate, the media shifted its narrative once again, revisiting its initial framing of Palin as independent and assertive. This time, however, that frame was filtered through the expectation that vice presidential candidates serve as "attack dogs"—presidential surrogates who do the campaign's dirty work so that the presidential candidate may calmly reside above the fray. A *New York Times* blog entry by Michael Falcone carried the subheading "Palin Relishes Attack Dog Role." Palin herself put a feminine spin on her job as GOP enforcer, announcing that "'the heels are on, the gloves are off.'"[46] The *New York Daily News* credited Palin for being a "quick study in the black art of attack-dog politics," but it also quoted an unnamed "Republican political operative" who referred to the vice presidential debate as "Gidget Goes to St. Louis" and insisted, "The question you have to ask yourself at the end of this is: did perky trump policy?" Similarly, the *St. Petersburg Times* dubbed Palin a "chipper and relentless attack dog."[47]

Because so much of the media-generated controversy surrounding Palin focused on issues related to her public image, she was perhaps more susceptible than some to being damaged by the revelation that the Republican National Committee reportedly spent more than $150,000 on her campaign wardrobe. At first glance, this story seems to function as another example of the ways in which journalistic media have historically fixated on women candidates' clothing and appearance more than men's. The *New York Times* rightly noted, however, that the story is akin to stories about "John McCain's multiple houses and John Edwards's $400 haircut." In context, the Palin wardrobe gaffe "joined the ranks" of other accounts of "symbolic political excess." On *Time.com* Jay Carney dubbed the story, "Palin's Excess-ories," and a report on the *CBS Evening News* noted that the $150,000 shopping spree "may not square with her image as a down-to-earth everywoman." Ed Rollins, a Republican consultant to Ronald Reagan, chided, "It looks like nobody with a political antenna was working on this. . . . It just undercuts Palin's whole image as a hockey mom, a 'one-of-us' kind of candidate." Even an Australian source noted the impact on public opinion polls: "She's dragging down the Republican ticket. She's been embroiled in a series of damaging controversies, the latest a Republican Party shopping spree."[48]

The wardrobe controversy was particularly damaging for Palin because it revealed the fallacy lurking within the postfeminist narrative of a privileged woman standing in for "every" woman. Moreover, it underscored the ways in which the power feminist strategy of using one's physical appearance and/or sex appeal to get ahead requires material, economic resources. The feminine attractiveness that tempered Palin's "attack dog" persona and made her more palatable to some voters came at a ($150,000) cost—a bill that not every woman could foot. The fact that the Republican National Committee, not Palin, covered the tab was not enough to displace the fact that this particular postfeminist hero was enjoying a unique position of privilege—a perch on which she could stand only after sacrificing the rugged individualism that made her persona initially so appealing.

As the final month dawned on the 2008 presidential campaign, the bounce that McCain enjoyed after adding Palin to the Republican ticket waned to a dribble. Anxieties mounted as Obama's polling numbers remained strong. Soon, McCain staffers and the media began the predictable scapegoating process. In late October, CNN reported that "several McCain advisers have . . . become increasingly frustrated with what one aide described as Palin 'going rogue.'"[49] The "going rogue" frame precipitated the attitudinal shift in which Palin went from being viewed as a maverick mom to a dangerous diva. Examination of the specific framing strategies illustrates the ways in which the "unruly woman" persona can quickly be transformed from an asset to a liability for political women.

One controversy in particular fed the narrative of Palin as especially reckless. Palin was under investigation for allegedly abusing her power as governor and acting unethically and/or illegally in relation to the firing of the chief of Alaska's state police. Critics charged that Palin precipitated the dismissal after the chief refused to fire Palin's former brother-in-law. Those launching the attacks argued that Palin sought retribution against her former brother-in-law after he and her sister were embroiled in a bitter divorce and child custody battle. Hearkening back to Bill Clinton's own scandal involving Arkansas state troopers, numerous sources labeled the incident "Troopergate."[50] The initial investigation concluded in October and found that Palin "acted within her proper and lawful authority," but it also stated that she "permitted a situation to continue where impermissible pressure was placed on several subordinates in order to advance a personal agenda."[51] Her conduct was an ethical violation. However, a second investigation, which concluded the day before the presidential election, exonerated the governor. The *New York Times* reported that "Sarah Palin did not apply improper pressure to try to dismiss a state trooper ... and did not violate state ethics laws in the firing of her public safety commissioner."[52] The new verdict was, however, too little too late. Throughout October and November 2008, the story was coupled with discussions of Palin's wardrobe excesses and her daughter's pregnancy. Cumulatively, a narrative emerged of a vice presidential candidate who was out of control. The maverick mom had become a dangerous diva.

Although all vice presidential candidates differ with their presidential counterparts on specific policy issues, Palin's differences with McCain became particularly problematic because they were situated within the narrative that cast McCain as presidential patriarch and Palin as his appropriately feminine running "mate." Early on, McCain attempted to use these differences as proof of the maverick nature of his campaign, telling CNN, "'By the way, you may figure out from time to time, Sarah and I don't agree on every issue,' [McCain] said. 'What do you expect of two mavericks, to agree on everything? Eh?'" Differences of opinion, however, developed into aloofness. *NBC Nightly News* reported that "McCain and Palin don't relate to each other like close friends. They've only really known each other for two months, and for most of that time they have been traveling in separate orbits across the continent."[53]

Aloofness quickly developed into diffidence, and in late October *Politico.com* announced that "Palin allies report rising camp tension." The tension was linked to Palin's independence, something that had initially been a selling point for the campaign. The media framing illustrates the possibility that the McCain camp was looking for a female running mate who would appear to be independent while still knowing her "proper" place. The *Politico* report explained that Palin "decided increasingly to disregard the advice of the former Bush aides tasked to handle her, creating occasionally tense situations." An unnamed senior Republican was quoted as saying, "Palin had begun to 'go rogue' in some of her public pronouncements and decisions."[54] Reporting for ABC's *Nightline*, George Stephanopoulos stated, "There is no question there is a rift between the Palin camps and McCain camps inside the campaign." Even the *Daily Show with Jon Stewart* got in on the act in its October 29, 2008 episode, which featured a montage of news clips demonstrating Palin's penchant for "going rogue." A male voice narrated the clips in the style of a movie trailer voiceover, saying, "They found her in the wild ... they taught her everything ... they set her loose ... but they forgot one thing ... she couldn't be contained. Now they have just six days to stop her from destroying everything they've worked for. This November, Sarah Palin is, 'Goin' Rogue.'" Stewart incisively critiqued the dominant media narrative by asking, "Is that what going rogue is in politics—talking?"[55]

The dangerous diva frame was completed when critics asserted that Palin's political ambition was the true source of the problem. In a *New York Times* op-ed, Frank Rich wrote that "there's a steady unnerving undertone to Palin's utterances, a consistent message of hubristic self-confidence and hyper-ambition. She wants to be president, she thinks she can be president, she thinks she will be president." The piece was accompanied by a drawing of a high heel with a squashed McCain on the sole. Jonathan Freedland wrote in a *Guardian* blog that "Palin won't go away; if you imagine she's going to settle for quiet obscurity in Alaska after the election, think again." Barrie Cassidy told ABC's *Insiders* that Palin's real goal was the US presidency and charged that she was "doing nothing to disabuse us of that notion." Soon, the "pit bull" persona that served Palin well in August and early September was transformed into a negative moniker. A *New York Post* headline announced: "Pit Bull Turns on McMaverick," and the corresponding story quoted a "McCain insider" who said that "she's now positioning herself for her own future. Of course, this is bad for John. It looks like no one is in charge." The "pit bull in lipstick" went from being an "attack dog" to an unpredictable "bitch." The *Politics Blog* in Britain reported that, according to McCain, "Palin is even more trouble than a pitbull." The relationship between the two was described as "tense," and the blog attributed the following joke to McCain: "What is the difference between Sarah Palin and a pitbull? The friendly canine eventually lets go." The information was credited to Nigel Sheinwald, the British ambassador to the United States.[56]

Implicit in this narrative is the "bitch" metaphor that framed First Lady Hillary Clinton when she was perceived to be too much of an independent force within her husband's presidential administration.[57] Lauren Sutton explains that "'bitch' represents the domesticated animal that has gone wrong, that bites the hand that feeds it. A female dog in heat or protecting her young will growl, threaten, or even bite her owner; she has reverted to her wild state; she is a *bitch,* uncontrollable." At the conclusion of the 2008 campaign, then, Palin experienced an antifeminist backlash against her post-feminist candidacy. Personal ambition (a requirement for anyone involved in presidential politics) was coded as inappropriate and framed with the gendered term *diva.* The *Chicago Tribune's* Mark Silva wrote that "the 'rogue diva' of the McCain campaign is starting to look out for her own future now." The day after Obama was elected president, the *New York Times* reported on "anger within the McCain camp that Ms. Palin harbored political ambitions beyond 2008."[58]

Sarah Palin went from maverick mom to dangerous diva in a short two-month span. The media framing of her candidacy illustrates not only the shortcomings of a postfeminist political identity but also the vulnerability of all women candidates to antifeminist backlash. To be sure, much of the criticism aimed at Palin was well deserved; however, this chapter illustrates the ways in which legitimate critique often gets wrapped up in gendered stereotypes, undercutting not only the force of the legitimate critique but also the credibility of women as presidential figures. The speed with which the McCain camp and the media turned from postfeminist praise to anti-feminist backlash in the fall of 2008 was remarkable. It is possible, however, that they were primed for backlash as a result of the antifeminist framing of Hillary Clinton during the 2008 Democratic primary.

The Four C's of Hillary Clinton's "Dangerous" Campaign

In the early days of the 2008 campaign, before Hillary Clinton officially announced that she was forming a presidential exploratory committee, conventional political wisdom positioned her as the clear frontrunner in the race for the Democratic nomination. The Gallup Poll News Service published a piece announcing that "Clinton Remains the Front-Runner among Democrats" and noting that she had been "the clear leader ... in every poll of Democrats Gallup has conducted since early 2005." Characteristic of media coverage at that time was Matt Towery's declaration: "Hang It Up Obama— It's Hillary's Nomination." Towery offered one explanation for Clinton's political fortitude, citing "the old Bill and Hillary Clinton machine [that] awaits, well-oiled and ready to rumble."[59]

When Clinton finally did announce her intention to form a presidential exploratory committee, she continued to enjoy favorable media coverage. On the day of her announcement, an Associated Press story stated, "With her immense star power, vast network of supporters and donors and seasoned team of political advisers, the 59-year-old Clinton long has topped every national poll of potential Democratic contenders." *US News* reported that, despite the number of candidates in the Democratic field, "party operatives and independent analysts still consider Clinton to be the frontrunner." The *Washington Post* ran the headline "Hillary Clinton Opens Presidential Bid: The Former First Lady Enters the Race as the Front-Runner for the Democratic Nomination." The Gallup Poll News Service published a story titled "Clinton Eclipses Obama and Edwards on Leadership," naming Hillary Clinton the "front-runner" on a number of issues, including "perceived leadership qualities," "positive personal characteristics," and "being qualified to be president and being a strong leader."[60]

In early 2007, Clinton's frontrunner status also dominated global headlines. The *Sunday Times* of London compared Hillary to Margaret Thatcher. The *Guardian* declared "Clinton Out in Front with 24-point Lead," citing polling data that "established Hillary Clinton as the front-runner for the Democratic presidential nomination, 24 hours after she declared her intention to seek to become the first woman to take the office." The *Daily Mail* of London called her the "clear favourite." The *Sydney Morning Herald* stated that "Hillary Rodham Clinton is the frontrunner to win the Democratic nomination for the presidency in 2008."[61]

The news media, of course, had a vested interest in suggesting that the nomination was still in play. In January 2007 the *Philadelphia Daily News* noted just how much of the race remained, declaring, "Democrats Scramble Begins: Clinton's the Front-Runner, but 'We're a Lifetime Away.'" A news narrative rife with potential conflict would attract readers and viewers more effectively than one that presented an uncomplicated story of Clinton's political strengths. A French news agency introduced this competing storyline even before Clinton's official announcement, stating that "New York Senator Hillary Rodham Clinton has been the front-runner for months, but polls show she remains a polarizing figure in US politics. Many Democrats hoping to be the other-than-Hillary candidate have since come forward."[62]

By the spring of 2007, Clinton's vulnerabilities as a candidate were beginning to be itemized in coverage of her campaign. Some of these reports exhibited the gendered framing to which so many women candidates are subjected. For example, in May 2007, although the *Economist* contended that "the smart money is on Hillary Clinton to win the White House in 2008" and her speech at a Cleveland high school was a "study in political professionalism," the article also determined that "for all that, there was something missing." What was not missing from the *Economist*'s coverage was a description of Clinton's physical attributes in the story's lead paragraph, where it touted her "perfectly choreographed performance—speaking without notes, displaying a remarkable knowledge of the school's achievements, and bringing a touch of glamour to a dull Ohio afternoon with her pearls and perfectly coiffed blonde hair."[63] The article, which referred to the sitting US senator and presidential frontrunner by using her marital title, "Mrs.

Clinton," quickly declared her frontrunner status "puzzling" and listed a litany of personal characteristics that invoke the double bind between femininity and competence: Clinton was "strong but brittle," "polarizing," and "sharp elbowed," in contrast to Obama, who, the article notes, spoke to "an overflow crowd" where the "atmosphere was electric."[64] Confirming the research summarized earlier in this chapter, the article also paid significant attention to Clinton's personal life and characterized Bill Clinton's personal failings as Hillary Clinton's political liabilities. In a paragraph itemizing her "striking weaknesses," the *Economist* article lists her "brittle" disposition, her (undefined) "political baggage," and her husband's "long record of suicidally risky sexual dalliance."[65] Although the numerous scandals that plagued Bill Clinton's presidency surely would impact Hillary Clinton in her own presidential bid, the magazine's choice to list his actions as one of *her* "striking weaknesses" illustrates the extent to which political women continue to be defined in personal and relational terms.

By June 2007, the narrative of Clinton's "inevitable" nomination was being displaced by a series of media frames that positioned her outside the norms of presidentiality. The *LA Times* picked up on the trend, calling Hillary Clinton "The Tough, but Vulnerable, Front-Runner."[66] What is interesting about 2007 is that within the space of twelve months, Clinton was framed in three radically different ways: the formidable frontrunner, the vulnerable female candidate, and the dangerously deviant woman. By December 2007, MSNBC anchor Chris Matthews was using violent and infanticidal metaphors to describe Clinton's campaign, asking, "Is the Hillary Clinton campaign trying to obliterate Obama's candidacy, not just *beat it* but *strangle it in the crib* before there's any chance he catches on?" [emphasis added].[67] In the next section of this chapter, we detail key moments in the misogynistic progression of the media coverage of the Clinton campaign, noting the rhetorical moves made to distract from, undermine, and eventually obliterate Clinton's presidentiality.

Cleavage

On July 20, 2007, Robin Givhan published a now infamous piece in the Arts & Living section of the *Washington Post* titled "Hillary Clinton's Tentative Dip into New Neckline Territory." In it, she offered a speculative critique of Clinton's Senate floor attire, which Givhan described as follows: "She was wearing a rose-colored blazer over a black top. The neckline sat low on her chest and had a subtle V-shape. The cleavage registered after only a quick glance. No scrunch-faced scrutiny was necessary. There wasn't an unseemly amount of cleavage showing, but there it was. Undeniable." On the surface, the article appeared to congratulate the senator on her "confidence and physical ease" because "it means that a woman is content being perceived as a sexual person in addition to being seen as someone who is intelligent, authoritative, witty, and whatever else might define her personality." Yet the article's rhetorical functions were not limited by the ostensible intentions of its author. In less than eight hundred words the article reminded readers of the perceived gap between feminine sexiness and political competence. Clinton's barely visible cleavage was deemed "a teasing display" and "a provocation" that was somehow "unnerving." Givhan contrasted the "conservative" choice of "uniform" favored by Clinton during her US Senate campaign—her black pantsuits—with the "wide array of suits and jackets" she donned as a presidential candidate, noting that Clinton tried out "everything from dull khaki to canary yellow and sofa florals. Once again, she is playing the fashion field." The implication is that although Clinton made dull but disciplined fashion decisions as a US senator, as president she would be less predictable—and potentially less reliable. Givhan ultimately disparaged Clinton by asserting that her attire marked her as "noncommittal" and by suggesting that Clinton's revelation was analogous to "catching a man with his fly unzipped."[68]

The article created more buzz than the *Washington Post* editors likely anticipated. A week after the publication of this story that ignited a range of commentary on Hillary Clinton's cleavage, *Washington Post* writer Howard Kurtz assessed the situation in an article titled "Cleavage and the Clinton Campaign Chest." Kurtz's framing of the controversy was important because, in addition to covering the media for the *Washington Post,* Kurtz also served as host of CNN's *Reliable Sources,* a program that scrutinizes journalistic ethics. By responding to the controversy, Kurtz was speaking, at least in part, from his privileged position as a respected and widely read media ethicist. In his column, Kurtz addressed the responses given both by Givhan and the Clinton campaign. The Clinton campaign, according to Kurtz, "rolled out a fundraising letter" using the story as leverage, calling Givhan's column "'grossly inappropriate' and 'insulting.'" Kurtz quoted Givhan, who suggested there was more to Clinton's cleavage than a fashion choice, calling it "surprising because of the location and because of the person. It's disingenuous to think that revealing cleavage, any amount of it, in that kind of situation is a nonissue." Kurtz ultimately concluded that the Clinton campaign's outrage was strategic, asserting, "For candidates, using criticism—real or perceived—to raise money is catching on as a political maneuver."[69]

Kurtz's framing of the controversy is interesting in a number of ways. First, consider the column's headline: "Cleavage and the Clinton Campaign Chest." A "campaign chest" typically refers to the money the candidate has amassed to purchase advertising. The pun intimates that Clinton was doing some political advertising of her own on the floor of the US Senate, and the double entendre also invokes the stereotype that women's professional gains are at some level related to their sexual advances. Second, even though numerous academic studies (of which Kurtz is likely aware) have demonstrated that journalists routinely scrutinize the physical appearance of women candidates more than they do men's, Kurtz begins his essay by listing a few prominent male candidates whose physical appearance has landed them in the headlines. These examples are in the clear minority, but because Kurtz identifies more stories about men's appearance than women's, his article suggests that the objections of the Clinton camp are baseless overreactions. Finally, Kurtz's article contains the seeds of the story that would grow into the narrative of Hillary Clinton as a calculating, conniving candidate. Kurtz not only suggests that Clinton used criticism about her appearance, specifically her cleavage, as a cynical "political maneuver" but also argues that her objections are somehow abnormal, even by political standards. Kurtz states, "Politicians often rip the media over what they see as unfavorable coverage, hoping to score points against an unpopular institution. But the cleavage letter is undoubtedly a first in the annals of campaign counterpunching."[70]

Kurtz's narrative of Clinton as simultaneously oversensitive and calculating is echoed in other journalistic accounts of the controversy. The *New York Daily News* headline read, "Clinton Hot and Bothered over Cleavage Report," and the opening sentence of the accompanying article stated that her campaign is "so outraged—outraged!" at the story "that they're urging equally miffed supporters to fight back by stuffing cash into her coffers." Clearly making light of the story, the report frames Clinton not as a candidate upset over sexist media coverage but as an opportunistic stripper hoping to benefit from the scandal. The story went on to quote a "longtime Democratic operative who is no Clinton fan," who said, "'She looks for every opportunity she can get to be the victim. It's her playbook.'" An associated content article from *Yahoo.com*, self-described as "the world's largest source of community-created content," was more overt, stating that "Clinton Uses Cleavage to Raise Cash" and suggesting that "all normalcies have been removed and the push to raise money at all costs has erupted." CNN's *Political Ticker* claimed that "Clinton Seeks 'Cleavage' Cash." Writing for the *Columbia Journalism Review*, Megan Garber was unable to resist the breast puns even in a piece that criticizes the *Post* for publishing the original article. Garber's piece, entitled "Oval Office or Bust," ruminates on "Clinton's *other* war chest" [emphasis in original]. Despite the puns, Garber capably articulates the primary problem with the coverage, or what she calls "the basic Catch-22 of Clinton's candidacy: that her political legitimacy is somehow inversely proportional to her sexuality. That the more she puts her femininity on display, the less presidential she seems." As Garber concludes, "Not only does sex not sell for Clinton; it could end up selling her out." As late as August 9, 2007, however, a CNN poll announced that Clinton was still "firmly positioned as Democratic front-runner."[71] The cleavage controversy was short lived, but it gave way to a second inexplicable campaign "conundrum": the "Clinton Cackle."

Cackle

In September 2007, the *New York Times* published a piece by Patrick Healy under the headline, "The Clinton Conundrum: What's behind the Laugh?" Healy describes the situation this way: "It was January 2005, and Senator Hillary Rodham Clinton had just finished a solemn speech about abortion rights—urging all sides to find 'common ground' on the issue and referring to abortion as 'a sad, even tragic choice to many, many women.' Stepping offstage, she took questions from reporters, and found herself being grilled about whether she was moderating her own pro-choice position. And suddenly it happened: Mrs. Clinton let loose a hearty belly laugh that lasted a few seconds. Reporters glanced at one another as if they had missed the joke. But nothing particularly funny had occurred; it was, instead a deployment of the Clinton Cackle." Healy then assesses a string of incidents in which Senator Clinton deployed her "huge cackle," as an (ostensibly) calculated effort at "sham[ing] her inquisitors." Healy also asserts that at one campaign event, when not cackling, Clinton "turned frosty and traded barbs with the audience member."[72] Gendered stereotypes undergird Healy's narrative. Clinton's unruliness manifested itself either as feminine excess (the uncontrolled cackle) or cold calculation.

Additional cackle commentary could be found at *Politico.com,* which on September 30, 2007, suggested that Senator Clinton's laugh "sounded like it was programmed by computer." The *Politico.com* article aggregated media coverage from the week of September 30, noting the ways in which Clinton was framed as "evasive," "ruthless in self-advancement," and "overreaching." The article also pointed out that the shift in media coverage presented "a genuine challenge for her in 2008: overcoming perceptions that she is a politician so infused with ambition and artifice that she cannot connect with ordinary voters." CNN's *Political Ticker* blogged on "Clinton's Cackle Coverage." In his *New York Times* op-ed column, Frank Rich wrote that "Mrs. Clinton is erupting in a laugh with all the spontaneity of an alarm clock buzzer."[73] The *Washington Post*'s Howard Kurtz stated, "Forget the cleavage. It's now about the cackle." Kurtz cited numerous examples from a variety of popular and journalistic outlets of pundits and comedians ruminating on the "Clinton Cackle": from Comedy Central's Jon Stewart and ABC's *Good Morning America* to conservative pundit Sean Hannity and MSNBC's *Hardball*—each had commented on Senator Clinton's "cackle."[74] Kurtz explained why this particular media narrative served the commercial interests of these media outlets: "The subtext here is that the media have collectively decided that the wife of the 42nd president is the inevitable nominee and a good bet to become the 44th Oval Office occupant. Lacking much of a horse race, since Clinton has maintained a 20-point national lead over Barack Obama all year, journalists are resorting to a classic general-election question: Are Americans ready to have this woman in their living rooms every night for four years? Are they comfortable with her personality? Do they like her voice?"[75]

The tide appeared to be shifting by September 2007. CBS News reported that Clinton was no longer just the "front-runner" but also the "target," "finding herself in her rival's cross-hairs." The article quoted Clinton's opponents, who "are starting to point out Clinton's potential vulnerabilities and question her electability" in an effort to "remain in the game." *USA Today* ran a headline that echoed the CBS story: "Clinton Debates as Front-Runner and Target." On October 11, 2007, the *Christian Science Monitor* posed the once confident declaration as a tentative question in a headline that asked, "Inevitable Hillary?" The corresponding article suggested that Clinton's status as the "presumptive winner" was weakening and noted the "danger in [the] perceived early coronation."[76]

An oft-quoted editorial by Charles Krauthammer, published in October 2007, homed in on Clinton's ambition as the problem: "Her liberalism, like her husband's—flexible, disciplined, calculated, triangulated—always leaves open the possibility that she would do the right thing for the blessedly wrong (i.e., self-interested, ambition-serving, politically expedient) reason."[77] Although Krauthammer included Bill Clinton in his indictment, unchecked ambition in women is punished more frequently in politics than is the same quality in men. In an article questioning the inevitability of a Hillary Clinton presidential nomination, the *Kiplinger Business Forecast* identified the negative associations that cluster around the image of the Clinton Cackle, calling them her "high 'H' quotient. Lots of folks simply hate her for messing up health care reform in 1993 and for her role in the Whitewater scandal. Some also think that she's too ambitious, lacks executive management experience and tells voters whatever they want to hear. They fear a Clinton dynasty. (And some even find her laugh insincere and calculated.)"[78]

By November 2007, relatively innocuous "controversies" over cleavage and cackles had generated a media narrative that was beginning to discredit Clinton's presidentiality in ways that were clearly informed by gendered stereotypes. The *Pittsburgh Post-Gazette* quoted Mark Halperin's assertion that Clinton "'fell off the tough-shrill balance beam onto the 'shrill' side—with a THUD.'" The December 13, 2007, issue of the *Economist* ran a story titled "The Cracks Begin to Show: Hillary Clinton No Longer Looks Inevitable." The art that accompanied the headline was a comically drawn Hillary-as-Joan-of-Arc, confidently brandishing a sword while pieces of her "mettle" fall off her body. Her unsure steed and complement of soldiers gaze warily at their delusionally overconfident commander. One section of the article captured the sentiment that often accompanied stories about the Democratic race from this period: "Mrs. Clinton's problems have forced her to abandon her high horse of inevitability for the boxing ring." In a section titled "Same Old Dirty Politics," the article reminded readers of Clinton's supposed character weaknesses, including being "cold," "scripted," and "calculating." By December 2007, *US News & World Report* had announced that "New York Senator Clinton's hoped-for coronation has turned into a battle royal with Illinois Sen. Barack Obama."[79] And the primaries had not yet begun.

Crying

In January 2008, at a campaign event in New Hampshire, Hillary Clinton responded to a question from a voter who asked how she was holding up during the grueling campaign, noting that "as a woman, I know how hard it is to get out of the house and get ready. Who does your hair?" Clinton responded, first, by cracking a joke. Karen Breslau of *Newsweek* described the scene as follows: "Clinton chuckled, made a few jokes about how she 'has help' on certain days (but those are never the pictures you see on Web sites, she joked). Then she paused. Her eyes grew red. The coffee shop, packed with about 100 members of the media and 16 outnumbered voters, grew silent. 'I just don't want to see us fall backward as a nation,' Clinton began, her voice strained, her eyes welling."[80]

Breslau noted that "even as [Clinton] spoke, a local television reporter was broadcasting live that Clinton had started crying. Other reporters tried to correct him, even as he was still on the air. No she didn't cry." The distinction between "welling up" and "crying" was an important one in Clinton's case since, as Breslau's initial report explained, "there will no doubt be comparisons to the teary press conference former Colorado representative Pat Schroeder held to announce that she wouldn't run for president, thus confirming that anyone who needed to carry a Kleenex in her purse was unfit for the highest office in the land."[81] There was a bit of that in the aftermath of the episode: one *New York Times* columnist recounted the reaction of a fellow "reporter who covers security issues." "We are at war," the columnist's supposedly cringing colleague said, adding, "Is this how she'll talk to Kim Jong-il?"[82] Yet, in a twenty-first-century context, crying is no longer anathema for US presidents. Bill Clinton's famous capacity for empathy served him well as president, and in the wake of the 9/11 attack George W. Bush cried publicly on more than one occasion. It is true that women are given less latitude in terms of emotional displays than are men—which explains why this episode of brief "welling up" was quickly recast by the press as "crying."

For Clinton, however, the episode was noteworthy because of what it supposedly revealed about her authenticity. On one hand, as Breslau suggested, "Hillary's teary moment" may help "a candidate who is seen as aloof and too tightly scripted to appear more vulnerable, more human and more appealing." On the other hand, the moment had the potential to be coded as yet another calculation by the Clinton campaign. Indeed, after Clinton made a better-than-expected showing in the New Hampshire primary, reporters were quick to jump on the bandwagon and ruminate about Clinton's calculated crying. Maureen Dowd's *New York Times* op-ed was headlined, "Can Hillary Cry Her Way Back to the White House?" Dowd described several journalists' reactions to seeing Senator Clinton well up, including one who "joked: 'That crying really seemed genuine. I'll bet she spent hours thinking about it beforehand.'" Christina Bellantoni of the *Washington Times* asked, "Did Hillary win N.H. crying game?" and acknowledged that the "Comeback Cry" "incited conspiracy theories, accusations and strong reactions from voters and the press." *USA Today* drew a clear distinction between Clinton's tears and presidential fitness: "Was she using the old trick of crying to get sympathy from voters? Possibly. But for a woman who said she was tough enough to handle the heat in the kitchen, this does not make her look very presidential." Rush Limbaugh declared, "Mrs. Clinton's calculated tears set back feminism fifty years."[83]

According to the media frame that began to take hold in late 2007, Clinton's real negatives had little to do with experience, policy stances, or even cleavage, cackling, and crying. The real c-words with which Clinton had to contend were "calculating," "cold," and "conniving."[84] Simply by setting her sights on the Oval Office, Clinton transgressed the boundaries of feminine propriety and demonstrated ambition, which, although often rewarded in men, served as proof of her unpalatability. Former Vermont governor Madeleine Kunin admitted that when she ran for governor, she was ambitious. "Anyone, male or female[,] who goes through the trials of a campaign must be ambitious. But can a woman be seen as openly seeking power? Power is an explosive word, particularly when applied to women. It is one of the arrows that is shot at Clinton. Women, many believe, are not supposed to want power."[85] Similarly, on *Hannity & Colmes* Alan Colmes questioned what is really happening when Clinton is characterized as ambitious: "When Hillary Clinton wants to be president, she's portrayed as ambitious. When a man wants to become president, somehow I don't hear that word applied. Sounds a little bit of sexism." The difference, according to one *Hannity & Colmes* panelist, is "being ambitious because you want to continue to serve your country and being ambitious for this odd sort of personal glory and gain. And Hillary Clinton thinks that she is God's gift to the country."[86] One journalist claimed, "Hillary, like her hubby, is consumed with herself. She's no altruist, no convention patriot, but an ego-driven, ambitious politician prepared to do anything to achieve her goal."[87] The media frame that dominated during the early months of 2008 was more similar to that posed by the *Washington Post,* referring to a piece in *Slate,* which likened Clinton to Tracy Flick, "the hyperactively ambitious teenager" played by Reese Witherspoon in the 1999 film *Election.* For Clinton, ambition was a sign of female irrationality. One columnist's piece announced in its headline that "Irrational Ambition Is Hillary Clinton's Flaw," and the caption under Clinton's picture in that article charged, "She wants so badly to win that she will try anything."[88]

If Clinton's ambition would be her personal undoing, it also had become a liability for the Democratic Party. Seeking to secure the nomination by seating the disputed Michigan and Florida delegations at the 2008 Democratic National Convention, Clinton was beginning to wear out her welcome—with the press and the party. Sean Hannity labeled the strategy her "nuclear option" and said that she "is so ambitious that she's going to try to seat these delegates from Michigan and Florida."[89] The "nuclear option" label was repeated in national newspapers, cable political talk shows, and blogs.[90] Scholar Larry Sabato was quoted in the *Huffington Post* saying, simply, "Wow. The nuclear option will yield nuclear winter for the Democratic party."[91] The *Sunday Express* explained the consequences for the party as follows:

> Desperate Hillary Clinton could be planning a "scorched earth" strategy as the White House race slips from her grasp. Senior Democrats fear that despite having no realistic chance of beating Barack Obama to the Presidential nomination, she will refuse to drop out. They believe that this frantic "clinging on" will mean that the final choice to lead the Democrats in the November election will be sorted out only at the party conference in August. This would lead to huge divisions within the party with the likely result that although Obama would win the nomination, he would lose the Presidential election to Republican John McCain. This would leave Obama looking [like] a spent force and pave the way for Mrs. Clinton to have another shot at the Presidency in 2012. . . . Senior party officials have called the plan the "nuclear option."[92]

Conniving

Given the sheer number of column inches devoted to Hillary Clinton's presidential candidacy, it is not surprising that diverse and even conflicting media frames emerged in 2007–8. Throughout the entire campaign, however, there was a persistent undertone in the narrative, one that portrayed her as a cold, calculating, and conniving candidate. It was a familiar narrative for Clinton, who was framed similarly during the campaign and first two years of Bill Clinton's initial presidential term.[93] For the first year of Clinton's official candidacy, the "cold and calculated" woman frame ran parallel to the inevitable frontrunner frame. For example, in an interview on Fox News on February 7, 2007, pollster Frank Luntz explained that the "challenge for Hillary" was that "there's no emotion. It all seems so calculated when she speaks." Luntz also acknowledged, however, that she was the "frontrunner." Writing for *Salon.com,* Tim Grieve quoted a New Hampshire resident about his reaction to Clinton's response on her Iraq war vote. He "says that Clinton's response was 'cold and calculated' and left him with the impression that she 'is what the media often describes her as, too political and not authentic.' 'We are looking for authentic this time.'" In a *Chicago Sun-Times* editorial in March 2007, Steve Huntley wrote, "No one uses words such as dithering or wavering when talking about Sen. Hillary Clinton. Calculating is the way she's often described. She was an assertive first lady, pushing a bold initiative for health care—too bold for the times, as it turned out." A year before the election, Clinton's opponents reinforced the narrative. According to the *Washington Post,* in a November 2007 speech, Senator Obama accused Senator Clinton "of following a campaign plan that prizes calculation over candor and that is aimed more at winning the election than uniting the country." The article claimed the comments were aimed at clarifying "his differences with the Democratic front-runner." Chris Matthews even used the term "she devil" when discussing Hillary Clinton on his November 18, 2007, broadcast.[94]

The Project for Excellence in Journalism reported that the week of February 11, 2008, was the turning point, the week "the media narrative for the Democratic presidential race shifted . . . anointing a definite frontrunner and an underdog." Barack Obama did not simply move into the frontrunner spot, the journalists' group reported, but he "vault[ed]," leaving Hillary Clinton behind with "some corners of the punditocracy unfriendly to Clinton . . . [preparing] her political obit." And media coverage did not merely shift, it struck a new low. Jake Tapper of *ABCNews.com* reported on one way Hillary Clinton could win the Democratic nomination. According to an anonymous Democratic official, he wrote, Clinton would need to exercise "'the Tonya Harding Option'—the idea that Clinton's only path to the gold medal is to destroy her leading competitor." A reporter writing for a Canadian newspaper suggested that when voters regarded Clinton, some "saw just another ambitious politician who didn't represent change of any kind, a no-holds-barred campaigner who possessed all the feminine charm of Lady Macbeth." *Politico.com* produced an entry titled "Mommie's Dearest," ostensibly about whether it was Bill or Chelsea who was the best surrogate for Hillary on the campaign trail, yet the headline framed the candidate as the infamously bad mother immortalized onscreen by Faye Dunaway. Ken Rudin, NPR's political editor, updated the cinematic reference when he appeared on CNN on April 27, 2008, and compared Hillary Clinton to Glenn Close's character in *Fatal Attraction:* "Let's be honest here, Hillary Clinton is Glenn Close in *Fatal Attraction.* She's going to keep coming back, and they're not going to stop her." According to *MediaMatters.com,* Glenn Close comparisons also were made by Monica Crowley on the *McLaughlin Group* and by *Atlantic* editor and blogger Andrew Sullivan.[95]

Since Clinton was being compared to icons of destructive female ambition, it was perhaps no surprise that the conclusion to this media narrative involved her demise. In discussing the possibility of debating in Indiana and North Carolina before the primaries in those states, *CNN.com*'s Jack Cafferty wrote, "She says that she will debate him any place at any time, adding that it could even be done on the back of a flat-bed truck. He would probably prefer to run over her with a flat-bed truck at this point." Similarly, MSNBC's

Keith Olbermann joked with Howard Fineman that when Clinton failed to withdraw from the Democratic primary, party officials needed to find "somebody who can take her into a room and only he comes out." Republican strategist Pete Snyder concurred, saying that "I think someone's going to have to go out there and take her behind the barn. You know, I grew up in Lancaster, Pennsylvania, and that's kind of the term you use for that."[96]

The Dangers of Political Ambition

When Eric Zorn's *Chicago Tribune* blog entry about the Democratic primary race appeared on January 23, 2008, under the heading "Hillary Clinton's Dangerous Game," it invoked the media frame that came to dominate both Palin's and Clinton's campaigns.[97] Analysis of the narratives and images deployed by political media in 2007–8 illustrates not just the sexism with which all women candidates have to contend but also a misogynistic positioning of Palin and especially Clinton as overly ambitious (and therefore) "dangerous" women. Near the end of Clinton's primary bid, the *Washington Post* captured Hillary Clinton's response to the sexism in the media during her campaign:

> In an interview after church services in Bowling Green on Sunday, Clinton for the first time addressed what women have been talking about for months, what she refers to as the "sexist" treatment she has endured at the hands of the pundits, media and others. The lewd T-shirts. The man who shouted "Iron my shirt" at a campaign event. The references to her cleavage and her cackle. "It's been deeply offensive to millions of women," Clinton said. "I believe this campaign has been a groundbreaker in a lot of ways. But it certainly has been challenging given some of the attitudes in the press, and I regret that, because I think it's been really not worthy of the seriousness of the campaign and the historical nature of the two candidacies we have here." Later, when asked if she thinks this campaign has been racist, she says she does not. And she circles back to the sexism. "The manifestation of some of the sexism that has gone on in this campaign is somehow more respectable, or at least more accepted, and . . . there should be equal rejection of the sexism and the racism when it raises its ugly head," she said. "It does seem as though the press at least is not as bothered by the incredible vitriol that has been engendered by the comments by people who are nothing but misogynists."[98]

What is most disturbing about the criticisms leveled against Sarah Palin and Hillary Clinton are the ways in which their political ambitions were framed as both inappropriate and excessive. The underlying message is that political ambition in a woman is dangerous; women are not supposed to desire political power. Recall our discussion in chapter 2 about the ways in which fictional presidentiality positioned female presidents onscreen. Neither Mackenzie Allen nor Laura Roslin was framed as having political ambition; each inherited the position of president through no ambition of her own. The media framing of campaign 2008 suggests that any woman who actively seeks the highest political office, rather than being passively ushered there from the vice presidency in a time of national crisis, is suspect. She's a danger to herself, her party, and, ultimately, to the nation.

Although the American public prides itself as having progressed through the overt sexism of the past, familiar patterns are hard to break. A fifty-five-year study of *Time* magazine coverage found "a tale of stability" in the language used to frame presidentiality. That study quoted Seymour Martin Lipset, who noted that "'the United States has developed a homogenous culture in the veneration accorded the Founding Fathers, Abraham Lincoln, Theodore Roosevelt, and their principles.' *Time* magazine is part of that homogeneity, part of that veneration. It keeps the waters calm."[99]

One way to "keep the waters calm" is to fit political news into the familiar frame of strategy, relying on metaphors of sports, war, and romance. Prior research has documented the deleterious effects of these frames for political agency. Our analysis suggests that they also work to place women and femininity outside the realm of presidentiality, reinforcing hegemonic masculinity. In 2007–8, journalistic coverage reached new misogynistic lows as Sarah Palin was framed as the maverick mother who became the dangerous diva in the span of two months. More alarmingly, Hillary Clinton was framed first as improperly sexual (cleavage), then as excessively performative (cackle), then as emotionally vulnerable (crying), and finally as conniving and dangerous. In fact, the image of a "cold and calculating" Clinton was the only consistent element of the media frame throughout Clinton's primary bid. That likely reveals more about US culture than it does about Clinton. As Roseann M. Mandziuk notes, "When we look at [Hillary Clinton], we see the reflection of our cultural instabilities, a set of unresolved conflicts conflated in mediated fragments and discursive depictions."[100] As the next chapter argues, however, the dangerous woman frame may not capture completely the level to which press framing has devolved. In chapter 5, we continue to assess journalistic and popular media from the 2008 campaign, uncovering a more insidious narrative to which the American audience appears to have become accustomed: the "pornification" of the presidential body.

Bodies Politic

"Porning" the Presidential Body

Presidential sexual dalliances have long been a topic of public discussion, debate, and comic derision. Sometimes, as in the case of Bill Clinton's extramarital affair with White House intern Monica Lewinsky, the convergence of serious and satirical discourses suggests that "public figures are engaged in a tawdry burlesque drama."[1] This prurient preoccupation with presidents' sexual exploits is not a phenomenon confined to the digital age or even to the twentieth century. During the 1884 presidential election, Grover Cleveland admitted to fathering a child out of wedlock. After a well-known political cartoonist satirized the scandal, Cleveland's political opponents began bringing children to his rallies and instructing them to chant, "Ma, Ma, where's my pa?" Cleveland supporters got the last laugh, however, after he won the presidential election. They countered the chant with the retort, "Gone to the White House. Ha! Ha! Ha!"[2]

Much of the humor that satirizes presidential sexuality historically has sprung from situations of the (male) president's own making—often his own adulterous behavior. During the 2008 campaign, however, pundits, citizens, and comedians sexualized the political images of Hillary Clinton and Sarah Palin. This sexualization was triggered not by a scandal or specifically illicit behavior. Instead, the mere fact that these prospective presidential figures were female opened the floodgates to imagistic exploitation unprecedented in previous presidential campaigns. Terms and depictions that were previously considered too crude for public consumption infiltrated political culture and were circulated by political pundits, journalists, and citizens through social and entertainment media, campaign paraphernalia, and viral videos.* In fact,

---

*We have chosen explicitly to spell out objectionable language in this chapter because acknowledging the actual words connoted by the acronyms and images included in this essay is part of the social critique in which we are engaging. Neglecting to spell out the terms, even under the guise of academic propriety, would obscure the rhetorical force of the framing that we are attempting to point out. When terms appear in direct quotations, we replicate the form in which they appeared in the original quotation.

the explicit consumption of the female presidential body was so speakable during the 2008 campaign that a new campaign frame emerged—one that fulfilled both the journalistic trend toward titillation and the cultural impetus to reinscribe traditional norms of political power. As we argue in chapter 4, the 2008 race was framed using the language of sports, war, and even romance. For the first time in US presidential campaign history, however, a new frame emerged—one that we are calling "pornification."

In this chapter, we argue that the female presidential body was "pornified" during the 2008 US presidential campaign.[3] Pornographic metaphors, images, and narratives infiltrated US political culture in ways similar to their earlier emergence in advertising and popular culture. Building on the literature review and analysis established in the previous chapter, we examine debates among feminists regarding the import and influence of pornographic discourses on women's agency. Next, we examine a diverse array of texts from the 2008 presidential campaign, including comments of broadcast journalists, viral videos, campaign paraphernalia, and political satire that pornified Palin, Clinton, and female voters as a group. We conclude by contending that the pornification of the presidential body in 2008 reveals the persistence of cultural stereotypes about women political leaders and women citizens, despite the progress evidenced by Clinton's and Palin's candidacies. These discourses were informed by antifeminist and postfeminist ideologies. Not only did the 2008 campaign produce discourse that reached a new low in terms of sexism but misogyny proved to be palatable to a mass audience. The emergence of the pornification frame signals a twenty-first-century backlash against the gains women have made in US presidential politics.

Media Fragments as Political Frames

In chapter 4 we summarize the academic literature on media framing of political campaigns, examining journalists' reliance on the strategy frame and its metaphors of sports, war, and romance. Since, as Robert M. Entman explains, frames that are culturally resonant must "use words and images highly salient in the culture, which is to say *noticeable, understandable, memorable,* and *emotionally charged,*" examination of campaign frames provides a snapshot of political culture, as well as its corresponding narratives, themes, assumptions, and power relationships during a given election cycle [emphasis in original].[4] Moreover, as political campaigns and news outlets struggle to catch the attention of an American citizenry increasingly distracted by fragmented relationships, economic hardship, and digital diversions, one way to make their discourse "noticeable, understandable, memorable, and emotionally charged" is to strategically participate in popular culture. Candidates make seemingly obligatory appearances on late-night talk shows and participate in self-deprecating satirical sketches; cable news stations infuse their programming with bombastic punditry and slick news productions. As culture has become increasingly coarse, so too has the campaign framing that is embedded in that culture. Of particular note during the 2008 campaign were the ways in which anachronistic stereotypes about femininity and women's leadership were repackaged and deployed in the polysemous postmodern political environment.

The metaphors used to describe, critique, and satirize political campaigns can both reveal and reinforce stereotypes, especially those that may not be explicitly stated in other communication forms. In his study of political framing, William A. Gamson stresses that as citizens negotiate meaning, the "public discourse people draw on is much broader than the news and takes many forms."[5] Consequently, in this chapter we examine a variety of journalistic and pop cultural texts, including news broadcasts, political punditry, blogs, viral videos, campaign paraphernalia, and satirical television. In the introduction to this book, we cited Michael Calvin McGee's assertion that one of the most important tasks undertaken by rhetorical critics is "inventing a text suitable for criticism," one that makes apparent the "'invisible text' which is never quite finished" but is "constantly in front of us."[6] The "invisible text" that this chapter reveals is the frame of "pornification" that encapsulated the female presidential body during the 2008 campaign. This frame is indicative of a progression in campaign framing and, more broadly, the political culture in which campaigns were first treated as competitions, then trivialized as romances, and finally transformed into cultural peep shows.

Our contention is that metaphors of pornography constructed women presidential candidates in ways that revealed the persistence of cultural stereotypes about women political leaders, despite the progress evidenced by Clinton's and Palin's candidacies. Additionally, these metaphors became instruments of cultural backlash disciplining female presidentiality and grew increasingly misogynistic as women closed in on the office of US president. Before examining the pornification of the presidential body, however, we analyze debates in feminist communities over the issue of pornography and, more broadly, women's agency.

Pornography and Women's Agency

Pornography is a highly contested subject within feminist communities. Although it is difficult to define what, exactly, constitutes pornography, antipornography feminists point to sexist objectification and the sometimes violent dehumanization of women as distinguishing features. Insofar as pornographic objectification dehumanizes women and presents them, in some cases, as providing and even gaining sexual gratification from their own victimization, antipornography feminists argue that pornography creates a cultural climate that reinforces male dominance and implicitly or explicitly

CHAPTER 5

condones violence against women. Additionally, some critics claim that the majority of women who participate in the production of pornography are exploited and their participation (whether voluntary or coerced) exemplifies patriarchal power relationships. For this reason, antipornography feminists of the 1970s and 1980s formed unlikely alliances with social conservatives, articulating political and intellectual objections to pornography and lobbying for legal restrictions on the distribution of pornography.[7]

In response to the efforts of antipornography feminists, some feminist critics took an oppositional approach that has been called "sex-positive," "pro-sex," or "sex-radical" feminism. Proponents of this view argue that antipornography feminists sometimes conflate pornography with erotica—a form of sexual display that is not inherently patriarchal. Moreover, sex-positive feminists advocate for an expanded range of accepted sexual inter-actions, display, and performance as long as the activities take place between consenting adults.[8] This strain of feminist thought contributed, in part, to the power feminist argument that women could and should revel in their sexuality as a source of personal agency.[9]

During the first decade of the twenty-first century, the pendulum began to swing again as academics, pundits, and public intellectuals reflected, once more, on the mainstreaming of pornographic themes and images in popular culture.[10] In part, the attention to porn as entertainment was triggered by the popularization of the "pimp culture" promoted in rap music, on popular television programs like MTV's *Pimp My Ride,* and in film with movies like *Hustle and Flow,* which produced the Academy Award–winning original song, "It's Hard Out Here for a Pimp." Pop music, too, was becoming in-creasingly pornified, with Britney Spears, Christina Aguilera, and others performing exaggerated versions of the Madonna/whore dichotomy in their music videos and concerts. Of course, popular culture has always transgressed the boundaries of social convention. However, in the effort to maintain a reputation as "cutting edge," stars, advertisers, and producers peddle increas-ingly exaggerated, patriarchal versions of (mostly) female sexuality in which women are objectified, dominated, and abused.

Feminist debates over pornography and popular culture typically focus on questions about women's agency (does a pornified culture inhibit women's personal and political power?) and violence against women (does the main-streaming of sadomasochistic images promote gendered violence?). For several decades thoughtful critics from a variety of interdisciplinary perspec-tives have participated in this debate; spatial constraints preclude an exhaus-tive examination of the arguments proffered by proponents and opponents of these various positions.[11] What has not been examined, however, is the increasing pornification of US *political* culture. This is an especially troubling trend insofar as it occurs within the realm of governance and public policy, redefining the woman citizen in the public mind. Moreover, it comes at a time when women have just begun to gain enough leadership credibility that they do well in national political contests. The continuum of pornification represents a twenty-first-century backlash against women's power that inhabits many guises: playful and prurient, satirical and sexist, masochistic and misogynistic.

Porning the Presidential Body

Before building a case for the claim that themes, images, and metaphors of pornography functioned as an important media frame for the 2008 presidential campaign, we first must explain how "pornification" as a rhetorical process differs from "pornography" as an artifact. Unlike pornography, pornification need not include actual nudity or explicit sex acts. Rather, we assert the following:

- Pornification is a process that mainstreams the narratives, metaphors, images, and frames culled from the realm of pornography.
- A pornified image need not be as explicit as actual pornography. Rather, it connotes interpretations that are hypersexual or sexually exploitative.
- Pornification highlights sexuality in contexts that otherwise are not normally sexualized and, through the use of crude humor or gender-based parody, disciplines individuals who do not conform to traditional gender norms.

Both male and female politicians' images can be pornified. Certainly many of the jokes and satirical images spurred by President Bill Clinton's affair with Monica Lewinsky could be categorized as "pornification." During the 2008 campaign, a photograph of a shirtless candidate Barack Obama in a swimsuit (taken while he was on vacation) appeared in magazines, YouTube videos, and other pop cultural contexts. In 2010, when Republican senatorial candidate Scott Brown was vying against Democratic candidate Martha Coakley to succeed the deceased Edward M. Kennedy in the US Senate, the media dug up a twenty-eight-year-old photograph of him posing nude for the magazine *Cosmopolitan* as the winner of the magazine's "America's sexiest man" contest.[12] The increasing prevalence of the pornification frame in stories about candidates of both genders coincides with the coarsening of US culture more broadly. Even so, the process is both more prevalent for women candidates and more problematic. As Kathleen Hall Jamieson explains, "Throughout history, women have been identified as bodies not minds."[13] Because women candidates perpetually combat the double bind between femininity and competence, media frames that cast them as sex objects undermine their credibility as leaders in ways that the same frames do not undercut male candidates.

The pornification of the US presidency exists on a continuum. At one end are relatively innocuous images of candidates as sexy and appealing and female voters as infatuated with the candidates they support. These discourses may occasionally be intended as compliments and are certainly less lurid than much of what is considered acceptable within mainstream entertainment culture. These images are pornified, however, by their appearance in the civic context of public, democratic politics, where they reinstantiate women citizens and leaders as vixens, sex objects, and/or nymphomaniacs. Importantly, unlike the pornography published in magazines like *Playboy* or *Hustler*, the pornified images of women politicians appear without their consent or participation and often are distributed under the guise of humor or parody. Thus, even images that purport to flatter or are distributed "in good fun" are exploitative in that they hijack a woman politician's image or persona to serve sexist, patriarchal, or misogynistic purposes. As the continuum expands, pornified political discourses become baser and more extreme until, at the opposite end of the spectrum, a sadomasochistic narrative emerges, explicitly depicting or defending sexualized violence against women as pleasurable, natural, or deserved.

During the 2008 presidential campaign, the images of candidates from both major parties were co-opted and pornified. Discourses emerged from supporters and opponents of Sarah Palin and Hillary Clinton and employed very different, but equally sexist, symbolic framing. The pornification of Palin's identity reflects a power feminist/postfeminist assumption that women's most potent form of power is sexual and that sex appeal can and should be employed to gain other forms of power (personal, economic, political). Palin's case reveals the danger intrinsic to this ideology. Ostensibly complementary discourses quickly morphed into a sexist dismissal of candidate Palin, sexualizing her public persona and trivializing her political accomplishments. Conversely, the pornification of Clinton's identity was an antifeminist disciplining of a woman seeking too much power. The attacks on Clinton illustrate the ways in which the pornification of political women can quickly degenerate into a violently misogynistic hatred of women.

Sarah Palin as National MILF

When Senator John McCain chose Sarah Palin, the relatively unknown governor of Alaska, to be his vice presidential running mate, political journalists and pundits were stunned. Although her résumé as a culturally conservative, western governor with professional connections to the oil and energy industry made her a potentially good strategic pick for McCain, journalistic discussions about Palin focused more attention than is usual for a vice presidential candidate on her physical appearance. Palin was a former beauty pageant contestant who exuded a western, rugged sex appeal. Whether she was riding a Harley Davidson, hunting big game, or ostensibly taking on special interests as governor of Alaska, Palin somehow negotiated the dangerous terrain between being either too feminine to lead or not feminine enough to be a "normal" woman. Palin's burgeoning national persona was cemented by her trademark up-do and glasses, which invoked one staple of pornographic entertainment, the "sexy librarian." The blog *stylelist* reported that Palin's "sexy librarian glasses spark[ed] interest in eyewear," and it noted that Palin "also has become the flavor of the month in the political thong industry." (Exactly when did political thongs become an industry?) An entry in a *New Republic* blog quoted former federal prosecutor David Lat, who "switched from supporting Hillary Clinton to supporting McCain-Palin": "Well, some of my reasons for supporting Palin are a bit idiosyncratic, and independent of the minutiae of policy platform or her record on various issues. . . . It's like being in love—reason flies out the window! . . . What I like about Palin is that she has [Obama's] glibness, his surface appeal but you can't help thinking that behind those librarian glasses, she knows she is playing a role—and playing it beautifully."[14]

Palin's sexy celebrity spawned a host of artifacts, from the picture of a fictional Alaskan license plate that read, "Alaska: O-MAMA! Where the air is cold, and the governor is hot!" to the political cartoon featuring two presidential campaign buttons that read, "'08 Obama/Biden" and "McCain/35–23–35 Palin."[15] Almost immediately after joining the ticket, Palin's head was Photoshopped onto a picture of a woman clad in a US flag bikini and holding a rifle. The picture spread like wildfire on the Internet, even after being revealed as a fake.[16] Palin's sex appeal was cheerfully lampooned more than once on *Saturday Night Live,* and that topic made the rounds in the late-night comedy monologues as well. The raciest of the early "pro-Palin" discourses were T-shirts, posters, and a *Saturday Night Live* skit that touted her as a "MILF," an acronym meaning "Mom I'd Like to Fuck."[17]

In less than a week, Palin went from being a rising star in the Republican Party and the first Republican woman to be nominated for the vice presidential ticket to being the national MILF. This transformation has the potential to undercut women's agency by reducing their power to mere sex appeal and rewarding their attractiveness with heterosexual male approval rather than respect. Framing women's political agency in terms of sexual influence is a familiar strategy, one that has shaped both ancient and contemporary narratives.[18] Reporting for *MSNBC.com,* Carrie Dann suggested that the MILF frame resonated with the public. After reviewing the results of a study analyzing "search term data compiled for NBC News by the online research company Hitwise," Dann reported that

about one in every five hundred web searches containing the phrase "Sarah Palin" during that week inquired about the Alaska governor's support for the pork project [which attempted to bring the infamous "Bridge to Nowhere" to Alaska], making "Sarah Palin Bridge to Nowhere" the 72nd most frequent search term on her list. But ranking far above the earmark investigation in popularity (among the 10 million internet users in Hitwise's sample) were "Sarah Palin legs" (No. 16), "Sarah Palin Vogue" (No. 18), and "Sarah Palin sexy photos" (No. 49).

In other words, while political operatives frenetically worried about how the public viewed the authenticity of Palin's claims, the online public was frenetically viewing—without particular worry about authenticity—doctored photos of a bikini-clad, gun-toting Alaska governor.[19]

If the business acumen of pornographer and *Hustler* founder Larry Flynt can be trusted, there's a market for images of a pornified Palin. Shortly after McCain made his choice public, the *New York Daily News* ran a headline about Flynt "Hustling up an Ala-skin flick with Sarah Palin look-alike." Sadly, Flynt's *Nailin' Paylin* was quickly produced, with edited clips featured on widely read political blogs such as the *Huffington Post,* which posted clips with nudity obscured so that they would be "safe for work" viewing. That same blog reported that as of October 2008, the Flynt video included "a threeway with Hillary and Condoleezza look-alikes" and was "being fast tracked for release before the election."[20] The *Huffington Post* certainly was not the only news outlet playing up the so-called "Sarah Palin porn flick." It became a featured entertainment news item in the weeks preceding the presidential election and also appeared on political news outlets such as *Salon.com, Politics Daily, Right Wing News,* and *DCRepublican.com.*[21] The unnamed blogger for *DCRepublican.com* lauded Flynt's film, asking, "Can anyone else think of another time in history where a conservative has become such an icon in pop-culture? While this isn't exactly the best form of publicity, I think it's great that the conservative movement has a woman standing up for our principles that is not only gorgeous, but intelligent at the same time."[22]

The pornification of Sarah Palin's political identity falls within the "soft-core" end of the continuum. The sitting governor of Alaska did not hide her status as a former beauty pageant contestant, and, like many male and female politicians, she chose to conform to mainstream standards of beauty and attractiveness. But the framing of her candidacy in blogs, political cartoons, journalistic sources, and political paraphernalia went well beyond noting her attractiveness. Sarah Palin was dubbed the national "MILF," a term that not only trades on the stereotype of an attractive older woman's sexual allure but also features the four-letter word for sexual intercourse. Surprisingly, however, that four-letter word was not the worst example of coarse characterization in campaign 2008. Before Sarah Palin was the national MILF, Democratic presidential primary contender Senator Hillary Clinton went from being a "bitch" to a "cunt."

Hillary Clinton Labeled "Rhymes with Blunt"

In January 1995, following the failed Clinton health care reform campaign and the midterm election that handed a congressional majority to the Republicans, journalist Connie Chung interviewed the mother of Speaker of the House Newt Gingrich. A now infamous portion of their exchange unfolded as follows:

CONNIE CHUNG. Mrs. Gingrich, what has Newt told you about President Clinton?

KATHLEEN GINGRICH. Nothing, and I can't tell you what he said about Hillary.

CHUNG. You can't?

GINGRICH. I can't.

CHUNG. Why don't you just whisper it to me, just between you and me.

GINGRICH. "She's a bitch." About the only thing he ever said about her. I think they had some meeting, you know, and she takes over.[23]

At the time, Kathleen Gingrich's explicit invocation of the term *bitch* was treated as a shocking departure from accepted norms of public, political discourse. A media debate over the use of the term ensued, with some pundits noting that there was only one label more offensive to women, and so far the "c-word" had not been sanctioned for public use.[24] One wonders if, during the 2008 campaign, Clinton viewed 1995 wistfully, as a time of relative cultural innocence. By July 2008, when Clinton was stumping for Democratic presidential nominee Barack Obama, one online respondent to a story about Clinton posted on the *Washington Post*'s website that "Clinton is a conniving ... well, never mind ... it rhymes with blunt."[25] Despite the temptation to dismiss the anonymous comment as an isolated incident or a rant from the digital fringe, the euphemistic rhyme invoked a term that was hurled explicitly at Clinton during the 2008 Democratic primary.

Fans of the television series *South Park* will not be surprised that it was at the forefront of this troubling trend. In the March 28, 2007, episode, "The Snuke," lead character Eric Cartman stumbles into a national security crisis when he helps to uncover a terrorist plot to detonate a nuclear bomb cleverly hidden inside Hillary Clinton's vagina. The episode, a spoof of the popular Fox series *24*, introduces the crisis with a bomb-sniffing pig discovering the bomb during Clinton's campaign rally in South Park. A CIA official quickly briefs his boss:

CIA OFFICIAL. Mr. Thompson, that kid who called in the warning was right. We recovered intel that terrorists have obtained a nuclear device and that they have most likely hidden it in Mrs. Clinton's ... well, in her ...

CIA DIRECTOR. In her what?
CIA OFFICIAL. In her snatch, sir.[26]

The episode features an x-ray of the bomb inside Clinton, with one technician describing it as "a suitcase nuke designed to fit in a woman's snizz. It's called a 'snuke.'" When both Cartman and the CIA are unsuccessful in tracking down the remote detonator, officials decide that "somebody is going to have to go in and try to disarm this nuke manually." The security officer responds, "No, it's too dangerous. That snatch has not seen action in over thirty years. It could be toxic!" The episode subjects the viewer to an extended exam of Clinton's "dark, cold" vagina, at which point the examiner discovers that something other than a nuclear device is hidden deep inside Clinton. Unfortunately, he is unable to identify it before it devours his head. The fact Trey Parker and the other writers working on "The Snuke" took the joke that far is telling. The myth of a ferocious "vagina dentata" is common in many cultures and typically signals a deep-seated fear of female sexual power.[27] When the meme is applied to Clinton, it shifts slightly, altering the myth to invoke fear of female power more broadly. In Clinton's case, the *South Park* episode connotes charges that have surrounded her since her tenure as US first lady—that her sexual frigidity and personal ambition made her the prototypical "castrating bitch."

The *South Park* episode "The Snuke" smartly satirizes racial profiling, the shortcomings of US intelligence gathering systems, and the inauthenticity of political candidates. What it fails to satirize is the sexism directed at Clinton. Instead, discussion of Clinton's private parts was played for laughs in *South Park's* uniquely shocking style. The episode aired on March 28, 2007, predating by several months the other, more mainstream examples of the "c-word" and its synonyms being directly associated with Clinton, as discussed in this chapter. Consequently, rather than critiquing a pop culture meme, *South Park's* "The Snuke" may have been instrumental in generating it.

After Clinton was positioned as the frontrunner for the Democratic nomination early in the primary season, explicit examples of Clinton as "cunt" began to surface in mainstream political culture. One photo that made the Internet rounds appeared to be an authentic picture of a T-shirt worn by an anonymous man. The shirt presented a series of simple images that corresponded to the words "I Love Country Music." Above the written text appeared an eye, a heart, a head shot of Hillary Clinton, a tree, and a musical staff.[28] An article on *Salon.com* introduced a new political action committee called "Citizens United Not Timid, aka CUNT." Not a spoof, this registered 527 organization was established to oppose Hillary Clinton's candidacy. Its logo was a red, white, and blue drawing shaped like a woman's crotch and with the tagline, "**C**itizens **U**nited **N**ot **T**imid: a 527 Organization to Educate the American Public About What Hillary Clinton Really Is" [emphasis in original]. The *Salon.com* article explains that the organization's purpose was to "sell $25 T-shirts emblazoned with the organization's charming name and its red, white, and blue logo. The logo is supposed to evoke a woman's crotch."[29]

Although the emergence of the word *cunt* in public, political discourse seems to have been triggered by the Clinton candidacy, it was not limited to her. Comedian Jon Stewart marked a different instance of the term's use during the June 11, 2008, edition of *The Daily Show*. His monologue was as follows:

> There's an old saying in Washington that the nastiest four-letter word in government is *cunt* [bleeped, but lips not obscured]. And you know, that adage is as true today as it was when the saying was first etched on the side of the Jefferson Memorial. Now, you may be sitting there wondering, (a) why you let the kids watch with you tonight, and (b) "Why the dry history lesson, Professor?" Well, it turns out that one of the gentlemen running for president has been accused of dropping the C-bomb while engaged in a heated debate on the floor of the living room of his own house. According to a new unauthorized biography, *The Real McCain,* one time, after his wife Cindy told him his hair didn't look good, Senator McCain responded, "At least I don't plaster on the makeup like a trollop, you c**t." Okay, seems a little harsh. But in his defense Senator McCain's a navy man. It's just salty navy talk. He's not trying to hide it. You've seen his campaign slogan [flash to a picture of McCain in front of a green campaign sign]: "John McCain: Experience You C**ts Can Count On." You know, you can't spell "count on" without c . . . [*trails off*].

Stewart concludes the bit by saying, "Is this story true? Who knows, but the important thing is, it's out there, signaling that we have officially moved into the character assassination portion of our presidential campaign."[30]

Although Stewart's satirization of the "cunt" story pointed to its inappropriateness in the context of a political campaign, it also furthered the introduction of a formerly taboo characterization into mainstream political pop culture. A one-liner tossed out by the comedian and HBO talk-show host Bill Maher lacked the critical edge of Stewart's bit. During a discussion about media censorship he joked, "Now they fined CBS a million dollars—a million dollars—for Janet Jackson's nipple. Think what they could get for Hillary Clinton's cunt!"[31]

Soon, that imagery migrated from the realm of entertainment and satire to serious political news shows. Consider, for example, the following exchange from MSNBC's political talk show *Tucker,* hosted by conservative pundit Tucker Carlson, and described on the *Media Matters for America* website:

On the October 15 edition of MSNBC's *Tucker*, discussing Sen. Hillary Rodham Clinton's (D-NY) presidential campaign with *Washington Post* columnist Eugene Robinson and Cliff May, president of the Foundation for the Defense of Democracies, host Tucker Carlson said: "Gene, this is an amazing statistic: 94 percent of women say they'd be more likely to vote if a woman were on the ballot. I think of all the times I voted for people just because they're male. You know? The ballot comes up, and I'm like, 'Wow. He's a dude. I think I'll vote for him. We've got similar genitalia. I'm—he's getting my vote.'" After asserting that "the Clinton campaign says: 'Hillary isn't running as a woman,'" Carlson stated: "Well, that's actually completely false, considering the Hillary campaign—and I get their emails—relentlessly pushes the glass ceiling argument. 'You should vote for her because she's a woman.' They say that all the time." May responded: "At least call her a Vaginal-American." Carlson replied: "Is that the new phrase? Boy, that's nasty. I don't think I can say that." Robinson interjected, "No, you don't say that," to which Carlson responded: "I shouldn't say that? I'm not going to attempt it. No, no."[32]

Despite Carlson's assessment of the term "Vaginal-American" as "nasty," the three men who participated in the discussion laughed, both at the specific "Vaginal-American" joke and at the notion that women would like to vote for a woman to be president. This anecdote also illustrates an only slightly toned-down version of the "cunt" discourse that surrounded Clinton's candidacy insofar as it explicitly calls attention to the female genitalia in a derogatory way.

It is important, at this juncture, to explain why the preceding examples fit onto the pornification continuum as we have constructed it. According to the second edition of the *Oxford English Dictionary*, the word *cunt* is defined both as "the female external genital organs" and as "a term of vulgar abuse" which is "applied to a person, esp[ecially] a woman." The entrance of this term into political discourse is evidence of more than just the coarsening of US culture. The term *cunt* itself is a pornified version of terms like the word *vagina*—one that is applied exclusively to women and represents not just sexism but a misogynistic hatred of women. By deploying it in the context of legally recognized political action committees, mainstream cable news shows, and political pop culture, proponents participate in the third type of pornification: highlighting sexuality in contexts that otherwise are not normally sexualized and, through the use of crude humor and gender-based parody, disciplining individuals who do not conform to traditional gender norms.

Using terms like "Vaginal-American" and "cunt" to describe Clinton's political identity was only one form of discipline exercised in political pop culture. Other strategies fit within the pornification frame insofar as they use gender-based parody to highlight her status as an abnormal or improper woman candidate. One image, credited to *FreakingNews.com*, which describes itself as a site for "News Photoshop Contests," takes a picture of a president giving a speech behind a lectern, with the first lady sitting to his right, and places Hillary Clinton's head on the male president's body, with Bill Clinton's head topping the figure of the first lady. Similarly, another Photoshopped image poses as a still shot taken from a security camera in a men's public restroom. Hillary Clinton is standing, wearing a skirt, looking around suspiciously, and using the urinal. The subtext of these examples is, of course, that any woman who seeks the office of US president is unnatural, dangerous, even deviant. The threat of the power-seeking woman was crystallized in the Hillary Clinton nutcracker. Consumers may purchase the functional nutcracker from Amazon.com as well as many other websites, where animated images show her nutcracking power in action (the nut is placed between her thighs). To ensure that this product is recognized as a reaction against her presidential bid, the nutcracker is wearing her signature black pantsuit and a "Hillary" campaign button.

Central to sadomasochistic pornography is the notion that women should be humiliated, violated, and abused. Occasionally, the abuse is taken to the extreme, causing the woman's death, either simulated or real, as in the genre of the "snuff" film. A review of discussions occurring on mainstream political talk shows demonstrates the cavalier invocation of threats of violence and death against candidate Clinton as they occurred within the off-hand comments and jokes of guests and hosts, particularly when the conventional wisdom was that Clinton was overstaying her welcome by refusing to bow out of the Democratic primary race. We alluded to some of these exchanges in the previous chapter, but they warrant additional consideration here. For example, on an episode of MSNBC's *Countdown* with Keith Olbermann, *Newsweek's* senior Washington correspondent Howard Fineman was discussing the need for Clinton to concede the primary race to Obama. Fineman's exchange with Olbermann unfolded as follows:

FINEMAN. There's some adults in the Democratic party to step in and stop this thing like a referee in a fight that could go on for thirty rounds. . . .
OLBERMANN. Right—somebody who can take her into a room and only he comes out.
FINEMAN. [*nodding*] Yes.[33]

Although Fineman chose the nonviolent metaphor of a referee, Olbermann responded with the image of a mob hit man, an imagistic switch with which Fineman easily concurred.

Similarly, on a CNN broadcast, NPR political editor Ken Rudin stated, "Well, first of all, let's be honest here, Hillary Clinton is Glenn Close in *Fatal Attraction*, she's going to keep coming back and they're not going to stop her."[34] In case there was any doubt about what should happen to the

Glenn Close version of Hillary Clinton, an Obama delegate was caught on tape saying, "Barack Obama's going to be the nominee of our party.... Senator Clinton, I thought when she said 'I'm going to support the Democratic nominee' was indicating kind of finally she was going to give up, but uh, like Glenn Close [she] should have stayed in that tub," referring to the drowning of the Glenn Close character in *Fatal Attraction*. On the Fox News program *Hannity & Colmes*, Republican strategist Pete Snyder encouraged the Democratic Party to essentially put Hillary down (a euphemism for killing an animal) in order to get her to withdraw from the Democratic primary race. He said, "You know, I think someone's going to have to go out there and take her behind the barn. You know, I grew up in Lancaster, Pennsylvania, and that's kind of the term you use for that."[35]

It may not be immediately evident why we place the aforementioned examples on the pornification continuum. Our argument is that pornification functions to sexualize, objectify, discipline, and sometimes dehumanize women candidates. The Glenn Close character in *Fatal Attraction* was not just psychotic. She was sexy, sexually available, obsessive, and psychotic. She becomes a cautionary tale in US culture because she took sexual obsession too far and demanded too much from her lover. She represents the unity of sex, obsession, power, and death. Importantly, at the end of *Fatal Attraction,* her death was a deserved death—one brought on by her choice to transgress established social boundaries for how the "other woman" should conduct herself. When that character becomes a pop cultural moniker for one of the leading candidates for the Democratic presidential nomination, pornification is at work.

Sarah Palin and Hillary Clinton were not the only presidential figures to be pornified during the 2008 campaign. Barack Obama's image also was sexualized in what became the most popular and widely acclaimed viral video of the campaign. The video trades on racist stereotypes of black masculinity. Interestingly, however, it also illustrates the ways in which the pornification of male presidentiality leaves intact—even bolsters—presidential qualities such as power, authority, and gravitas. At the same time, images of the young women who willingly participate in the pornification of male presidentiality reinforce stereotypes about young women voters: they are nymphomaniacs who are primarily interested in presidential candidates' sexual, rather than political, appeal. This type of political pornification is palatable to a mass audience, in part, because the sexualization of women's power has been embraced by some young feminists. Astrid Henry explains that some young women who ascribe to the "third-wave feminist" label have stressed the "liberating potential of sexuality" and focused on "a woman's right to pleasure." Henry lauds this "important—if limited—vision of female empowerment," which celebrates "both women's power and women's sexuality," creating a "world where one can be both feminist and sexual."[36] It is true that the recognition that women have just as much potential for/right to sexual pleasure as men is a productive feminist cultural development. Unfortunately, popular culture often conflates feminist sexual freedom with more traditionally sexist depictions of women's sexuality. When this happens in political culture, associated discourses "promot[e] the notion that women voters, like women in general, are sexual rather than political beings, seeking out the affection of their elected officials while touting their own sexual attractiveness."[37]

Porning Obama and Young Female Voters

The website YouTube has facilitated the explosion of a seemingly endless barrage of political parody. Some of these viral videos present thoughtful political critique. Many take on the tone of a political rant. A few, however, reach an audience outside the confines of YouTube. During the 2008 Democratic primary, perhaps the most infamous of these videos was Obama Girl's "I Got a Crush . . . on Obama."[38] Posted in June 2007, "Crush on Obama" launched the now popular website *BarelyPolitical.com* and was touted on that website as being "named one of 2007's 10 best videos by *Newsweek*, *People* Magazine, the AP and YouTube."[39] The video instantly received attention from national news outlets. A *Washington Post* political blog called *Channel '08* described the video as follows: "Alternately dressed in a bikini, some very short shorts and a tight white-and-pink top that reads 'I GOT A CRUSH ON OBAMA,' she pole dances on a subway stop, sings to a stranger on a park bench and gets on top of an office desk and starts dropping it like it's hot. Lyrics include such gems as: 'You're into border security. Let's break this border between you and me . . . Universal health care reform, it makes me warm. . . . You can Barack me tonight.'"[40]

The video patterns itself after the form of R&B and hip hop videos and invokes stereotypes about black male and female sexuality, situating the female star/Obama campaigner as a sex-starved "ho" and Obama as the stud she is eager to service. The hypersexualized black male is a mainstay of racist imagery, and Murali Balaji explains that "black masculinity—and the performance of it—in music videos is a manifestation of identity and body politics steeped in the normative assumptions of Black men's behavior."[41] Using a double entendre based on the myth of black men's predation on white women, Obama Girl coos, "Baby you're the best candidate. / I like it when you get hard / on Hillary in debate." Similarly, the song invokes the notion of Obama's male endowment with the line, "In the new Oval Office / You'll get your head of state."[42]

The rhetorical force of the song's lyrics is multiplied by the video's visual imagery. Obama Girl writhes around in skimpy attire, pole-dancing on a subway train, and performing for male coworkers on top of an office desk. Obama's image, culled from speech clips and still photos, is a ubiquitous character in the video. The video positions him in the role ascribed to African American men in the so-called "pimp culture" of hip hop music— an environment in which "pimps" (as highly sexualized patriarchs) are "elevated to the status of a hero."[43]

Of course, one can mine the vast depths of the Internet and turn up just about anything. "Crush on Obama" is a significant artifact of presidentiality because of the myriad ways it was repurposed and deployed in mainstream news outlets and political talk shows during the 2008 campaign. The phenomenon was similar to that described by Eric King Watts and Mark P. Orbe in their assessment of the successful Budweiser "Whassup" campaign, in which the pop cultural artifact "signif[ies] a pleasure principle orienting white consumption of blackness."[44] Ettinger's personal website showcases videos of her multiple appearances on Fox News, ABC News, and MSNBC programs.[45] Her debut video was featured on several different National Public Radio news programs, discussed in major national newspapers, and referenced in news magazines.[46] Matt Bai, writing for the *New York Times,* asserted that the "Crush on Obama" video "probably had more to do with shaping Obama's complicated public image . . . than any Internet appeal devised by the candidate's own aides."[47]

The video's popularity spawned a cottage industry of similar videos for other candidates, including Rudy Giuliani and Hillary Clinton. The viral music video backing candidate Clinton was called "Hott 4 Hill" and appeared on YouTube several weeks after the release of "Crush on Obama."[48] Stylistically, the video borrows from the 1980s Van Halen music video "Hot for Teacher," in that it depicts a young, attractive teacher dancing in front of her elementary school class as she pines for her candidate. In one shot, the teacher takes a seductive bite out of the middle of a cake with Clinton's picture on it, singing, "The USA would be a better place / if everyone could just get a taste / of you." Invoking the popular girl-on-girl porn motif, the teacher sings, "I know you're not gay / but I'm hoping for bi," and after a brief pause a voiceover adds "lingual!" The allusions to body parts and sexual terms, finished by words that turn the suggestion toward politics, is one strategy employed throughout the video. It is telling that the "Hott 4 Hill" video was envisioned with a female, rather than male, teacher (played by Taryn Southern). In addition to tacitly acknowledging the many actual charges of lesbianism leveled at Clinton throughout her public life, the video's parody of recognizable pop rock video form is what lends cultural salience and makes it successful as a parody.

These videos made multiple appearances on MSNBC's *Hardball,* where roundtable discussants reviewed them at length.[49] "Crush on Obama" was promoted on the *New York Times*'s political blog *The Caucus,* was discussed during the Sunday morning roundtable on ABC's *This Week . . . with George Stephanopoulos,* and appeared on ABC's *World News Sunday,* to name just a few major news sources.[50] The popularity of "Crush on Obama" and "Hott 4 Hill" also earned their stars occasional interviews on major cable news shows. For example, Southern, Ettinger, and the short-lived "Giuliani Girl" (Adolina Kristina) were invited to appear with Chris Matthews on his political news show *Hardball*. In response to Matthews's question, "What do you like about Rudy Giuliani?" Kristina stated, "I like his leadership skills, what he was able to"—cutting her off in midsentence, Matthews goaded and teased her:

MATTHEWS. That's the name of the book you're reading. Is that where you got the word from?
KRISTINA. No.
MATTHEWS. Come on, I saw you with the book today, Adolina, that said leadership on it. It looked to me like a talking point.

After extracting a coherent answer from Kristina, despite his efforts to the contrary, Matthews asks the women if they are registered to vote, inquires about their political affiliation, and concludes that "with no insult intended to Pat Buchanan and the other people I usually have on this show, I would rather be with these people."[51] Matthews makes clear how much personal pleasure he derives from consuming both the women and their cultural productions.

Both "Crush on Obama" and "Hott 4 Hill" invoke the stylistic tropes of their respective music video genres (R&B, hip hop, and female pop). Academic research has thoroughly established the implications for women's identity and agency contained in this form of entertainment.[52] This chapter extends that argument to the realm of women's political agency. Although viral videos certainly do not impinge on anyone's right or ability to vote, to the extent that these images form media frames, especially for positioning young female voters, they undermine and rhetorically dismiss women's political agency. The 2008 campaign also reveals the risks latent in the post-feminist accentuation of women's sexual power. Conforming to traditional, sexist gender norms enhanced the personal and economic power of women like Ettinger and Southern. They were granted access to serious political talk shows like *Hardball* and were praised by media personalities like Matthews, who often uses his platform to ridicule and dismiss liberal feminist political figures such as Hillary Clinton. Their access comes at a price, however, and that price is paid by the women candidates and female voters, whose degradation finds sanction in videos like "Crush on Obama."

At this point, some may question whether the aforementioned examples do any actual harm to women in politics. After all, the Internet is full of fringe humor and offensive discourse, and in an environment of twenty-four-hour cable news, people are bound to say things they might later regret.

Concerned citizens have the option to avoid certain websites, delete objectionable emails, and turn off the television. Of course, that does not solve the problem of individuals who seek and share material like this because they think it is funny or apropos. Even so, does Clinton's formidable primary campaign not demonstrate that these discourses have little material impact? The cloak of humor allowed pornified political discourses to infiltrate "serious" political discussion to the extent that even "jokes" about killing candidate Clinton passed, unremarked upon, by cable news program hosts and contributors. That is a stunning cultural devolution. It illustrates the extent to which misogyny continues to be speakable in US culture.

Pornification and Political Consequences

Perpetrators of the pornification frame actively attempt to subjugate political actors who only recently have begun to experience meaningful political agency. Women, who make up more than 50 percent of the population and have had the right to vote in the United States for nearly a century, in 2010 comprised just less than 17 percent of the US House of Representatives (72 out of 435 plus a delegate each from Guam, the Virgin Islands, and Washington, DC), 17 percent of the US Senate (17 out of 100), and six state governorships.[53] Women have made inroads in presidential administrations during the past two decades, with women from both major political parties serving key Cabinet posts, including secretary of state. As the visibility of women's political power increased during the 2008 campaign, however, they experienced a cultural backlash—digitally disciplined in a wide array of cultural contexts through humor, punditry, and parody that fixated on women's bodies.

It is important to note at this juncture in the argument that observations about the symbolic impact of the pornification of political discourse do not rely on them being the only, or the most prominent, or even a frequent news frame. Unlike the argument about horse race journalism—which is premised on the ubiquity of the frame in campaign reporting—the argument about political pornification is one of presence and palatability. The *presence* of the romance narrative is a marker of the narrative fidelity that heterosexual romantic norms continue to have in twenty-first-century popular culture— even popular *political* culture, where the notion of romance would seem disjunctive with civic republicanism. The frame is unremarkable because it somehow "fits" within accepted cultural notions of political relationships. We have grown to expect that our candidates for public office will "court" and "woo" us as suitors instead of "persuading" us as interlocutors. Once the romance frame was employed frequently enough to sound familiar, it was not too far a leap from gendered romance to sexist compliment, from sexist compliment to dirty joke, from dirty joke to hard-core exploitation, and finally to symbolic (and then political) annihilation. Consequently, the second part of our argument about the impact of political pornification is one of palatability.

Just a decade ago, "the c-word" was still unspeakable in public political dialogue. Calling a candidate a "bitch," while all too common in everyday parlance, was a shocking departure from the norms of public civility when Connie Chung's infamous interview with Newt Gingrich's mother aired in 1995. Just twelve years later, Senator Hillary Clinton's bid for the Democratic presidential nomination was inundated with words, images, and slogans that made "bitch" sound almost quaint. As an article in the *New Orleans Times-Picayune* pointed out, Clinton faced "an onslaught of open misogynistic expression," and the writer admonished readers to "step lightly through that thickly settled province of the Web you could call anti-Hillaryland," for they could too easily find themselves "knee-deep in 'bitch,' 'slut,' 'skank,' 'whore,' and, ultimately, what may be the most toxic four-letter word in the English language. We have never been here before."[54] As the web becomes the source of choice for political news, in a climate where newspapers are shuttering their doors and consumers are customizing their online news delivery by subscribing only to their preferred pundits and bloggers, the web can no longer be dismissed as the chaotic ramblings of the cultural and political fringe. As this chapter has demonstrated, even the mainstream cable political talk shows and print media picked up on many of the pornified images, recycling them sometimes under the protective guise of condemnation, but often presenting them as simply the latest political joke to be told around whatever the cyberspace equivalent is of the office water cooler.

It is the *presence* and *palatability* of political pornification that is critically significant. The analysis in this chapter does not claim, and does not need to claim, that the examples selected for examination are representative of all campaign discourse. Thankfully, they are not. But they are *indicative* of the persistent, pernicious backlash against women's political gains. Even—or perhaps especially—as women approach the last glass ceiling of US electoral politics, they are disciplined by increasingly base, vile, and violent discourses that reinscribe the worst kind of misogynistic patriarchy. It is a misogyny that most US voters would recoil from if asked about it in those surveys that gauge whether Americans are "ready to vote for a qualified woman presidential candidate." But surveys and focus groups are losing credibility as the best measurements of public opinion. In the age of the Internet, researchers are now turning to social networking sites, blogs, and other digital repositories of public opinion, many of which are regarded for their ability to record candid opinion due to contributor anonymity (in blog comments, for example), or their ability to quickly access the opinions of large numbers of "real people" (on Twitter, Facebook, and MySpace).[55] This chapter demonstrates that analysis of political pop culture can serve as another important gauge of public opinion. Communication scholars have long recognized that opinion polls are problematic sources of public attitudes because factors such as the wording and ordering of questions can make poll results unreliable.[56] Critical assessment such as that undertaken in this chapter reveals the persistence of stereotypes that many people insist have been vanquished from the public dialogue. If postfeminism refers to a time in which the goals of the feminist movement have largely been achieved, our analysis demonstrates that, regrettably, the postfeminist era is not yet upon us. Critics and citizens have more work to do in order to ensure that women are equitably represented—in language, in culture, and in positions of political leadership.

In this respect, political pornification functions like epithets, such as "bitch," hurled at women who have transgressed the boundaries of appropriate behavior for their gender and wielded too much public power. The term *bitch* functions as a rhetoric of containment in contemporary political culture, one that is particularly debilitating for women because it relies on the logic of the double bind between femininity and competence.[57] Male leaders can be tough and (appropriately) masculine. Female leaders can be either tough or (appropriately) feminine. Pulling off both at the same time is not impossible, but it is tricky terrain to navigate. Women candidates have worked diligently to break down the logic of that particular double bind during the past two decades. As they succeed in displacing the "bitch" charge, however, a new rhetoric of containment emerges to discipline them once more. This "new" pornified political parlance, however, simply repurposes old stereotypes about gender and sex. When male candidates are pornified, they are typically still cast in positions of power: jokes about Bill Clinton situated him in the Oval Office with a woman hiding under his desk; the tabloid photo of a shirtless Barack Obama immortalized in the "Crush on Obama" viral video was intercut with images of a swooning, scantily clad groupie pole-dancing in a subway car. Women candidates, on the other hand, are cast in the power*less* roles of "MILF" and "cunt"—roles that erode their credibility as candidates and leaders. As noted by New York writer Emily Gould, "Men are typically seen as having agency and women are typically seen as being acted upon in romantic relationships. . . . So then even when those stereotypical power dynamics aren't really the ones at play, the culture-making machinery will simplify whatever the real story is until it is a more familiar . . . narrative."[58]

If journalistic and political pop cultural environments are purveying increasingly oversimplified versions of political identity, that trend can be seen in other entertainment contexts as well. In the next chapter, we examine political parody, assessing the ways in which much of the most popular political parody of the 2008 campaign normalized rather than challenged traditional understandings of presidentiality, once again putting women candidates at a disadvantage.

Parodying Presidentiality

A (Not So) Funny Thing Happened on the Way to the White House

On September 13, 2008, Tina Fey made a triumphant return to *Saturday Night Live* (*SNL*), the television series that launched her comedy career. Appearing alongside Amy Poehler's incarnation of former presidential hopeful Hillary Rodham Clinton, Fey portrayed Alaska governor and Republican vice presidential nominee Sarah Palin. In the episode's "cold open," Fey's Palin and Poehler's Clinton preside over a joint press conference, billed as "A Nonpartisan Message from Sarah Palin and Hillary Clinton."[1] Fey's Palin explained that she and Clinton were "crossing party lines to address the now very ugly role that sexism is playing in the campaign." *People* magazine accepted that the explicit purpose of the Fey/Poehler skit was to "skewer issues of sexism surrounding the presidential election," but *About.com*'s Daniel Kurtzman focused instead on the "barbs that took aim at Palin's lack of experience, Clinton's bitterness over Palin's ascendance, and the media's fawning coverage of Palin."[2] Poehler's Clinton then pointed out the differences between the two women, and this exchange followed:

CLINTON. I don't want to hear you compare your road to the White House to my road to the White House. I scratched and clawed through mud and barbed wire, and you just glided in on a dog sled wearing your pageant sash and your Tina Fey glasses!

PALIN. What an amazing time we live in. To think that just two years ago I was a small town mayor of Alaska's crystal meth capital. And now I am just one heartbeat away from being president of the United States. It just goes to show that anyone can be president!

CLINTON. [*exasperated, sarcastic*] Anyone! Anyone! Anyone!

That excerpt of the sketch touches on a central question addressed in this book. Can "anyone" be president? What does an analysis of, for example, presidential parody reveal about our culture's acceptance of women in that role? The preceding chapter provides a partial response to that question: parodies sometimes sexualize and even pornify the presidential body in order to attract an audience or launch a partisan critique. As a distinct rhetorical genre, however, presidential parody occupies a more complex role in postmodern political culture.

Parody can levy both partisan and cultural critique, and reviews of the aforementioned *SNL* sketch focused on its partisan message. David Zurawik of the *Baltimore Sun* lauded *SNL*'s executive producer, Lorne Michaels, saying, "He knew what the politically savvy core audience of *SNL* wanted and he gave it to them before anyone even yelled 'Live from New York.'" Indeed, *SNL* served up some satirical raw meat to audience members unsupportive of Palin's candidacy. CBS News's Scott Conroy asserted that "one of the more biting pieces of satire came at the beginning of the sketch when Amy Poehler's rendition of Hillary Clinton standing beside Palin said, 'I believe that diplomacy should be the cornerstone of any foreign policy.' 'And I can see Russia from my house,' Fey as Palin replied." Jeffrey P. Jones asserts that parodic form allowed Fey to "strip the encounter bare and offer up the essence of the situation instead—a governor who was a political novice and intellectual lightweight seeking to charm her way through a campaign and into an office that she was ill-prepared to fill."[3] Conroy's article suggests that the real Palin, who watched the bit live from her chartered campaign flight, "had a good laugh along with the press corps in the back of the plane and millions of Americans at home."[4]

Parody, of course, does more than simply entertain. Robert Hariman argues that "political humor and particularly its core modality of parody are essential for an engaged, sustainable, democratic public culture." Hariman links parody with the epideictic genre of communication, contending that parody puts "social conventions on display for collective reflection."[5] At the same time, Roderick P. Hart and E. Johanna Hartelius warn, parodic political performances sometimes run the risk of exacerbating our already cynical view of politics and are especially dangerous in a "self-sealing world where no claim can be proven false and all claims retain an air of plausibility."[6] Parody, like all rhetoric, may be used for good or ill. Our purpose in this chapter is neither to condemn nor to exonerate parody as a genre of communication. Nor is it to assess the full range of parodic discourses that populate the postmodern political environment. Rather, our examination of select parodic episodes salient to the 2008 presidential campaign suggests that despite its oppositional design and rootedness in paradox, parodic presidentiality often normalizes rather than challenges traditional understandings of presidential power. In particular, although key parodic episodes of the 2008 campaign aptly skewered the mainstream media and questioned the partisan motives of candidates themselves, much of their humor was derived from reinforcement of, rather than challenge to, traditional gender norms. In that respect, the parodies of campaign 2008 contributed to the backlash against female presidentiality in ways similar to the media framing discussed in earlier chapters. After briefly discussing the structure and function of parody, we examine key parodic texts from 2007–8, focusing specifically on *SNL* parodies of Hillary Clinton, Sarah Palin, and Barack Obama.[7]

Parodic Politics as Resistant and/or Assimilative

Mikhail Bakhtin recognized the ubiquity of parody, noting that "there never was a single strictly straightforward genre, no single type of direct discourse—artistic, rhetorical, philosophical, religious, ordinary everyday—that did not have its own parodying and travestying double." Gary Saul Morson concurs, noting that parody can be found "under the names of 'mimicry,' 'mockery,' 'spoofing,' 'doing a takeoff,' and so forth—in the most diverse forms and most various contexts of everyday life." Parodic discourse is consequential because of its educational function in society. Hariman states that although people can "acquire knowledge of the formal conventions and social assumptions of public speech" from "subcultures of democratic participation such as interscholastic debate, electoral campaigning, and legislative service," most citizens "never go there." Consequently, for "many people, that education is provided by parody and other forms of political humor."[8]

Parody's educational capacity is rooted in imitation. Hariman notes that the literal translation of the word *parody* is "beside the song," and parodic humor works by placing communication "beside itself," so to speak. Following Bakhtin, Morson explains that parody's "double-voiced words" are meant to convey to its audience "both a version of the original utterance as the embodiment of its speaker's point of view . . . *and* the second speaker's evaluation of that utterance from a different point of view" [emphasis in original].[9] Hariman states that this "comic doubling" introduces "a profound ambiguity into the direct address. What once seemed to have one meaning now can have more than one meaning."[10] So, in the *SNL* skit cited at the beginning of this chapter, Fey's performance both enacted the heroic individualism that formed the basis of Sarah Palin's political identity ("it just goes to show that anyone can be president") *and* it critiqued the notion that Palin's success was related in any way to her individual merit (by illustrating Clinton's superior qualifications). Morson identifies three criteria that must be met in order for communication to function parodically:

- It must "evoke or indicate another utterance," also called the "target."
- It must be "in some respect, antithetical to its target."
- It must clearly indicate that "it is intended by its author to have higher semantic authority than the original."[11]

Priscilla Marie Meddaugh explains that Bakhtin located parody within what he saw as the democratic space of carnival, a "social space outside of official life" where "hierarchies of social, economic, and political structures are suspended to allow egalitarian contact among citizens." Parody's carnival "challenges authoritative claims to the 'center' of discourse" and "positions audiences as insiders, in contrast to their traditional roles as outsiders of official discourse and authorized modes of communication." She concludes that the parodic carnival "provides a temporary suspension from officialdom, inviting audiences to observe and question the shortcomings of political life through parody and satire. It does so through participation rather than instruction, subversion rather than hierarchy, possessing a keen understanding of rhetorical situation and historical reality."[12] In postmodern society, the carnival often is located in the digital spaces of television and the Internet. Audiences critique the absurdities of politics by enthymematically supplying parody's punchlines. The *SNL* parody of Palin is funny only when placed in the context of the broader campaign—a context that contains references to her lack of experience, her physical attractiveness, and her meteoric rise to (potentially undeserved) political prominence.

Complicating this view of carnival's democratic nature, Linda Hutcheon observes that although the medieval carnival subverted the social norms of its time, it also was, as Bakhtin noted, "'consecrated by tradition,' both social and ecclesiastical. Therefore, although this popular festival and its manifest forms exist apart from 'serious official, ecclesiastical, feudal, and political cult forms and ceremonials,' in so being, they in fact also posit those very norms." To put it more simply, "Parody's transgressions ultimately remain authorized—authorized by the very norm it seeks to subvert."[13] In that respect, too, the postmodern carnival resembles its premodern precursor. It is no longer the exclusive space of the jester; *SNL* and other late-night comedy programs routinely host candidates and even sitting presidents. By participating in parody, the power structure both sanctions and infiltrates the parodic space.

Hariman reconciles Meddaugh's and Hutcheon's apparently contradictory readings of Bakhtin by contending that parody is "neither radical nor conservative, but both at once," since the original discourse, once parodied, is "cut down to size, corrected against the 'backdrop of a contradictory reality,' positioned to be set aside or otherwise not obeyed, and challenged to adapt toward the critique in order to continue to hold an audience." Key to parody's radical potential is its leveling function—the "deft political satire of those who richly deserve it."[14] Of course, an audience's conception of "who deserves it" is inextricably linked to the audience members' values and assumptions. Democrats target Palin. Republicans target Obama. Everyone targets the media, and so on. Because a popular network television program like *SNL* is interested in garnering the broadest possible audience, it stands to reason that the parody proffered on its stage will be polyvalent—audience members will find different aspects of the sketches funny depending upon their personal beliefs, values, and political leanings.[15] This chapter is particularly concerned with parodies of gender and leadership that resonated broadly in popular culture during the 2008 presidential campaign.

Because we closely analyze each text, we had to delimit this chapter's textual scope. Since our discussion of presidential bodies critiques many artifact types that function satirically and comically (e.g., T-shirts, viral videos, campaign paraphernalia), we chose, in this chapter, to focus exclusively on *SNL* parodies. Chris Smith and Ben Voth discuss the consequentiality of *SNL* parodies of presidential candidates, arguing that they play "a critical synthetic role in informing political views."[16] In our estimation, these texts also reveal cultural assumptions that may be sublimated in other arenas but still powerfully influence political culture. Although the sketch we referred to at the beginning of this chapter levied both a partisan critique of Palin and a broader indictment of sexism in politics, that sketch may be the exception that proves true the rule. More common was the tendency for parodic performances to rely on gender stereotypes as a source of (rather than target of) their humor.

Parodic Presidentiality as Normative Performance

We began this chapter by referring to the *SNL* sketch that positioned Clinton and Palin as spokeswomen against the sexism of politics. Unlike many of the *SNL* sketches from the 2008 political season, including others featuring Fey's Palin and Poehler's Clinton, this skit did, indeed, critique sexism. Picking up on a theme discussed earlier in this book, the skit drew attention to the inappropriate sexualization of both Clinton's and Palin's images:

CLINTON. But, Sarah, one thing we can agree on is that sexism can never be allowed to permeate an American election.
PALIN. So, please, stop Photoshopping my head on sexy bikini pictures!
CLINTON. And stop saying I have cankles!
PALIN. Don't refer to me as a MILF!
CLINTON. Don't refer to me as a "flurge"—I Googled what it stands for, and I do not like it.
PALIN. Reporters and commentators, stop using words that diminish us! Like "pretty," "attractive," "beautiful" . . .
CLINTON. "Harpy," "shrew," "boner shrinker" . . .

This segment contrasts the stereotypes that undergird what Kathleen Hall Jamieson has identified as the double bind between femininity and competence, where "the evaluated woman has deviated from the female norm of femininity while exceeding or falling short of the masculine norm of competence. She is too strident and abrasive or not aggressive or tough enough."[17] In addition to highlighting the stereotypes that most often constrain political women, the *SNL* sketch attempted to distinguish between sexism and legitimate partisan critique. Near the end of the skit, Fey's Palin invited the media to "be vigilant for sexist behavior." Poehler's Clinton replied, "Although it is never sexist to question female politicians' credentials. Please, ask this one about dinosaurs." The satire in that line skewers Palin's creationist beliefs, but it also draws a distinction between objections rooted in policy differences and those that stem from cultural prejudices. In that respect, then, the sketch appears, as Hariman suggested, to "nurture public culture" by "portraying public life as a dynamic field of competing voices forever commenting on each other."[18]

To understand why the preceding *SNL* sketch was notable in terms of its treatment of gender issues, it is helpful to contrast it with other *SNL* sketches from the 2008 Democratic primary season featuring Poehler's Clinton, Fred Armisen's Barack Obama, and cameo appearances by the real Clinton and Obama. During the November 3, 2007, episode, when Clinton was still considered the Democratic frontrunner, *SNL* featured a Halloween costume party hosted by the Clintons at their home in Chappaqua, New York, and attended by the other Democratic presidential contenders.[19] As the sketch opens, Hillary Clinton welcomes John Edwards to the party:

CLINTON. I just thought it would be good for all of us Democrats to get together after Tuesday's debate. [*exaggerated laughter*]
EDWARDS. Agreed.
CLINTON. You know, because even though things can get heated, come next November we all have to support the Democratic nominee, no matter who she may be.

Edwards replies to Clinton's assertion of her dominance in the pack of candidates by complimenting Clinton, dressed in a bridal gown, on her costume:

EDWARDS. And may I just say that is a great witch costume.
CLINTON. I'm actually a bride.
EDWARDS. Oh, okay, now I see it. All in how you wear it, I guess.

That particular joke is funny only if the audience supplies the missing enthymematic premise that Clinton is somehow "witchlike" and that she deserves to be skewered for her "witchiness"—remember Hariman's claim that when parody is funny, it is because the audience believes the target "richly deserves it." It is no accident that the word "witch" rhymes with "bitch" and often replaces that epithet on broadcast television programs that restrict the

Parodying Presidentiality

use of certain terms. Clinton's history with the term "bitch" and her persona as an improperly aggressive woman was efficiently evoked by *SNL's* parodic display.[20] Additionally, the joke about Clinton being mistaken for a witch is carried through to the end of the sketch, becoming the dominant theme of the bit. Thus, unlike in the Fey/Poehler press conference sketch, the humor in the "Halloween Party" sketch works to reinforce, rather than challenge, the stereotype that successful women politicians are too aggressive.

The rhetorical force of the parody of Clinton is bolstered by the ways in which other characters are parodied in contrast. In the sketch, the characters' costumes exaggerate the defining characteristics of their public identity: Bill Clinton is a lovable lothario, John Edwards comes dressed as a hobo (mocking the way in which the millionaire trial lawyer crafted a public persona linked to poverty), and Bill Richardson is an eager Al Gore (lobbying Hillary about his vice presidential potential). After Richardson has an obsequious exchange with Hillary, Bill and Hillary trade lines that underscore Hillary's "witch" stereotype:

BILL CLINTON. Man, he really does want to be your vice president.
HILLARY CLINTON. How come every time someone says something nice to me you say it's because they want to be my vice president? People are nice to you all the time. Do they want to be your vice president?
BILL CLINTON. People like me.

A few seconds later, after commenting on how attractive Dennis Kucinich's wife is, Bill Clinton remarks, "There's a marriage he won't regret in thirty years." The rhetorical force of the "witch" theme culminates, however, when a party guest in an Obama mask greets the Clintons:

BILL CLINTON. Hey, great Obama mask.
HILLARY CLINTON. Yeah, who is that under there? [The party guest removes the mask to reveal the real Barack Obama—extended applause from the studio audience.]
OBAMA. Hello, Hillary. Hello, Bill.
HILLARY CLINTON. Nice to see you, Barack. So, you dressed as yourself?
OBAMA. Well, you know, Hillary, I have nothing to hide. I enjoy being myself. I'm not going to change who I am just because it's Halloween.
HILLARY CLINTON. [*ruefully*] Well that's . . . that's great.
OBAMA. And may I say, you make a lovely bride.
BILL CLINTON. She's a witch.
HILLARY CLINTON. Bill!

Not only is Obama the only personality satirized for a good quality (he's "too" authentic), he also treats his political rival with more care and concern than her own husband or any of the other partygoers. The choice to compliment Obama in this particular sketch is perhaps understandable, given his cameo appearance on the show. The theme of Obama's attractiveness and Hillary's unattractiveness as presidential figures, however, was sustained throughout numerous *SNL* sketches during 2007–8. Our analysis of those bits will reveal two important insights: first, presidential parodies reinforce the double bind between femininity and competence, illustrating the contemporary impact of this ancient stereotype, and second, in a postfeminist political climate, sexism is perceived to be both innocuous and funny in ways that racism is not.

Take, for example, the March 1, 2008, sketch entitled "Democratic Debate #2."[21] The sketch begins with Poehler's Clinton and Armisen's Obama seated at a debate being hosted by NBC News anchor Brian Williams (played by Will Forte) and NBC News Washington bureau chief Tim Russert (played by Darrell Hammond). The skit opens with Williams addressing the debate audience:

WILLIAMS. If you're just joining us, the first segment of tonight's debate, all three hours and forty minutes of it, was entirely given over to a discussion of health care, and sweet Georgia Brown it was more boring than you could possibly imagine. A vitally important issue to be sure, but when this one here [*gestures to a smiling Clinton*] gets to talking about it, it's all a person can do to keep the mind alive.
RUSSERT. I'll be honest, Brian, I blanked out for most of it.
WILLIAMS. Well, you didn't miss a thing.
CLINTON. Brian, could I say something here?
WILLIAMS. Uh, is it about health care? Because if it is, I swear I'm gonna lose it.
CLINTON. Never mind.

Russert then engages Clinton in a question that first extends *SNL*'s running joke about the media's tendency to go easier on Obama than on Clinton in debates.[22] Second, he references the real Clinton's critique of Obama, and third (importantly, for our purposes), he invokes stereotypes about Clinton (specifically) and women leaders (generally):

RUSSERT. Senator Clinton, you often allude to Senator Obama's eloquence. And let's be honest. He is really, really eloquent. Amazingly eloquent. Quite astonishingly eloquent. Really.
CLINTON. I get it, Tim, he's eloquent.
RUSSERT. But you seem to dismiss it by arguing that he can only talk about change where you can make change happen. Explain that.
CLINTON. Well, Tim, take health care, for example.

Russert. No, please, no, God . . .

Clinton. All right. Energy policy. The big oil companies are quite happy with the status quo. They're earning record profits, and pretty speeches are not going to make them give up power. It's going to take a fighter, not a talker. Someone who is *aggressive* enough, and *relentless* enough, and *demanding* enough to take them on. Someone so *annoying*, so *pushy*, so *grating*, so *bossy* and *shrill*, with a *personality so unpleasant* that at the end of the day the special interests will have to go "Enough! We give up! Life is too short to deal with this *awful woman!* Just give her what she wants so she'll shut up and leave us in peace." And I think the American people will agree, *that someone is me* [emphasis added].

The response of the studio audience—extended applause and laughter—suggests that the joke that Clinton's competence was necessarily accompanied by "shrill" bossiness and "grating" aggressiveness resonated with the dominant narrative framing Clinton's candidacy. It is especially interesting to note that although the real Clinton does not appear in this sketch, she did make a cameo appearance immediately following the sketch. Clinton's presence on the set did not trigger the deference that Obama's presence on the set had garnered for him in November 2007.

Clinton's cameo on the March 1, 2008, episode of *SNL* immediately followed the "Democratic Debate #2" and completed the show's "cold open."[23] Billed as an "Editorial Response from Senator Hillary Clinton," the skit showed the real Hillary Clinton seated at a desk, assuring the *SNL* audience that the preceding debate sketch was "not an endorsement of one candidate over another—I can say this confidently because, when I asked if I could take it as an endorsement I was told, 'absolutely not.'" The audience gave Clinton an extended round of applause when she first appeared on camera, and the humor of the bit came from the real Clinton encountering her *SNL* doppelganger, Poehler's Clinton, with the two women dressed exactly alike. The bit was short and Clinton gamely went along with *SNL*'s premise in the preceding skit that she was competent but grating, saying, "But I still enjoyed that sketch a great deal." Poehler's Clinton laughed in an exaggerated, obnoxious manner (a hallmark of Poehler's Clinton parody that invoked the "Clinton Cackle" discussed in chapter 4), and this exchange followed:

The Real Clinton. Do I really laugh like that?
Poehler's Clinton. Uh, well . . .
The Real Clinton. Yeah, well, okay . . .

Again, extended audience laughter suggests that the image of a well-meaning but grating presidential candidate resonated with the public.

The sketch played well for Clinton insofar as it gave her the opportunity to react charitably to the negative stereotypes about her and even demonstrate that she was in on the joke. To some extent, all politicians have to "play along" when they appear on late-night comedy shows. What is interesting about this exchange, however, is that the humor informing the sketches from 2007 and 2008 drew from different wells depending on who they were parodying. Parodies of Obama pertained to his positive qualities and the media's fawning support of his candidacy. Parodies of Clinton, conversely, played up her persona as an overly aggressive, unpleasant, and inappropriately bossy leader. Whereas the real Obama got to be magnanimous and even chivalrous in his 2007 *SNL* cameo, the real Clinton had no choice but to laugh at herself and her ostensible foibles.

Dora Apel notes that "caricature depends on the immediate recognition of the object being caricatured."[24] Attention to the specific parodic narratives chosen by *SNL* reveals that the cultural dynamics that constructed the double bind between femininity and competence centuries ago retains rhetorical force. Morson notes that the job of the parodist is to "reveal the otherwise covert aspects" of the situation being parodied, "including the unstated motives and assumptions of both the speaker and the assumed and presumably sympathetic audience."[25] In this case, the audience is "sympathetic" to the view that, despite her competence and dogged determination, Clinton is ultimately annoying. Her presence disrupts the more idealized version of republican leadership into which Obama, because of his masculinity, fits more neatly. It should be noted at this juncture that because parodic texts are inherently complex and contradictory, they are also polyvalent. Different audiences may laugh at the same joke for very different reasons. Our analysis suggests, however, that the bulk of *SNL*'s 2007–8 presidential parodies skewered women leaders rather than the cultural forces that constrain them. Women, or more precisely, women as leaders, were the parodic targets. The jokes did not reveal sexism; they relied on sexism for their comic effect. In this respect, the humor was particularly postfeminist. Audiences were liberated by a postfeminist assumption that sexism is no longer dangerous to women. If sexism is inconsequential, humor based on sexism may be treated as similarly inconsequential. Anyone who points out the latent sexism informing the joke is positioned as an overreactor—an old-school "angry feminist" who cannot adjust to a postmodern environment of parodic play. Once feminism is made the scapegoat for women's frustrations, postfeminism becomes the vehicle that ushers in increasingly misogynistic humor *even as* it denies the existence of misogyny. This postfeminist parodic modus operandi is most clearly visible when compared to the ways in which *SNL* addressed race/racism in parodic discourses related to Obama.

During the February 23, 2008, episode of *SNL,* former cast member Tina Fey appeared on the "Weekend Update" segment—a long-standing *SNL* sketch that parodies broadcast news. Although Fey's appearance preceded her more widely publicized stint as Sarah Palin during the general election campaign, it still caused a stir. The *Boston Globe* characterized Fey's appearance as a "thinly veiled exhortation to young women to quit Obama and get with the Hillary bandwagon."[26] The spot also illustrates how tricky it is to challenge the double bind between femininity and competence while maintaining a parodic performance that will be positively received by a mass audience.

In the "Weekend Update" segment, Fey was billed as a "special women's news correspondent." After poking fun at a variety of current events stories involving gender, Fey turned to a discussion of Clinton's primary battle with Obama: "And, finally, the most important women's news item there is—we have our first serious female presidential candidate in Hillary Clinton. [*audience applause*] And, yes, women have come so far as feminists that they don't feel obligated to vote for a candidate just because she's a woman. Women today feel perfectly free to make whatever choice Oprah tells them to [*picture of Obama with Oprah Winfrey flashes on screen*]."[27]

After taking a jab at Obama's female supporters, Fey invokes the stereotype that married women politicians are pawns of their spouses—or at least that Bill Clinton would inevitably overshadow his wife: "Which raises the question, why are people abandoning Hillary for Obama? Some say that they are put off by the fact that Hillary can't control her husband and that we would end up with co-presidents. 'Cause that would be terrible—having two intelligent, qualified people working together to solve problems, yuck."

Fey's next joke played on the rumor that the Clinton marriage is a political, rather than personal, arrangement designed to foster each partner's professional goals. That conception of the Clinton marriage is bolstered by the image of Hillary as an unnatural woman incapable of meeting her husband's sexual needs: "You know, what's it, America? What it is? Are you weirded out that they are married? Because I can promise you that they are having exactly as much sex with each other as George Bush and Jeb Bush are."

The portion of the sketch that got the most attention in subsequent media accounts addressed the question of Clinton's public persona directly:

FEY. Maybe what bothers me the most is that people say that Hillary is a bitch. And let me say something about that. Yeah. She is [*smiling*]. And so am I. And so is this one [*camera shot widens as Fey points to Poehler*].
POEHLER. [*smiling*] Yeah. Deal with it.
FEY. You know what? Bitches get stuff done. That's why Catholic schools use nuns as teachers and not priests. Those nuns are mean old clams and they sleep on cots and they're allowed to hit you. And at the end of the school year you hated those bitches, but you knew the capital of Vermont. So I'm saying it's not too late, Texas and Ohio! Get on board! Bitch is the new black!

Embracing a negative term and imbuing it with a more positive connotation is one strategy of resistance that has yielded positive results for some groups. The LGBTQ community's revisioning of words such as *gay* and *queer* is perhaps the most widely accepted example. Some feminists have advocated a similar strategy for the word *bitch*, but research has documented the ways in which that can be a problematic strategy for women in electoral politics.[28] Even if people accept that "bitches get stuff done," the term still posits women's power as unpleasant, unnatural, and potentially threatening. Our discussion in the preceding chapters illustrates the ways in which Clinton was disciplined by media commentators and some voters throughout her presidential bid—not for her policy stances but for her gender identity. Having said that, however, the tone of Fey's monologue did critique sexist assumptions while simultaneously reinforcing them. The parody reified sexism because the joke stemmed from cultural resonance with stereotypes about women's power. Absent that recognition there would be no laughter. It also, however, challenged sexism by suggesting that bitches can be appealing—as Fey and Poehler are—and that a bitch might also make a capable president. It was this narrative that *SNL* picked up on explicitly in the "Democratic Debate #2" sketch one week later, when Poehler's Clinton promised to wear down the special interests with her sheer unpleasantness. A *Boston Globe* article included a quoted comment that summarized the impact of the *SNL* debate parodies as follows: "'In less than a minute, the *SNL* skit crystallized Hillary's complaints [about unfair media treatment] and upgraded them from media inside baseball to the conventional wisdom,' said Matthew Felling, former media analyst for CBS.com."[29]

Media accounts credited Fey, Poehler, and *SNL* with bolstering Clinton's performance in the polls. Reporting on March 5, 2008, the *New York Times*'s Katharine Q. Seelye attributed a tonal shift in the Democratic primary contest to *SNL*'s parodies that "mocked the news media for treating Mr. Obama more gently than it treated Mrs. Clinton. Mrs. Clinton amplified that view later in a debate, and her aides stoked it all week, practically browbeating reporters. Now comes evidence that the publicizing by the Clinton campaign and the news media may have helped flip the coverage as it questioned Mr. Obama more aggressively."[30]

Interestingly, that same article replicates the portrayal of Clinton as an aggressive leader (aided by browbeaters, no less) quoting a study published by the Pew Research Center that stated, "With the Clinton media narrative focused on her being a candidate *firmly in combat mode*, she enjoyed a respite from recent coverage that had focused on her post–Super Tuesday losing streak and her campaign's strategic shortcomings" [emphasis added].[31] In other words, the "bitch" is back.

Perhaps because Fey's "Weekend Update" monologue was so successful as both partisan strategy and parodic entertainment, *SNL* revived the bit several weeks later, this time giving former cast member Tracy Morgan (also Fey's costar on the successful NBC series *30 Rock*) the opportunity to both stump for Barack Obama and offer a rebuttal to Fey's contention that "bitch is the new black."[32] Unlike the comedy that dominated *SNL*'s Obama parodies, Morgan's monologue was explicitly focused on race. "Weekend Update" cohost Seth Meyers explained that Morgan was invited to comment after a much-publicized statement made by former vice presidential candidate Geraldine Ferraro:

MEYERS. This week the issue of race once again became the focal point for the Democratic presidential candidates. Hillary Clinton's longtime advisor Geraldine Ferraro said, "If Barack Obama was a white man he would not be in this position, and if he was a woman he would not be in this position. He happens to be very lucky to be who he is." Here to comment, an old friend of ours, Tracy Morgan.

MORGAN. Thank you, Seth. [*shaking his head*] Mm, mm, mm, why is it that every time a black man in this country gets too good at something there's always someone to come around and remind us that he's black. First Tiger, then Donovan McNabb, then me! Now Barack. I got a theory about that. It's a little complicated but it basically goes like this: We are a racist country. The end. [*audience laughter*] Maybe not the people in this room, but . . .

After excusing the *SNL* audience from their connection to racism in the United States, Morgan plays on stereotypes about black masculinity for comic effect, referring to a successful political commercial aired by the Clinton campaign entitled "3 A.M. Phone Call."[33] That campaign ad suggested voters would want her experience in times of crisis: "But if we're not a racist country, how did Hillary convince everybody in Texas and Ohio that Barack didn't know how to answer the phone at three in the morning? Let me tell you something, Barack knows how to answer that phone. He's not going to answer it like, 'Hello [*voice high, feminized*], I'm scared, what's going on?' He's gonna answer it like I would get a phone call at three in the morning 'Yeah, who's this? [*voice lower, aggressive*] This better be good or I'm gonna come down there and put somebody in a wheelchair.'"

Next, Morgan's monologue continues to link Obama's persona to stereotypical and dangerous versions of black identity: "People are saying he's not a fighter. Let me tell you something. He's a gangster. He's from Chicago!"

Since parody's comic effect relies on recognition of common tropes and stories, Morgan, like Fey, chooses to reinforce certain stereotypes. Interestingly, however, whereas Fey identified herself and Hillary as fellow "bitches," Morgan reinforces stereotypes about black identity while *exempting* Obama from those that would be most damaging to his presidential persona: "Barack is not just winning because he's a black man. If that was the case, I would be winning and I'm way blacker than him! I used to smoke Newports and drink Old English. I grew up on government cheese. I prefer it!"

Morgan then took on Clinton's qualifications, suggesting that her marriage to Bill Clinton was the only qualification she possessed: "Barack is qualified. Personally, I want to know what qualifies Hillary Clinton to be the next president. Is it because she was married to the president? If that were the case then Robin Givens would be the heavyweight champion of the world [*extended audience laughter*]!"

With that joke, Morgan echoed a claim made by Chris Matthews several months earlier: that Clinton's political achievements should be credited to her marital affiliations. Dismissing her performance in the New Hampshire Democratic primary, Matthews stated, "The reason she's a US senator, the reason she's a candidate for president, the reason she may be a front-runner is her husband messed around."[34] Thus, a postfeminist performance made an antifeminist attack palatable.

Morgan's narrative also invoked the same stereotype about the Clinton marriage that Fey raised, with a notably antifeminist conclusion: "If Hillary's last name wasn't Clinton she'd be some crazy white lady with too much money and not enough lovin.' That's where I come in. I know women like that and you do NOT want them on the phone at three in the morning!"

Morgan closed with an explicit reference to Fey's monologue: "In conclusion, three weeks ago my girl, Tina Fey, she came on the show and she declared that 'bitch is the new black.' And you know I love you, Tina. You know you're my girl. But I have something to say: bitch may be the new black, but black is the new president, bitch [*extended audience cheering and applause*]."

Morgan's material performance of the closing line is especially important to understand. Throughout most of the monologue, Morgan exhibited the good-natured obtuseness that is a characteristic of his comic persona. When uttering the last line, however, he dropped his parodic style, looked straight at the camera, and gravely announced, "Black is the new president, bitch." Whereas Fey's "bitch is the new black" invoked a phrase from the fashion world (where "the new black" is not a racial identifier but refers instead to whatever is in style), Morgan's usage both identified "black" with race and used "bitch" as a slur—the inflection was the same as that used when the term is invoked in hip hop culture.

In their "Weekend Update" segments, Fey and Morgan spoke from positions that, paradoxically, were both privileged and powerless. As successful stars coming back to the series that launched their careers, they inhabited a position of privilege. They employed their privilege to articulate what appeared to be personally held political convictions. Yet, they also spoke as members of groups that possess less power in US political culture than do white men. Fey's strategy accepted the stigmas applied to women in politics but sought to transform them. Morgan similarly invoked negative stereotypes about black masculinity but exempted Obama from those that were most damaging. Both monologues starkly illustrate the ways in which power and assertiveness get coded as positive qualities for male politicians and as liabilities for female politicians.

The last two examples of parodied presidentiality taken from the *SNL* spoofs of the 2008 campaign season provide additional illustration of the ways in which parody is not an "equal opportunity" offender. Linda Hutcheon points out that modern parody can have a broad "range of intent—from the ironic and playful to the scornful and ridiculing" and that although parody always imitates through "ironic inversion," the imitation is not always performed "at the expense of the parodied text."[35] Morson makes an important distinction between "shallow" and "deep" parodies, suggesting that "shallow parody is sometimes used to pay an author [subject/target] an indirect compliment. The opposite of damning with faint praise, this parody with faint criticism may be designed to show that no more fundamental criticism *could* be made" [emphasis in original]. Conversely, deep parody is directed at "fundamental faults of the original."[36] The depiction of Obama in the "Halloween Party" sketch discussed earlier in this chapter is an excellent example of "shallow" parody, insofar as Obama's character, unlike those of all the other candidates portrayed in the sketch, was spared critique. If anything, the sketch suggested, Obama was too authentic, too polite, and too generous. That same sketch contained "deep" parody of Clinton, whose status as a "witch" represented the antifeminist parodic critique of her "fundamental faults."

The 2007 "Halloween Party" sketch is not the only example of *SNL*'s tendency to reserve "deep" parody for Clinton and other targets such as journalistic media and to subject Obama to largely complimentary "shallow" parody. After Obama won the general election, *SNL* aired a sketch called "Obama Plays It Cool" and starring Armisen's Obama.[37] The skit came closer than the others described in this chapter to associating Obama with stereotypes connected to his ethnicity; however, the stereotypes had positive connotations. Obama enters a darkened stage and sits on a single chair—the set evokes the atmosphere of a jazz club. Dressed in a suit and tie, with light jazz playing in the background, Obama explains that he will be a good president because of his ability to "keep it cool": "Hello. I'm Barack Obama. The past few weeks my transition team and I have been in Chicago laying the groundwork for my presidency. One thing has become clear. No matter the circumstances, I am going to keep it cool."

Obama's first example to support *SNL*'s contention that "Barack is one cool cat" addresses Hillary Clinton specifically.[38] Armisen's Obama says, "Let's take Hillary Clinton. You remember her? She ran against me in the Democratic primary. Told superdelegates I couldn't win in a general election. Hey, she brought up William Ayers before anyone. Did I exact political revenge? Nope. I brought her in. Why? Because I keep it cool."

Taking personal credit for his primary opponent's move to support him during the general election (a standard expectation of any politician), Armisen's Obama continues to laud his own coolness: "I take my kids to school. I don't lose my temper. It's my only rule. I keep it cool."

Interestingly, that riff explicitly displaces negative stereotypes about black masculinity, associating Obama with involved fatherhood and self-discipline. One reason for this approach may be that although racial and gender stereotypes are both widely recognizable, gender stereotypes can acceptably be played for laughs in ways that racial stereotypes cannot be. Although we certainly endorse any effort to challenge stereotypes of all kinds, it is instructive to consider the ways in which *SNL* gingerly avoided linking Obama to the negative stereotypes associated with black masculinity even as they repeatedly portrayed Clinton's gender in a negative light.

Take, for example, a sketch that appeared during the 2008 Democratic primary and spoofed Clinton's "3 A.M. Phone Call" ad. Again starring Poehler in the Hillary Clinton role, the sketch parodies the ad directly, preceding the ad with the obligatory candidate statement, which casts Clinton in a negative (though not particularly gendered) light. A smiling Clinton states, "I'm Hillary Clinton, and I approved this unfair and deceptive message."[39] The ad depicts images of sleeping Americans that resemble the images in the real "3 A.M. Phone Call" ad. The *SNL* version, however, features a long telephone conversation between a calm and confident Clinton and a panicked Obama, paralyzed by a nuclear crisis involving North Korea. The sketch's parody engages in both a partisan and a gendered critique. The script lambastes the real Clinton's contention that Obama's lack of experience would be a detriment in the case of a national emergency. The *SNL* sketch portrays an overly naïve and emotional Obama reacting in ways not consistent with the actual Obama's public persona at the time. This suggests that the premise of the actual "3 A.M. Phone Call" ad is patently ridiculous. Interestingly, part of the reason the ad is so easy to parody is that the stereotype of an illogical, irrational, overly emotional leader is at odds with Obama's gender. Thus, the parody is funny because as it invokes Clinton's ad it reifies the notion that Obama is calm and rational—thus Clinton's portrayal of him becomes ridiculous. Conversely, the gendered parody of Clinton emerges immediately in the sketch's visuals. The images that accompany the conversation are black-and-white stills of Obama and Clinton. Obama is calling from the Oval Office, dressed in a suit. Clinton is answering the telephone from her bedroom, looking ridiculous with curlers, face cream, and a dowdy nightgown. The "expertise" she demonstrates is completely routine knowledge that everyone would know. Finally, as in the other skits involving Clinton, *SNL* includes a jab at the Clinton marriage. When Obama asks if Bill is there, an exasperated Hillary responds, "It's 3:00 A.M., what do you think?" The *SNL* sketch, then, reinforces the narrative that Obama is a credible presidential figure and

Clinton is a self-important, cynical politician who could not hang on to her husband.

When Play Is Punishment

Jeffrey P. Jones notes that when citizens engage politics in mediated contexts their encounters are "often related to pedestrian pursuits of pleasure, distraction, curiosity, community, sociability, and even happenstance."[40] Indeed, much of what makes parody pleasurable is its rootedness in laughter and play. Modern conceptions of culture distinguish the "political-normative" realm from the "aesthetic-expressive" realm, placing "art and affect, pleasure and play" squarely within the aesthetic sphere.[41] Postmodern perspectives on culture, however, challenge this dichotomy, in part because of the proliferation of texts like *SNL*, a program that fits Geoffrey Baym's formulation of a "televisual spectacle created for the public screen that crisscrosses the boundaries between the political-normative and the aesthetic-expressive." Baym suggests that we are living in an "age of aestheticized politics" where parodic texts treat "politics as play."[42] As noted earlier in this chapter, however, that does not minimize the significance of politics or its many parodies. One potential advantage of parodic form is the way in which it "creates a virtual world in which one may play with what has been said and so think about it without direct consequences of reprimand, censorship, or punishment."[43]

The rub comes when the parody itself turns from play to punishment. Our analysis of *SNL* parodies during the 2008 presidential campaign season illustrates the ways in which presidential parodies often reinforce the sexist narratives they ostensibly set out to critique. Functionally, they allow antifeminist attacks to be sublimated within postfeminist parodic form. Hariman accounts for the potentially deleterious effects of political parody by acknowledging that "good jokes are better than bad jokes, and fine wit is better than contrived gags, and satire on behalf of social justice is better than humor used to enforce hierarchies of domination. But it's a package deal. To take humor seriously, one has to be prepared to step outside the norms of deliberation, civility, and good taste."[44] We take humor seriously in this chapter not because we are sidestepping deliberative norms but because careful analysis of humor reveals the beliefs, attitudes, and values that shape those same norms.

Our analysis of humor in this chapter focuses attention on the sexism inherent in parodies of Hillary Clinton, sexism with which she was expected to "play along." Humorous portrayals of Barack Obama, on the other hand, presented him as above the fray, too genuine or generous, and outside the stereotypes of black masculinity parodied. Viewers were asked to participate with their laughter in popular culture's fortification of gender stereotypes and the femininity/ competence double bind, without questioning the larger implications for doing so. Is a woman president really so funny? In this instance, laughter is not a tool of resistance but a sign of complicity.

Throughout this book we have detailed case after case, and each demonstrates the ways in which the masculine norms of presidentiality are rigidly performed and reinforced to the detriment of female political candidates, whether in the oratory of the candidates themselves or the punditry of political journalists, in everything from televisual representations to comedic play. In the concluding chapter, we reflect on the ways in which postfeminism has become a Trojan horse, smuggling antifeminist backlash into postmodern political culture.

Conclusion

Our Candidates, Ourselves

When author and *New York Times* columnist Jodi Kantor was promoting her book about the Obama marriage, she recounted the following anecdote to Terry Gross, host of the National Public Radio interview program *Fresh Air*. According to Kantor, when Barack Obama was considering whether or not to make a bid for the US presidency, his wife, Michelle, "in front of everybody, asks her husband a very dramatic question. She says, 'What do you think you can bring to this that the other candidates can't?'" Kantor continued, saying that "it was a good question because at that point, John Edwards's agenda and Hillary Clinton's agenda looked pretty similar to a Barack Obama agenda. And [Obama] paused, and he said, 'I really think that if I became president, it would inspire people all over the world to think of new possibilities.'"[1]

Indeed, the widespread appeal Obama had in the popular and political culture of 2008 is attributable, in part, to the ways in which his candidacy disrupted the hegemonic subject's ultimate signifier: the US presidency. If presidential whiteness could be displaced, what other "new possibilities" would be available to members of postmodern polities? Unfortunately, as our analysis makes clear, Obama's candidacy did nothing to challenge the more intransigent hegemonic masculinity of US presidentiality. Instead, the 2008 presidential contest became a site where normative presidentiality was reinforced—time and time again—in campaign oratory, news framing and punditry, and popular culture. We recount Kantor's anecdote here because it typifies the ways in which many people either overlook or discipline the transgressive and inspirational potential of female presidential candidates. Even with Hillary Clinton as a presumptive presidential contender, Obama deemed his candidacy unique in its potential to inspire "new possibilities." When Clinton eventually lost the Democratic nomination to Obama, it was more than a failed campaign. It was a repudiation—both of female presidentiality and of the second-wave feminism that Clinton relied on for the opportunity to be treated equally, that she employed in her rhetorical strategy, and that she came to represent in the broader political culture. Our examination of Clinton's and Palin's candidacies illustrates the ways in which their rhetorical choices reveal more about "us" (the American people) than they do about them (the candidates). The 2008 campaign also is important because it marks a key moment when postfeminism shifted from being the fruit of the culture of depoliticization to a seed germinating political grass roots.

We conclude our book by reflecting on the failed presidential/vice presidential bids of Hillary Clinton and Sarah Palin, arguing that although pundits point out specific missteps made by each campaign, too little attention has been paid to the broader cultural milieu that has constrained women presidential candidates for more than one hundred years. That cultural context not only affects women candidates but also constructs women as voters, citizens, and leaders more broadly. We herald the concrete gains women have made in politics: sitting as justices on the Supreme Court, rising to the position of Speaker of the House, serving as US secretaries of state, secretary of homeland security, and attorneys general. And we do not wish to diminish the poll results that contend that most Americans claim they are ready to vote for a qualified woman presidential candidate.[2] Yet, our study demonstrates that despite these gains, there remains a deep cultural resistance to women wielding presidential power. In fact, we argue that the very gains women have made in the political realm have spurred a cultural backlash not unlike the one that followed the push for gender equity in the 1960s and 1970s. By examining gender and US presidential culture, we can more fully understand women's political agency, generational political action, and the evolution of feminist politics in the twenty-first century.

The central claim of this book is that the hegemonic masculinity of the US presidency retains significant rhetorical force in the twenty-first century because it is so uniformly and thoroughly constituted by rhetorics of presidentiality. Antifeminist stereotypes are made more palatable by postfeminist narratives that herald women candidates' equality even as they contain female presidentiality. To be sure, Barack Obama's election should not be taken as evidence that we live in a postracial age any more than Clinton's and Palin's candidacies prove we live in a postfeminist age. Yet, Obama's performance of presidentiality thus far has allowed him to inhabit both a transformative multiracial *and* a normative presidential space. The US presidency as a rhetorical performance, synecdochical symbol, and normative paradigm disciplines our cultural imagination such that we have, to date, neither unmasked nor overcome that which privileges above all else the masculinity of the office. This book offers one step in that direction. Our purpose, however, is not to produce more reliable predictions about when a woman will be elected US president or what rhetorical characteristics she will possess. Rather, we contribute our insights to the larger project of transforming the ideology of presidentiality in US culture, for only when we can credibly and consistently *imagine* women as presidents will we be poised to elect them as such.

Unmasking the Norms of Presidential Culture

Our introduction to this book begins the process of demystifying presidentiality as a rhetorical performance that has been constituted over time such that the paradigmatic American president exemplifies white heterosexual masculinity. The ideal democratic citizen and national patriarch, the US president historically has relied on a cast of supporting characters to complement and reinforce his performance. Chief among them are a traditionally feminine spouse and an appropriately deferential vice president. When women attempt to enter the fray as something other than supportive spouse or submissive vice president, their presence challenges cultural and political norms. The ensuing cultural cognitive dissonance is assuaged by disciplining political women for their transgressions. This disciplining occurs in a variety of political and cultural spheres—this book has observed the battle over presidentiality that has been waged in fictionalized and parodic representations of presidentiality, political oratory, campaign journalism, and popular culture.

In chapter 1 we introduce the reader to eleven women prior to Hillary Clinton who launched bids for the US presidency, noting the ways in which their campaigns were characterized as pioneering and examining the extent to which each candidate embraced the pioneer metaphor. When Theodore Roosevelt envisioned a resurgence in American exceptionalism spurred by citizens' renewed dedication to the "'strenuous life' of their ancestors on the frontier," both women and men were included, but they were given distinct and complementary roles. Leroy G. Dorsey explains that Roosevelt declared in a speech entitled "The Strenuous Life" "that the 'woman must be the housewife' and 'the wise and fearless mother of many healthy children,'" while men should not shirk their duties by "fearing to work or to wage 'righteous war.'"[3] When women presidential candidates attempt to capitalize on the imagery of the frontier, they are positioned as cowgirls—rugged and strong but still the helpmates and partners of the presidential cowboys. When the pioneer frame is ascribed to political women, their difference from archetypal presidentiality, rather than fidelity to that narrative, is underscored. Female presidential candidates are unruly, radical, and (ultimately) symbolic pioneers in name only.

Evaluation of a vice presidential pioneer such as Sarah Palin reveals the inherent conservativeness of the metaphor. A postmodern inhabitant of the Alaskan frontier, Palin responds to Theodore Roosevelt's call for women to live the "strenuous life" by "embracing their natural roles as mothers and bearing many healthy children."[4] She is a beauty pageant winner, wife and mother of five, and a self-described "hockey mom" whose political ambition stemmed from her desire to improve schools for her children. Palin's justifications for women's public involvement also invoke the "Christian feminism" of the Women's Christian Temperance Union (WCTU), whose nineteenth-century members "believed that through Christianity, their 'status' would be 'elevated' and they would become more socially aware and proud of their womanhood."[5] By coding her political motivations as primarily maternal and spiritual, Palin fails to challenge the central tenets of presidentiality. Her status as a vice presidential figure makes her rhetorical choices strategically sound, since the vice presidency has, itself, been a historically feminized role.

As Carmen Heider's research on discourse produced by the Nebraska WCTU in 1879–82 reveals, however, even conservative justifications of women's political agency have the potential to be radicalized. Her analysis suggests that when "activists situated arguments for self-determined womanhood within the frameworks of home protection and religion," they used conservative arguments to "make radical demands."[6] In chapter 3, we examine the campaign oratory of Sarah Palin and Hillary Clinton. Speaking from the intimate space of a living room and choosing to define her campaign with a "conversation" metaphor, Clinton's announcement speech was informed by second-wave feminism's emphasis on consciousness-raising rhetoric. Her attempt to create an alternative face of presidentiality was disciplined, however, by political pundits, journalistic frames, pop culture depictions, and satirical send-ups. Palin's oratory, on the other hand, was infused with norms of post-feminism, through which she presented herself first as a supportive running "mate" and later as an independent co-president.

In chapter 2, we assess another location where the hegemonic white masculinity of US presidentiality is reinforced: television and film. Mary Douglas Vavrus argues that "news texts about political women in the 1990s act as 'technologies of gender' by privileging a particular perspective on women and power while overlooking others. These stories overlap and enhance one another at times, and at times they are contradictory, but by publicly commenting on women's relationships to power, they always suggest what is and what is not appropriate for women."[7] Our analysis reveals the ways in which films and television series can, similarly, function as "technologies of gender." Even in films and television series that feature female presidential figures in leading roles, their presence is marked as somehow exceptional in both senses of the word—they are "exceptional" in terms of their skills and abilities since, propositionally, the images of fictionalized presidency discussed in chapter 2 argue that women are as qualified as men to be president. Yet the fictionalized presidential figures are also the "exceptions" that prove the rule true that presidents should be male; suppositionally, the films and television series argue that presidentiality itself is masculine, militaristic, and patriarchal. Further, the women presidential figures examined in chapter 2 highlight the ways in which women, even fictionalized women presidents, are cast as primarily sexual, maternal, and humanitarian and are, therefore, ill suited to the demands of presidentiality.

The study of fictional presidentiality reveals cultural biases and assumptions germane to the rhetorical situations encompassing real presidential candidates. First, women may serve in positions of power if called upon to do so, but they should not seek them out. *Commander in Chief*'s Mackenzie Allen and *Battlestar Galactica*'s Laura Roslin accede to the presidency as a result of calamity, and both are cast as disinterested in executive power. *The Contender*'s Laine Hanson also is tapped by a sitting president to serve as vice president, and her confirmation is coded as his political victory. The presidential status of Kathryn Bennett in *Air Force One* is never fully realized since the true commander in chief maintains control of the situation even though he is a prisoner of his own hijacked airplane. Only two fictional presidents—Leslie McCloud in *Kisses for My President* and *24*'s Allison Taylor—are elected to the office of US president, and they are each relieved of duty by their respective narrative's conclusion. In the real world, a candidate like Palin, who responds to the call of her prospective president and exhibits a willingness to serve her country, is more palatable than a figure like Clinton, who actively seeks the Oval Office. When Clinton's political strength is undermined by media frames that position her as cold, calculating, and conniving, those narratives resonate with fictional portrayals of failed female presidentiality.

A second component of the presidential rhetorical situation revealed in fictional depictions of presidentiality is the continued salience of traditional gender norms in factual and fictional presidential narratives. Even in fantastical contexts, like the *Battlestar Galactica* universe, women presidents confirm, rather than challenge, stereotypes about femininity, relationships, and gender norms. Laura Roslin and William Adama are the yin/yang of leadership—with feminine leadership qualities assigned to Roslin and masculine characteristics assigned to Adama. The futuristic sci-fi rendition of presidentiality ends as a conventional tragic romance. Similarly, consider the ways in which a series such as *24* constituted diverse presidentiality. Whereas the African American David Palmer (the presidential hero from *24*'s initial seasons) was a quintessentially ideal presidential figure—strong, resolute, a person of character and conviction—the female president, Allison Taylor, became a cautionary tale about gendered presidentiality. Each of her stereotypically feminine traits quickly became a liability, the damage from which was mitigated only by the perpetually heroic masculinity of Jack Bauer.

Fictional presidentiality, then, both constitutes and reflects the norms of actual presidential culture. So, too, does journalism and punditry. In chapter 4, we demonstrate that many of the stereotypes of gendered presidentiality present in fictionalized depictions also populate mainstream political journalism and punditry. Hillary Clinton, like the fictional Allison Taylor inspired by Clinton's prospective candidacy, was judged to be cynically ambitious and then disciplined for being cold, calculating, and conniving. Clinton's ambition was framed as not only inappropriate but dangerous. The conclusion of the narrative spun in journalistic and pop cultural spheres suggested that this "dangerous" candidate deserved to be punished, and punished she was. Not only was her candidacy destroyed but her public image was symbolically annihilated time and again. In chapter 6, we detail the ways in which Clinton was obligated to smile and play along with parodic sketches that exaggerated her unpalatability as a presidential figure. More problematic was the pornification of political identities discussed in chapter 5, in which our analysis illustrates the ways in which powerful political women are bound and gagged into submission.

When unmasked, the norms of presidential culture are unsurprisingly consistent, but the culture that surrounds presidentiality is perpetually in flux. Our examination of gendered presidentiality speaks not only to the constraints facing women presidential candidates and the cultural discourses that constitute them; as we contend in the introduction of this book, our analysis also reveals the ways in which misogyny is being repurposed for public consumption—a task made even easier by the postmodern media environment and the postfeminist cultural mood.

A Twenty-First-Century Backlash

Each of the case studies from the 2008 presidential election season presented in this book illustrates the resurgence of a backlash against women's political power at the historical moment when women are, once again, making significant political gains. As Susan Faludi observed in 1991, "A backlash against women's rights is nothing new in American history. Indeed, it's a recurring phenomenon: it returns every time women begin to make some headway toward equality, a seemingly inevitable early frost to the culture's brief flowering of feminism." Faludi likened the progress of American women through history to "a corkscrew tilted slightly to one side, its loops inching closer to the line of freedom with the passage of time . . . [an] asymptotic spiral, turning endlessly through the generations, drawing ever nearer to her destination without ever arriving."[8] Perhaps it is no wonder, then, that in 2008 American women felt another turn of the screw.

This time, however, the backlash is informed by postfeminism, a cultural moment and political mode that followed both the second wave of feminism and the ensuing backlash of the 1980s. Angela McRobbie posits that Faludi's work charted "anti-feminist interventions that are coterminous with feminism more or less as it happens." By contrast, McRobbie argues that "post-feminism positively draws on and invokes feminism as that which can be taken into account, to suggest that equality is achieved, in order to install a whole repertoire of new meanings which emphasise [*sic*] that it is no longer needed, it is a spent force."[9] Similarly, Mary Douglas Vavrus explains that "postfeminists claim that women have made gains because of feminism, but these gains have been exhausted for all intents and purposes; they take for granted rights that first- and second-wave feminists fought for . . . but simultaneously argue that feminism actually harms women, overall, because it gives women unrealistic expectations."[10] Bonnie J. Dow concurs, contending that "postfeminism represents . . . a hegemonic negotiation of second-wave ideals, in which the presumption of equality for women in the public sphere has been retained. . . . At the same time, the most radical aspects of feminism, those centered in sexual politics and a profound awareness of power differences between the sexes at all levels and in all arenas, have been discarded as irrelevant or threatening."[11] In addition to rejecting feminism's collective radicalism, postfeminism "encourages women's private, consumer lifestyles rather than cultivating a desire for public life and political activism."[12] For that reason, postfeminism is sometimes regarded as apolitical; however, it should be understood instead as a highly political ideology—one that, like any ideology, privileges certain political interests and sublimates others.

Susan J. Douglas prefers the term *enlightened sexism* to *postfeminism*, in part because the term *postfeminist* "suggests that somehow feminism is at the root of this when it isn't—it's good, old-fashioned, grade-A sexism that reinforces good, old-fashioned, grade-A patriarchy." Douglas's definition of "enlightened sexism" is worth repeating in its extended form, because although her definition applies to culture, writ large, it highlights many of the dynamics specifically in play during the 2008 presidential campaign. Douglas states that "enlightened sexism is a manufacturing process that is produced, week in and week out, by the media. Its components—anxiety about female achievement; a renewed and amplified objectification of young women's bodies and faces; the dual exploitation and punishment of female sexuality; the dividing of women against each other by age, race, and class; rampant branding and consumerism—began to swirl around in the early 1990s, consolidating as the dark star it has become in the early twenty-first century."[13]

In 2007–8, the "enlightened sexism" of postfeminist political culture produced each and every dynamic that Douglas identified. The first component of enlightened sexism—anxiety about women's achievements—appeared after Clinton's assiduous organization and broad political experience produced one of the most stunning primary leads in modern political history. The cultural anxiety over Clinton's impending "coronation" as the Democratic presidential nominee triggered a backlash that turned attention to trivialities (cleavage and cackles), diminished Clinton's presidential gravitas (crying), and shrouded her in suspicion (conniving). The second feature of this new sexism is a renewed and amplified objectification of young women's bodies and faces, and the pornification of Clinton's and Obama's presidential bodies was aided by the commodification of "Obama Girl" and the "Hott 4 Hill" girl, who gained entrée into mainstream political news stories and talk shows, further amplifying their objectification. Nothing illustrates the paradoxical third dynamic of dual exploitation and punishment of female sexuality more clearly than the modalities by which Palin and Clinton were pornified. Palin's sexuality was exploited, by her own actions and by the McCain campaign, news organizations, her political opponents, pundits and parodists, and the public who lapped up these images. Clinton's sexuality, conversely, was punished as abnormal, threatening, excessive, and dangerous. The MILF/cunt dyad is the 2008 campaign shorthand for such "dual exploitation." The fourth dynamic, that of pitting women against each other by age, race, and class, could be seen when young women's failure to enthusiastically support Clinton over Obama was characterized as a betrayal of their mothers' second-wave feminist battles. At the same time, black women were asked to rank-order their loyalties to their race and gender. Later, when older women voters refused to see supporting Palin as a sign of feminist sisterhood, they were lambasted for betraying their convictions. Women's groups such as the National Organization for Women and the Feminist Majority Foundation were skewered in the media when they did not endorse the candidacy of Sarah Palin.[14] Leslie Sanchez asks, "Why didn't more prominent women's groups come to Sarah Palin's defense? Or, to put it more bluntly, why were some so set on her demise?"[15] Although arguments about what it means to be a feminist, and what the role of feminism is in contemporary politics, got lost in the fray, what registered in the public consciousness was another catfight—women battling with each other over who gets to represent a movement that, according to popular sentiment, was no longer needed.

Ironically, however, the discourse of the 2008 campaign proves that feminism, as a social and political movement, is still desperately needed. Faludi argues that in each backlash period "a 'crisis of masculinity' has erupted" in which is manifested a "ludicrous overreaction to women's modest progress."[16] The "ludicrous overreaction" to Clinton's progress disciplined her transgressions through violent metaphors, increasingly misogynistic media frames, patriarchal parodies, and pornification. The more real political power a woman gains, the more vicious the attacks must become in order to assert hegemonic control over her. But many of the discourses that framed Clinton's (and Palin's) campaigns were not viewed as misogynistic—many were seen as not even particularly problematic. Rather, they were consumed as entertainment, as spectacle, and as farce. In that respect, the 2008 presidential campaign functioned through what Eric King Watts and Mark P. Orbe have described as "operations of spectacular consumption."[17] In their assessment of racialized tropes in commercial images, Watts and Orbe assess a phenomenon in which the dominant white audience's ambivalence over anxiety about black culture collides with the market appeal of "authentic" black imagery, creating a media sensation. A similar dynamic occurred in the 2008 campaign. Consider, for example, Obama Girl's "I Got a Crush . . . on Obama" viral video. Watts and Orbe explain that the ads they studied conflate blackness with cultural authority, *even as* they reinstantiate hegemonic whiteness. Similarly, Obama Girl's viral video lauds a popular African American presidential candidate *even as* it replicates the stereotypical black hypermasculinity of hip hop culture. Watts and Orbe discuss spectacular consumption as it relates to race and popular culture. This study suggests the ways in which their insights also might be applied to gender and political culture. Recall our discussion in chapter 5 regarding the Obama Girl video and the clones it inspired. Taryn Southern's "Hott 4 Hill" invoked a "girl-on-girl" motif (a mainstay of mainstream pornography), locating the video squarely within dominant, heterosexual male fantasy *even as* it articulated tongue-in-cheek support for protofeminist candidate Clinton and her progressive political agenda—exemplifying the mechanics of spectacular consumption. Although "Hott 4 Hill" singer Southern never garnered Obama Girl Amber Lee Ettinger's level of fame, she was invited to appear with Chris Matthews on his show *Hardball*, along with Ettinger and Adolina Kristina, the short-lived "Giuliani Girl." After asking his interviewees whether they were registered to vote and inquiring about their political affiliation Matthews concluded that "with no insult intended to Pat Buchanan and the other people I usually have on this show, I would rather be with these people," making clear how much personal pleasure he derived from his spectacular consumption of both the women and their cultural productions.[18]

Discourses of postfeminism complicate critical assessment of both the popular culture and news commentary produced during the 2008 campaign. Ettinger, Southern, and Kristina—like Clinton and Palin—are independent women pursuing the professional path of their own choosing. They chose publicity—deciding whether to capitalize on their sexuality and/or their private relationships. Yet complicity in a sexist frame does not negate its sexism, and although candidates Clinton and Palin willingly stepped into the limelight, each clearly was subjected to a level of misogyny that exceeds the typical "rough and tumble" of the political sphere. However, because such misogynistic discourses are both dismissed as "humor" and glorified as "power feminism," their rhetorical force is often discounted, even by those who purport to study such discourses.

Perhaps that is why the political scientist Thomas L. Dumm breezily ignored both the formidable campaign waged by Clinton in the 2008 Democratic primary and her widespread political appeal, asserting instead that "Hillary Clinton has not been able to rise positively above the din of her own resentments to articulate a vision anywhere close to that offered by Obama." In that same paragraph, Dumm surmised that Clinton had "not been able to speak to gender as Obama has been able to speak to race," perhaps because of the pace of the campaign, the "artificiality of the projection of persona," or *"simply her constitutional inability to grow as a human being"* [emphasis added].[19] How quickly Dumm jumps from a reflection on the challenges entailed in speaking to issues of gender in US culture to a summary judgment about Clinton's abilities "as a human being." That is a leap that would have been out of reach except for the bridge built almost imperceptibly by the textual fragments compiled in this book—fragments that are like stones so smooth they barely cause a ripple when water trickles over them but strong enough when assembled to form a wall that can dam the very current of progress.

Despite the machinations of misogyny, however, women are progressing. One hopeful sign of women's continued insurgence against a patriarchal political power is the resurgence of the word *feminist* and the breadth of its use in the 2008 campaign. Reflecting on Palin's penchant to identify as a feminist (despite the loud objections of many feminists), Rebecca Traister has noted the ways in which "Palin's candidacy had empowered Republican women eager to claim their share of the feminist legacy." Young women, too, discovered a more robust version of feminism than their postfeminist culture had peddled. Traister notes that "for a long period during my adolescence and early adulthood it seemed that I would not live to hear the word *feminist* uttered in earnest by anyone my age or younger. Just a decade into the new century it was back, embraced in a manner that broadened its reach, relaxed the rules about how it might be deployed, extended it so far outward that, yes, it became imperiled again. But its return also meant that someday feminism's legacy would bear fruit with regard to the presidency, even if it's not so sweet as many of us might have hoped."[20]

The 2008 campaign was certainly "not so sweet" for the variety of reasons detailed in this book, most importantly the level of misogyny hurled against Clinton and Palin in ways that not only objectified but dehumanized them. Cheris Kramarae and Paula A. Treichler proposed that "feminism is the radical notion that women are people."[21] If feminists, women and men alike, continue to do feminism's work, perhaps the twenty-first century will be the time in which US voters accept the radical notion that women are also presidents.

Notes

Works included in the bibliography are cited here in shortened author/title format.

Introduction

1. Stacy Lambe and Adam Smith, "Texts from Hillary," Tumblr, April 4, 2012, http://texts fromhillaryclinton.tumblr.com/page/4.

2. Phoebe Connelly, "Texts from Hillary: Your New Favorite Political Tumblr," *Yahoo News,* April 5, 2012, http://abcnews.go.com/Politics/OTUS/texts-hillary-favorite-political -tumblr/story?id=16081728; Helen A. S. Popkin, "'Texts from Hillary' Tumblr Shows Clinton at Her Coolest," *Digital Life on Today,* April 6, 2012, http://digitallife.today.msnbc.msn.com /_news/2012/04/06/11055577-texts-from-hillary-tumblr-shows-clinton-at-her-coolest?lite; Megan Carpentier, "Texts from Hillary: Everyone Wants to Know What's behind Those Shades," *Guardian* (UK), April 12, 2012, http://www.guardian.co.uk/commentisfree/cifamerica /2012/apr/12/texts-from-hillary-clinton-tumblr; Howard Fineman, "The 'Clinton Party' Wins in Pennsylvania: Is 2016 Next?" *Huffington Post,* April 25, 2012, http://www.huffingtonpost .com/2012/04/25/hillary-clinton-president-2016-bill-clinton_n_1452182.html?1335369750. Also see Tim Mak, "Hillary Clinton 2016: Democrats' Top Choice, Poll Suggests," *Politico,* April 17, 2012, http://www.politico.com/news/stories/0412/75258.html.

3. For example, some critics emphasize the ways in which postfeminism depoliticized the feminist movement, encouraging "women's private, consumer lifestyles rather than cultivating a desire for public life and political activism." Vavrus, *Postfeminist News,* 2. Others describe postfeminism as a movement that "explores the possibilities afforded to women in the wake of feminist legal gains while at the same time reassert[ing] and renaturaliz[ing] what in the nineteenth century was framed as the separate spheres of gender." Gerhard, "*Sex and the City,*" 41. Gerhard's essay provides a helpful overview of the emergence of postfeminism in academia and popular culture in the 1980s and 1990s, explaining the ways in which it has been conceived alternately as a machination of antifeminism, a cultural mash-up of conflicting attitudes about feminism and femininity, and even as a poststructuralist and postcolonial critique of the gender binarism of second-wave feminism.

4. Steve Kornacki, "The Resurrection of Hillary Clinton," *Salon,* April 18, 2012, http://www .salon.com/2012/04/18/the_resurrection_of_hillary_clinton/; Benjy Sarlin, "Hillary Boomlet Hits New Gear as 'Texts from Hillary' Explodes," *Talking Points Memo,* April 9, 2012, http:// 2012.talkingpointsmemo.com/2012/04/the-hillary-clinton-boomlet-hits-high-gear.php.

5. Howard Kurtz, "How Hillary Clinton Got Hot after Years of Being Stuck with a Cold Image," *Daily Beast,* April 13, 2012, http://www.thedailybeast.com/articles/2012/04/13/how -hillary-clinton-got-hot-after-years-of-being-stuck-with-a-cold-image.html; Paul Begala, "Paul Begala on Hillary Clinton's Coming Run for the White House in 2016," *Daily Beast,*

April 14, 2012, http://www.thedailybeast.com/articles/2012/04/14/paul-begala-on-hillary-clinton-s-coming-run-for-the-white-house-in-2016.html.

6. Faludi, *Backlash*, xviii, xix.

7. Michael A. Memoli, "As Perry and Romney Spar, Michele Bachmann Fades," *Los Angeles Times*, September 7, 2011, http://articles.latimes.com/2011/sep/07/news/la-pn-michele-bachmann-debate-20110907; Jason Linkins, "The Spectacular Gullibility of Michele Bachmann," *Huffington Post*, updated May 25, 2011, http://www.huffingtonpost.com/2009/02/18/the-spectacular-gullibili_n_167954.html. The meme of Bachmann as a "crazy" presidential candidate quickly took off. See, for example, Tim Murphy, "Michele Bachmann: Crazy Like a Fox," *Mother Jones*, August 15, 2011, http://motherjones.com/politics/2011/08/michele-bachmann-iowa-frontrunner; Julian Brookes, "Taibbi on 'Batshit Crazy' Michele Bachmann," *Rolling Stone.com*, June 22, 2011, http://www.rollingstone.com/politics/blogs/national-affairs/matt-taibbi-on-batshit-crazy-michele-bachmann-20110622; and "The 10 Craziest Michele Bachmann Quotes," *BuzzFeed*, n.d., http://www.buzzfeed.com/mjs538/the-10-craziest-michele-bachmann-quotes (accessed December 30, 2011). *Slate* columnist Jessica Grose pinpointed several of the mainstream media stories that were used to frame Bachmann as "crazy," arguing that the frame was more readily applied to the woman in the Republican primary field even though male candidates such as Rick Perry made similarly outrageous statements and held nearly identical policy positions. See Jessica Grose, "Crazy vs. Stupid: Why Do the Media Treat Michele Bachmann and Rick Perry Differently?" *Slate*, September 27, 2011, http://www.slate.com/articles/double_x/doublex/2011/09/crazy_vs_stupid.html.

8. Karen Tumulty, "Michele Bachmann's Campaign Flameout," *Washington Post*, December 29, 2011, http://www.washingtonpost.com/politics/michele-bachmanns-campaign-flameout/2011/12/29/gIQAuydIPP_story.html.

9. Although some studies suggest that women candidates raise money as effectively as male candidates when other factors (such as incumbency and political experience) are comparable, women running for US president may still experience disparity in their ability to raise funds. See, for example, Seltzer, Newman, and Leighton, *Sex as a Political Variable*; and Whicker and Isaacs, "Maleness of the American Presidency," 221–32.

10. Whicker and Isaacs, "Maleness of the American Presidency." For a broader discussion of women's political recruitment in the United States and in other countries see, for example, Norris, ed., *Passages to Power*.

11. Jamieson, *Dirty Politics*; Cappella and Jamieson, *Spiral of Cynicism*; Rule, "Parliaments of, by, and for the People"; Amy, *Real Choices / New Voices*; Falk, *Women for President*; Carlin and Winfrey, "Have You Come a Long Way, Baby?"; Heldman, Carroll, and Olson, "'She Brought Only a Skirt'"; and Iyengar et al., "Running as a Woman."

12. See, for example, Edwards, ed., *Gender and Political Communication in America*; Anderson and Sheeler, *Governing Codes*; Marshall and Mayhead, eds., *Navigating Boundaries*; Anderson, "'Rhymes with Rich'"; Campbell, "Discursive Performance of Femininity"; Jamieson, *Beyond the Double Bind*; Anderson, "From Spouses to Candidates"; T. Parry-Giles and S. J. Parry-Giles, "*The West Wing*'s Prime-Time Presidentiality"; Kimmel, *Manhood in America*, 36–38; and Campbell, "Rhetorical Presidency."

13. McGee, "Text, Context, and the Fragmentation of Contemporary Culture," 274, 288.

14. Ibid., 287.

15. Dow and Condit, "State of the Art in Feminist Scholarship in Communication," 449.

16. "Matthews: '[S]ome Men' Say Sen. Clinton's Voice Sounds Like 'Fingernails on a Blackboard," *Media Matters for America*, November 8, 2006, http://mediamatters.org/mmtv/200908210041; "Buchanan: Clinton's Raised Voice Is One 'Every Husband in America . . . Has Heard at One Time or Another," *Media Matters for America*, February 26, 2008, http://mediamatters.org/research/200802260002; Amanda Fortini, "The Feminist Reawakening," *New York*, April 13, 2008, http://nymag.com/news/features/46011/; Amanda Fortini, "The Feminist

Reawakening: Hillary Clinton and the Fourth Wave," *New York,* April 13, 2008, http://nymag .com/news/features/46011/; Marie Cocco, "Misogyny I Won't Miss," *Washington Post,* May 15, 2008, A15, www.lexisnexis.com.

17. Carlin and Winfrey, "Have You Come a Long Way, Baby?," 330; Falk, *Women for President,* 1.

18. McRobbie, "Post-Feminism and Popular Culture," 255. For examples of the work that popularized postfeminism in the 1990s, see Sommers, *Who Stole Feminism?;* and Fox-Genovese, *Feminism Is Not the Story of My Life.*

19. See, for example, Dow, *Prime-Time Feminism;* Vavrus, "Putting Ally on Trial"; Dubrofsky, "Ally McBeal as Postfeminist Icon"; Gerhard, "*Sex and the City*"; Hammers, "Cautionary Tales of Liberation and Female Professionalism"; Tasker and Negra, eds., *Interrogating Postfeminism;* and Southard, "Beyond the Backlash."

20. Edwards, "Symbolic Womanhood and Sarah Palin"; McCarver, "Rhetoric of Choice and 21st-Century Feminism."

21. Sarah Palin, Address to the Susan B. Anthony List, May 14, 2010, http://www.viddler .com/explore/rightscoop/videos/31/.

22. The phrase "rhetorical presidency" was coined by James Ceaser, Glen Thurow, Jeffrey Tulis, and Joseph M. Bessette and originated as a derisive label for modern US presidential leadership. See Ceaser, Thurow, Tulis, and Bessette, "Rise of the Rhetorical Presidency." In his book-length expansion of the argument, Tulis contends that the presidencies of Theodore Roosevelt and Woodrow Wilson ushered in an era in which "popular or mass rhetoric [became] the principal tool of presidential governance." Tulis presents this development as an institutional change in the office of the presidency, one that was at odds with the president's role as conceived in the US Constitution because it prompted presidents to appeal directly to the electorate regarding matters of policy—a process that, according to Tulis, eventually facilitates presidential demagoguery. When Tulis laments the modern "rhetorical presidency," he is decrying what he understands to be a "twentieth-century invention" that "prescribed" rather than "proscribed" a president's use of popular, rhetorical appeals. Tulis, *Rhetorical Presidency,* 4–5. Responding to Tulis, Martin J. Medhurst explains that Tulis's work and other early studies on the rhetorical presidency subscribe to an institutional view, one that approaches the US presidency primarily as a "constitutional office" but gives short shrift to the import of rhetoric. Conversely, scholars in the field of Communication Studies take "rhetoric" as the "principal subject of investigation" so that "rhetoric is the subject matter and presidential rhetoric the specific arena of investigation." Medhurst, *Beyond the Rhetorical Presidency,* xiv. See also Kernell, *Going Public,* 4th ed. For additional explication of a robustly rhetorical view of rhetorical presidencies, see Ivie, "Tragic Fear and the Rhetorical Presidency," esp. 157–66; Dorsey, *Presidency and Rhetorical Leadership,* 3–19; and Stuckey, "Rethinking the Rhetorical Presidency and Presidential Rhetoric."

23. T. Parry-Giles and S. J. Parry-Giles, "*The West Wing's* Prime-Time Presidentiality," 209.

24. Lucas, "George Washington and the Rhetoric of Presidential Leadership," 60; Dorsey, *Presidency and Rhetorical Leadership,* 253.

25. Goffman, *Interaction Ritual;* Bitzer, "Rhetorical Situation"; Burke, *Grammar of Motives.*

26. Lancaster, "Performative Language Games of *Dramapolitik,*" 1044.

27. Ibid., 1045. Also see Barthes, *Mythologies.*

28. Lancaster, "Performative Language Games of *Dramapolitik,*" 1043.

29. For explication of the theory of constitutive rhetoric, see Charland, "Case of the *Peuple Québécois.*" For studies that explore the constitutive functions of the US presidency, see, for example, Campbell and Jamieson, *Presidents Creating the Presidency;* Murphy, "To Form a More Perfect Union"; Stuckey, *Defining Americans;* Beasley, *You, the People;* and Zarefsky, *President Johnson's War on Poverty.* Of course, constitutive performances sometimes fall short of their policy goals and at other times do not interpellate audiences according to the speaker's inten-

tion. See Carcasson, "Ending Welfare as We Know It"; and Zagacki, "Constitutive Rhetoric Reconsidered."

30. Ivie, "Tragic Fear and the Rhetorical Presidency," 162.

31. Campbell, "Rhetorical Presidency," 180–81.

32. Ibid., 180, 188.

33. T. Parry-Giles and S. J. Parry-Giles, *Prime-Time Presidency,* 2; Goodale, "Presidential Sound," 167; Lucas, "George Washington and the Rhetoric of Presidential Leadership," 60; Campbell and Jamieson, *Presidents Creating the Presidency,* 33; Zarefsky, "Presidency Has Always Been a Place for Rhetorical Leadership," 21; Darsey, "Barack Obama and America's Journey," 94.

34. Campbell, "Rhetorical Presidency," 188.

35. Caroli, *First Ladies,* 33–57.

36. Wertheimer, "First Ladies' Fundamental Rhetorical Choices," 3.

37. See, for example, Wertheimer, *Inventing a Voice;* Mayo and Meringolo, *First Ladies;* and Caroli, *First Ladies.*

38. Burns, "Collective Memory and the Candidates' Wives in the 2004 Presidential Campaign," 687.

39. Campbell and Jamieson, *Presidents Creating the Presidency,* 2.

40. Kathleen Parker, "Obama: Our First Female President," *Washington Post,* June 30, 2010, A17.

41. See, for example, Shome, "Outing Whiteness"; Stuckey, "Rethinking the Rhetorical Presidency and Presidential Rhetoric"; T. Parry-Giles and S. J. Parry-Giles, *Prime-Time Presidentiality;* Stuckey and Morris, "Other Side of Power"; Sinclair-Chapman and Price, "Black Politics, the 2008 Election and the (Im)Possibility of Race Transcendence"; and Dumm, "Barack Obama and the Souls of White Folk."

42. Stuckey, "Rethinking the Rhetorical Presidency and Presidential Rhetoric," 44; Daughton, "Women's Issues, Women's Place," *Communication Quarterly,* 114; Stuckey, "Rethinking the Rhetorical Presidency and Presidential Rhetoric," 43; Kimmel, *Manhood in America,* 36–37, 38; Goodale, "Presidential Sound," 167.

43. Kimmel, *Manhood in America,* 267, 269, 296, 297.

44. Anderson and Sheeler, *Governing Codes,* 123. Also see Anderson, "'Rhymes with Rich.'" Quoted material can be found in Michael Barone, "Bad News for Boomer Liberals," *US News & World Report,* August 29, 1994, 32; and Scott Steele, "A Man of Hope (Ark.)," *Maclean's,* November 16, 1992, 42.

45. Malin, *American Masculinity under Clinton,* 15. For additional discussion of the Clinton presidency as an example of a crisis in masculinity, see D. Nelson, *National Manhood,* 226–27.

46. Lancaster, "Performative Language Games of *Dramapolitik,*" 1044; Fahey, "French and Feminine."

47. Stuckey, "Rethinking the Rhetorical Presidency and Presidential Rhetoric," 44; C. E. Morris, ed., *Queering Public Address;* Murphy, "Heroic Tradition in Presidential Rhetoric."

48. Jamieson, *Beyond the Double Bind,* 120, 121.

49. For scholarly evaluation of Hillary Rodham Clinton's public persona and the implications for gender norms in US culture, see, for example, Muir and Taylor, "Navigating Gender Complexities"; Falk, "Gender Bias and Maintenance"; S. J. Parry-Giles, "Mediating Hillary Rodham Clinton"; Mattina, "Hillary Rodham Clinton"; Anderson, "'Rhymes with Rich'"; Campbell, "The Discursive Performance of Femininity"; Jamieson, *Beyond the Double Bind,* chap. 2; Muir and Benitez, "Redefining the Role of the First Lady"; Sullivan and Turner, *From the Margins to the Center,* chap. 4; Winfield, "'Madame President'"; and Campbell, "Shadowboxing with Stereotypes."

50. Anderson and Sheeler, *Governing Codes,* 6. Also see, for example, Anderson, "From Spouses to Candidates"; and Anderson, "Hillary Rodham Clinton as 'Madonna.'" Karlyn

Kohrs Campbell persuasively argues that "because members of the largely white male political elite face fewer rhetorical challenges, their discourse is a less fertile field for rhetorical research" than is assessment of "the rhetoric of outgroups," who "must discover ways to subvert popular belief and overcome unusually significant persuasive obstacles." Campbell asserts that, for this reason, members of outgroups "must be more inventive than their advantaged counterparts." Campbell, "Sound of Women's Voices," 212. Thus, many studies of historical and contemporary political women illustrate the ways in which women have used rhetoric to challenge, contest, and redefine cultural and political norms.

51. S. J. Parry-Giles and T. Parry-Giles, "Gendered Politics and Presidential Image Construction," 342. For additional discussion of masculinity as a hegemonic cultural force, see, for example, Lélièvre, "In the Laboratory of Masculinity"; Kimmel, *Manhood in America;* and D. Nelson, *National Manhood.*

52. See, for example, Caruso, ed., *First Woman President;* Gutgold, *Paving the Way for Madam President;* Lawless and Fox, *It Takes a Candidate;* Watson and Gordon, eds., *Anticipating Madam President.*

53. Anderson, "From Spouses to Candidates," 123, 126. For additional assessment of women as presidential candidates see, for example, Gutgold, *Paving the Way for Madam President;* and Reiser, "Crafting a Feminine Presidency."

54. Watson and Gordon, *Anticipating Madam President,* 16; Kunin, *Pearls, Politics & Power,* 178; Jeffrey M. Jones, "Some Americans Reluctant to Vote for Mormon, 72-Year-Old Presidential Candidates," *Gallup News Service,* February 20, 2007, http://www.gallup.com/poll/26611 /some-americans-reluctant-vote-mormon-72yearold-presidential-candidates.aspx; AlaraJRogers, comment on "Hillary Sexism Watch: If a Woman Is President, Who Will Iron the Shirts?" *Feministing.com,* January 8, 2008, http://www.feministing.com/archives/008362.html.

55. Darsey, "Barack Obama and America's Journey," 100.

56. Center for American Women and Politics, "Republican Women Follow National Winning Pattern."

1. The First Shall Be Last

1. Karen Tumulty, "Hillary Gets Ready to Run," *Time,* August 19, 2006, www.time.com; cover image, *Time,* August 28, 2006.

2. Poll results, White House Project, http://www.thewhitehouseproject.org/v2/researchand reports/roperreport/White%20House%20Project%20poll%209–05.pdf (accessed November 5, 2006). According to its mission statement, the White House Project is a "national, nonpartisan, not-for-profit organization [that] aims to advance women's leadership in all communities and sectors, up to the US presidency." See http://www.feminist.com/resources/quotes/ (accessed November 5, 2006).

3. Jeffrey M. Jones, "Six in 10 Americans Think US Ready for a Female President: Vast Majority Think Country Would not Accept Atheist or Gay President," Gallup Poll News Service, October 3, 2006, http://www.cawp.rutgers.edu/Facts/Elections/Gallup_6in10.pdf.

4. Prior to the 2010 midterm election, women held seventeen seats in the US Senate (17 percent) and seventy-three seats in the US House of Representatives (16.8 percent). See the White House Project website for the most up-to-date data, http://www.thewhitehouseproject.org /culture/facts/ (accessed July 23, 2010).

5. "Women in National Parliaments," November 30, 2010, chart available on the Interparliamentary Union website, http://www.ipu.org/wmn-e/classif.htm.

6. The notion of Senator Clinton trading on presidential ambitions for the role of Senate majority/minority leader was posted on the *Carpetbagger Report* (blog), August 3, 2006, http:// www.thecarpetbaggerreport.com/archives/8107.html. Also see the *Left Coaster* blog, October 1, 2006, http://www.theleftcoaster.com/archives/008893.php. The theory gained wider circulation when it appeared on broadcast political talk shows such as the *Chris Matthews Show,* No-

vember 5, 2006, transcript available at http://www.thechrismatthewsshow.com/. Two weeks earlier, Matthews and his panelists discussed the positive prospects for a 2008 Barack Obama presidential bid. See *Chris Matthews Show*, October 22, 2006, transcript available at http://www .thechrismatthewsshow.com/.

7. On the founding mothers of colonial times, see Pearson, "Conflicting Demands in Correspondence"; and Norton, *Founding Mothers & Fathers*. On abolitionists, see Daughton, "Fine Texture of Enactment"; Browne, *Angelina Grimké*; and Zaeske, *Signatures of Citizenship*. On Progressive Era activists, see Campbell, *Man Cannot Speak for Her*, 2 vols.; Huxman, "Perfecting the Rhetorical Vision of Woman's Rights"; Slagell, "Rhetorical Structure of Frances E. Willard's Campaign for Woman Suffrage"; Heider, "Suffrage, Self-Determination, and the Women's Christian Temperance Union in Nebraska, 1879–1882"; Tonn, "Militant Motherhood"; and Burt, "Working Women and the Triangle Fire." On later twentieth-century women candidates and officeholders, see Dow and Tonn, "'Feminine Style' and Political Judgment in the Rhetoric of Ann Richards"; Jamieson, *Beyond the Double Bind*; Sullivan and Turner, *From the Margins to the Center*; Norris, ed., *Women, Media, and Politics*; Vavrus, "Working the Senate from the Outside In"; Marshall and Mayhead, eds., *Navigating Boundaries*; Mayhead and Marshall, *Women's Political Discourse*; and Anderson and Sheeler, *Governing Codes*. On women's power to swing elections, see Vavrus, "From Women of the Year to 'Soccer Moms'"; Conway, Steuernagel, and Ahern, *Women and Political Participation*; and O'Connor, Brewer, and Fisher, *Gendering American Politics*.

8. Anderson, "From Spouses to Candidates"; Watson and Gordon, *Anticipating Madam President*; and Gutgold, *Paving the Way for Madam President*.

9. See Whitaker, ed., *Women in Politics*, 221; Kimmel, *Manhood in America*, 36–38; Murphy, "Heroic Tradition in Presidential Rhetoric"; Anderson, "From Spouses to Candidates"; T. Parry-Giles and S. J. Parry-Giles, *Prime-Time Presidency*; and Edwards, ed., *Gender and Political Communication in America*, 233–50.

10. See Braden, *Women Politicians and the Media*; S. J. Parry-Giles, "Mediating Hillary Rodham Clinton"; Devitt, "Framing Gender on the Campaign Trail," 11, http://www.appcpenn .org/political/archive/wlfstudy.pdf (accessed June 11, 2003); Bystrom, "Advertising, Web Sites, and Media Coverage"; Carroll, *Women as Candidates in American Politics*; Norris, *Women, Media and Politics*; Carroll, *Women and American Politics*; and Falk, *Women for President*, 2nd ed.

11. See Watson and Gordon, *Anticipating Madam President*, 3; Gutgold, *Paving the Way for Madam President*, 116–17; and Anderson, "From Spouses to Candidates," 121.

12. An exception to this rule is Hillary Clinton, who, as of October 2006, had maintained a virtual lock on major funding sources for Democratic presidential candidates. She was surpassed by then-Senator Barack Obama in early 2008, and she ended up raising $229.4 million by May 2008. That economic viability made her the most talked-about contender for the 2008 Democratic presidential nomination early in the race—a fact that made the early buzz surrounding relative newcomer Obama even more striking. For more information on candidate fundraising and spending, see opensecrets.org.

13. See Watson and Gordon, *Anticipating Madam President*, 4–10.

14. See, for example, Anderson and Sheeler, *Governing Codes*; Dickinson and Anderson, "Fallen"; Anderson, "Hillary Rodham Clinton as 'Madonna'"; Marshall and Mayhead, *Navigating Boundaries*; Anderson, "'Rhymes with Rich'"; Campbell, "Discursive Performance of Femininity"; and Jamieson, *Beyond the Double Bind*.

15. Iyengar et al., "Running as a Woman," 79. For additional discussion of the variety of gendered ways in which women candidates are framed, see Edwards, *Gender and Political Communication in America*; and Mayhead and Marshall, *Women's Political Discourse*.

16. Carlin and Winfrey, "Have You Come a Long Way, Baby?," 328.

17. Ibid., 326–43; Mandziuk, "Dressing Down Hillary," 315; Falk, "Press, Passion, and Portsmouth," 61; Shepard, "Confronting Gender Bias, Finding a Voice"; Harp, Loke, and Bachmann, "First Impressions of Sarah Palin," 304.

18. For a more detailed discussion of gender and metaphor in contemporary US politics, see Anderson and Sheeler, *Governing Codes.*

19. M. Nelson, "Introduction: Rossiter Revisited," xxiv–xxv.

20. Falk, *Women for President,* 36.

21. Dodwell, "From the Center"; Carpenter, "Frederick Jackson Turner and the Rhetorical Impact of the Frontier Thesis," 117.

22. Dorsey, "Myth of War and Peace in Presidential Discourse."

23. Quoted in Murphy, "Barack Obama, the Exodus Tradition, and the Joshua Generation," 399.

24. Rushing, "Evolution of 'The New Frontier' in *Alien* and *Aliens,*" 1.

25. Calder, *There Must Be a Lone Ranger,* 160, 165.

26. Anderson and Sheeler, *Governing Codes,* 15.

27. Ibid., 46.

28. Quoted in Underhill, *Woman Who Ran for President,* xiii.

29. Quoted in ibid., 7–8.

30. "Victoria Woodhull-Martin Papers: Biography," Morris Library, Southern Illinois University Carbondale, http://www.lib.siu.edu/Plonetest/departments/speccoll/inventories/015 (accessed November 5, 2006).

31. Ellen Goodman, "First Woman Candidate Shot Down," Boston Globe Newspaper Company, March 19, 1999, http://www.texnews.com/1998/1999/opinion/good0319.html (accessed November 5, 2006).

32. National Women's History Museum, "Belva Ann Bennett McNall Lockwood."

33. Norgren, "Before It Was Merely Difficult," 33.

34. Belva A. Lockwood, "How I Ran for the Presidency," *National Magazine* 17 (March 1903): 729.

35. Norgren, "Before It Was Merely Difficult," 34, 35.

36. Kevin Miller, "Margaret Chase Smith Paved the Way, but Will the Governor's Mansion Remain Elusive?," *Bangor Daily News,* July 30, 2010, www.bangordailynews.com.

37. "Nation: Madam President," *Time,* February 7, 1964, www.time.com.

38. Quoted in ibid.

39. R. Lakoff, *Language and Woman's Place.*

40. Shelley, "Leave It to the Girls."

41. Freeman, "Shirley Chisholm's 1972 Presidential Campaign."

42. Quoted in Gloria Steinem, "The Ticket That Might Have Been," *Ms.,* January 1973, http://www.pbs.org/pov/pov2005/chisholm/special_ticket.html (accessed November 5, 2006).

43. James Barron, "Shirley Chisholm, 'Unbossed' Pioneer in Congress, Is Dead at 80," *New York Times,* January 3, 2005, www.nytimes.com; Suzanne C. Ryan, "'Chisholm '72' Is Riveting Portrait of a Pioneer," *Boston Globe,* February 7, 2005, www.boston.com.

44. Center for American Women and Politics, "Women Presidential and Vice Presidential Candidates," Eagleton Institute of Politics, Rutgers University, 2008, http://www.cawp.rutgers .edu/fast_facts/levels_of_office/documents/prescand.pdf (accessed November 26, 2010).

45. "Documentary on Pioneer Congresswoman Patsy Mink to Screen Oct. 30," press release, Japanese American National Museum, October 23, 2010, http://www.janm.org/press /release/247/.

46. Center for American Women and Politics, "Women Presidential and Vice Presidential Candidates"; Gilroy, *Shared Vision.*

47. Center for American Women and Politics, "Women Presidential and Vice Presidential Candidates."

48. Anderson and Sheeler, *Governing Codes,* 14.

49. Dan Balz, "Hoping to Be 'Part of History': Elizabeth Dole Is Wowing Women Voters, but Her Bid to Overtake George W. Bush for the GOP Prize Remains an Uphill Struggle,"

Washington Post, July 15, 1999, www.lexisnexis.com; "Dole Drops Out: Lack of Money Chases Former Red Cross Head from Race," *ABCNews.com*, October 20, 1999.

50. See, for example, Richard L. Berke, "Eye on 2000, Elizabeth Dole Leaves Red Cross," *New York Times*, January 5, 1999, www.lexisnexis.com; and Lynn Rosellini, Marianne Lavelle, and Dana Hawkins, "The Woman Who Could Beat Him," *US News & World Report*, March 15, 1999, www.lexisnexis.com.

51. Balz, "Hoping to Be 'Part of History.'"

52. B. Drummond Ayres Jr., "Political Briefing: Women to the Rescue of Elizabeth Dole," *New York Times*, July 22, 1999, www.lexisnexis.com.

53. "Dole Drops Out."

54. Robin Givhan, "One Small Step for Womankind: Elizabeth Dole's Candidacy Became Merely the Symbol She Avoided," *Washington Post*, October 21, 1999, www.lexisnexis.com; quoted in Bill Hemmer and Jeff Greenfield, "Elizabeth Dole: 'It's More Important to Raise Issues Than to Raise Campaign Funds,'" *CNN Live Event/Special*, October 20, 1999, www.lexisnexis.com.

55. Steve Kornacki, "Moseley-Braun Launches Historic Bid for the White House," *Politics NJ.com*, February 20, 2003.

56. Ken Rudin, "Former Sen. Carol Moseley Braun," *National Public Radio's Morning Edition*, May 6, 2003, www.NPR.org; Kornacki, "Moseley-Braun Launches Historic Bid for the White House."

57. Campbell, "Rhetoric of Women's Liberation."

58. Anderson, "Hillary Rodham Clinton as 'Madonna.'"

59. Trent, "Presidential Surfacing," 282. Trent also outlines a third component of speeches during the surfacing stage: addressing campaign issues. We omitted that factor from our analysis because the other two were more central to our questions regarding gender and US presidential identity and the pioneer metaphor.

60. Woodhull, "And the Truth Shall Make You Free."

61. Quoted in Underhill, *Woman Who Ran for President*, 77–78.

62. "Power feminism" was first articulated by Naomi Wolf and emphasizes that women already possess the power to assert their own individual, material, economic, and sexual agency. Wolf's conception both of "power" and of "feminism" is contested by feminists who argue that power feminists speak from a position of racial and class privilege and that continued political and structural changes are needed in order for feminism's promise to be realized. See, for example, Wolf, *Fire with Fire*; hooks, "Dissident Heat"; Rowe, "Subject to Power—Feminism without Victims"; S. K. Foss and K. A. Foss, "Our Journey to Repowered Feminism"; and Hains, "Power Feminism, Mediated."

63. S. K. Foss and K. A. Foss, "Our Journey to Repowered Feminism," 57.

64. Woodhull, "Lecture on Constitutional Equality."

65. Browne, "Encountering Angelina Grimké," 56, 70.

66. Chisholm, Brooklyn Announcement. All quotations from Chisholm's announcement address are taken from this source.

67. Burke, *Rhetoric of Motives*, 22.

68. Freeman, "Shirley Chisholm's 1972 Presidential Campaign."

69. Quoted in James Barron, "Shirley Chisholm, 'Unbossed' Pioneer in Congress, Is Dead at 80," *New York Times*, January 5, 2005, http://www.nytimes.com/2005/01/03/obituaries/03chisholm.html?ex=1180152000&en=e64ded3e79a24f25&ei=5070.

70. Dole, Exploratory Committee Announcement Speech. All quotations from Dole's speech are taken from this source.

71. Edwards, "Traversing the Wife-Candidate Double Bind," 180.

72. Reiser, "Crafting a Feminine Presidency."

73. Quoted in Victoria Pope, Jerelyn Eddings and Margaret Loftus, "An Iron Fist in a Vel-

vet Glove," *US News & World Report,* August 11, 1996, http://www.usnews.com/usnews/news/articles/960819/archive_034919.htm.

74. See, for example, Kathy Rudy, "Elizabeth Dole and Conservative Feminist Politics," *Genders* 30 (1990): n.p., http://www.genders.org/g30/g30_rudy.html#n37 (accessed January 10, 2012).

75. Moseley Braun, Announcement Speech, September 22, 2003. All quotations from the speech are taken from this source.

76. Kim Gandy, "NOW/PAC Endorses Carol Moseley Braun for President," August 26, 2003, http://www.now.org/press/08-03/08-26.html.

77. "Former Sen. Carol Moseley Braun." interview by Bob Edwards, *National Public Radio,* May 6, 2003, http://www.npr.org/programs/specials/democrats2004/transcripts/braun_trans.html.

78. All quoted in Chris Matthews, *The Chris Matthews Show,* October 22, 2006, transcript at www.thechrismatthewsshow.com.

79. Ibid.

80. Ibid.

2. Fictional Presidentiality

1. "Bart to the Future," *The Simpsons,* season 11, episode 17, aired March 19, 2000, www.rocktube.us/Funny/The_Simpsons_Bart_to_the_Future-W90MBRmdUvx.html. All quotes are from this source. Of course, including the qualifier "straight" is a satirical recognition of rumors swirling around many powerful female politicians that they are closeted lesbians. It also calls out the heteronormativity of the US presidency.

2. Hariman, "Political Parody and Public Culture," 250, 248, respectively; T. Parry-Giles and S. J. Parry Giles, "*The West Wing*'s Prime-Time Presidentiality," 209; Murphy, "Heroic Tradition in Presidential Rhetoric," 467.

3. Quoted in David Zurawik, "Power Suits Her: Geena Davis as *Commander in Chief* Leads an Army of Strong, Smart Women into TV's Fall Lineup," *Baltimore Sun,* September 25, 2005, 1E, www.lexisnexis.com.

4. Quoted in Lauren Beckham Falcone, "'Chief' Followers: Show's Fans Say TV's Female President Could Shape Political Reality," *Boston Herald,* October 18, 2005, 41, www.lexisnexis.com.

5. Melanie McFarland, "A Female 'Chief'? We Have a Ways to Go," *Seattle Post-Intelligencer,* October 21, 2005, http://www.seattlepi.com/tv/245366_tv21.html.

6. Spigel and Mann, eds., *Private Screenings,* xiii; Dow, *Prime-Time Feminism,* xiii.

7. *Kisses for My President,* directed by Curtis Bernhardt (1964; Burbank, CA: Warner Home Video, 1992), VHS; *Air Force One,* directed by Wolfgang Petersen (1997; Los Angeles: Columbia TriStar Home Video, 1998), DVD; *The Contender,* directed by Rod Lurie (2000; Universal City, CA: Dreamworks Home Entertainment, 2001), DVD; *Battlestar Galactica* (New York: Sci-Fi Channel, 2004–9), streaming video or DVD recording; *Commander in Chief* (Burbank, CA: ABC, 2005–6), streaming video or DVD recording; *24* (Beverly Hills, CA: Fox, 2001–10), streaming video or DVD recording. All quotations from these films and television series have been transcribed directly from the source material cited here.

8. See, for example, Fiske, "Television: Polysemy and Popularity"; Condit, "Rhetorical Limits of Polysemy"; and Ceccarelli, "Polysemy."

9. Ceccarelli, "Polysemy," 408.

10. Meyers, "Fracturing Women," 12; Dow, *Prime-Time Feminism,* 8; Shugart, Waggoner, and Hallstein, "Mediating Third-Wave Feminism," 198; Shugart, "Reinventing Privilege," 68.

11. Stanley Kauffmann, "Stanley Kauffmann on Films," *New Republic,* August 25, 1997, 24, EBSCO Academic Search Premier.

12. T. Parry-Giles and S. J. Parry Giles, "*West Wing*'s Prime-Time Presidentiality."

13. Ibid., 211. Certainly, insofar as media texts are "polyvalent," audience responses are varied and sometimes contradictory. See Cohen, "'Relevance' of Cultural Identity in Audiences' Interpretations of Mass Media." Nonetheless, texts themselves invoke ideological perspectives, the implication of which can and should be assessed critically. See Wander, "Third Persona."

14. Christensen and Haas, *Projecting Politics,* 4, 16; T. Parry-Giles and S. J. Parry-Giles, "*The West Wing*'s Prime-Time Presidentiality," 210, 212 (quote).

15. T. Parry-Giles and S. J. Parry-Giles, "*The West Wing*'s Prime-Time Presidentiality," 210.

16. "Filmography by TV Series for Rod Lurie," Internet Movie Database, http://www.imdb .com/name/nm0527109/filmoseries#tt0429455 (accessed December 12, 2010).

17. "Diversity Training," *Newsweek,* February 2, 2008, http://www.newsweek.com/2008/02 /02/diversity-training.html.

18. Quoted in Zurawik, "Power Suits Her"; quoted in Falcone, "'Chief' Followers."

19. Kate Aurthur, "Hail to the 'Chief," *New York Times,* September 29, 2005, E2, www.lexis nexis.com; Walt Belcher, "For Bergen, White House Roles Spur Fantasies of Having a Woman President," *Tampa Tribune,* January 24, 2006, 4, www.lexisnexis.com.

20. Melanie McFarland, "ABC's 'Chief' Is No Longer in Command," *Seattle Post-Intelligencer,* May 4, 2006, http://www.seattlepi.com/tv/268898_commander04.html.

21. Neil Genzlinger, "*Commander in Chief:* Geena Davis as President," *New York Times,* September 24, 2005, http://www.nytimes.com/2005/09/24/arts/television/25tv-cover.html, including Lurie quote.

22. "Pilot," *Commander in Chief,* aired September 27, 2005. Subsequent quotations in the text, as noted, are from the pilot episode.

23. T. Parry-Giles and S. J. Parry-Giles, "*The West Wing*'s Prime-Time Presidentiality," 210.

24. "First Strike," *Commander in Chief,* aired October 11, 2005.

25. "First Choice," *Commander in Chief,* aired October 4, 2005.

26. "Rubie Dubidoux and the Brown Bound Express," *Commander in Chief,* aired November 15, 2005.

27. "The Wind beneath My Wing," *Commander in Chief,* aired January 24, 2006.

28. Robin Givhan, "In the Oval Office, Pumps and Circumstance," *Washington Post,* May 5, 2006, http://www.washingtonpost.com/wp-dyn/content/article/2006/05/04/AR200605 0401778.html; Tom Shales, "Geena Davis Sweeps Up the Oval Office," *Washington Post,* September 27, 2005, C01, www.lexisnexis.com; Connie Schultz, "Female President? Think Outside Box," *Cleveland Plain Dealer,* October 10, 2005, D1, www.lexisnexis.com.

29. "Rubie Dubidoux and the Brown Bound Express," *Commander in Chief,* aired November 15, 2005.

30. Susan Page, "Call Her Madame President," *USA Today,* October 11, 2005, 1D, www .lexisnexis.com.

31. "Pilot," *Commander in Chief,* aired September 27, 2005.

32. "First Dance," *Commander in Chief,* aired October 18, 2005.

33. See, for example, Campbell, *Man Cannot Speak for Her,* vol. 1; and Johnston, *Sexual Power.*

34. See, for example, Ruddick, "Maternal Thinking"; and Gilligan, *In a Different Voice.* See Dow, *Prime-Time Feminism,* 164–202, for her discussion of the implications of "difference" or "cultural" feminism.

35. "Pilot," *Commander in Chief,* aired September 27, 2005. Subsequent quotes are also from this episode.

36. Mercer and Shingler, *Melodrama,* 1. Importantly, the authors note that within film studies, "melodrama" is highly contested. Thus, there is no single, generally accepted definition of the term.

37. Mercer and Shingler, *Melodrama,* 7.

38. Ibid., 12–14.

39. "Rubie Dubidoux and the Brown Bound Express," *Commander in Chief,* aired November 15, 2005.

40. McFarland, "Female 'Chief'?"

41. Dana Stevens, "Smell the History: ABC's *Commander in Chief* Is Cheesy Good Fun," *Slate,* September 27, 2005, http://www.slate.com/id/2126991/.

42. "Unfinished Business," *Commander in Chief,* aired June 14, 2006. Subsequent dialogue comes from this episode.

43. Critics of the "Unfinished Business" episode argue that time limits for ratification have expired. Therefore, state-by-state ratification of the ERA would need to commence from the beginning, so the episode lacks real-world application. However, some scholars dispute that time-limit restrictions apply to the ERA. See Held, Herndon, and Stager, "Equal Rights Amendment."

44. Heather Havrilesky, in "Will You Miss *The West Wing?*" *Salon,* January 24, 2006, http://mobile.salon.com/ent/tv/feature/2006/01/24/west_wing/index.html; Joshua Alston, "Clinton and Obama May Be Breaking New Presidential Ground, but Hollywood Beat Them to the Top Decades Ago," *Newsweek,* February 2, 2008 http://www.newsweek.com/2008/02/02/diversity-training.html.

45. Alston, "Clinton and Obama May Be Breaking New Presidential Ground." It is notable that Bochco, too, was gone by the final episode. The explicitly feminist tone of the final episode was the work of Bochco's replacement. *Showrunner* is the Hollywood term for the executive producer responsible for a television program's management and content. A showrunner is comparable to the director of a film.

46. Bosley Crowther, "The Screen: 'Kisses for My President': Fred MacMurray and Polly Bergen Star," *New York Times,* August 22, 1964, nytimes.com.

47. Jessica Milner Davis, *Farce,* 2nd ed. (New Brunswick, NJ: Transaction, 2003), 2.

48. Bostdorff, "Vice-Presidential Comedy and the Traditional Female Role," 2. Also see Bostdorff, "Hillary Rodham Clinton and Elizabeth Dole as Running 'Mates' in the 1996 Campaign."

49. Quoted in Haas, "Women, Politics, and Film," 274.

50. In *Commander in Chief,* Lurie repeated this notion that appointing the first female president was the legacy of her male predecessor. See "First Scandal," *Commander in Chief,* aired November 8, 2005.

51. *Battlestar Galactica,* Internet Movie Database, http://www.imdb.com/title/tt0314979/episodes (accessed December 27, 2010).

52. Eberl, ed., *Battlestar Galactica and Philosophy,* ix.

53. Goulart and Joe, "Inverted Perspectives on Politics and Morality in *Battlestar Galactica,*" 180; "Ronald D. Moore," Internet Movie Database, http://www.imdb.com/name/nm0601822/ (accessed December 27, 2010). For discussion of Moore's involvement with the *Star Trek* franchise, along with the history of the screen revival of *Battlestar Galactica,* see John Hodgman, "Ron Moore's Deep Space Journey," *New York Times,* July 17, 2005, http://www.nytimes.com/2005/07/17/magazine/17GALACTICA.html.

54. Goulart and Joe, "Inverted Perspectives on Politics and Morality in *Battlestar Galactica,*" 180.

55. Hodgman, "Ron Moore's Deep Space Journey," including Moore quote. For analysis of the series' intellectual and political themes, see Goulart and Joe, "Inverted Perspectives on Politics and Morality in *Battlestar Galactica*"; and Eberl, *Battlestar Galactica and Philosophy.*

56. The character's name may be an homage to the first ladies whose husbands were in office during the initial series run (Rosalynn Carter) and the subsequent premiere of the remake (Laura Bush).

57. Conly, "Is Starbuck a Woman?," 239; Goulart and Joe, "Inverted Perspectives on Politics and Morality in *Battlestar Galactica,*" 190.

58. The linkage between betrayal and gender first appears with the introduction of Caprica Six, a gorgeous blond woman who effuses sexual power. Her ability to bewitch Dr. Gaius Balter into betraying the human race situates her as an "Eve" figure—responsible for the downfall of humanity. Reinforcing this theme, a human character, Lieutenant Sharon "Boomer" Valerii, is revealed to be a covert Cylon sleeper agent, and Admiral Cain's leadership is an illustration in the corrupt excess of female power. This examination of the series also explores the mysticism of President Roslin and the questions about her credibility. It should be noted, however, that white masculinity does not go unscathed in *Battlestar Galactica*. The series star is Commander Adama, played by the Latino actor Edward James Olmos. However, Adama is surrounded by white men. His second in command, Colonel Saul Tigh, is an alcoholic reviled by many of his subordinate crew members. Another primary white male character, Dr. Gaius Baltar, is a sniveling egomaniac who lacks the courage or moral conviction to fight for anyone other than himself. These portrayals of white masculinity, however, are tempered by characters such as Captain Lee "Apollo" Adama (played by Jamie Bamber, who lacks the external markers of ethnicity exhibited by Olmos's Adama) and Lieutenant (later Captain) Karl "Helo" Agathon. Both Apollo and Helo exhibit independence, strength, courage, and heroism throughout the series, escaping some (though not all) of the morally dubious choices made by other characters in the series.

59. Cloud, "Hegemony or Concordance?," 122.

60. Other linguistic habits that diverge from contemporary US parlance include the substitution of "oh my gods" for the more familiar version of the expression that refers to the deity in singular form (this, of course, reflects the Colonies' polytheistic religious beliefs) and the safe-for-broadcast-television substitution of the word *frak* for the more familiar expletive beginning with the letter "f."

61. Hodgman, "Ron Moore's Deep Space Journey."

62. Quoted in ibid.

63. Hodgman, "Ron Moore's Deep Space Journey."

64. "Epiphanies," *Battlestar Galactica*, aired January 20, 2006. President Adar is upset because he wanted to use violence against the union in order to deter further strikes.

65. "Battlestar Galactica: The Miniseries," *Battlestar Galactica*, aired December 8–9, 2003. Subsequent quotes are from this two-part miniseries.

66. Quoted in Kate O'Hare, "President Roslin Speaks—Q&A with 'Battlestar Galactica's' Mary McDonnell," *Kate O'Hare's Hot Cuppa TV*, February 23, 2009, http://blog.zap2it.com /kate_ohare/2009/02/president-roslin-speaks-qa-with-battlestar-galacticas-mary-mcdonnell .html.

67. "Battlestar Galactica: The Miniseries," *Battlestar Galactica*, aired December 8–9, 2003. Subsequent quotes are from this two-part miniseries.

68. Gilligan, *In a Different Voice*, 159.

69. Blahuta, "Politics of Crisis," 42.

70. Dunn, "Being Boomer," 131.

71. Cooke, "'Let It Be Earth.'"

72. Goulart and Joe, "Politics and Morality in *Battlestar Galactica*," 187.

73. Ibid., 188.

74. Blahuta, "Politics of Crisis," 43.

75. "Lay Down Your Burdens, Part 2," *Battlestar Galactica*, aired March 10, 2006.

76. See "Gemenon Liner 1701," *Battlestar Galactica Wiki*, http://en.battlestarwiki.org/wiki /Gemenon_Liner_1701 (accessed December 29, 2010).

77. "Resistance," *Battlestar Galactica*, aired August 5, 2005.

78. As noted in the *Battlestar Galactica Wiki*, Helo is "young, capable, and resourceful with an acute sense of right and wrong, something which he is prepared to articulate and act upon, even at risk to his own standing." "Karl Agathon," *Battlestar Galactica Wiki*, http://en .battlestarwiki.org/wiki/Karl_Agathon (accessed December 29, 2010).

79. On Cylon Number Six, see Goulart and Joe, "Politics and Morality in *Battlestar Galactica*," 191–94.

80. O'Hare, "President Roslin Speaks."

81. "Daybreak, Part 2," *Battlestar Galactica*, aired March 20, 2009.

82. Quoted in Goulart and Joe, "Politics and Morality in *Battlestar Galactica*," 196.

83. Joshua Alston, "Jack Bauer's Parting Shots," *Newsweek*, May 25, 2010, http://www.newsweek.com/2010/05/25/jack-bauer-s-parting-shots.print.html.

84. Quoted in Anthony C. Ferrante, "Exclusive Interview: Howard Gordon Gives the Early Scoop on '24'—season 7: Version 3.0," *If*, September 11, 2007, http://web.archive.org/web/20070911120151/http://www.ifmagazine.com/feature.asp?article=2257.

85. Nellie Andreeva, "Jones Moves into '24' Oval Office," *Reuters*, July 20, 2007, http://www.reuters.com/article/idUSN2027850820070721.

86. Ferrante, "Exclusive Interview: Howard Gordon." Season seven, featuring President Allison Taylor, was slated to premiere in January 2008, and Clinton was the Democratic frontrunner when season seven was in the early stages of development. Due to the 2007–8 Writers Guild of America strike, however, the season seven premiere was pushed back to January 2009. See "Fox: '24' on Shelf until Next January," *CNN.com*, February 14, 2008, http://web.archive.org/web/20080314212629/http://www.cnn.com/2008/SHOWBIZ/TV/02/14/tv.24delay.ap/index.html.

87. *24*'s executive producer Howard Gordon confirmed his view that *24* is a tragedy. See Ferrante, "Exclusive Interview: Howard Gordon."

88. David Palmer, the popular and principled African American president introduced in the first season, struggled with disloyal cabinet members, was taken in by a conniving wife, and eventually was assassinated. John Keeler's presidency was cut short when he was incapacitated in a terrorist attack that ushered the corrupt Charles Logan into power. Other characters who briefly inhabited the role of US president include Wayne Palmer (incapacitated by a cerebral hemorrhage) and Noah Daniels (who served out Wayne Palmer's term only to be beaten at the polls by Allison Taylor).

89. Peacock, *Reading "24,"* 5; Chamberlain and Ruston, "*24* and Twenty-First Century Quality Television," 14.

90. See, for example, Peacock, *Reading "24."*

91. Cynthia Fuchs, "*24*: Season Seven Premiere," *PopMatters*, January 11, 2009, http://www.popmatters.com/pm/review/68894-twenty-four/.

92. "Redemption," *24*, aired November 23, 2008.

93. "Day 7: 8:00 A.M.–9:00 A.M.," *24*, aired January 11, 2009.

94. "Day 7: 10:00 A.M.–11:00 A.M.," *24*, aired January 12, 2009.

95. Ibid.

96. "Day 7: 1:00 P.M.–2:00 P.M.," *24*, aired January 26, 2009.

97. Ibid.

98. "Day 7: 3:00 P.M.–4:00 P.M.," *24*, aired February 9, 2009.

99. "Day 7: 3:00 A.M.–4:00 A.M.," *24*, aired April 27, 2009.

100. "Day 7: 8:00 A.M.–9:00 A.M.," *24*, aired January 11, 2009.

101. "Day 7: 5:00 P.M.–6:00 P.M.," *24*, aired February 23. 2009.

102. "Day 7: 11:00 P.M.–12:00 A.M.," *24*, aired March 30, 2009.

103. "Day 7: 7:00 A.M.–8:00 A.M.," *24*, aired May 18, 2009.

104. Ibid.

105. "Day 8: 5:00 A.M.–6:00 A.M.," *24*, aired April 5, 2010.

106. "Day 8: 10:00 A.M.–11:00 A.M.," *24*, aired April 26, 2010.

107. Ibid.

108. Alston, "Jack Bauer's Parting Shots."

109. "Day 8: 9:00 A.M.–10:00 A.M.," *24*, aired April 19, 2010.

110. Ibid.

111. "Day 8: 3:00 P.M.–4:00 P.M.," *24*, aired May 24, 2010.

112. Delaney, "'She May Be a Little Weird,'" 192.

113. "Jack's Back! A Guide to the Seventh Season of Fox's '24,'" *St. Petersburg Times*, January 10, 2009, http://license.icopyright.net/user/viewFreeUse.act?fuid=MTExNzAxNjg%3D.

114. Alston, "Jack Bauer's Parting Shots."

115. T. Parry-Giles and S. J. Parry-Giles, *Prime-Time Presidency*, 24. Also see Peacock, *Reading "24."*

116. "Day 8: 2:00 P.M.–3:00 P.M.," *24*, aired May 24, 2010.

117. "Day 8: 3:00 P.M.–4:00 P.M.," *24*, aired May 24, 2010.

118. Dow, *Prime-Time Feminism*, 161.

119. See Anderson and Stewart, "Politics and the Single Woman"; Gring-Pemble and Blair, "Best-Selling Feminisms"; Lotz, "Communicating Third-Wave Feminism and New Social Movements," 3–4; and Orr, "Charting the Currents of the Third Wave," 34.

120. See T. Parry-Giles and S. J. Parry-Giles, *Prime-Time Presidency*. For other discussions of the norms of masculinity, militarism, and whiteness that govern fictional and empirical discussions of the US presidency, see, for example, Anderson, "From Spouses to Candidates," 123–25; Campbell, "Rhetorical Presidency"; Christensen and Haas, *Projecting Politics*, chaps. 13 and 14; Daughton, "Women's Issues, Women's Place," *Communication Quarterly*, 106–19; Jamieson, *Beyond the Double Bind;* Kimmell, *Manhood in America*, 36–38; and Keyishian, *Screening Politics.*

3. Presidential Campaign Oratory

1. Hillary Clinton, Presidential Exploratory Committee Announcement, video transcript, January 20, 2007, http://www.4president.org/speeches/hillary2008announcement.htm. All subsequent quotations are taken from this source, which includes Clinton's e-mail announcement text as well.

2. Daughton, "Women's Issues, Women's Place," in *Presidential Campaign Discourse*, 223, 232.

3. Jorgensen, "Constructed Masculinities," 56.

4. Ibid., 55–56.

5. See George H. W. Bush, 1988 Republican National Convention, Acceptance Address, August 18, 1988, http://www.americanrhetoric.com/speeches/georgehbush1988rnc.htm. For discussion of Bush's struggle with the "wimp" label, see Anderson, "'Rhymes with Rich.'"

6. Anderson, "'Rhymes with Rich'"; Campbell, "Rhetorical Presidency"; Campbell, "Shadowboxing with Stereotypes."

7. Jorgensen, "Constructed Masculinities," 59.

8. Daughton, "Women's Issues, Women's Place," in *Presidential Campaign Discourse*, 233.

9. Anderson and Sheeler, *Governing Codes*, 167.

10. Elizabeth Dole, "Speaking before the Republican National Convention," *PBS Newshour,* August 14, 1996, http://www.pbs.org/newshour/convention96/floor_speeches/elizabeth_dole.html.

11. Anderson and Sheeler, *Governing Codes*, 167.

12. S. J. Parry-Giles and T. Parry-Giles, "Gendered Politics and Presidential Image Construction," 346, 348.

13. See G. Lakoff, *Moral Politics*, 65–107, for a discussion of strict father morality, and 108–41, on nurturant parent morality.

14. Cienki, "Bush's and Gore's Language and Gestures in the 2000 US Presidential Debates."

15. Roper, "*Contemporary Presidency*," 142; Coe et al., "Masculinity as Political Strategy," 49.

16. John Kerry, Text of John Kerry's Acceptance Speech at the Democratic National Con-

vention, *Washington Post,* July 29, 2004, www.washingtonpost.com. All quotations from the speech are taken from this source.

17. Fahey, "French and Feminine," 133. See also Harris, "In My Day It Used to Be Called a Limp Wrist."

18. Bystrom et al., *Gender and Candidate Communication,* 219; Gordon and Miller, "Gender, Race, and the Oval Office," 154–55; Lawless, "Women, War, and Winning Elections," 487; Falk and Kenski, "Issue Saliency and Gender Stereotypes," 2.

19. Dow, "Review Essay: Reading the Second Wave," 100.

20. Hillary Clinton, Announcing Suspension of Presidential Campaign, June 7, 2008, http://www.americanrhetoric.com/speeches/hillaryclintoncampaignsuspensionspeech.htm.

21. Campbell, "Rhetoric of Women's Liberation," 75.

22. Jamieson, *Eloquence in an Electronic Age.*

23. Campbell, "Rhetoric of Women's Liberation," 79.

24. Ibid.

25. R. Lakoff, *Language and Woman's Place.*

26. Jamieson, *Beyond the Double Bind.*

27. See, for example, Campbell, "Discursive Performance of Femininity"; and Anderson, "'Rhymes with Rich.'"

28. Quoted in Anderson and Sheeler, *Governing Codes,* 125.

29. Julie Vorman, "A Listening Tour? It Worked for Hillary," *Paper Trail,* September 21, 2010, http://www.publicintegrity.org/blog/entry/2432/.

30. Hillary Clinton, "Remarks on Government Reform at St. Anselm College in Manchester, New Hampshire," April 13, 2007, *American Presidency Project,* ed. Gerhard Peters and John T. Woolley, www.presidency.ucsb.edu.

31. Clinton, "Remarks on Government Reform at St. Anselm College, in Manchester, New Hampshire," April 13, 2007, in *The American Presidency Project, ed.* Gerhard Peters and John T. Woolley, www.presidency.ucsb.edu. Clinton made this statement on many occasions over the next several months, including numerous events in early primary states such as Iowa and New Hampshire.

32. Clinton, "Remarks at the Every County Counts Kickoff in Council Bluffs, Iowa," December 16, 2007, in *The American Presidency Project,* ed. Gerhard Peters and John T. Woolley, www.presidency.ucsb.edu. Clinton also made this statement in New Hampshire.

33. Hillary Clinton, "Remarks on Foreign Policy at George Washington University in Washington, DC," February 25, 2008, in *The American Presidency Project,* ed. Gerhard Peters and John T. Woolley, www.presidency.ucsb.edu.

34. Hillary Clinton, "Hillary Clinton Speech and Q&A on Innovation," May 31, 2007, in *The American Presidency Project,* ed. Gerhard Peters and John T. Woolley, www.presidency.ucsb .edu.

35. Quoted in Anderson, "Hillary Rodham Clinton as 'Madonna,'" 7. This essay reveals similarities between Clinton's political persona in the 1990s and the persona she cultivated during the 2008 Democratic primary.

36. Hillary Clinton, "Remarks to the Urban League," July 27, 2007, in *The American Presidency Project,* ed. Gerhard Peters and John T. Woolley, www.presidency.ucsb.edu.

37. Hillary Clinton, "Remarks at the New Hampshire Democratic Party 100 Club Dinner in Milford," January 4, 2008, in *The American Presidency Project,* ed. Gerhard Peters and John T. Woolley, www.presidency.ucsb.edu.

38. Hillary Clinton, "Remarks at the Center for a New American Security in Washington, DC," June 27, 2007, in *The American Presidency Project,* ed. Gerhard Peters and John T. Woolley, www.presidency.ucsb.edu.

39. Hillary Clinton, "Remarks at the Granite State Independent Living Forum in Manchester, New Hampshire," November 2, 2007, in *The American Presidency Project,* ed. Gerhard

Peters and John T. Woolley, www.presidency.ucsb.edu; Clinton, "Remarks at the New Hampshire Democratic Party 100 Club Dinner in Milford"; Clinton, "Remarks at Every County Counts Kickoff."

40. Hillary Clinton, "Remarks—Modern Progressive Vision: Shared Prosperity," May 29, 2007, in *The American Presidency Project,* ed. Gerhard Peters and John T. Woolley, www.presidency.ucsb.edu.

41. Hillary Clinton, "Remarks at the Iowa Jefferson-Jackson Dinner in Des Moines," November 10, 2007, in *The American Presidency Project,* ed. Gerhard Peters and John T. Woolley, www.presidency.ucsb.edu.

42. Hillary Clinton, "Remarks at the Virginia Jefferson-Jackson Dinner," February 9, 2008, in *The American Presidency Project,* ed. Gerhard Peters and John T. Woolley, www.presidency.ucsb.edu.

43. Hillary Clinton, "Excerpt of Remarks in Clear Lake, Iowa," December 3, 2007, in *The American Presidency Project,* ed. Gerhard Peters and John T. Woolley, www.presidency.ucsb.edu.

44. Clinton, "Remarks at the Every County Counts Kickoff."

45. Clinton, "Remarks on Foreign Policy at George Washington University."

46. Bostdorff, "Vice-Presidential Comedy and the Traditional Female Role," 2.

47. Ibid., 7.

48. John McCain, "McCain Introduces Palin as Running Mate," *CQ Transcripts Wire,* August 29, 2008, http://www.washingtonpost.com/wp-dyn/content/article/2008/08/29/AR2008 082901882.html.

49. Ibid.

50. For more on "perspective by incongruity," see Burke, *Permanence and Change,* rev. ed.

51. We address these interviews in the next chapter, but pundits and journalists lambasted Palin's performance. See, for example, Alessandra Stanley, "A Question Reprised, but the Words Come None Too Easily for Palin," *New York Times,* September 26, 2008, www.lexisnexis.com; David Goldstein, "Palin Allure Fading in Glare of TV Light," *Newark Star-Ledger,* September 27, 2008, www.lexisnexis.com; Kathleen Parker, "The Palin Problem," *Washington Post,* September 28, 2008, www.lexisnexis.com; and Toby Harnden, "Sarah Palin's Train Wreck Interview with Katie Couric," *Telegraph* (London), September 28, 2008, http://blogs .telegraph.co.uk/news/tobyharnden/5307777/Sarah_Palin%C3%A2s_train_wreck_interview _with_Katie_Couric/.

52. Sarah Palin, "Transcript: Palin's Speech in Dayton, Ohio," NPR, August 29, 2008, http://www.npr.org/templates/story/story.php?storyId=94118910.

53. Sarah Palin, Republican Vice Presidential Nomination Acceptance Speech, September 3, 2008, http://www.americanrhetoric.com/speeches/convention2008/sarahpalin2008rnc .htm (accessed March 14, 2011).

54. Anderson and Sheeler, *Governing Codes,* 52.

55. Ibid., 57–58.

56. Palin, Republican Vice Presidential Nomination Acceptance Speech.

57. Kahl and Edwards, "Epistolary Epilogue," 272.

58. Gibson and Heyse, "'Difference between a Hockey Mom and a Pit Bull.'" For additional discussion of "femiphobia," see Ducat, *Wimp Factor.*

59. Gibson and Heyse, "'Difference between a Hockey Mom and a Pit Bull,'" 236, 245.

60. Palin, Republican Vice Presidential Nomination Acceptance Speech.

61. Bostdorff, "Vice-Presidential Comedy and the Traditional Female Role," 6–7.

62. Palin, "Transcript: Palin's Speech in Dayton, Ohio."

63. Michael Scherer and Alice Park, "How Healthy Is John McCain?" *Time,* May 14, 2008, http://www.time.com/time/politics/article/0,8599,1779596,00.html.

64. Bostdorff, "Vice-Presidential Comedy and the Traditional Female Role," 9.

65. Liz Sidoti, "Palin Says Daughter, 17, Is Pregnant," *Associated Press Online,* September 1,

2008, www.lexisnexis.com; Patrick Healy and Michael Luo, "$150,000 Wardrobe for Palin May Alter Tailor-Made Image," *New York Times,* October 22, 2008, www.nytimes.com. "Troopergate" was the label given to the charge that Palin abused her power as governor in firing an Alaska state trooper who refused to fire Palin's former brother-in-law, who was involved in a messy divorce and custody battle with Palin's sister. See, for example, "Palin Makes Troopergate Assertions That Are Flatly False," *Political Punch* (blog), October 12, 2008, ABCNews.com. Also see John Nichols, "Troopergate Conclusion: Palin Abused Her Office," *Nation* (blog), October 10, 2008; Nathan Thornburgh, "Palin and Troopergate: A Primer," *Time.com,* September 11, 2008; and Serge F. Kovaleski, "Alaska Inquiry Concludes Palin Abused Powers," *New York Times,* October 10, 2008, nytimes.com.

66. Sarah Palin, "Palin Campaign Speech in Johnstown, Pennsylvania," October 11, 2008, C-SPAN, http://www.c-spanvideo.org/program/281734–1. See also Sarah Palin, "Palin Speech in Jeffersonville, Indiana," October 29, 2008, C-SPAN, http://www.c-spanvideo.org/program /PalinS; Sarah Palin, "Palin Speech in Marietta, Ohio," November 2, 2008, C-SPAN, http:// www.c-spanvideo.org/program/Mariet.

67. Palin, "Palin Campaign Speech in Johnstown, Pennsylvania"; Sarah Palin, "Palin Speech in Loveland, Colorado," October 20, 2008, C-SPAN, http://www.c-spanvideo.org/program /Lovel; Sarah Palin, "Palin Campaign Speech in Fort Wayne, Indiana," October 25, 2008, C-SPAN, http://www.c-spanvideo.org/program/Wayne; Palin, "Palin Speech in Jeffersonville, Indiana"; Palin, "Palin Speech in Marietta, Ohio"; Sarah Palin, "Governor Palin in Dubuque, Iowa," November 3, 2008, C-SPAN, http://www.c-spanvideo.org/program/Dubu.

68. Palin, "Palin Campaign Speech in Johnstown, Pennsylvania" (first quote); Palin, "Palin Speech in Marietta, Ohio"; Palin, "Palin Speech in Jeffersonville, Indiana"; Palin, "Palin Campaign Speech in Fort Wayne, Indiana" (second quote); Palin, "Palin Speech in Loveland, Colorado"; Palin, "Palin Campaign Speech in Fort Wayne, Indiana" (third quote); Palin, "Palin Campaign Speech in Johnstown, Pennsylvania"; Palin, "Palin Speech in Loveland, Colorado"; Palin, "Palin Speech in Fort Wayne, Indiana"; Palin, "Palin Speech in Jeffersonville, Indiana" (fourth quote).

69. Joe Biden, "Transcript: Joe Biden's Acceptance Speech," August 27, 2008, NPR, http:// www.npr.org/templates/story/story.php?storyId=94048033; quoted in Lynn Sweet, "Joe Biden at Seattle Fund Raiser Transcript Says Obama Will Be Tested," *Chicago Sun-Times,* October 21, 2008, http://blogs.suntimes.com/sweet/2008/10/joe_biden_seattle_fund_raiser.html.

70. Palin, "Palin Campaign Speech in Johnstown, Pennsylvania"; Palin, "Palin Speech in Loveland, Colorado"; Palin, "Palin Campaign Speech in Fort Wayne, Indiana"; Palin, "Palin Speech in Jeffersonville, Indiana"; Palin, "Palin Speech in Marietta, Ohio"; Palin, "Governor Palin in Dubuque, Iowa."

71. Palin, "Palin Speech in Loveland, Colorado"; Palin, "Palin Campaign Speech in Fort Wayne, Indiana"; Palin, "Palin Speech in Marietta, Ohio."

72. See, for example, http://www.foulmouthshirts.com/Political-t-shirts/shirtpages/OIL -PALIN-TWO-THINGS-IN-ALASKA-ID-LIKE-TO-DRILL.htm (accessed February 12, 2012). Similarly, cafepress.com sold a woman's thong with Palin's picture and the tagline, "I'd Drill That." See http://www.cafepress.com/+id_drill_palin_classic_thong,299696599 (accessed February 12, 2012).

73. Palin, "Palin Speech in Loveland, Colorado"; Palin, "Palin Campaign Speech in Fort Wayne, Indiana."

74. Palin, "Palin Speech in Johnstown, Pennsylvania."

4. Political Journalism and Punditry

1. All quotations from "Special Coverage for the DNC—Tuesday, August 26," MSNBC, http://www.msnbc.msn.com/id/26422936/ns/msnbc_tv-hardball_with_chris_matthews/ (accessed July 28, 2008).

2. Ibid.

3. Entman, "Framing: Toward Clarification."

4. Entman, *Projections of Power*, 5, 6.

5. Entman, "Framing Bias," 163.

6. Patterson, *Out of Order*, 60.

7. Entman, "Framing: Toward Clarification," 55.

8. Messner, *Power at Play*, 151.

9. Howe, "Metaphor in Contemporary American Political Discourse"; Jansen and Sabo, "Sport/War Metaphor"; Carpenter, "America's Tragic Metaphor."

10. Hahn, *Political Communication*, 136, 167, 170.

11. Ibid., 163.

12. Jamieson, *Dirty Politics*, 186.

13. Amy Goldstein and Michael D. Shear, "A Tenacious Reformer's Swift Rise," *Washington Post*, August 30, 2008, www.lexisnexis.com.

14. Michael Grunwald and Jay Newton-Small, "Why McCain Picked Palin," *Time*, August 29, 2008, www.time.com; Dan Balz, "With Pick, McCain Reclaims His Maverick Image," *Washington Post*, August 30, 2008, www.lexisnexis.com; Emily Ramshaw, "Elections '08 President 'I Have Found the Right Partner' Palin Seen as Way to Woo Values Voters as Well as Women," *Dallas Morning News*, August 30, 2008, www.lexisnexis.com; David R. Sands, "Palin's Rise a Model for Maverick Politicians," *Washington Times*, August 30, 2008, www.lexisnexis .com; Grunwald and Newton-Small, "Why McCain Picked Palin."

15. Charlotte Allen, "The Last Frontier: In Alaska, the Folks Are Self-Reliant and Prefer to Take Care of Things Themselves; And They Like Sarah Palin," *Weekly Standard*, October 27, 2008, www.lexisnexis.com.

16. Corky Siemaszko, "Meet John McCain's Mooseburger-eatin,' Salmon-fishin,' Gun-totin' Pick for Running Mate," *New York Daily News*, August 30, 2008, www.lexisnexis.com.

17. See, for example, Tim Harper, "A 'Gun-Toting' Mother: McCain's Surprise VP Pick Appeals to Republican Base but Carries Huge Risks," *Toronto Star*, August 30, 2008, www .lexisnexis.com; Joan Walsh, "What Sarah Palin Means," *Salon*, August 29, 2008, www.lexis nexis.com; "John Baer: So, There's No Rhetoric in Minnesota? Cue the Eye Roll," *Philadelphia Daily News*, September 2, 2008, www.lexisnexis.com; Allen, "Last Frontier"; and Daphne Bramham, "Palin Confounds the Theories about Female Politicians: What Impressed Women about Hillary Clinton Drove Men Away; With Sarah Palin, the Polling Numbers Show the Opposite," *Vancouver Sun*, October 18, 2008, www.lexisnexis.com.

18. Ibid. (This description appeared in numerous journalists' reports.)

19. Camille Paglia, "Fresh Blood for the Vampire," *Salon*, September 10, 2008, www.lexis nexis.com.

20. Ibid.; "Sarah Palin's Background and Political Career," *Saturday Today*, NBC News, August 30, 2008, www.lexisnexis.com; Chip Reid, "John McCain Chooses Governor Sarah Palin of Alaska as Running Mate," *CBS Evening News*, August 29, 2008, www.lexisnexis.com.

21. "Just Who Is Sarah Palin?" *Hannity & Colmes*, Fox News Network, August 29, 2008, www.lexisnexis.com.

22. "Transcript: Palin and McCain Interview," CBS News, September 30, 2008, http:// www.cbsnews.com/8301–18563_162–4490788.html?tag=contentMain;contentBody. Subsequent quotations from the interview are taken from this source.

23. Associated Press, "McCain to Choose Alaska Governor as Running Mate," *El Paso Times*, August 29, 2008, www.lexisnexis.com.

24. Abdon M. Pallasch, "'Hockey Mom' Gets the Nod: McCain's Choice of Alaska Gov as Running Mate Seeks to Woo Hillary Supporters, Beef Up Appeal to Conservatives," *Chicago Sun-Times*, August 30, 2008, www.lexisnexis.com; Jim Tharpe, "State Republicans Like McCain's 'Bold' Pick: Palin Expected to Bring 'Buzz' to GOP Convention," *Atlanta Journal-*

Constitution, August 30, 2008, www.lexisnexis.com; Adam Nagourney, Jim Rutenberg, and Jeff Zeleny, "Campaigns Shift as McCain Choice Alters the Race," *New York Times,* August 31, 2008, www.lexisnexis.com; Tom Curry, "Palin Is McCain's Boldest Gamble," *MSNBC.com,* August 29, 2008, www.lexisnexis.com.

25. Stokes, "Clinton, Post-Feminism, and Rhetorical Reception on the Campaign Trail," 131.

26. Peggy Fikac and Hillary Sorin, "Campaign 2008 Republican Convention: Palin's Surprise; Pregnancy Announcement Draws GOP Support; Running Mate True to Consistent, 'Pro-Life Message,'" *Houston Chronicle,* September 2, 2008, www.lexisnexis.com.

27. Liz Sidoti, "Palin Says Daughter, 17, Is Pregnant," *Associated Press Online,* September 1, 2008, www.lexisnexis.com; G. N. Miller, Carl Campanile, and Chuck Bennett, "This Is No Way to Treat a Lady—GOPers Stand Up for Sarah," *New York Post,* September 3, 2008, www.lexisnexis.com.

28. Macer Hall, "McCain's Secret Weapon, a Beauty Queen," *Express* (UK), August 30, 2008, www.lexisnexis.com; Toby Harnden, "Feminine Touch Lifts McCain's Campaign," *Daily Telegraph* (London), August 30, 2008, www.lexisnexis.com; Toby Harnden, "Former Beauty Queen Is McCain's Number 2," *Daily Telegraph* (London), August 30, 2008, www.lexisnexis.com; "Miss Alaska Runner-Up Could Make History," *Birmingham Post* (UK), August 30, 2008, www.lexisnexis.com.

29. Frank Newport, "Republicans' Enthusiasm Jumps after Convention," *Gallup.com,* September 8, 2008.

30. Ibid.; Bill Weir and Kate Snow, "Hockey Mom in the Heartland: Sarah Palin Hits the Trail," *Good Morning America,* ABC News Transcript, September 6, 2008, www.lexisnexis.com.

31. Harry Smith and John Blackstone, "Palin Mania Raging across Country Following Sarah Palin's Introduction to the Nation at the Republican National Convention," *Early Show,* CBS News Transcripts, September 5, 2008, www.lexisnexis.com.

32. "McCain's Image Improves—with Big Assist from Palin," Pew Research Center for the People and the Press, September 10, 2008, http://pewresearch.org/pubs/946/mccain-image-palin-coverage.

33. Vavrus, *Postfeminist News,* 23.

34. Media Lizzy, "Sarah Palin: Every Woman." *Media Lizzy & Friends—Love, Politics, and Playing with Fire* (blog), September 1, 2008, http://medializzy.wordpress.com/category/im-every-woman/; Ed Kilgore, "Everywoman or Superwoman?" *Democratic Strategist: A Journal of Public Opinion and Political Strategy,* September 3, 2008, http://www.thedemocraticstrategist.org/; MichaelW, "Palin as Everywoman," *QandO Blog: Free Markets, Free People* (blog), September 2, 2008, http://www.qando.net/details.aspx?Entry=9208; Michelle D. Bernard, "Sarah Palin: An Everywoman Qualified by What She's Done," *Townhall.com,* September 12, 2008 (accessed January 20, 2012).

35. Kim Mance, "RNC Speech Proves Sarah Palin Is Not 'Every Woman,'" *Huffington Post,* September 4, 2008, huffingtonpost.com; Sarah Wildman, "Will the Real Sarah Palin Please Stand Up? *Guardian* (UK), October 4, 2008, www.guardian.co.uk.

36. Paglia, "Fresh Blood for the Vampire."

37. The transcript of the interview by Charles Gibson is available at http://abcnews.go.com/Politics/Vote2008/full-transcript-gibson-interviews-sarah-palin/story?id=9159105 (accessed February 4, 2012). Katie Couric's interview with Sarah Palin was broadcast in segments over multiple days. See "Sarah Palin on the Financial Crisis," *CBS Evening News,* September 24, 2008, www.lexisnexis.com; and "Sarah Palin on Foreign Policy," *CBS Evening News,* September 25, 2008, www.lexisnexis.com.

38. Michael Abramowitz, "Many Versions of 'Bush Doctrine': Palin's Confusion in Interview Understandable, Experts Say," *Washington Post,* September 13, 2008, www.lexisnexis.com.

39. See, for example, Carlin and Winfrey, "Have You Come a Long Way, Baby?"; and P. C. Wasburn and M. H. Wasburn, "Media Coverage of Women in Politics."

40. Alessandra Stanley, "Showing a Confidence, in Prepared Answers," *New York Times,* September 11, 2008, www.nytimes.com; Editorial, "Gov. Palin's Worldview," *New York Times,* September 13, 2008, www.lexisnexis.com; Jim Rutenberg, "In First Big Interview, Palin Says 'I'm Ready' for the Job," *New York Times,* September 12, 2008, www.lexisnexis.com.

41. Russell Goldman, "Palin Takes Hard Line on National Security, Softens Stance on Global Warming," *ABCNews.com,* September 11, 2008; Wesley Johnson, "'Eager Student' Palin Leaves Questions after TV Grilling," *Birmingham Post* (UK), September 13, 2008, www.lexis nexis.com; Howard Kurtz, "The ABCs of Sarah Palin," *Washington Post,* September 12, 2008, www.washingtonpost.com; Jack Shafer, "Palin vs. Gibson, Round 1," *Slate.com,* September 11, 2008.

42. The exchange is quoted in Ben W. Heineman Jr., "The Inside Story of Ferraro's 1984 Debate Prep," *Atlantic,* March 27, 2007, http://www.theatlantic.com/politics/archive/2011/03/the-inside-story-of-ferraros-1984-debate-prep/73070/.

43. Romesh Ratnesar, "Viewpoint: Sarah Palin's Foreign Policy Follies," *Time,* September 27, 2008, www.time.com; "Sarah Palin Chances Another Interview with Katie Couric," *Show Tracker* (blog), *LA Times,* September 29, 2008, www.latimesblogs.

44. "A Nonpartisan Message from Sarah Palin & Hillary Clinton," *Saturday Night Live,* September 13, 2008, http://www.nbc.com/saturday-night-live/video/palin—hillary-open/656281; "Sarah Palin on Foreign Policy," *CBS Evening News.*

45. "The Vice Presidential Debate," *New York Times,* October 2, 2008, www.nytimes.com; McKinney, Rill, and Watson, "Who Framed Sarah Palin?"; Brian Williams and Andrea Mitchell, "Assessment of Last Night's VP Debate," *NBC Nightly News,* October 3, 2008, www.lexis nexis.com; Ann Curry, Matt Lauer, and Andrea Mitchell, "Assessment of Thursday's Debate between Sarah Palin and Joe Biden," *Today,* NBC News Transcripts, October 3, 2008, www.lexisnexis.com; Alessandra Stanley, "A Candidate Recaptures Her Image," *New York Times,* October 3, 2008, www.lexisnexis.com; Joe Klein, "Palin Was Fine, but This Debate Was No Contest," *Time,* October 3, 2008, www.time.com.

46. Michael Falcone, "The Early Word: Palin Relishes Attack Dog Role," *Caucus* (blog), *New York Times,* October 6, 2008, thecaucus.blogs.nytimes.com.

47. Thomas M. DeFrank, "Six-Packin' Sarah Hold [*sic*] Her Own, But Question Is: 'Did Perky Trump Policy' Notes GOP," *New York Daily News,* October 3, 2008, www.lexisnexis.com; Adam C. Smith, "Palin Goes on the Attack," *St. Petersburg Times,* October 7, 2008, www.lexis nexis.com.

48. Patrick Healy and Michael Luo, "$150,000 Wardrobe for Palin May Alter Tailor-Made Image," *New York Times,* October 22, 2008, www.nytimes.com; Jay Carney, "Palin's Excessories," *Time.com,* October 23, 2008; Katie Couric and Nancy Cordes, "Republican Party Buys Wardrobe for Sarah Palin," *CBS Evening News,* October 22, 2008, www.lexisnexis.com; Rollins quoted in Healy and Luo, "$150,000 Wardrobe for Palin May Alter Tailor-Made Image"; Mark Simkin, "Palin Spending Spree Costs Republican Votes," *Lateline* (Australia), ABC Transcripts, October 24, 2008, www.lexisnexis.com.

49. Dana Bash, Peter Hamby, and John King, "Palin's 'Going Rogue,' McCain Aide Says," *CNN Politics,* October 25, 2008, articles.cnn.com.

50. Laura Strickler, "State Probing Palin's Troopergate," *CBSNews.com,* September 3, 2008.

51. "Palin Makes Troopergate Assertions That Are Flatly False," *Political Punch* (blog), *ABC-News.com,* October 12, 2008. Also see John Nichols, "Troopergate Conclusion: Palin Abused Her Office," *Nation* (blog), October 10, 2008; Nathan Thornburgh, "Palin and Troopergate: A Primer," *Time.com,* September 11, 2008; Serge F. Kovaleski, "Alaska Inquiry Concludes Palin Abused Powers," *New York Times,* October 10, 2008, nytimes.com.

52. William Yardley and Serge F. Kovaleski, "Report Backs Palin in Firing of Commissioner," *New York Times,* November 3, 2008, nytimes.com.

53. Peter Hamby, "McCain and Palin Joke Away Differences on ANWR Drilling," *CNN*

Politics (blog), September 18, 2008, politicalticker.blogs.cnn.com; Brian Williams, "In Depth: Sarah Palin on False Allegations about Her, Her Life Is an Open Book, and Her Political Future," *NBC Nightly News*, October 24, 2008, www.lexisnexis.com.

54. Ben Smith, "Palin Allies Report Rising Camp Tension," *Politico.com*, October 25, 2008.

55. Terry Moran and George Stephanopoulos, "Nightline Report Card: Palin Goes Rogue," *Nightline*, ABC News Transcripts, October 27, 2008, www.lexisnexis.com; "Goin' Rogue," *Daily Show with Jon Stewart*, Comedy Central, October 29, 2008, http://www.thedailyshow.com /watch/wed-october-29–2008/goin—rogue.

56. Frank Rich, "Pitbull Palin Mauls McCain," *New York Times* (opinion), October 4, 2008, nytimes.com; Jonathan Freedland, "Palin Won't Go Away," *Comment Is Free* (blog), *Guardian* (UK), October 23, 2008, www.guardian.co.uk; Barrie Cassidy, "Gap Closes in US Presidential Campaigns," *Insiders*, ABC Transcripts, October 26, 2008, www.lexisnexis.com; Carl Campanile and Ginger Adams Otis, "Pit Bull Turns on McMaverick," *New York Post*, October 26, 2008, nypost.com (accessed January 20, 2012); Nicholas Watt, "McCain's Verdict on Palin: More Trouble Than a Pitbull." *Politics Blog, Guardian* (UK), November 5, 2008, www.guardian .co.uk/politics/blog/2008/nov005/john-mccain-sarah-palin.

57. Anderson, "'Rhymes with Rich.'"

58. Sutton, "Bitches and Skankly Hobags," 561; Mark Silva, "Sarah Palin: 'Rogue . . . Diva . . . Elephant?,'" *The Swamp* (blog), *Chicago Tribune*, October 26, 2008, swamppolitics.com; Elisabeth Bumiller, "Internal Battles Divided McCain and Palin Camps," *New York Times*, November 5, 2008, nytimes.com.

59. Frank Newport, "Clinton Remains the Front-runner among Democrats; McCain and Giuliani Are Front-runners among Republicans," Gallup Poll News Service, January 18, 2007, www.lexisnexis.com; Matt Towery, "Hang It Up Obama—It's Hillary's Nomination," *Human Events Online*, January 18, 2007, www.lexisnexis.com.

60. Beth Fouhy, "Hillary Clinton Launches White House Bid," *Associated Press Online*, January 20, 2007, www.lexisnexis.com; Dan Gilgoff, "Hillary Clinton: 'I'm in to Win,'" *USNEWS.com*, January 20, 2007, www.lexisnexis.com; Dan Balz, "Hillary Clinton Opens Presidential Bid: The Former First Lady Enters the Race as the Front-Runner for the Democratic Nomination," *Washington Post*, January 21, 2007, www.lexisnexis.com; Lydia Saad, "Clinton Eclipses Obama and Edwards on Leadership: Obama Enjoys a Softer Image as Likable, a Uniter," Gallup Poll News Service, January 31, 2007, www.lexisnexis.com.

61. Sarah Baxter, "Hillary Runs for the White House as 'New Thatcher,'" *Sunday Times* (London), January 21, 2007, www.lexisnexis.com; Ewen MacAskill, "US Election 2008: Polls; Clinton Out in Front with 24-point Lead," *Guardian* (UK), January 22, 2007, www.lexisnexis .com; David Gardner, "Hillary Tops Poll of Democrats in Presidential Race," *Daily Mail* (London), January 22, 2007, www.lexisnexis.com; "The Clinton Dynasty," *Sydney Morning Herald*, January 23, 2007, www.lexisnexis.com.

62. John F. Morrison, "Democrats' Scramble Begins: Clinton's the Front-Runner, but 'We're a Lifetime Away,' Another Candidate Noted, *Philadelphia Daily News*, January 22, 2007, www .lexisnexis.com; "The 2008 US Presidential Hopefuls," *Agence France Presse*, April 1, 2007, www .lexisnexis.com.

63. "The Candidates: Hillary Clinton," *Economist*, May 17, 2007, http://www.economist .com/node/9196231.

64. Ibid. The *Economist*, like the *New York Times*, eschews use of professional titles such as "Senator," favoring the personal titles "Mr." and "Mrs." However, because the *Economist* chooses "Mrs." as opposed to the more neutral "Ms." (which would be parallel to "Mr."), the story highlights Clinton's marital status and draws attention to her personal life in ways that other titling choices would not.

65. "The Candidates: Hillary Clinton," *Economist*.

66. Ronald Brownstein, "The Tough, but Vulnerable, Front-Runner," *LA Times* (opinion),

June 13, 2007, http://www.latimes.com/news/opinion/commentary/la-oe-brownstein13jun13,0, 821331.column.

67. Chris Matthews, "Hardball," *MSNBC.com,* December 20, 2007.

68. Robin Givhan, "Hillary Clinton's Tentative Dip into New Neckline Territory," *Washington Post,* July 20, 2007, http://www.washingtonpost.com/wp-dyn/content/article/2007/07/19 /AR2007071902668.html.

69. Howard Kurtz, "Cleavage and the Clinton Campaign Chest," *Washington Post,* July 28, 2007, http://www.washingtonpost.com/wp-dyn/content/article/2007/07/27/AR2007072702369 .html.

70. Ibid.

71. Kenneth Bazinet, "Clinton Hot and Bothered over Cleavage Report," *New York Daily News,* July 28, 2007, http://www.nydailynews.com/news/national/2007/07/28/2007–07–28_clin ton_hot_and_bothered_over_cleavage_r-1.html; Mike White, "Clinton Uses Cleavage to Raise Cash," *Yahoo.com,* August 1, 2007, http://www.associatedcontent.com/article/331619/clin ton_uses_cleavage_to_raise_cash.html?cat=75; Alexander Mooney, "Clinton Seeks 'Cleavage' Cash," *Political Ticker* (blog), *CNN.com,* July 28, 2007, http://politicalticker.blogs.cnn.com /2007/07/28/clinton-seeks-cleavage-cash/; Megan Garber, "Oval Office or Bust: The Latest Campaign Frivolity Analyzes Clinton's *Other* War Chest," *Columbia Journalism Review,* August 2, 2007, http://www.cjr.org/behind_the_news/oval_office_or_bust.php?page=2; "Poll: Clinton Firmly Positioned as Democratic Front-Runner," *CNN.com,* August 9, 2007, http:// articles.cnn.com/2007–08–09/politics/2008.dems.poll_1_obama-and-edwards-clinton-cam paign-democratic-front-runner?_s=PM:POLITICS.

72. Patrick Healy, "The Clinton Conundrum: What's behind the Laugh?," *New York Times,* September 30, 2007, http://www.nytimes.com/2007/09/30/us/politics/30clinton.html.

73. Mike Allen and John F. Harris, "Clinton Hits Turbulence," *Politico.com,* September 30, 2007, http://www.politico.com/news/stories/0907/6088.html; Jeanne Moos, "Clinton's Cackle Coverage," *Political Ticker* (blog), *CNN.com,* October 2, 2007, http://politicalticker.blogs.cnn .com/2007/10/02/clintons-cackle-coverage/; Frank Rich, "Is Hillary Clinton the New Old Al Gore?," *New York Times,* September 30, 2007, *www.nytimes.com.*

74. Howard Kurtz, "Hillary Chuckles; Pundits Snort; Clinton's Robust Yuks Lead to Analysis of Appeal of Laughter," *Washington Post,* October 3, 2007, www.lexisnexis.com. See also Howard Kurtz, "Chucklegate," *Washington Post,* October 2, 2007, www.lexisnexis.com; "The Race to '08: Laughing in the Face of Critics," *Good Morning America,* October 1, 2001, ABC News Transcripts, www.lexisnexis.com; and "Hillary Clinton's Laughter," *Hannity & Colmes,* Fox News Network, October 1, 2007, www.lexisnexis.com.

75. Kurtz, "Hillary Chuckles."

76. "Hillary Clinton: Front-Runner and Target," *CBSNews.com,* September 22, 2007, http:// www.cbsnews.com/stories/2007/09/22/politics/main3288426.shtml; "Clinton Debates as Front-Runner and Target," *USA Today,* September 27, 2007, http://www.usatoday.com/news/politics /election2008/2007–09–26-democratic-debate_N.htm; "Inevitable Hillary?" *Christian Science Monitor,* October 11, 2007, http://www.csmonitor.com/2007/1011/p08s01-comv.html.

77. Charles Krauthammer, "Hillary Clinton Has No Principles; Therein Lies the Strange Allure of Her Candidacy," *Charleston (WV) Gazette,* October 13, 2007, www.lexisnexis.com.

78. Richard Sammon, "Hillary Clinton: Is the Democratic Nomination All Hers? *Kiplinger Business Forecasts,* October 22, 2007, www.lexisnexis.com.

79. Jack Kelly, "Hillary's in Trouble: Her Support Is Solidifying at Less than 50 Percent," *Pittsburgh Post-Gazette,* November 4, 2007, http://www.post-gazette.com/pg/07308/830711–373. stm; "The Cracks Begin to Show: Hillary Clinton No Longer Looks Inevitable," *Economist,* December 13, 2007, http://www.economist.com/node/10286068?story_id=10286068; Kenneth T. Walsh, "It's Gotten Too Close to Call," *US News & World Report,* December 20, 2007, http:// www.usnews.com/news/politics/articles/2007/12/20/its-gotten-too-close-to-call.html.

80. Karen Breslau, "Hillary Tears Up," *Newsweek,* January 7, 2008, http://www.newsweek.com/2008/01/06/hillary-tears-up.html.

81. Ibid.

82. Maureen Dowd, "Can Hillary Cry Her Way Back to the White House?," *New York Times,* January 9, 2008, www.lexisnexis.com.

83. Breslau, "Hillary Tears Up"; Dowd, "Can Hillary Cry Her Way Back to the White House?"; Christina Bellantoni, "Did Hillary Win N.H. Crying Game?" *Washington Times,* January 10, 2008, www.lexisnexis.com; "Choking Up on Campaign Trail Won't Cut It in White House," *USA Today,* January 11, 2008, www.lexisnexis.com; "Mrs. Clinton's Calculated Tears Set Back Feminism Fifty Years," *Rush Limbaugh Show,* January 7, 2008, transcript, http://www.rushlimbaugh.com/home/daily/site_010708/content/01125110.guest.html.guest.html.

84. See, for example, "Sally Quinn of the Washington Post on Hillary Clinton's Presidential Race," *Early Show,* CBS News Transcripts, June 5, 2008, www.lexisnexis.com; "It Seems Time for Senator Clinton to Face Facts and Admit Defeat," *Press* (Christchurch, New Zealand), May 10, 2008, www.lexisnexis.com; "Sexism Big Part of Primary Season," *East Lansing (MI) State News,* March 24, 2008, www.lexisnexis.com; Jodi Enda, "Clinton a Constant Target of Sexist Remarks," *San Jose (CA) Mercury News,* January 20, 2008, www.lexisnexis.com; Lisa Stevens, "Hillary-Baiting Shows Extra Barriers Ambitious Women Face," *Western Mail* (Cardiff, Wales), June 6, 2008, www.lexisnexis.com.

85. Madeleine M. Kunin, "Who's Ready for a Female President?," *Washington Post,* January 11, 2008, www.lexisnexis.com.

86. "Hillary Dropping in Polls," *Hannity & Colmes,* Fox News Network, April 1, 2008, www.lexisnexis.com.

87. Peter Worthington, "Oh, Just Wait Until 2012," *Portage (Manitoba) Daily Graphic,* May 9, 2008, www.lexisnexis.com.

88. Libby Copeland, "Belittled Women," *Washington Post,* May 16, 2008, www.washingtonpost.com; Anne Applebaum, "Irrational Ambition Is Hillary Clinton's Flaw," *Telegraph* (UK), May 8, 2008, http://www.telegraph.co.uk/comment/3558075/Irrational-ambition-is-Hillary-Clintons-flaw.html.

89. Sean Hannity, "Analysis with Karl Rove," *Hannity & Colmes,* Fox News Network, May 5, 2008, www.lexisnexis.com.

90. See, for example, Katharine Q. Seelye, "Q. & A. on Democrats and Disputed Delegates," *New York Times,* May 31, 2008, www.lexisnexis.com; Wolf Blitzer, William Schneider, Carol Costello, Donna Brazile, Abbi Tatton, Jack Cafferty, Mary Snow, Ed Henry, and Brian Todd, "DNC Rules & Bylaws Committee Meeting Set to Discuss Florida & Michigan Delegates; McCain Confronts Anti-War Hecklers," *Situation Room,* CNN, May 27, 2008, www.lexisnexis.com; Doug Mataconis, "Hillary Clinton's Nuclear Option," *Below the Beltway,* May 5, 2008, http://belowthebeltway.com/2008/05/05/hillary-clintons-nuclear-option/.

91. Thomas B. Edsall, "Clinton Camp Says It Will Use the Nuclear Option," *Huffington Post,* May 5, 2008, http://www.huffingtonpost.com/2008/05/04/clinton-camp-considering_n_100051.html.

92. Paul Thompson, "Hillary 'to Let McCain Win So She Can Return,'" *Sunday Express* (UK), May 18, 2008, www.lexisnexis.com.

93. See, for examples, Anderson, "'Rhymes with Rich'"; and Campbell, "Discursive Performance of Femininity."

94. "Interview with Frank Luntz, Michael Brown," *Hannity & Colmes,* Fox News Network, February 7, 2007, www.lexisnexis.com; Tim Grieve, "Clinton's Iraq Questioner: Her Answer Was 'Cold and Calculated,'" *Salon.com,* February 15, 2007, www.lexisnexis.com; Steve Huntley, "Senate to White House Is Tough Road to Travel," *Chicago Sun-Times,* March 16, 2007, www.lexisnexis.com; Dan Balz, "Obama Criticizes Clinton's Drive to Win," *Washington Post,* November 4, 2007, www.lexisnexis.com; *Chris Matthews Show,* transcript, *MSNBC.com,* November 18, 2007.

95. "Media Narrative Vaults Obama into Frontrunner Slot," *Journalism.org,* February 11–17, 2008, http://www.journalism.org/node/9828; Jake Tapper, "Dems Fear Clinton's 'Tonya Harding' Option," *ABCNews.com,* March 26, 2008, http://abcnews.go.com/GMA/Vote2008/story?id =4526203&page=1; Mary Lou Finlay, "There's Always Next Time," *Ottawa Citizen,* June 5, 2008, www.lexisnexis.com; Amie Parnes, "Mommie's Dearest," *Politico.com,* April 25, 2008, http:// www.politico.com/news/stories/0408/9876.html; Ken Rudin, interviewed on *Sunday Morning,* CNN, April 27, 2008; "Monica Crowley Compares Clinton to 'Glenn Close at the End of Fatal Attraction': 'You Think She's Dead and Then She Sits Bolt-Upright in the Bathtub," *Media-Matters for America,* January 14, 2008, http://mediamatters.org/research/200801140006?f=s _search; "Andrew Sullivan Declared Clintons Have 'a Touch of the Zombies about Them: Un-killable, They Move Relentlessly Forward,'" *MediaMatters for America,* March 10, 2008, http:// mediamatters.org/research/200803100008.

96. Jack Cafferty, "Should Obama Have Accepted Another Debate?" *Cafferty File* (blog), *CNN.com,* April 28, 2008, http://caffertyfile.blogs.cnn.com/2008/04/28/should-obama-have-accepted-another-debate/; Olbermann and Fineman quoted in "Hillary Clinton—Rising above Sexism & Misogyny," video montage, May 19, 2008, http://www.youtube.com/watch?v=lbz T2YqhGT4; "GOP Strategist on *Hannity & Colmes:* '[S]omeone Is Going to Have to Go Out There and Take [Clinton] behind the Barn,'" *MediaMatters for America,* February 26, 2008, http://mediamatters.org/mmtv/200802260006.

97. Eric Zorn, "Audio: Hillary Clinton's Dangerous Game," *Chicago Tribune,* January 23, 2008, http://blogs.chicagotribune.com/news_columnists_ezorn/2008/01/audio-hillary-c.html.

98. Lois Romano, "Clinton Puts up a New Fight: The Candidate Confronts Sexism on the Trail and Vows to Battle On," *Washington Post,* May 20, 2008, www.lexisnexis.com.

99. Quoted in Hart et al., *Political Keywords,* 163.

100. Mandziuk, "Dressing Down Hillary," 312.

5. Bodies Politic

1. Benoit et al., "A Fantasy Theme Analysis of Political Cartoons on the Clinton-Lewinsky-Starr Affair," 383. Also see Robertson and Walker, "Clinton a Go-Go," 14.

2. The cartoon and corresponding information about the Cleveland scandal can be found at Daryl Cagle, "Grover Cleveland's Love Child," *Daryl Cagle's Political Cartoonists Index,* May 19, 2011, http://www.cagle.com/2011/05/grover-clevelands-love-child/.

3. The terms *pornified, porning,* and *pornification* have appeared in a number of books, including Paul, *Pornified;* Ingraham, *Power to the People;* and Sarracino and Scott, *Porning of America.*

4. Entman, "Cascading Activation," 417.

5. Gamson, *Talking Politics,* 118.

6. McGee, "Text, Context, and the Fragmentation of Contemporary Culture," 287–88.

7. See, for example, Dworkin, *Pornography;* Dworkin and MacKinnon, *Pornography and Civil Rights;* Kimmel, ed., *Men Confront Pornography;* and Duggan and Hunter, *Sex Wars.*

8. See, for example, Rubin, "Thinking Sex"; McElroy, *XXX;* Kipnis, *Bound and Gagged;* and Strossen, *Defending Pornography.*

9. See, for example, Wolf, *Fire with Fire;* and Paglia, *Vamps and Tramps.*

10. See Paul, *Pornified;* Ingraham, *Power to the People;* and Sarracino and Scott, *Porning of America.*

11. For discussions of academic and legal perspectives on pornography and feminism, see, for example, Duggan and Hunter, *Sex Wars;* and Kipnis, *Bound and Gagged.*

12. See Ashley Womble, "Senator Is the Centerfold," *Cosmopolitan,* September 22, 2009, http://www.cosmopolitan.com/celebrity/news/scott-brown-nude-in-cosmo.

13. Jamieson, *Beyond the Double Bind,* 53.

14. "Palin's Sexy Librarian Glasses Spark Interest in Eyewear," *stylelist,* September 9, 2008,

www.stylelist.com; Christopher Orr, "Sarah Palin as Sexy Librarian," *The Plank* (blog), *New Republic,* September 5, 2008, http://blogs.tnr.com/tnr/blogs/the_plank/archive/2008/09/05/sarah-palin-as-sexy-librarian.aspx.

15. Many of the images assessed in this study spread virally as e-mail attachments or blog postings. When possible, we have tracked the image to its original source. Otherwise we cite the e-mail or blog source where we found the image. See Royce Williams, "O-Mama Spoof of Alaska Statehood Plate," *AKPL8S,* September 6, 2008, http://blog.akplates.org/2008/09/o-mama-spoof-of-alaska-statehood-plate.html; tabtoons@telus.net [author credit], "Campaign Buttons," *Calgary (Alberta) Sun,* August 29, 2008, *www.caglecartoons.com.*

16. Charlotte Hilton Anderson, "Sarah Palin Bikini Pictures: Fake Photos Hit the Web," *Huffington Post,* September 2, 2008, http://www.huffingtonpost.com/charlotte-hilton-andersen/sarah-palin-bikini-pictur_b_123234.html.

17. See, for example, the *MILF McCain '08* website at http://milfmccain.com/ (accessed October 20, 2008), and the poster with Palin's picture and the caption "MILF" on the *cafepress* website at http://art.cafepress.com/item/sarah-palin-milf-small-poster/302525295 (accessed October 20, 2008). The narrative of the experienced woman engaging an eager younger man in sex is a staple of popular culture, exemplified in characters such as *The Graduate's* Mrs. Robinson, *Desperate Housewives'* Gabrielle, *Lipstick Jungle's* Nico, and in the Fountains of Wayne hit song, "Stacy's Mom Has Got It Goin' On."

18. The biblical story of Esther is the archetypal example of this phenomenon—a narrative that Elizabeth Cady Stanton strongly rejected in her version of *The Woman's Bible.* Contemporarily, the influence of political spouses has been reduced to "pillow talk," suggesting (usually) that female spouses of political leaders accessed political power primarily via the conjugal bed.

19. Carrie Dann, "Desperately Searching for Sarah: What Web Searches Say about What We Really Want to Know," *Decision '08 Archive–NBCNews.com,* September 28, 2008, http://www.msnbc.msn.com/id/26903680/page/2/.

20. "Larry Flynt Is Hustling Up an Ala-skin Flick with Sarah Palin Look-Alike," *New York Daily News,* October 2, 2008, www.NYDailyNews.com; "Nalin' Paylin: Another Minute of Hustler Palin-Spoof Porn," *Huffington Post,* October 24, 2008, http://www.huffingtonpost.com/2008/10/24/nailin-paylin-another-min_n_137592.html; "'Nailin Paylin': *Hustler's* Palin Porn Details," *Huffington Post,* October 3, 2008, http://www.huffingtonpost.com/2008/10/03/nailin-paylin-hustlers-pa_n_131581.html.

21. Tracy Clark-Flory, "Sneak Peek: The Palin Porno," *Salon.com,* October 20, 2008, www.lexisnexis.com; Tommy Christopher, "Hustler Endorses 'Serra Paylin,'" *Politics Daily,* October 21, 2008, http://www.politicsdaily.com/2008/10/21/hustler-releases-palin-inspired-porn-flick/; "Nailin' Paylin: The Palin Porn Flick," *Right Wing News,* October 15, 2008, www.lexisnexis.com; and "Is Larry Flint [*sic*] Nailin' Palin?" *DCRepublican.com,* October 21, 2008, http://dcrepublican.com/2008/10/21/is-larry-flint-nailin-palin/.

22. "Is Larry Flint [*sic*] Nailin' Palin?"

23. Transcript reprinted in "Gingrich Cries Foul over Mom's Whisper," *Sacramento Bee,* January 5, 1995, A1, www.lexisnexis.com. Also see Roger Simon, "Just Answer in a Whisper: Can Connie Be Trusted?," *Baltimore Sun,* January 6, 1995, final edition, 2A, www.lexisnexis.com.

24. Anderson, "'Rhymes with Rich.'"

25. Anonymous comment in response to Perry Bacon Jr., "Clinton: GOP Should Apologize to America," *The Trail: A Daily Diary of Campaign 2008* (blog), July 13, 2008, http://blog.washingtonpost.com/44/2008/07/13/clinton_gop_should_apologize_t.html.

26. "The Snuke," *South Park* (New York: Comedy Central, aired March 28, 2007), http://www.southparkstudios.com/full-episodes/s11e04-the-snuke. Subsequent quotes were transcribed from this source.

27. See, for example, Hobby, "*Independence Day;* and Walker, *Woman's Dictionary of Symbols and Sacred Objects,* 1036.

28. Katherine Meiszkowski, "More Ways to Call Hillary Clinton the C-Word," *broadsheet* (blog), January 25, 2008, www.Salon.com.

29. Carol Lloyd, "The C-Word as a Political Tool," *broadsheet* (blog), January 24, 2008, www.Salon.com (accessed October 20, 2008). The IRS filing for Citizens United Not Timid is available at *Talking Points Memo Document Collection,* January 23, 2008, http://www.talking pointsmemo.com/docs/citizens-not-timid/.

30. Jon Stewart, *The Daily Show,* June 11, 2008, http://www.thedailyshow.com/video/index .jhtml?videoId=173064&title=indecision-2008-obama-fist-bump.

31. Quoted in "Hillary Clinton—Rising Above Sexism & Misogyny," video montage, May 19, 2008, http://www.youtube.com/watch?v=lbzT2YqhGT4.

32. The exchange was described on the *Media Matters for America* website, which also contained video of the full conversation. See Eric Boehlert and Jamison Foser, "Cliff May on Sen. Clinton: 'At Least Call Her a Vaginal-American,'" *Media Matters for America,* October 16, 2007, http://mediamatters.org/items/200710160010?f=s_search.

33. Quoted in "Hillary Clinton—Rising Above Sexism & Misogyny."

34. "NPR's Rudin: 'Hillary Clinton Is Glenn Close in *Fatal Attraction,*" *Media Matters for America,* April 28, 2008, http://mediamatters.org/research/200804280002. Rudin later called his statement a "facile and dumb comparison." See "NPR's Rudin Said 'I Wish I Hadn't' Compared Clinton to Glenn Close in *Fatal Attraction,*" *Media Matters for America,* May 30, 2008, http://mediamatters.org/research/200805030001.

35. Obama delegate quoted in "Hillary Clinton—Rising above Sexism & Misogyny"; "GOP Strategist on *Hannity & Colmes:* '[S]omeone Is Going to Have to Go Out There and Take [Clinton] behind the Barn," *Media Matters for America,* February 26, 2008, http://media matters.org/mmtv/200802260006.

36. Henry, "Orgasms and Empowerment," 74, 82.

37. Anderson and Stewart, "Politics and the Single Woman," 606.

38. Obama Girl [Amber Lee Ettinger], "I Got a Crush . . . on Obama," produced by Ben Relles, June 13, 2007, http://www.youtube.com/watch?v=wKsoXHYICqU.

39. "About Us: The Barely Political Team," *www.BarelyPolitical.com* (accessed October 21, 2008).

40. Jose Antonio Vargas, "Obama Crush . . . with Eyeliner," June 14, 2007, *Channel '08* (blog), http://blog.washingtonpost.com/channel-08/2007/06/obama_crush_with_eyeliner.html.

41. Balaji, "Owning Black Masculinity," 22. See also Jackson, *Scripting the Black Masculine Body;* and R. Richardson, *Black Masculinity and the US South.*

42. Obama Girl [Amber Lee Ettinger], "I Got a Crush . . . on Obama."

43. Kelley, "Kickin' Reality, Kickin' Ballistics," 142.

44. Watts and Orbe, "Spectacular Consumption of 'True' African American Culture"; hooks, *Black Looks.*

45. *Amber Lee,* http://www.amberleeonline.com (accessed January 31, 2010).

46. See "Beyond 'Obama Girl," *All Things Considered,* October 1, 2008, NPR transcript, www.lexisnexis.com; Liane Hansen, "Campaign Songs Then and Now," *Weekend Edition,* September 16, 2007, NPR transcript, www.lexisnexis.com; Matt Bai, "The Web Users' Campaign," *New York Times,* December 9, 2007, 29, www.lexisnexis.com; Ben Goldberger, "Hott4Hill Takes on Obama Girl," *Chicago Sun-Times,* July 12, 2007, 30, www.lexisnexis.com; Jonathan Storm, "Jonathan Storm: Puncturing Pols Online," *Philadelphia Inquirer,* April 13, 2008, H01, www .lexisnexis.com; Karen Breslau, "How to Run for President, YouTube Style," *Newsweek,* January 7, 2008, 69, www.lexisnexis.com; and Rob Long, "Oh No You Can't—Amateur Propagandists in the YouTube Age," *National Review,* April 7, 2008, www.lexisnexis.com.

47. Bai, "Web Users' Campaign."

48. Taryn Southern, "Hott 4 Hill," July 2, 2007, http://www.youtube.com/watch?v=-Sudw 4ghVe8.

49. See, for example, Chris Matthews, "Hardball for June 25, 2007," *Hardball*, June 25, 2007, www.lexisnexis.com; Chris Matthews, "Hardball for July 13, 2007," *Hardball*, July 13, 2007, www .lexisnexis.com; Chris Matthews, "Hardball for July 16, 2007," *Hardball*, July 16, 2007, www.lexis nexis.com; and Chris Matthews, "Hardball for July 24, 2007," *Hardball*, July 24, 2007, www .lexisnexis.com.

50. Kate Phillips, "2008: Obama Girl and More," June 13, 2007, *The Caucus* (blog), http:// thecaucus.blogs.nytimes.com/2007/06/13/2008-obama-girl-and-more/; George Stephanopou-los, "Roundtable," *This Week . . . with George Stephanopoulos*, ABC News, June 17, 2007, www .lexisnexis.com; Dan Harris and David Wright, "Obamagirl; Video Rocks Presidential Cam-paign," *World News Sunday*, June 17, 2007, www.lexisnexis.com. .

51. Matthews, "Hardball for July 24, 2007."

52. This argument is powerfully illustrated in the *Dreamworlds* documentary trilogy produced by Sut Jhally and the *Media Education Foundation*. See an unabridged preview of *Dreamworlds 3* at http://www.mediaed.org/cgi-bin/commerce.cgi?preadd=action&key=223 (ac-cessed October 21, 2008).

53. "Facts on Women in Congress 2010," Center for American Women and Politics, http:// www.cawp.rutgers.edu/fast_facts/levels_of_office/Congress-CurrentFacts.php (accessed Feb-ruary 2, 2011); "Women in Statewide Elective Office 2011," Center for American Women and Politics, http://www.cawp.rutgers.edu/fast_facts/levels_of_office/Statewide-Current.php (ac-cessed February 2, 2011).

54. Jonathan Tilove, "Woman-Hating Glee Club," *New Orleans Times-Picayune*, Decem-ber 11, 2007, http://www.nola.com/news/tp/index.ssf?/base/living9/1197354420308740.xml&coll=1 &thispage=1.

55. See, for example, Emily Steel, "The New Focus Groups: Online Networks; Proprietary Panels Help Consumer Companies Shape Products, Ads," *Wall Street Journal*, January 14, 2008, http://online.wsj.com/article/SB120027230906987357.html; and Alex Cohen, "Artists Use Social Media for Public Feedback," *All Things Considered*, June 18, 2009, www.npr.org.

56. Hogan, "George Gallup and the Rhetoric of Scientific Democracy."

57. Anderson, "'Rhymes with Rich.'"

58. Quoted in Rebecca Dana, "Why Women Don't Have Sex Scandals," *Daily Beast*, De-cember 11, 2009, http://www.thedailybeast.com/articles/2009/12/11/why-women-dont-have-sex -scandals.html.

6. Parodying Presidentiality

1. "A Nonpartisan Message from Sarah Palin and Hillary Clinton," *Saturday Night Live*, September 13, 2008, http://www.nbc.com/saturday-night-live/video/palin—hillary-open/656281. All references to the sketch were transcribed from streaming video.

2. Brian Orloff, "Tina Fey Parodies Sarah Palin on *SNL* Premiere," *People*, September 14, 2008, http://www.people.com/people/article/0,,20225679,00.html; Daniel Kurtzman, "Tina Fey Skewers Sarah Palin on *Saturday Night Live*," *About.com*, September 14, 2008, http:// politicalhumor.about.com/b/2008/09/14/tina-fey-skewers-sarah-palin-on-saturday-night -live.htm.

3. David Zurawik, "*SNL* Vet Tina Fey's Palin Skit Stole the Show," *Baltimore Sun*, Sep-tember 15, 2008, www.baltimoresun.com/entertainment/bal-te.to.review15sep15,0,375092.story; Scott Conroy, "The Real Sarah Palin Laughs Along with Tina Fey's Impression," *CBSNews .com*, September 14, 2008, http://www.cbsnews.com/8301-502443_162-4448143-502443.html; Jones, *Entertaining Politics*, 4.

4. Conroy, "Real Sarah Palin Laughs Along with Tina Fey's Impression."

5. Hariman, "Political Parody and Public Culture," 248, 251.

6. Hart and Hartelius, "Political Sins of Jon Stewart," 270.

7. We examine sketches that stream in their entirety in the "Political Gallery" collection at the *SNL* website. See http://www.nbc.com/saturday-night-live/video/categories/political-gallery/33501/ (accessed January 9, 2011).

8. Bakhtin, *Dialogic Imagination,* 53; Morson, "Parody, History, and Metaparody," 63; Hariman, "Political Parody and Public Culture," 264.

9. Hariman, "Political Parody and Public Culture," 249; Morson, "Parody, History, and Metaparody," 65.

10. Hariman, "Political Parody and Public Culture," 254.

11. Morson, "Parody, History, and Metaparody," 67.

12. Meddaugh, "Bakhtin, Colbert, and the Center of Discourse," 379, 380, 387.

13. Hutcheon, "Modern Parody and Bakhtin," 99, 100.

14. Hariman, "Political Parody and Public Culture," 254; Hariman, "In Defense of Jon Stewart," 274.

15. For discussion of "polyvalence" as it relates to television viewing, see Ceccarelli, "Polysemy"; and Condit, "Rhetorical Limits of Polysemy."

16. Smith and Voth, "Role of Humor in Political Argument," 114.

17. Jamieson, *Beyond the Double Bind,* 121.

18. Hariman, "Parody and Public Culture," 257.

19. "Halloween Party," *Saturday Night Live,* November 3, 2007, http://www.nbc.com/saturday-night-live/video/halloween-party/229116/. All references to the sketch were transcribed from streaming video.

20. For a discussion of Clinton's history with the word *bitch,* see Anderson, "'Rhymes with Rich.'"

21. "Democratic Debate #2," *Saturday Night Live,* March 1, 2008, http://www.nbc.com/saturday-night-live/video/democratic-debate-2/229111/. All subsequent quotes are from this streaming video.

22. During the February 23, 2008, episode, *SNL* aired a debate sketch premised entirely on the contention that the journalists hosting the debate were going easier on Obama than they were on Clinton.

23. "Editorial Response from Senator Hillary Clinton," *Saturday Night Live,* March 1, 2008, http://www.nbc.com/saturday-night-live/video/response-sen-clinton/229110/?__cid=thefilter. All references to the sketch were transcribed from streaming video.

24. Apel, "Just Joking?," 137.

25. Morson, "Parody, History, and Metaparody," 71.

26. Peter S. Canellos, "Swing in Momentum May Alter Media's Focus," *Boston Globe,* March 5, 2008, http://www.boston.com/news/nation/articles/2008/03/05/swing_in_momentum_may_alter_medias_focus/. Repost of article's full text available at http://mediachannel.org/wordpress/2008/03/05/swing-in-momentum-may-alter-medias-focus/ (accessed January 9, 2011).

27. "Tina Fey on Update," *Saturday Night Live,* February 23, 2008, http://www.nbc.com/Saturday-night-live/video/tina-fey-on-update/221773/.

28. See Anderson, "'Rhymes with Rich.'"

29. Canellos, "Swing in Momentum May Alter Media's Focus."

30. Katharine Q. Seelye, "News Coverage Changes, and So Does Tone of the Campaign," *New York Times,* March 5, 2008, http://www.nytimes.com/2008/03/05/us/politics/05press.html?_r=1.

31. Ibid.

32. "Weekend Update: Tracy Morgan," *Saturday Night Live,* March 15, 2008, http://www

.nbc.com/saturday-night-live/video/update-tracy-morgan/1145548/. All references to the sketch were transcribed from streaming video.

33. See Chris Cillizza, "Clinton's '3 A.M. Phone Call' Ad," *The Fix* (blog), February 29, 2008, http://voices.washingtonpost.com/thefix/eye-on-2008/hrcs-new-ad.html.

34. "After Vowing Not to Underestimate Clinton, Matthews asserted, '[T]he Reason She May Be a Front-Runner Is Her Husband Messed Around," *Media Matters for America*, January 9, 2008, http://mediamatters.org/research/200801090008.

35. Hutcheon, "Modern Parody and Bakhtin," 87–88.

36. Morson, "Parody, History, and Metaparody," 73.

37. "Obama Plays It Cool," *Saturday Night Live*, December 6, 2008, http://www.nbc.com/saturday-night-live/video/obama-plays-it-cool/866342. All references to the sketch were transcribed from streaming video.

38. "Barack is one cool cat" is the subtitle listed below the video on the *SNL* videos page. See http://www.nbc.com/saturday-night-live/video/obama-plays-it-cool/866342 (accessed January 9, 2011).

39. "3 A.M. Phone Call," *Saturday Night Live*, March 8, 2008, http://www.nbc.com/saturday-night-live/video/3am-phone-call/229104/. All references to the sketch were transcribed from streaming video.

40. Jones, "Cultural Approach to the Study of Mediated Citizenship," 366.

41. Baym, "Representation and the Politics of Play," 361.

42. Ibid., 361, 373.

43. Hariman, "Political Parody and Public Culture," 255.

44. Ibid., 247.

Conclusion

1. Terry Gross, "Michelle and Barack Obama: A Powerful Partnership," *Fresh Air*, January 10, 2012, http://www.npr.org/2012/01/10/144324472/michelle-and-barack-obama-a-powerful-partnership. The book under discussion was Jodi Kantor, *The Obamas* (London: Penguin Books, 2012).

2. In February 2007, when Clinton was the frontrunner for the Democratic presidential nomination, Gallup reported that 88 percent of Americans polled said they would vote for a woman for US president. See Jeffrey M. Jones, "Some Americans Reluctant to Vote for Mormon, 72-Year-Old Presidential Candidates," *Gallup*, February 20, 2007, http://www.gallup.com/poll/26611/Some-Americans-Reluctant-Vote-Mormon-72YearOld-Presidential-Candidates.aspx.

3. Dorsey, "Theodore Roosevelt, 'The Strenuous Life' (10 April 1899)," 6, 7.

4. Ibid., 7.

5. Heider, "Suffrage, Self-Determination, and the Women's Christian Temperance Union in Nebraska," 88–89.

6. Ibid., 100.

7. Vavrus, *Postfeminist News.* 14.

8. Faludi, *Backlash*, 46, 46–47.

9. McRobbie, *Aftermath of Feminism*, 11, 12.

10. Vavrus, *Postfeminist News*, 22.

11. Dow, *Prime-Time Feminism*, 88.

12. Vavrus, *Postfeminist News*, 2.

13. Douglas, *Enlightened Sexism*, 10.

14. See, for example, Cathy Young, "Why Feminists Hate Sarah Palin," *Wall Street Journal* (opinion), September 15, 2008, http://online.wsj.com/article/SB122143727571134335.html.

15. Sanchez, *You've Come a Long Way, Maybe*, 79.

16. Faludi, *Backlash*, 62, 64.

17. Watts and Orbe, "Spectacular Consumption of 'True' African American Culture."

18. Chris Matthews, "Hardball for July 24, 2007," *Hardball*, July 24, 2007, www.lexisnexis .com.

19. Dumm, "Barack Obama and the Souls of White Folk," 320.

20. Traister, *Big Girls Don't Cry*, 284, 287.

21. The quotation is widely attributed to Kramarae and Treichler. See, for example, Mulvaney, "Gender Differences in Communication," 221.

Bibliography

Achter, Paul. "Racing Jesse Jackson: Leadership, Masculinity, and the Black Presidency." In *Gender and Political Communication in America: Rhetoric, Representation and Display,* edited by Janis L. Edwards, 107–27. Lanham, MD: Lexington Books, 2009.

Amy, Douglas J. *Real Choices / New Voices.* New York: Columbia University Press, 2002.

Anderson, Karrin Vasby. "The First Lady: A Site of 'American Womanhood." In *Inventing a Voice: The Rhetoric of American First Ladies of the Twentieth Century,* edited by Molly Meijer Wertheimer, 17–30. Lanham, MD: Rowman & Littlefield, 2004.

———. "From Spouses to Candidates: Hillary Rodham Clinton, Elizabeth Dole and the Gendered Office of US President." *Rhetoric & Public Affairs* 5, no. 1 (2002): 105–32.

———. "Hillary Rodham Clinton as 'Madonna': The Role of Metaphor and Oxymoron in Image Restoration." *Women's Studies in Communication* 25, no. 1 (2002): 1–24.

———. "'Rhymes with Rich': 'Bitch' as a Tool of Containment in Contemporary American Politics." *Rhetoric & Public Affairs* 2, no. 4 (1999): 599–623.

———, and Kristina Horn Sheeler. *Governing Codes: Gender, Metaphor, and Political Identity.* Lanham, MD: Lexington Books, 2005.

———, and Jessie Stewart. "Politics and the Single Woman: The 'Sex and the City Voter' in Campaign 2004." *Rhetoric & Public Affairs* 8, no. 4 (2005): 595–616.

Apel, Dora. "Just Joking? Chimps, Obama and Racial Stereotype." *Journal of Visual Culture* 8, no. 2 (2009): 134–42.

Bacon, Jacqueline. "'Acting as Freemen': Rhetoric, Race, and Reform in the Debate over Colonization in *Freedom's Journal,* 1827–1828." *Quarterly Journal of Speech* 93, no. 1 (2007): 58–83.

Bakhtin, Mikhail. *The Dialogic Imagination.* Edited by Michael Holquist. Translated by Caryl Emerson and Michael Holquist. Austin: University of Texas Press, 1981.

Balaji, Murali. "Owning Black Masculinity: The Intersection of Cultural Commodification and Self-Construction in Rap Music Videos." *Communication, Culture & Critique* 2, no. 1 (2009): 21–38.

Barthes, Roland. *Mythologies*. Translated by Annette Lavers. 1957. Reprint, New York: Hill and Wang, 1972.

Baym, Geoffrey. "Representation and the Politics of Play: Stephen Colbert's 'Better Know a District.'" *Political Communication* 24, no. 4 (2007): 359–76.

Beasley, Vanessa B. *You, the People: American National Identity in Presidential Rhetoric.* College Station: Texas A&M University Press, 2004.

Benoit, William L., Andrew A. Klyukovski, John P. McHale, and David Airne. "A Fantasy Theme Analysis of Political Cartoons on the Clinton-Lewinsky-Starr Affair." *Critical Studies in Media Communication* 18, no. 4 (2001): 377–94.

Bitzer, Lloyd F. "The Rhetorical Situation." *Philosophy & Rhetoric* 1, no. 1 (1968): 1–14.

Black, Edwin. "The Invention of Nixon." In *Beyond the Rhetorical Presidency*, edited by Martin J. Medhurst, 104–21. College Station: Texas A&M University Press, 1996.

Blahuta, Jason P. "The Politics of Crisis: Machiavelli in the Colonial Fleet." In *Battlestar Galactica and Philosophy*, edited by Jason T. Eberl, 40–51. Malden, MA: Blackwell, 2008.

Blankenship, Jane, and Deborah C. Robson. "A 'Feminine Style' in Women's Political Discourse: An Exploratory Essay." *Communication Quarterly* 43, no. 3 (1995): 353–66.

Bostdorff, Denise M. "Hillary Rodham Clinton and Elizabeth Dole as Running 'Mates' in the 1996 Campaign: Parallels in the Rhetorical Constraints of First Ladies and Vice Presidents." In *The 1996 Campaign: A Communication Perspective*, edited by Robert E. Denton, 199–228. Westport, CT: Praeger, 1998.

———. "Vice-Presidential Comedy and the Traditional Female Role: An Examination of the Rhetorical Characteristics of the Vice Presidency." *Western Journal of Speech Communication* 55, no. 1 (1991): 1–27.

Braden, Maria. *Women Politicians and the Media*. Lexington: University Press of Kentucky, 1996.

Brands, H. W. "Politics as Performance Art: The Body English of Theodore Roosevelt." In *The Presidency and Rhetorical Leadership*, edited by Leroy G. Dorsey, 115–28. College Station: Texas A&M University Press, 2002.

Braun, Carol Moseley. Announcement Speech. September 22, 2003. http://www.4president.us/speeches/carolmoseleybraun2004announcement.htm.

Browne, Stephen H. *Angelina Grimké: Rhetoric, Identity, and the Radical Imagination.* East Lansing: Michigan State University Press, 1999.

———. "Encountering Angelina Grimké: Violence, Identity, and the Creation of Radical Community." *Quarterly Journal of Speech* 82, no. 1 (1996): 55–73.

Burke, Cindy, and Sharon R. Mazzarella. "A Slightly New Shade of Lipstick: Gendered Mediation in Internet News Stories." *Women's Studies in Communication* 31 (fall 2008): 395–418.

Burke, Kenneth. *A Grammar of Motives*. New York: Prentice-Hall, 1945.

———. *Permanence and Change*. Rev. ed. Berkeley and Los Angeles: University of California Press, 1954.

———. *A Rhetoric of Motives*. 1950. Berkeley and Los Angeles: University of California Press, 1969.

Burns, Lisa M. "Collective Memory and the Candidates' Wives in the 2004 Presidential Campaign." *Rhetoric & Public Affairs* 8, no. 4 (2005): 684–88.

Burt, Elizabeth V. "Working Women and the Triangle Fire: Press Coverage of a Tragedy." *Journalism History* 30 (winter 2005): 189–99.

Bush, George W. Address to a Joint Session of Congress following 9/11 Attacks. September 20, 2001. http://www.americanrhetoric.com/speeches/gwbush911joint sessionspeech.htm.

Bystrom, Dianne. "Advertising, Web Sites, and Media Coverage: Gender and Communication along the Campaign Trail." In *Gender and Elections: Shaping the Future of American Politics,* edited by Susan J. Carroll and R. L. Fox, 169–88. New York: Cambridge University Press, 2006.

———, Mary Christine Banwart, Lynda Lee Kaid, and Terry A. Robertson. *Gender and Candidate Communication: VideoStyle, WebStyle, NewsStyle.* New York: Routledge, 2004.

Calder, Jenni. *There Must Be a Lone Ranger.* London: Hamish Hamilton, 1974.

Campbell, Karlyn Kohrs. "The Discursive Performance of Femininity: Hating Hillary." *Rhetoric & Public Affairs* 1, no. 1 (1998): 1–19.

———. *Man Cannot Speak for Her.* 2 vols. Westport, CT: Praeger, 1989.

———. "The Rhetorical Presidency: A Two-Person Career." In *Beyond the Rhetorical Presidency,* edited by Martin J. Medhurst, 179–95. College Station: Texas A&M University Press, 1996.

———. "The Rhetoric of Women's Liberation: An Oxymoron." *Quarterly Journal of Speech* 59 (February 1973): 74–86.

———. "Shadowboxing with Stereotypes: The Press, the Public, and the Candidates' Wives." Research paper R-9, President and Fellows of Harvard College, 1993.

———. "The Sound of Women's Voices." *Quarterly Journal of Speech* 75, no. 2 (1989): 212–20.

———, and Kathleen Hall Jamieson. *Presidents Creating the Presidency: Deeds Done in Words.* Chicago: University of Chicago Press, 2008.

Cappella, Joseph N., and Kathleen Hall Jamieson. "News Frames, Political Cynicism, and Media Cynicism." *Annals of the American Academy of Political and Social Science Media and Politics* 546 (July 1996): 71–84.

———, and ———. *Spiral of Cynicism: The Press and the Public Good.* New York: Oxford University Press, 1997.

Carcasson, Martin. "Ending Welfare as We Know It: President Clinton and the Rhetorical Transformation of the Anti-Welfare Culture." *Rhetoric & Public Affairs* 9, no. 4 (2006): 655–92.

Carlin, Diana B., and Kelly L. Winfrey. "Have You Come a Long Way, Baby? Hillary Clinton, Sarah Palin, and Sexism in 2008 Campaign Coverage." *Communication Studies* 60, no. 4 (2009): 326–43.

Caroli, Betty Boyd. *First Ladies.* New York: Oxford University Press, 1995.

Carpenter, Ronald H. "America's Tragic Metaphor: Our Twentieth-Century Combatants and Frontiersmen." *Quarterly Journal of Speech* 76, no. 1 (1990): 1–22.

———. "Frederick Jackson Turner and the Rhetorical Impact of the Frontier Thesis." *Quarterly Journal of Speech* 63, no. 2 (1977): 117–29.

Carroll, Susan J. *Women and American Politics: New Questions, New Directions.* New York: Oxford University Press, 2003.

———. *Women as Candidates in American Politics.* Bloomington: Indiana University Press, 1994.

Caruso, Joseph, ed. *The First Woman President.* New York: Nova Science, 2007.

Catt, Carrie Chapman, and Nettie Rogers Shuler. *Woman Suffrage and Politics.* New York: Charles Scribner's Sons, 1926. http://www.infoplease.com/t/hist/suffrage-inner-story/chapter4.html.

Ceaser, James, Glen Thurow, Jeffrey Tulis, and Joseph M. Bessette. "The Rise of the Rhetorical Presidency." *Presidential Studies Quarterly* 11, no. 2 (1981): 158–71.

Ceccarelli, Leah. "Polysemy: Multiple Meanings in Rhetorical Criticism." *Quarterly Journal of Speech* 84, no. 4 (1998): 395–415.

Center for American Women and Politics. "Republican Women Follow National Winning Pattern: Newcomers Take Many House Races, But Only One New Senate Seat, Three New Governors; Many House Incumbents Fall." *Center for American Women and Politics: Election Watch,* November 23, 2010. http://www.cawp.rutgers.edu/press_room/news/documents/PressRelease_11–23–10.pdf.

Chamberlain, Daniel, and Scott Ruston. "*24* and Twenty-First Century Quality Television." In *Reading "24": TV against the Clock,* edited by Steven Peacock, 13–24. New York: I. B. Taurus, 2007.

Charland, Maurice. "Constitutive Rhetoric: The Case of the *Peuple Québécois.*" *Quarterly Journal of Speech* 73, no. 2 (1987): 133–50.

Chisholm, Shirley. Brooklyn Announcement. http://www.4president.org/speeches/shirleychisholm1972announcement.htm. Accessed January 25, 2011.

Christensen, Terry. *Reel Politics: American Political Movies from "Birth of a Nation" to "Platoon."* New York: Basil Blackwell, 1987.

———, and Peter J. Haas. *Projecting Politics: Political Messages in American Films.* Armonk, NY: M. E. Sharpe, 2005.

Cienki, Alan J. "Bush's and Gore's Language and Gestures in the 2000 US Presidential Debates: A Test Case for Two Models of Metaphors." *Journal of Language and Politics* 3, no. 3 (2004): 409–40.

Clift, Eleanor, and Tom Brazaitis. *Madam President: Shattering the Last Glass Ceiling.* New York, Scribner, 2000. Reissued as *Madam President: Women Blazing the Leadership Trail.* New York: Routledge, 2003.

Cloud, Dana L. "Hegemony or Concordance? The Rhetoric of Tokenism in 'Oprah' Winfrey's Rags to Riches Biography." *Critical Studies in Mass Communication* 13, no. 2 (1996): 115–37.

Coe, Kevin, David Domke, Meredith M. Bagley, Sheryl Cunningham, and Nancy Van Leuven. "Masculinity as Political Strategy: George W. Bush, the 'War on Terrorism,' and an Echoing Press." *Journal of Women, Politics, and Policy* 29, no. 1 (2007): 31–55.

Cohen, Jodi R. "The 'Relevance' of Cultural Identity in Audiences' Interpretations of Mass Media." *Critical Studies in Mass Communication* 8, no. 4 (1991): 442–54.

Collins, Michael. "The American Character." *Contemporary Review.* http://findarticles.com/p/articles/mi_m2242/is_1657_284/ai_n6141795/. Accessed November 9, 2010.

Condit, Celeste Michelle. "The Rhetorical Limits of Polysemy." *Critical Studies in Mass Communication* 6, no. 2 (1989): 103–22.

Conley, Donovan S. "Virtuoso." *Communication and Critical/Cultural Studies* 5, no. 3 (2008): 307–11.

Conly, Sarah. "Is Starbuck a Woman?" In *Battlestar Galactica and Philosophy,* edited by Jason T. Eberl, 230–40. Malden, MA: Blackwell, 2008.

Conroy, Meredith. "Political Parties: Advancing a Masculine Ideal." In *Rethinking Madam President: Are We Ready for a Woman in the White House?,* edited by Lori Cox Han and Caroline Haldman, 133–46. Boulder, CO: Lynne Rienner, 2007.

Conway, M. Margaret, Gertrude A. Steuernagel, and David W. Ahern. *Women and Political Participation: Cultural Change in the Political Arena.* 2nd ed. Washington, DC: CQ Press, 2005.

Cooke, Elizabeth F. "'Let It Be Earth': The Pragmatic Virtue of Hope." In *Battlestar Galactica and Philosophy,* edited by Jason T. Eberl, 218–29. Malden, MA: Blackwell, 2008.

Darsey, James. "Barack Obama and America's Journey." *Southern Communication Journal* 74, no. 1 (2009): 88–103.

Daughton, Suzanne. "The Fine Texture of Enactment: Iconicity as Empowerment in Angelina Grimké's Pennsylvania Hall Address." *Women's Studies in Communication* 18 (spring 1995): 19–43.

———. "Women's Issues, Women's Place: Gender-Related Problems in Presidential Campaigns." *Communication Quarterly* 42, no. 2 (1994): 106–19.

———. "Women's Issues, Women's Place: Gender-Related Problems in Presidential Campaigns." In *Presidential Campaign Discourse: Strategic Communication Problems,* edited by Kathleen E. Kendall, 221–39. Albany: State University of New York Press, 1995.

Delaney, Paul. "'She May Be a Little Weird': Chloe O'Brian." In *Reading "24": TV against the Clock,* edited by Steven Peacock, 191–200. New York: I. B. Taurus, 2007.

Denton, Robert E., Jr., ed. *The 2008 Presidential Campaign: A Communication Perspective.* Lanham, MD: Rowman & Littlefield, 2009.

Devitt, James. "Framing Gender on the Campaign Trail: Female Gubernatorial Candidates and the Press." *Journalism and Mass Communication Quarterly* 79, no. 2 (2002): 445–63.

Devitt, James. "Framing Gender on the Campaign Trail: Women's Executive Leadership and the Press." Women's Leadership Fund, 1999. http://www.appcpenn.org/political/archive/wlfstudy.pdf. Accessed June 11, 2003. Paper archived at https://mmm1102.verio-web.com/thewh5/v2/researchandreports/framinggender/Framing_Gender_Report.pdf. Accessed March 15, 2011.

deVreese, Claes. "The Effects of Strategic News on Political Cynicism, Issue Evaluations, and Policy Support: A Two-Wave Experiment." *Mass Communication and Society* 7, no. 2 (2004): 191–214.

Dickinson, Greg. "Selling Democracy: Consumer Culture and Citizenship in the Wake of September 11." *Southern Communication Journal* 70 (2005): 271–84.

———, and Karrin Vasby Anderson. "Fallen: OJ Simpson, Hillary Rodham Clinton and the Recentering of White Patriarchy." *Communication and Critical/Cultural Studies* 1, no. 3 (2004): 271–96.

Dodwell, Karen. "From the Center: The Cowboy Myth, George W. Bush, and the War with Iraq." *Americanpopularculture.com*, March 2004. http://www.american popularculture.com/archive/politics/cowboy_myth.htm.

Dolan, Kathleen. "Women Candidates in American Politics: What We Know, What We Want to Know." Paper presented at the Annual Meeting of the Midwest Political Science Association, Chicago, IL, April 20–23, 2006.

Dole, Elizabeth. Exploratory Committee Announcement Speech. March 10, 1999. http://www.4president.org/speeches/2000/elizabethdole2000announcement.htm.

Dorsey, Leroy G. "The Myth of War and Peace in Presidential Discourse: John Kennedy's 'New Frontier' Myth and the Peace Corps." *Southern Communication Journal* 62 (fall 1996): 42–55.

———, ed. *The Presidency and Rhetorical Leadership.* College Station: Texas A&M University Press, 2002.

———. "Theodore Roosevelt, 'The Strenuous Life' (10 April 1899)." *Voices of Democracy* 3 (2008): 1–16.

Douglas, Susan J. *Enlightened Sexism: The Seductive Message That Feminism's Work Is Done.* New York: Times Books, 2010.

Dow, Bonnie J. *Prime-Time Feminism: Television, Media Culture, and the Women's Movement since 1970.* Philadelphia: University of Pennsylvania Press, 1996.

———. "Review Essay: Reading the Second Wave." *Quarterly Journal of Speech* 91 (February 2005): 89–107.

———, and Celeste M. Condit. "The State of the Art in Feminist Scholarship in Communication." *Journal of Communication* 55, no. 3 (2005): 448–78.

———, and Mari Boor Tonn. "'Feminine Style' and Political Judgment in the Rhetoric of Ann Richards." *Quarterly Journal of Speech* 79 (August 1993): 286–302.

Dubrofsky, Rachel. "Ally McBeal as Postfeminist Icon: The Aestheticizing and Fetishizing of the Independent Working Woman." *Communication Review* 5, no. 4 (2002): 265–84.

Ducat, Stephen J. *The Wimp Factor: Gender Gaps, Holy Wars, and the Politics of Anxious Masculinity.* Boston: Beacon Press, 2004.

Duerst-Lahti, Georgia. "Reconceiving Theories of Power: Consequences of Masculinism in the Executive Branch." In *The Other Elites: Women, Politics, and Power in the Executive Branch,* edited by MaryAnne Borrelli and Janet M. Martin, 11–32. Boulder, CO: Lynne Rienner, 1997.

Duggan, Lisa, and Nan D. Hunter. *Sex Wars: Sexual Dissent and Political Culture.* New York: Routledge, 1995.

Dumm, Thomas L. "Barack Obama and the Souls of White Folk." *Communication and Critical/Cultural Studies* 5, no. 3 (2008): 317–20.

Dunn, George A. "Being Boomer: Identity, Alienation, and Evil." In *Battlestar Galactica and Philosophy*, edited by Jason T. Eberl, 127–40. Malden, MA: Blackwell, 2008.

Dworkin, Andrea. *Pornography: Men Possessing Women*. New York: Penguin, 1981.

———, and Catharine MacKinnon. *Pornography and Civil Rights: A New Day for Women's Equality*. Minneapolis: Organization against Pornography, 1988.

Dyer, Richard. *White*. New York: Routledge, 1997.

Eberl, Jason T., ed. *Battlestar Galactica and Philosophy*. Malden, MA: Blackwell, 2008.

Edelman, Murray. *Constructing the Political Spectacle*. Chicago: University of Chicago Press, 1988.

Edwards, Janis L., ed. *Gender and Political Communication in America: Rhetoric, Representation, and Display*. Lanham, MD: Lexington Books, 2009.

———. "Symbolic Womanhood and Sarah Palin: Running against the Feminist Grain." In *Studies of Identity in the 2008 Presidential Campaign*, edited by Robert E. Denton Jr., 25–40. Lanham, MD: Lexington, 2010.

———. "Traversing the Wife-Candidate Double Bind." In *Gender and Political Communication in America*, edited by Janis L. Edwards, 165–85. Lanham, MD: Lexington Books, 2009.

Entman, Robert M. "Cascading Activation: Contesting the White House's Frame after 9/11." *Political Communication* 20, no. 4 (2003): 415–32.

———. "Framing: Toward Clarification of a Fractured Paradigm." *Journal of Communication* 43, no. 4 (1993): 51–58.

———. "Framing Bias: Media in the Distribution of Power." *Journal of Communication* 57, no. 1 (2007): 163–73.

———. *Projections of Power: Framing News, Public Opinion, and US Foreign Policy*. Chicago: University of Chicago Press, 2004.

Fahey, Anna Cornelia. "French and Feminine: Hegemonic Masculinity and the Emasculation of John Kerry in the 2004 Presidential Race." *Critical Studies in Media Communication* 24, no. 2 (2007): 132–50.

Falk, Erika. "Gender Bias and Maintenance: Press Coverage of Senator Hillary Clinton's Announcement to Seek the White House." In *Gender and Political Communication in America: Rhetoric, Representation and Display*, edited by Janis L. Edwards, 219–31. Lanham, MD: Lexington Books, 2009.

———. "Press, Passion, and Portsmouth: Narratives about 'Crying' on the Campaign Trail." *Argumentation and Advocacy* 46 (summer 2009): 51–63.

———. *Women for President: Media Bias in Eight Campaigns*. Urbana: University of Illinois Press, 2008.

———. *Women for President: Media Bias in Nine Campaigns*. 2nd ed. Urbana: University of Illinois Press, 2010.

———, and Kate Kenski. "Issue Saliency and Gender Stereotypes: Support for Women as Presidents in Times of War and Terrorism." *Social Science Quarterly* 87, no. 1 (2006): 1–18.

Fallows, James. *Breaking the News: How the Media Undermine American Democracy.* New York: Vintage, 1997.

Faludi, Susan. *Backlash: The Undeclared War against American Women.* New York: Crown, 1991.

Faure, Christine, ed. *Political and Historical Encyclopedia of Women.* Translated by Richard Dubois et al. London: Routledge, 2003.

Fiske, John. "Television: Polysemy and Popularity." *Critical Studies in Mass Communication* 3, no. 4 (1986): 391–408.

Foss, Sonja K., and Karen A. Foss. "Our Journey to Repowered Feminism: Expanding the Feminist Toolbox." *Women's Studies in Communication* 32, no. 1 (2009): 36–62.

Fox-Genovese, Elizabeth. *Feminism Is Not the Story of My Life: How Today's Feminist Elite Has Lost Touch with the Real Concerns of Women.* New York: Doubleday, 1996.

Frankenberg, Ruth, ed. *Displacing Whiteness: Essays in Social and Cultural Criticism.* Durham, NC: Duke University Press, 1998.

Freeman, Jo. "Shirley Chisholm's 1972 Presidential Campaign." *JoFreeman.com,* February 2005. http://www.jofreeman.com/polhistory/chisholm.htm,

Gamson, William A. *Talking Politics.* New York: Cambridge University Press, 1992.

Garber, Megan. "Oval Office or Bust: The Latest Campaign Frivolity Analyzes Clinton's *Other* War Chest." *Columbia Journalism Review,* August 2, 2007. http://www.cjr.org/behind_the_news/oval_office_or_bust.php?page=2.

Gerhard, Jane. "*Sex and the City:* Carrie Bradshaw's Queer Postfeminism." *Feminist Media Studies* 5, no. 1 (2005): 37–49.

Gibson, Katie L. "Undermining Katie Couric: The Discipline Function of the Press." *Women and Language* 32, no. 1 (2009): 51–59.

———, and Amy L. Heyse. "'The Difference between a Hockey Mom and a Pit Bull': Sarah Palin's Faux Maternal Persona and Performance of Hegemonic Masculinity at the 2008 Republican National Convention." *Communication Quarterly* 58 (July–September 2010): 235–56.

Gilligan, Carol. *In a Different Voice: Psychological Theory and Women's Development.* Cambridge, MA: Harvard University Press, 1982.

Gilroy, Jane H. *A Shared Vision: The 1976 Ellen McCormack Presidential Campaign.* Parker, CO: Outskirts Press, 2010.

Goffman, Erving. *Interaction Ritual.* New York: Anchor Books, 1967.

Goodale, Greg. "The Presidential Sound: From Orotund to Instructional Speech, 1892–1912." *Quarterly Journal of Speech* 96, no. 2 (2010): 164–84.

Gordon, Ann, and Jerry Miller. "Gender, Race, and the Oval Office." In *Anticipating Madam President,* edited by Robert P. Watson and Ann Gordon, 145–55. Boulder, CO: Lynne Rienner, 2003.

Goulart, Woody, and Wesley Y. Joe. "Inverted Perspectives on Politics and Morality in *Battlestar Galactica.*" In *New Boundaries in Political Science Fiction,* edited by Donald M. Hassler and Clyde Wilcox, 179–97. Columbia: University of South Carolina Press, 2008.

Gring-Pemble, Lisa M., and Diane M. Blair. "Best-Selling Feminisms: The Rhetorical Production of Popular Press Feminists' Romantic Quest." *Communication Quarterly* 48, no. 4 (2000): 360–79.

Gutgold, Nichola. *Almost Madam President: Why Hillary Clinton 'Won' in 2008.* Lanham, MD: Lexington Books, 2009.

———. *Paving the Way for Madam President.* Lanham, MD: Lexington Books, 2006.

Haas, Elizabeth Ann. "Women, Politics, and Film: All About Eve?" In *Projecting Politics: Political Messages in American Films,* edited by Terry Christiansen and Peter J. Haas, 249–76. Armonk, NY: M. E. Sharpe, 2005.

Hahn, Dan F. *Political Communication: Rhetoric, Government, and Citizens.* State College, PA: Strata, 2003.

Hains, Rebecca C. "Power Feminism, Mediated: Girl Power and the Commercial Politics of Change." *Women's Studies in Communication* 32, no. 1 (2009): 89–113.

Halperin, Mark, and John Heilemann. *Game Change.* New York: HarperCollins, 2010.

Hammers, Michelle L. "Cautionary Tales of Liberation and Female Professionalism: The Case against Ally McBeal." *Western Journal of Communication* 69, no. 2 (2005): 167–82.

Hariman, Robert. "In Defense of Jon Stewart." *Critical Studies in Media Communication* 24, no. 3 (2007): 273–77.

———. "Political Parody and Public Culture." *Quarterly Journal of Speech* 94 (August 2008): 247–72.

Harp, Dustin, Jaime Loke, and Ingrid Bachmann. "First Impressions of Sarah Palin: Pit Bulls, Politics, Gender Performance, and a Discursive Media (Re)contextualization." *Communication, Culture, and Critique* 3, no. 3 (2010): 291–309.

Harris, W. C. "In My Day It Used to Be Called a Limp Wrist: Flip-Floppers, Nelly Boys, and Homophobic Rhetoric in the 2004 US Presidential Campaign." *Journal of American Culture* 29, no. 3 (2006): 278–95.

Hart, Roderick P., and E. Johanna Hartelius. "The Political Sins of Jon Stewart." *Critical Studies in Media Communication* 24, no. 3 (2007): 263–72.

———, Sharon E. Jarvis, William P. Jennings, and Deborah Smith-Howell. *Political Keywords: Using Language That Uses Us.* New York: Oxford University Press, 2005.

Heider, Carmen. "Suffrage, Self-Determination, and the Women's Christian Temperance Union in Nebraska, 1879–1882." *Rhetoric & Public Affairs* 8 (spring 2005): 85–108.

Held, Allison L., Sheryl L. Herndon, and Danielle M. Stager. "The Equal Rights Amendment: Why the ERA Remains Legally Viable and Properly before the States." *William & Mary Journal of Women and the Law* 3, no. 1 (1997): 113–36.

Heldman, Caroline, Susan J. Carroll, and Stephanie Olson. "'She Brought Only a Skirt': Print Media Coverage of Elizabeth Dole's Bid for the Republican Presidential Nomination." *Political Communication* 22, no. 3 (2005): 315–35.

Henry, Astrid. "Orgasms and Empowerment: *Sex and the City* and the Third Wave Feminism." In *Reading "Sex and the City,"* edited by Kim Akass and Janet McCabe, 65–82. London: I. B. Tauris, 2004.

Hobby, Teresa Santerre. "*Independence Day:* Reinforcing Patriarchal Myths about Gender and Power." *Journal of Popular Culture* 34, no. 2 (2000): 39–55.

Hogan, J. Michael. "George Gallup and the Rhetoric of Scientific Democracy." *Communication Monographs* 64, no. 2 (1997): 161–79.

hooks, bell. *Black Looks: Race and Representation.* Boston: South End Press, 1992.

———. "Dissident Heat: *Fire with Fire.*" In *"Bad Girls"/"Good Girls": Women, Sex, and Power in the Nineties,* edited by Nan Bauer Maglin and Donna Perry, 57–64. New Brunswick, NJ: Rutgers University Press, 1996.

Howe, Nicholas. "Metaphor in Contemporary American Political Discourse." *Metaphor and Symbol* 3, no. 2 (1988): 87–104.

Hutcheon, Linda. "Modern Parody and Bakhtin." In *Rethinking Bakhtin: Extensions and Challenges,* edited by Gary Saul Morson and Caryl Emerson, 87–103. Evanston, IL: Northwestern University Press, 1989.

Huxman, Susan Schultz. "Perfecting the Rhetorical Vision of Woman's Rights: Elizabeth Cady Stanton, Anna Howard Shaw, and Carrie Chapman Catt." *Women's Studies in Communication* 23 (fall 2000): 307–36.

Ingraham, Laura. *Power to the People.* Washington, DC: Regnery Publishing, 2007.

Ivie, Robert L. "Tragic Fear and the Rhetorical Presidency." In *Beyond the Rhetorical Presidency,* edited by Martin J. Medhurst, 153–78. College Station: Texas A&M University Press, 1996.

———, and Oscar Giner. "American Exceptionalism in a Democratic Idiom: Transacting the Mythos of Change in the 2008 Presidential Campaign." *Communication Studies* 60, no. 4 (2009): 359–75.

Iyengar, Shanto, Nicholas A. Valentino, Stephen Ansolabehere, and Adam F. Simon. "Running as a Woman: Gender Stereotyping in Political Campaigns." In *Women, Media, and Politics,* edited by Pippa Norris, 77–98. New York: Oxford University Press, 1997.

Jackson, R. L. *Scripting the Black Masculine Body: Identity, Discourse, and Racial Politics in Popular Media.* Albany: State University of New York Press, 2006.

Jamieson, Kathleen Hall. *Beyond the Double Bind: Women and Leadership.* New York: Oxford University Press, 1995.

———. *Dirty Politics: Deception, Distraction and Democracy.* New York: Oxford University Press, 1992.

———. *Eloquence in an Electronic Age.* New York: Oxford University Press, 1988.

———. "The Subversive Effects of a Focus on Strategy in News Coverage of Presidential Campaigns." In *1–800-President: The Report of the Twentieth Century Fund Task Force on Television and the Campaign of 1992,* 35–61. New York: Twentieth Century Fund Press, 1993.

———, and Paul Waldman. *The Press Effect: Politicians, Journalists, and the Stories That Shape the Political World.* New York: Oxford University Press, 2003.

Jansen, Sue Curry, and Don Sabo. "The Sport/War Metaphor: Hegemonic Masculinity, the Persian Gulf War, and the New World Order." *Sociology of Sport Journal* 11 (March 1994): 1–17.

Johnston, Carolyn. *Sexual Power: Feminism and the Family in America.* Tuscaloosa: University of Alabama Press, 1992.

Jones, Jeffrey P. "A Cultural Approach to the Study of Mediated Citizenship." *Social Semiotics* 16, no. 2 (2006): 365–83.

———. *Entertaining Politics: Satiric Television and Political Engagement.* 2nd ed. Lanham, MD: Rowman and Littlefield, 2010.

Jorgensen, Karin Wahl. "Constructed Masculinities in US Presidential Campaigns: The Case of 1992." In *Gender, Politics, and Communication,* edited by Annabelle Sreberny and Liesbet van Zoonen, 53–77. Cresskill, NJ: Hampton Press2000.

Kahl, Mary L., and Janis L. Edwards. "An Epistolary Epilogue: Learning from Sarah Palin's Vice Presidential Campaign." In *Gender and Political Campaign Communication in America,* edited by Janis L. Edwards, 267–77. Lanham, MD: Lexington Books, 2009.

Kelley, Robin D. G. "Kickin' Reality, Kickin' Ballistics: Gangsta Rap and Postindustrial Los Angeles." In *Droppin' Science: Critical Essays on Rap Music and Hip Hop Culture,* edited by William Eric Perkins, 117–58. Philadelphia: Temple University Press, 1996.

Kerbel, Matthew R. *netroots: Online Progressives and the Transformation of American Politics.* Boulder, CO: Paradigm, 2009.

Kernell, Samuel. *Going Public: New Strategies of Presidential Leadership.* Washington, DC: CQ Press, 1986.

———. *Going Public: New Strategies of Presidential Leadership.* 4th ed. Washington, DC: CQ Press, 2006.

Kerry, John. Text of John Kerry's Acceptance Speech at the Democratic National Convention. *Washington Post,* July 29, 2004. www.washingtonpost.com.

Keyishian, Harry. *Screening Politics: The Politician in American Movies, 1931–2001.* Lanham, MD: Scarecrow Press, 2003.

Kimmel, Michael. *Manhood in America: A Cultural History.* New York: Free Press, 1996.

———, ed. *Men Confront Pornography.* New York: Meridian, 1990.

Kipnis, Laura. *Bound and Gagged.* Durham, NC: Duke University Press, 1999.

Kramarae, Cheris, and Paula A. Treichler with Ann Russo. *A Feminist Dictionary.* Boston: Pandora Press, 1985.

Kunin, Madeleine. *Pearls, Politics & Power: How Women Can Win and Lead.* White River Junction, VT: Chelsea Green, 2008.

Lakoff, George. *Moral Politics: How Liberals and Conservatives Think.* Chicago: University of Chicago Press, 2002.

Lakoff, Robin. *Language and Woman's Place.* New York: Harper & Row, 1975.

Lancaster, Kurt. "The Performative Language Games of *Dramapolitik:* How Abraham Lincoln Became an Intellectual Patriot and George W. Bush Became a Cowboy Diplomat." *International Journal of Communication* 2 (2008): 1043–79.

Lawless, Jennifer L. "Women, War, and Winning Elections: Gender Stereotyping in the Post-September 11th Era." *Political Research Quarterly* 57, no. 3 (2004): 479–90.

———, and Richard L. Fox. *It Takes a Candidate: Why Women Don't Run for Office.* New York: Cambridge University Press, 2005.

Lawrence, Regina G. "Game-Framing the Issues: Tracking the Strategy Frame in Public Policy News." *Political Communication* 17, no. 2 (2000): 93–41.

Leff, Michael, and Ebony A. Utley. "Instrumental and Constitutive Rhetoric in Martin Luther King, Jr.'s 'Letter from Birmingham Jail.'" *Rhetoric & Public Affairs* 7, no. 1 (2004): 37–52.

Lélièvre, Simon Lindgren Maxime. "In the Laboratory of Masculinity: Renegotiating Gender Subjectivities in MTV's *Jackass*." *Critical Studies in Media Communication* 26, no. 5 (2009): 393–410.

Lotz, Amanda D. "Communicating Third-Wave Feminism and New Social Movements: Challenges for the Next Century of Feminism Endeavor." *Women and Language* 26, no. 1 (2003): 2–9.

Lucas, Stephen E. "George Washington and the Rhetoric of Presidential Leadership." In *The Presidency and Rhetorical Leadership,* edited by Leroy G. Dorsey, 42–72. College Station: Texas A&M University Press, 2002.

Lum, Lydia. "The Obama Era: A Post-Racial Society?" *Diverse Issues in Higher Education,* February 5, 2009. http://diverseeducation.com/article/12238/.

Malin, Brenton J. *American Masculinity under Clinton: Popular Media and the Nineties "Crisis of Masculinity."* New York: Peter Lang Publishing, 2005.

Mandel, Ruth B. "She's the Candidate! A Woman for President." In *Women and Leadership: The State of Play and Strategies for Change,* edited by Barbara Kellerman and Deborah L. Rhode. Hoboken, NJ: Jossey-Bass, 2007. Chapter online at http://www.cawp.rutgers.edu/research/research_by_cawp_scholars/index.php#Shes Candidate.

Mandziuk, Roseann. "Boundaries of Display and Performance: The Rhetorical Dimensions of the National Cowgirl Museum and Hall of Fame." Paper presented at the National Communication Association conference, San Diego, CA, November 20, 2008. Available online at *Communication & Mass Media Complete, EBSCOhost,* http://www.allacademic.com/meta/p260187_index.html.

———. "Dressing Down Hillary." *Communication and Critical/Cultural Studies* 5, no. 3 (2008): 312–16.

Marshall, Brenda DeVore, and Molly A. Mayhead, eds. *Navigating Boundaries: The Rhetoric of Women Governors.* Westport, CT: Praeger, 2000.

Martyn, Carlos. *Wendell Phillips: The Agitator.* New York: Funk and Wagnalls, 1890.

Mattina, Anne F. "Hillary Rodham Clinton: Using Her Vital Voice." In *Inventing a Voice: The Rhetoric of American First Ladies of the Twentieth Century,* edited by Molly Meijer Wertheimer, 417–33. Lanham, MD: Rowman & Littlefield, 2004.

Mayhead, Molly A., and Brenda DeVore Marshall. *Women's Political Discourse: A 21st-Century Perspective.* Lanham, MD: Rowman and Littlefield, 2005.

Mayo, Edith P., and Denise D. Meringolo. *First Ladies: Political Role and Public Image.* Washington, DC: Smithsonian Institution Press, 1994.

McCain, John. Announcement Speech. Portsmouth, New Hampshire, April 25, 2007. http://www.4president.org/speeches/2008/mccain2008announcement.htm.

McCarver, Virginia. "The Rhetoric of Choice and 21st-Century Feminism: Online Conversations about Work, Family, and Sarah Palin." *Women's Studies in Communication* 34, no. 1 (2011): 20–41.

McElroy, Wendy. *XXX: A Woman's Right to Pornography.* New York: St. Martin's Press, 1995.

McGee, Michael Calvin. "Text, Context, and the Fragmentation of Contemporary Culture." *Western Journal of Speech Communication* 54, no. 3 (1990): 274–89.

McKinney, Mitchell S., Leslie A. Rill, and Rebekah G. Watson. "Who Framed Sarah Palin? Viewer Reactions to the 2008 Vice Presidential Debate." *American Behavioral Scientist* 55, no. 3 (2011): 212–31.

McRobbie, Angela. *The Aftermath of Feminism: Gender, Culture, and Social Change.* Thousand Oaks, CA: Sage, 2009.

———. "Post-Feminism and Popular Culture." *Feminist Media Studies* 4, no. 3 (2004): 255–64.

Meddaugh, Priscilla Marie. "Bakhtin, Colbert, and the Center of Discourse: Is There No 'Truthiness' in Humor?" *Critical Studies in Media Communication* 27, no. 4 (2010): 376–90.

Medhurst, Martin J., ed. *Beyond the Rhetorical Presidency.* College Station: Texas A&M University Press, 1996.

Mercer, John, and Martin Shingler. *Melodrama: Genre Style, Sensibility.* London: Wallflower Press, 2004.

Messner, Michael A. *Power at Play: Sports and the Problem of Masculinity.* Boston: Beacon Press, 1992.

Meyers, Marian. "Fracturing Women." In *Mediated Women: Representations in Popular Culture,* edited by Marian Meyers, 3–24. Cresskill, NJ: Hampton Press, 1999.

Morris, Charles E., ed. *Queering Public Address: Sexualities and American Rhetorical Discourse.* Columbia: University of South Carolina Press, 2007.

Morris, Dick, and Eileen McGann. *Condi vs. Hillary: The Next Great Presidential Race.* New York: ReganBooks, 2005.

Morson, Gary Saul. "Parody, History, and Metaparody." In *Rethinking Bakhtin: Extensions and Challenges,* edited by Gary Saul Morson and Caryl Emerson, 63–86. Evanston, IL: Northwestern University Press, 1989.

Muir, Janette Kenner, and Lisa M. Benitez. "Redefining the Role of the First Lady: The Rhetorical Style of Hillary Rodham Clinton." In *The Clinton Presidency: Images, Issues, and Communication Strategies,* edited by Robert E. Denton Jr. and Rachel L. Holloway, 139–58. Westport, CT: Praeger, 1996.

Muir, Janette Kenner, and Anita Taylor. "Navigating Gender Complexities: Hillary and Bill Clinton as a Political Team." In *Gender and Political Communication in America: Rhetoric, Representation and Display,* edited by Janis L. Edwards, 1–21. Lanham, MD: Lexington Books, 2009.

Mulvaney, Becky Michelle. "Gender Differences in Communication." In *Intercultural Communication: A Global Reader,* edited by Fred E. Jandt, 221–29. Thousand Oaks, CA: Sage, 2004.

Murphy, John M. "Barack Obama, the Exodus Tradition, and the Joshua Generation." *Quarterly Journal of Speech* 97, no. 4 (2011): 387–410.

———. "The Heroic Tradition in Presidential Rhetoric." *Rhetoric & Public Affairs* 3,
no. 3 (2000): 466–70.

———. "'Our Mission and Our Moment': George W. Bush and September 11th."
Rhetoric & Public Affairs 6 (2003): 607–32.

———. "To Form a More Perfect Union: Bill Clinton and the Art of Deliberation."
Rhetoric & Public Affairs 8, no. 4 (2005): 657–78.

Nakayama, Thomas K., and Robert Krizek. "Whiteness: A Strategic Rhetoric."
Quarterly Journal of Speech 81, no. 3 (1995): 291–309.

———, and Judith N. Martin, eds. *Whiteness: The Communication of Social Identity.*
Thousand Oaks, CA: Sage, 1999.

National Women's History Museum. "Belva Ann Bennett McNall Lockwood." http://
www.nwhm.org/education-resources/biography/biographies/bennet-mcnall
-lockwood/. Accessed November 24, 2010.

———. "Margaret Chase Smith." http://www.nwhm.org/education-resources/biog
raphy/biographies/margaret-chase-smith/. Accessed November 24, 2010.

Nelson, Dana D. *National Manhood: Capitalist Citizenship and the Imagined Fraternity of White Men.* Durham, NC: Duke University Press, 1998.

Nelson, Michael. "Introduction: Rossiter Revisited." In *The American Presidency,* by
Clinton Rossiter, xi–xxix. 2nd ed. Baltimore: Johns Hopkins University Press, 1987.

Norgren, Jill. "Before It Was Merely Difficult: Belva Lockwood's Life in Law and
Politics." *Journal of Supreme Court History* 24, no. 1 (1999): 16–42.

Norris, Pippa, ed. *Passages to Power: Legislative Recruitment in Advanced Democracies.*
New York: Cambridge University Press, 1997.

———, ed. *Women, Media, and Politics.* New York: Oxford University Press, 1997.

———. "Women's Representation and Electoral Systems." In *Encyclopedia of Electoral Systems,* edited by Richard Rose. Washington, DC: CQ Press, n.d. Chapter
available online http://www.hks.harvard.edu/fs/pnorris/Acrobat/WOMENELE
.PDF. Accessed March 15, 2010.

Norton, Mary Beth. *Founding Mothers & Fathers: Gendered Power and the Forming of
American Society.* New York: Vintage Books, 1997.

Obama, Barack. Announcement Address. Springfield, Illinois, February 10, 2007. http://
www.barackobama.com/2007/02/10/remarks_of_senator_barack_obam_11.php.

———. Democratic National Convention Acceptance Address. Denver, Colorado,
August 28, 2008. http://www.cbsnews.com/stories/2008/08/28/politics/main4394
905.shtml.

"Obama Proved Them Wrong: Historical Speculation on the Prospects of a Black
President." *Journal of Blacks in Higher Education* 66 (2009–10). Reprinted at *The
DefendersOnline.com,* April 9, 2010. http://www.thedefendersonline.com/2010
/04/09/obama-proved-them-wrong-historical-speculation-on-the-prospects-of
-a-black-president/.

O'Connor, Karen, Sarah E. Brewer, and Michael Philip Fisher. *Gendering American
Politics: Perspectives from the Literature.* New York: Pearson Longman, 2006.

Orr, Catherine M. "Charting the Currents of the Third Wave." *Hypatia* 12, no. 3 (1997): 29–45.

Paglia, Camille. *Vamps and Tramps.* New York: Vintage Books, 1994.

Palin, Sarah. *Going Rogue: An American Life.* New York: HarperCollins, 2009.

Parry-Giles, Shawn J. "Mediating Hillary Rodham Clinton: Television News Practices and Image-Making in the Postmodern Age." *Critical Studies in Media Communication* 17, no. 2 (2000): 205–26.

———, and Trevor Parry-Giles. "Gendered Politics and Presidential Image Construction: A Reassessment of the 'Feminine Style.'" *Communication Monographs* 63, no. 4 (1996): 337–53.

Parry-Giles, Trevor, and Shawn J. Parry-Giles. *The Prime-Time Presidency: "The West Wing" and US Nationalism.* Urbana: University of Illinois Press, 2006.

———, and Shawn J. Parry-Giles. "*The West Wing*'s Prime-Time Presidentiality: Mimesis and Catharsis in a Postmodern Romance." *Quarterly Journal of Speech* 88, no. 2 (2002): 209–27.

Patterson, Thomas E. *Out of Order.* New York: Knopf, 1993.

Paul, Pamela. *Pornified: How Pornography Is Transforming Our Lives, Our Relationships, and Our Families.* New York: Times Books, 2005.

Pauley, Garth E. "W. E. B. Du Bois on Woman Suffrage: A Critical Analysis of His Crisis Writings." *Journal of Black Studies* 30 (2000): 383–410.

Peacock, Steven, ed. *Reading "24": TV against the Clock.* New York: I. B. Taurus, 2007.

Pearson, Judy C. "Conflicting Demands in Correspondence: Abigail Adams on Women's Rights." *Today's Speech* 23 (fall 1975): 29–33.

Perloff, Richard M. *Political Communication: Politics, Press, and Public in America.* Mahwah, NJ: Lawrence Erlbaum Associates, 1998.

Peters, Gerhard, and John T. Woolley, eds. *The American Presidency Project.* http://www.presidency.ucsb.edu. Accessed January 23, 2012.

Podhoretz, John. *Can She Be Stopped? Hillary Clinton Will Be the Next President of the United States Unless. . . .* New York: Crown Forum, 2006.

Reiser, Kim. "Crafting a Feminine Presidency: Elizabeth Dole's 1999 Presidential Campaign." In *Gender and Political Communication in America: Rhetoric, Representation and Display,* edited by Janis L. Edwards, 41–61. Lanham, MD: Lexington Books, 2009.

Richardson, R. *Black Masculinity and the US South: From Uncle Tom to Gangsta.* Athens: University of Georgia Press, 2007.

Robertson, Lori, and Child Walker. "Clinton a Go-Go." *American Journalism Review* 20 (October 1998).

Roper, Jon. "*The Contemporary Presidency:* George W. Bush and the Myth of Heroic Presidential Leadership." *Presidential Studies Quarterly* 34 (March 2004): 132–42.

Rossiter, Clinton. *The American Presidency.* 2nd ed. Baltimore: Johns Hopkins University Press, 1987.

Rowe, Aimee Carrillo. "Subject to Power—Feminism without Victims." *Women's Studies in Communication* 32, no. 1 (2009): 12–35.

Rubin, Gayle. "Thinking Sex: Notes for a Radical Theory of the Politics of Sexuality." In *Pleasure and Danger: Exploring Female Sexuality,* edited by Carole S. Vance, 267–319. Boston: Routledge, 1984.

Ruddick, Sarah. "Maternal Thinking." *Feminist Studies* 6, no. 2 (1980): 342–67.

Rule, Wilma. "Parliaments of, by, and for the People: Except for Women?" *Electoral Systems in Comparative Perspective: Their Impact on Women and Minorities,* edited by Wilma Rule and Joseph F. Zimmerman, 15–30. Westport, CT: Greenwood Press, 1994.

Rushing, Janice Hocker. "Evolution of 'The New Frontier' in *Alien* and *Aliens:* Patriarchal Co-Optation of the Feminine Archetype." *Quarterly Journal of Speech* 75, no. 1 (1989): 1–24.

———. "The Rhetoric of the American Western Myth." *Communication Monographs* 50 (1983): 14–32.

Ryfe, David Michael. *Presidents in Culture: The Meaning of Presidential Communication.* New York: Peter Lang, 2005.

Sarracino, Carmine, and Kevin Scott. *The Porning of America: Rise of Porn Culture, What It Means, and Where We Go from Here.* Boston: Beacon Press, 2008.

Sanchez, Leslie. *You've Come a Long Way, Maybe: Sarah, Michelle, Hillary, and the Shaping of the New American Woman.* New York: Palgrave Macmillan, 2009.

Saxonberg, Steven. "Women in East European Parliaments." *Journal of Democracy* 11 (April 2000): 145–58.

Seltzer, Richard A., Jody Newman, and Melissa Voorhees Leighton. *Sex as a Political Variable: Women as Candidates and Voters in US Elections.* Boulder, CO: Lynne Rienner, 1997.

Shelley, Gladys. "Leave It to the Girls." Margaret Chase Smith Library, University of Maine. http://www.mcslibrary.org/program/library/song.htm. Accessed November 26, 2010.

Shepard, Ryan. "Confronting Gender Bias, Finding a Voice: Hillary Clinton and the New Hampshire Crying Incident." *Argumentation and Advocacy* 46 (summer 2009): 64–77.

Shome, Raka. "Outing Whiteness." *Critical Studies in Media Communication* 17, no. 3 (2000): 366–71.

Shugart, Helene A. "Reinventing Privilege: The New (Gay) Man in Contemporary Popular Media." *Critical Studies in Media Communication* 20, no. 1 (2003): 67–91.

———, Catherine Egley Waggoner, and D. Lynn O'Brien Hallstein. "Mediating Third-Wave Feminism: Appropriation as Postmodern Media Practice." *Critical Studies in Media Communication* 18, no. 2 (2001): 194–210.

Sinclair-Chapman, Valeria, and Melanye Price. "Black Politics, the 2008 Election and the (Im)Possibility of Race Transcendence." *PS: Political Science and Politics* 41, no. 4 (October 2008): 739–45.

Slagell, Amy R. "The Rhetorical Structure of Frances E. Willard's Campaign for Woman Suffrage, 1876–1896." *Rhetoric & Public Affairs* 4 (spring 2001): 1–23.

Smith, Chris, and Ben Voth. "The Role of Humor in Political Argument: How 'Strategery' and 'Lockboxes' Changed a Political Campaign." *Argumentation and Advocacy* 39 (fall 2002): 110–29.

Sommers, Christina Hoff. *Who Stole Feminism? How Women Have Betrayed Women.* New York: Simon and Schuster, 1994.

Southard, Belinda A. Stillion. "Beyond the Backlash: *Sex and the City* and Three Feminist Struggles." *Communication Quarterly* 56, no. 2 (2008): 149–67.

Spigel, Lynn, and Denise Mann, eds. *Private Screenings: Television and the Female Consumer.* Minneapolis: University of Minnesota Press, 1992.

Stanton, Elizabeth Cady. "This Is the Negro's Hour." *National Anti-Slavery Standard,* December 26, 1865. Reprinted in *Selected Papers of Elizabeth Cady Stanton and Susan B. Anthony,* edited by Ann D. Gordon, 1:564–65. New Brunswick, NJ: Rutgers University Press, 1997.

Stein, Sarah R. "The '1984' Macintosh Ad: Cinematic Icons and Constitutive Rhetoric in the Launch of a New Machine" *Quarterly Journal of Speech* 88, no. 2 (2002): 169–92.

Stokes, Ashli Quesinberry. "Clinton, Post-Feminism, and Rhetorical Reception on the Campaign Trail." In *The 2008 Presidential Campaign: A Communication Perspective,* edited by Robert E. Denton Jr., 127–47. Lanham, MD: Rowman and Littlefield, 2009.

Strossen, Nadine. *Defending Pornography: Free Speech, Sex, and the Fight for Women's Rights.* New York: New York University Press, 2000.

Stuckey, Mary E. *Defining Americans: The Presidency and National Identity.* Lawrence: University Press of Kansas, 2004.

———. "Rethinking the Rhetorical Presidency and Presidential Rhetoric." *Review of Communication* 10, no. 1 (2010): 38–52.

———, and Richard Morris. "The Other Side of Power: Who Is Left Out of Presidential Rhetoric?" In *Presidential Frontiers: Underexplored Issues in White House Politics,* edited by Ryan J. Barilleaux, 179–93. Westport, CT: Praeger, 1998.

Sullivan, Patricia A., and Lynn H. Turner. *From the Margins to the Center: Contemporary Women and Political Communication.* Westport, CT: Praeger, 1996.

Sutton, Lauren A. "Bitches and Skankly Hobags: The Place of Women in Contemporary Slang," *Locating Power: Proceedings of the Second Berkeley Women and Language Conference, Berkeley, California, April 4–5, 1992,* edited by Kira Hall, Mary Bucholtz, and Birch Moonwoman, 560–72. Berkeley, CA: Berkeley Women and Language Group, 1992.

Tasker, Yvonne, and Diane Negra, eds. *Interrogating Postfeminism: Gender and the Politics of Popular Culture.* Durham, NC: Duke University Press, 2007.

Thurow, Glen E. "Dimensions of Presidential Character." In *Beyond the Rhetorical Presidency,* edited by Martin J. Medhurst, 15–29. College Station: Texas A&M University Press, 1996.

Tonn, Mari Boor. "Militant Motherhood: Labor's Mary Harris 'Mother' Jones." *Quarterly Journal of Speech* 82 (February 1996): 1–21.

Traister, Rebecca. *Big Girls Don't Cry: The Election That Changed Everything for American Women.* New York: Free Press, 2010.

Trent, Judith S. "Presidential Surfacing: The Ritualistic and Crucial First Act." *Communication Monographs* 45 (November 1978): 281–92.

Tulis, Jeffrey K. "Revising the Rhetorical Presidency." In *Beyond the Rhetorical Presidency,* edited by Martin J. Medhurst, 1–14. College Station: Texas A&M University Press, 1996.

———. *The Rhetorical Presidency.* Princeton, NJ: Princeton University Press, 1987.

Tyrrell, R. Emmett, with Mark W. Davis. *Madame Hillary: The Dark Road to the White House.* Washington, DC: Regnery, 2004.

Underhill, Lois Beachy. *The Woman Who Ran for President: The Many Lives of Victoria Woodhull.* Bridgehampton, NY: Bridge Works Publishing, 1995.

Valentino, Nicholas A., Matthew N. Beckmann, and Thomas A. Buhr. "A Spiral of Cynicism for Some: The Contingent Effects of Campaign News Frames on Participation and Confidence in Government." *Political Communication* 18, no. 4 (2001): 347–67.

———, Thomas A. Buhr, and Matthew N. Beckmann. "When the Frame Is the Game: Revisiting the Impact of 'Strategic' Campaign Coverage on Citizens' Information Retention." *Journalism and Mass Communication Quarterly* 78, no. 1 (2001): 93–112.

Vaughn, Justin S., and Jennifer R. Mercieca, eds. *The Rhetoric of Heroic Expectations: Establishing the Obama Presidency.* College Station: Texas A&M University Press (forthcoming).

Vavrus, Mary Douglas. "From Women of the Year to 'Soccer Moms': The Case of the Incredible Shrinking Women." *Political Communication* 17 (April–June 2000): 193–213.

———. *Postfeminist News: Political Women in Media Culture.* Albany: State University of New York Press, 2002.

———. "Putting Ally on Trial: Contesting Postfeminism in Popular Culture." *Women's Studies in Communication* 23, no. 3 (2000): 412–28.

———. "Working the Senate from the Outside In: The Mediated Construction of a Feminist Political Campaign." *Critical Studies in Mass Communication* 15 (September 1998): 213–35.

"Victoria Woodhull-Martin Papers: Biography." Southern Illinois University Carbondale Morris Library. http://www.lib.siu.edu/Plonetest/departments/speccoll/inventories/015. Accessed November 5, 2006.

Walker, Barbara G. *The Woman's Dictionary of Symbols and Sacred Objects.* New York: Harper Collins, 1988.

Wander, Philip. "The Third Persona: An Ideological Turn in Rhetorical Theory." *Central States Speech Journal* 35 (winter 1984): 197–216.

Wasburn, Philo C., and Mara H. Wasburn. "Media Coverage of Women in Politics: The Curious Case of Sarah Palin." *Media, Culture, & Society* 33, no. 7 (2011): 1027–41.

Watson, Robert P., and Ann Gordon, eds. *Anticipating Madam President.* Boulder, CO: Lynne Rienner, 2003.

Watts, Eric King, and Mark P. Orbe. "The Spectacular Consumption of 'True' African American Culture." *Critical Studies in Media Communication* 19, no. 1 (2002): 1–20.

Wertheimer, Molly Meijer. "First Ladies' Fundamental Rhetorical Choices: When to Speak? What to Say? When to Remain Silent?" In *Inventing a Voice: The Rhetoric of American First Ladies of the Twentieth Century*, edited by Molly Meijer Wertheimer, 1–15. Lanham, MD: Rowman & Littlefield, 2004.

———, ed. *Inventing a Voice: The Rhetoric of American First Ladies of the Twentieth Century*. Lanham, MD: Rowman & Littlefield, 2004.

Whicker, Marcia Lynn, and Hedy Leonie Isaacs. "The Maleness of the American Presidency." In *Women in Politics: Outsiders or Insiders?*, edited by Lois Duke Whitaker, 221–32. Upper Saddle River, NJ: Prentice Hall, 1999.

Whitaker, Lois Duke, ed. *Women in Politics: Outsiders or Insiders?* Upper Saddle River, NJ: Prentice Hall, 1991.

"Who's Talking." *White House Project.* www.thewhitehouseproject.org/research/who_talking_overview.html. Accessed June 10, 2003.

Winfield, Betty Houchin. "'Madame President': Understanding a New Kind of First Lady." *Media Studies Journal* 8, no. 2 (1994): 59–71.

Wolf, Naomi. *Fire with Fire: The New Female Power and How It Will Change the 21st Century.* New York: Random House, 1993.

Woodhull, Victoria. "Lecture on Constitutional Equality." February 16, 1871. http://lcweb2.10c.gov/cgi-bin/query/r?ammem/naw:@field(DOCID+@lit(rbnawsan1569divo)).

———. "And the Truth Shall Make You Free: A Speech on the Principles of Social Freedom." November 20, 1871. http://gos.sbc.edu/w/woodhull.html.

Zaeske, Susan. *Signatures of Citizenship: Petitioning, Antislavery, and Women's Political Identity.* Chapel Hill: University of North Carolina Press, 2003.

Zagacki, Kenneth S. "Constitutive Rhetoric Reconsidered: Constitutive Paradoxes in G. W. Bush's Iraq War Speeches." *Western Journal of Communication* 71, no. 4 (2007): 272–93.

Zarefsky, David. "The Presidency Has Always Been a Place for Rhetorical Leadership." In *The Presidency and Rhetorical Leadership*, edited by Leroy G. Dorsey, 20–41. College Station: Texas A&M University Press, 2002.

———. *President Johnson's War on Poverty: Rhetoric and History.* Tuscaloosa: University of Alabama Press, 1986.

Index

Huntley, Steve, 128–29
Hutcheon, Linda, 155, 166

If magazine, 76
"I Got a Crush ... on Obama," 146–48, 178
inevitability argument, woman president,
  12–13, 21. *See also* postfeminism
Insiders, 118
Internet announcement, Hillary Clinton's,
  89, 94
Interparliamentary Union, 16
invisible text, scholar's task, 4, 134
Ivie, Robert L., 7–8
Iyengar, Shanto, 18–19

Jack Bauer character, in *24* television show,
  76–77, 79–80, 83, 84–85, 174
Jack Hathaway character, in *The Contender,* 62
Jackson Evans character, in *The Contender,*
  61, 63, 65
James Marshall character, in *Air Force One,*
  58–59
Jamieson, Kathleen Hall, 8, 9, 12, 108, 136,
  156–57
Jansen, Sue Curry, 107
Jason Pillar character, in *24* television show,
  85–86
Jim Gardner character, in *Commander in
  Chief,* 45
Joe, Wesley Y., 65–66, 73
Joe Stevens character, in *24* television show,
  78, 79
John Keeler character, in *24* television show,
  193*n*88
Johnson, Lyndon B., 10
Johnson, Sonia, 26
Jones, Cherry, 77
Jones, Jeffrey P., 153, 168
Jorgensen, Karin Wahl, 90–91
Journal of Supreme Court History, 23
journey metaphor, Obama's, 8, 13, 37
Juma character, in *24* television show, 77–78

Kae-Kazim, Hakeem, 77
Kahl, Mary L., 100
Kaid, Lynda Lee, 52
Kamistan, in *24* television show, 82–84
Kane, Robert, 57
Kanin character (Ethan), in *24* television
  show, 78, 80–81, 83–84
Kantor, Jodi, 170
Kara Thrace character (Starbuck), in *Battle-
  star Galactica,* 66, 67, 73–74

Karl "Helo" Agathon character, in *Battlestar
  Galactica,* 75, 192*n*58, *n*78
Kathryn Bennett character, in *Air Force One,*
  58–61
Kauffman, Stanley, 41
Kay, Katty, 36
Keaton character (Warren), in *Commander
  in Chief,* 47
Keeler character (John), in *24* television
  show, 193*n*88
Kennedy, John F., 10, 20
Kenski, Kate, 93
Kerry, John, 11, 92
Kharkov character (Dmitri), in *Commander
  in Chief,* 52
Kharkov character (Mrs.), in *Commander in
  Chief,* 52
Kilgore, Ed, 112
Kimmel, Michael, 10
Kiplinger Business Forecast, 125
Kisses for My President, 56–58, 174
kitchen table politics, 96–97
Klein, Joe, 17, 36–37, 115
Korshunov character, in *Air Force One,* 59, 60
Kramarae, Cheris, 179
Krauthammer, Charles, 124
Kristina, Adolina, 148, 178
Kucinich, Dennis, 158
Kunin, Madeleine, 12–13, 127
Kurtz, Howard, 2, 113, 122–23, 124
Kurtzman, Daniel, 152

Laine Hanson character, in *The Contender,*
  61–65
Lakoff, George, 91
Lambe, Stacy, 1
Lancaster, Kurt, 7, 11
Lat, David, 138
LA Times, 114, 121
Lauer, Matt, 115
Laura Roslin character, in *Battlestar Galac-
  tica,* 66, 67, 68–74, 174
Lawless, Jennifer, 52–53
leaderless element, liberal feminism, 95
"Leave It to the Girls," 24
Ledbetter Fair Pay Act, 110
Lee "Apollo" Adama character, in *Battlestar
  Galactica,* 69, 70–71, 73, 74, 174, 192*n*58
Leslie McCloud character, in *Kisses for My
  President,* 56–58
Lewinsky, Monica, 132, 136
liberal feminism, second-wave, 38, 93, 95,
  170–71, 176. *See also* Clinton, Hillary

Limbaugh, Rush, 127
Lincoln, Abraham, 7
linguistic patterns: *Battlestar Galactica,* 67,
    192*n*60; in Hillary Clinton's conversation
    approach, 95; hedge characteristic, 24, 32;
    Palin's interviews, 114–15
Lipset, Seymour Martin, 131
lipstick joke, 100
Lisa Simpson character, in *The Simpsons,* 39
Lockwood, Belva Ann, 23
Logan character (Charles), in *24* television
    show, 82–83, 84, 193*n*88
Lucas, Stephen E., 7, 8
Luntz, Frank, 128
Lurie, Rod, 43–44, 49, 55, 61

machismo theme, nominating conventions,
    90. *See also* heroic masculinity
MacMurray, Fred, 56
Maher, Bill, 142
Malin, Brenton J., 11
Mandziuk, Roseann M., 131
Mann, Denise, 40
marital status frame: of Hillary Clinton,
    120–21, 165, 201*n*64; in fictional presidenti-
    ality, 49, 80–81. *See also* first spouse role
Marshall character (James), in *Air Force One,*
    58–60
Matthews, Chris: as antifeminist example, 5;
    Hillary Clinton coverage, 105, 106, 121, 129,
    165; music video coverage, 148, 178; Obama
    coverage, 36–37
maverick identity, Palin's, 99–104, 108–109,
    113–14, 117–18
May, Cliff, 143
McCain, John: in *Daily Show* monologue,
    142; maverick identity cultivation, 109,
    117; in Palin's rhetoric, 101–103, 104; vice-
    presidential choice, 98, 99
McCloud character (Leslie), in *Kisses for My
    President,* 56–58
McCloud character (Mr.), in *Kisses for My
    President,* 56–58
McCormack, Ellen, 25–26
McDonnell, Mary, 66, 69
McFarland, Melanie, 40
McGee, Michael Calvin, 4, 134
McKenzie Allen character. *See* Allen charac-
    ter (McKenzie), in *Commander in Chief*
McKinney, Mitchell S., 115
McLaughlin Group, 129
McRobbie, Angela, 6, 175–76
Meddaugh, Priscilla Marie, 155

Medhurst, Martin J., 183*n*22
media coverage: Chase Smith candidacy, 24;
    fictional presidentiality, 48, 53–54, 55, 76–
    77; *SNL* skits, 162, 163
media coverage, framing approaches:
    overview, 5–6, 106–108, 130–31, 174–75;
    Bachmann candidacy, 3, 182*n*7; Demo-
    cratic National Convention, 105–106;
    and democratic participation, 18–19, 108;
    Palin candidacy, 108–19. *See also* Clinton,
    Hillary (media frames of); pornification
    processes; *Saturday Night Live,* skits
Media Lizzy & Friends, 112
MediaMatters.com, 129
Media Matters for America, 142–43
melodrama genre, 52–55
Mercer, John, 52
Messner, Michael, 107
Meyers, Marian, 41
Michaels, Lorne, 153
MichaelW, 112
Michigan, delegate conflict, 128
MILF frame, 138–39, 205*n*17
Milhouse character, in *The Simpsons,* 39
militarism theme: in *Air Force One,* 59; in Hil-
    lary Clinton's rhetoric, 97–98; in conven-
    tion coverage, 105–106; in fitness for office
    rhetoric, 91–93; in media framing, 105–106,
    107; in Palin's rhetoric, 101. See also *Battle-
    star Galactica; Commander in Chief*
Miller, Jerry, 52
Miller, Kevin, 23–24
Mink, Patsy, 25
Mitchell, Andrea, 115
Mondale, Walter, 98
Moore, Ronald D., 65–66, 67–68
Morgan, Tracy, 164–65
Morson, Gary Saul, 154, 161, 166
Moseley Braun, Carol, 26–27, 33–36
Motobou character, in *24* television show, 77
MSNBC, 1, 5, 129–30, 142–43, 144, 147. *See also*
    Matthews, Chris
MSNBC.com, 111, 138–39
Murphy, John M., 39–40
music, functions of, fictional presidentiality:
    Commander in Chief, 52, 53
Myers, Seth, 164
mysticism theme, in *Battlestar Galactica,* 67,
    73–74

Nailin' Paylin, 139
Nathan Templeton character. *See* Templeton
    character (Nathan), in *Commander in Chief*

Russians, 82–84, 114
Ruston, Scott, 76

Sabato, Larry, 128
Sabo, Don, 107
Salon/Salon.com, 2, 55, 128, 141–42
Sanchez, Leslie, 177
San Pasquale episode, *Commander in Chief,*
    46–47
Sarlin, Benjy, 2
Saturday Night Live, skits: Hillary Clinton-
    Palin press conference, 152–53, 154, 156–57;
    Democratic debates, 159–60, 163; Hallow-
    een party, 157–58, 166; Palin as MILF, 138;
    Palin on Russia, 114; sexism's foundation,
    159, 161, 168–69; Weekend Update seg-
    ments, 161–66. *See also* parody, overview
Saul Tigh character, in *Battlestar Galactica,*
    192n58
Schroeder, Patricia, 26, 126
Schultz, Connie, 48
science fiction genre. *See Battlestar Galactica*
second-wave feminism, 38, 93, 95, 170–71, 176.
    See also Clinton, Hillary
Seelye, Katharine Q., 163
Senate campaign, Hillary Clinton's, 96
Sengala episode, *24* television show, 77–78
servant-leader identity, Dole's, 32–33
Sex and the City (Gerhard), 181n3
sexism, critiques/ridicule of: in fictional
    presidentiality, 45–46, 56–57, 59–60, 62–63,
    64–65, 86–87; *Saturday Night Live* skits,
    156–57, 162–63. *See also* media coverage,
    framing approaches; pornification pro-
    cesses
sexuality/sex appeal: cleavage frame of Hil-
    lary Clinton, 121–23; in fictional presi-
    dentiality, 48, 57, 61–62, 63, 75; pillow talk
    frame, 205n8. *See also* Palin, Sarah *entries;*
    pornification processes
Shales, Tom, 48
shallow parody, 166
A Shared Vision (Gilroy), 26
Sharon "Boomer" Valerii character, in *Battle-*
    star Galactica, 192n58
Sheinwald, Nigel, 118
Sheldon Runyon character, in *The Contender,*
    62–63, 64–65
Shingler, Martin, 52
showrunner, defined, 191n45
Shugart, Helene A., 41
Silva, Mark, 119

Simon, Adam F., 18–19
The Simpsons, 39, 189n1
Slate, 53, 113, 127, 182n7
Smith, Adam, 1
Smith, Chris, 156
"The Snuke" episode, *South Park,* 140–41
Snyder, Pete, 130, 145
soap opera comparison, 105
song, Chase Smith campaign, 24
Southern, Taryn, 147
South Park, 140–41
Spigel, Lynn, 40
sports metaphors, 90–91, 97, 105, 107
spouse role. *See* first spouse role
St. Petersburg Times, 116
Stanley, Alessandra, 115
Stanton, Elizabeth Cady, 205n18
Starbuck character, in *Battlestar Galactica,*
    66, 67, 73–74
Steinem, Gloria, 22
Stephanopoulos, George, 118, 147
Stevens, Dana, 53
Stevens character (Joe), in *24* television
    show, 78, 79
Stewart, Jon, 118, 142
Stockwell, Dean, 59
Stokes, Ashli Quesinberry, 111
Stow, Marietta, 23
strict father model, 91–92, 97
structural barriers, women candidates. *See*
    specific topics, e.g., media coverage, framing
    approaches; postfeminism; women presi-
    dential candidates, history overview
Stuckey, Mary E., 10, 11
student frame of Palin, 113–14
stylist blog, 138
substantive framing, 107
Sullivan, Andrew, 129
Sunday Express, 128
Sunday Times, 120
suppositional arguments, fictional presiden-
    tiality: in *Air Force One,* 60; in *Battlestar*
    Galactica, 67, 68, 73–75; in *Commander*
    in Chief, 47–52, 55; in *The Contender,* 61,
    63–65; in *Kisses for My President,* 57–58; as
    masculinity reinforcement, 40, 42–43, 87–
    88; in *24* television show, 76, 79–86
Supreme Court, U.S., 23
surfacing phase, rhetoric's functions, 28,
    188n59
Sutherland, Donald. *See* Templeton character
    (Nathan), in *Commander in Chief*

Watson, Robert P., 12
Watts, Eric King, 147, 177–78
Wayne Palmer character, in *24* television
show, 193*n*88
Webster character (Reginald), in *The Contender*, 62, 64
Weekly Standard, 109
Wertheimer, Molly Meijer, 9
The West Wing, 41, 42
"Whassup" campaign, 147
White House Project, 16, 40, 44
Wildman, Sarah, 113
Williams, Brian, 159
Wilson, Marie C., 40
Wilson, Woodrow, 183*n*22
Winfrey, Kelly L., 5–6, 19
Winfrey, Oprah, 162
witch joke, *Saturday Night Live*, 157–58
Wolf, Naomi, 188*n*62
The Woman's Bible (Stanton), 205*n*18
The Woman Who Ran for President (Underhill), 22

women presidential candidates, history
overview: announcement rhetoric,
28–36; backlash phenomenon, 3, 4, 171,
175–79; barriers summarized, 3–4, 18–21;
campaigns summarized, 22–27. *See also*
specific topics, e.g., Clinton, Hillary *entries;*
feminism; sexism, critiques/ridicule of
Women's Christian Temperance Union, 33,
173
Woodhull, Victoria, 22, 28–29
World News Sunday, 147–48

Yahoo.com, cleavage frame, 123
Yahoo group, for *Battlestar Galactica*, 67–68
Yahoo News, Tumblr text joke, 1
YouTube video. *See* Obama Girl

Zarefsky, David, 8
Zarek character (Tom), in *Battlestar Galactica*, 75
Zorn, Eric, 130
Zurawik, David, 153